International Environmental Law and Policy Series

Animal Welfare in Europe

European Legislation and Concerns

The International Environmental Law and Policy Series

Series General Editor
Stanley P. Johnson

Advisory Editor
Günther Handl

Other titles in the series

Transferring Hazardous Technologies and Substances, G. Handl, R.E. Lutz
(ISBN 0-86010-704-3)
Understanding US and European Environmental Law: A Practitioner's Guide, T.T. Smith,
P. Kromarek
(ISBN 1-85333-305-0)
*Air Pollution Control in the European Community: Implementation of the EC Directives in the Twelve
Member States*, G. Bennett (ed.)
(ISBN 1-85333-567-3)
International Responsibility for Environmental Harm, F. Francioni and T. Scovazzi (eds.)
(ISBN 1-85333-579-7)
Environmental Protection and International Law, W. Lang, H. Neuhold, K. Zemanek (eds.)
(ISBN 1-85333-611-4)
International Law and Global Climate Change, R. Churchill, D. Freestone (eds.)
(ISBN 1-85333-629-7)
International Legal Problems of the Environmental Protection of the Baltic Sea, M. Fitzmaurice
(ISBN 0-7923-1402-6)
Basic Documents of International Environmental Law, H. Hohmann (ed.)
(ISBN 1-85333-628-9)
The Antarctic Environmental and International Law, J. Verhoeven, P. Sands, M. Bruce (eds.)
(ISBN 1-85333-630-0)
Environmental Pollution Control: An Introduction to Principles and Practice of Administration,
J. McLoughlin, E.G. Bellinger
(ISBN 1-8533-577-0)
The Earth Summit: The United Nations Conference on Environment and Development (UNCED),
S.P. Johnson
(ISBN 1-85333-784-6)
*Amazonia and Siberia: Legal Aspects of the Preservation of the Environment and Development in the
Last Open Spaces*, M. Bothe, T. Kurzidem, C. Schmidt (eds.)
(ISBN 1-85333-903-2)
Pollution Insurance: International Survey of Coverages and Exclusions, W. Pfennigstorf (ed.)
(ISBN 1-85333-941-5)
Civil Liability for Transfrontier Pollution, G. Betlem
(ISBN 1-85333-951-2)
Transboundary Movements and Disposal of Hazardous Wastes in International Law, B. Kwiatowska,
A.H.A. Soons
(ISBN 0-7923-1667-3)
The Legal Regime for Transboundary Water Pollution: Between Discretion and Constraint,
A. Nollkaemper
(ISBN 0-7923-2476-5)
The Environment after Rio: International Law and Economics, L. Campiglio, L. Pineschi,
D. Siniscalco, T. Treves (eds.)
(ISBN 1-85333-949-0)
Overcoming National Barriers to International Waste Trade, E. Louka
(ISBN 1-7923-2850-7)

Precautionary Legal Duties and Principles in Modern International Environmental Law, H. Hohmann
(ISBN 1-85333-911-3)
*Negotiating International Regimes: Lesson Learned from the UN Conference on Environment and
Development*, B. Spector, G. Sjöstedt, I. Zartman (eds.)
(ISBN 1-85966-077-0)
Conserving Europe's Natural Heritage: Towards a European Ecological Network, G. Bennett (ed.)
(ISBN 1-85966-090-8)
US Environmental Liability Risks, J.T. O'Reilly
(ISBN 1-85966-093-2)
Environmental Liability and Privatization in Central and Eastern Europe, G. Goldenman *et al* (eds.)
(ISBN 1-85966-094-0)
German Environmental Law, G. Winter (ed.)
(ISBN 0-7923-3055-2)
The Peaceful Management of Transboundary Resources, G.H. Blake *et al* (eds.)
(ISBN 1-85966-173-4)
Pollution from Offshore Installations, M. Gavouneli
(ISBN 1-85966-186-6)
Sustainable Development and International Law, W. Lang
(ISBN 1-85966-179-3)
Canada and Marine Environmental Protection, D. Vanderzwaag
(ISBN 90-411-0856-4)
The Environmental Policy of the European Communities, S.P. Johnson, G. Corcelle
(ISBN 90-411-0862-9)
International Law and the Conservation of Biological Diversity, M. Bowman, C. Redgwell (eds.)
(ISBN 90-411-0863-7)
Participation in World Treaties on the Protection of the Environment: A Collection of Data,
M.C. Maffei, L. Pineschi, T. Scovazzi, T. Treves (eds.)
(ISBN 90-411-0879-3)
Global Forests and International Environmental Law, Canadian Council on International Law/Conseil
canadien de Droit international (ed.)
(ISBN 90-411-0897-1)
Codification of Environmental Law, H. Bocken, D. Ryckbost (eds.)
(ISBN 90-411-0888-2)
The Biodiversity Convention, F. McConnell
(ISBN 90-411-0917-X)
Oceans Law and Policy in the Post-UNCED Era: Australian and Canadian Perspectives,
L.K. Kriwoken *et al* (eds.)
(ISBN 90-411-0937-4)
The Law of Caribbean Marine Pollution, Anderson
(ISBN 90-411-0662-6)
The Scarcity of Water, Brans, de Haan, Rinzema, Nollkaemper
(ISBN 90-411-0657-X)

European Environmental Law, J. Salter (Looseleaf Service)
Basic Work ISBN 1-85966-050-9)

(Please order by ISBN or title)

International Environmental Law and Policy Series

Animal Welfare in Europe

European Legislation and Concerns

Edited by

David B. Wilkins, M.A., MRCVS
Director of Eurogroup for Animal Welfare

KLUWER LAW
INTERNATIONAL
LONDON – THE HAGUE – BOSTON

Published by
Kluwer Law International Ltd
Sterling House
66 Wilton Road
London SW1V 1DE
United Kingdom

Sold and distributed in the USA
and Canada by
Kluwer Law International
675 Massachusetts Ave
Cambridge, MA 02139
USA

Kluwer Law International Ltd incorporates
the publishing programmes of
Graham & Trotman Ltd,
Kluwer Law & Taxation Publishers
and Martinus Nijhoff Publishers

In all other countries, sold and distributed
by Kluwer Law International
P.O. Box 858889
2508 CN The Hague
The Netherlands

ISBN 90-411-0663-4
© Kluwer Law International 1997
First published 1997

British Library Cataloguing in Publication Data

A catalogue record for this book is available from the British Library.

Library of Congress Cataloguing in Publication Data is available.

Typeset in 11/12 pt Times by EXPO Holdings Sdn. Bhd., Malaysia
Printed and bound in Great Britain by Hartnolls Ltd, Bodmin, Cornwall

Contents

**PART II   SUMMARY OF LEGISLATION RELATIVE TO
ANIMAL WELFARE AT THE LEVELS OF THE
EUROPEAN COMMUNITY AND THE COUNCIL
OF EUROPE**

Foreword

The two documents which have been brought together for the first time in this single volume started life at the instigation of members of the European Parliament.

In July 1983 several MEPs from all political groups formed an Intergroup on Animal Welfare – later to be retitled the Intergroup on the Welfare and Conservation of Animals. The European Parliament, unlike many national parliaments, lacks a central library or an information, particularly technical/scientific information, resource. Those members of the European Parliament who were interested in animal welfare issues and wanted information, turned to Eurogroup for Animal Welfare to redress the situation.

Eurogroup for Animal Welfare was formed in 1980 and brought together the leading animal welfare organisations in the Member States of the European Union. The objective is to provide a unified animal welfare voice with which to lobby the European Institutions – particularly the European Commission, the Parliament and the Council of Ministers. Eurogroup's work also involves providing sound scientific evidence and detailed factual information to support our arguments for legislative change in the field of animal welfare. In addition to regular briefing reports on matters of topical interest and concern we agreed to produce two comprehensive reference books.

The 'Analysis of Major Areas of Concern for Animal Welfare in Europe' was first produced in February 1984. The document has two purposes. The first is to provide a guide to the main aspects of animal welfare which are, or could be, affected by European Community legislation and influence, or which might fall within the scope of work by the Council of Europe. The second is to suggest ways in which areas of concern might be addressed. Revised at intervals since 1994 to take account of new developments, it is now in its fifth edition.

The 'Summary of Legislation' was prepared at the same time as the 'Analysis' but under different authorship. It was first published in 1983 and has been revised on five occasions, this being the sixth revision. Initially there was little relevant legislation to document and much of the first edition contained a wide-ranging report on matters under discussion both at the level of the European Institutions and the Council of Europe. This latest revision concentrates on specifically animal welfare matters and only refers to the major species conservation and habitat protection measures.

Since 1992 the Maastricht Treaty has come into force which has necessitated amendments to the section on the background to the European Union and its institutions. Another new section added in 1995 was that concerning those judgments of the European Court of Justice having the most importance to animal welfare.

Every effort has been made to ensure that the information in this reference book is as accurate and up to date as possible. Should any errors, misinterpretations or omissions be evident, we apologise and it would be appreciated if they could be communicated to Eurogroup for Animal Welfare.

Over the years many people have assisted in the research and work necessary to produce these documents. Revising the text is always a painstaking and exacting task. For this latest revision I am particularly grateful to the help given by two members of Eurogroup's staff, Dr Doris Ponzoni and Geneviève Daloze. For the revision of the section in Wildlife, my thanks go to David Bowles of the Royal Society for the Prevention of Cruelty to Animals (RSPCA) in the UK.

David B. Wilkins, MA VET MB MRCVS
Director, Eurogroup for Animal Welfare

Research

This document was revised and brought up to date on 1 February 1997.

The original document was produced as a result of the following Minute contained within the Action Report of the inaugural meeting of the Intergroup on Animal Welfare, (in September 1994 it was re-titled 'Intergroup on the Welfare and Conservation of Animals'), at the European Parliament held in Strasbourg on 7 July 1983.

DOCUMENTATION

In order to assist the Intergroup in its future deliberations, Eurogroup was asked to prepare a dossier on:

1. existing Community legislation relative to animal welfare;

2. matters currently under discussion at the Commission and Council of the European Communities, together with all past initiatives of the European Parliament in this area; and

3. recommendations for future action.

This Summary aims to address points 1 and 2. Recommendations for future action (3) are contained in a separate volume entitled *Analysis of Major Areas of Concern for Animal Welfare in Europe.*

Note: Whilst the contents of this document have been as fundamentally and carefully researched as possible, it represents the first document to be produced on the subject of animal welfare legislation enacted within the legislative bodies of the European Economic Community and the Council of Europe. Should any errors, misinterpretations or omissions be evident, it would be appreciated if they could be communicated to Eurogroup for Animal Welfare.

Glossary

KEY TO EUROPEAN INSTITUTIONAL TERMS USED IN THIS DOCUMENT

European Union

EU	European Union (Established by the Treaty on European Union of 1992 for the closer union of European peoples through economic and social progress, common citizenship, and the pursuit of common aims in foreign policy, security, home affairs and justice. Founded on and compromising the European Community, the European Coal and Steel Community, and the European Atomic Energy Community.)
EC	European Community (Formerly the European Economic Community. The EC is still the legal body through which legislation on commercial, financial, social, agricultural and environmental matters – and therefore animal welfare – is enacted.)
EP	European Parliament (Composed of 626 Members elected from the Member States every five years by universal suffrage. Membership will increase following accession of new Member States.)
COUNCIL	Council of Ministers of the European Union (Composed of Ministers from Member State Governments.)
COMMISSION	Commission of the European Union (Administrative arm of the EU.)
ESC/EcoSoc	Economic and Social Committee (EC advisory committee.)
COREPER	Committee of Permanent Representatives (Body of national government representatives which prepares the work of the Council of Ministers.)
REGULATION	EC legal measure, binding in its entirety and directly applicable to all Member States.

DIRECTIVE	EC legal measure, binding equally on all Member States as regards the objectives to be achieved but allows flexibility in the method of implementation.
DECISION	EC legal measure, binding on those to whom it is addressed. Often used to confer Community approval on international conventions.

Council of Europe

COUNCIL OF EUROPE	Founded in 1949, the Council of Europe now has a membership of 40 countries. Its Legal Affairs Division has drafted five Conventions on animal welfare. The Council of Europe also provides the administration for the Convention on the conservation of European wildlife and habitats.
CONVENTION	Agreement, open to signature and ratification by Member States, which comes into force following ratification by a specified number of countries. Must be expressed through national legislation by those countries which ratify it.
RECOMMENDATION	Policy statement proposing a common course of action. Generally drafted under the terms of a Convention.

PART I

Analysis of Major Areas of Concern for Animals in Europe

Chapter 1

Farmed Animals

TRANSPORT OF FARM ANIMALS

Reasons for concern

Farm animals of all species are most commonly transported by road, some-times over considerable distances. Although some are despatched for use as breeding stock or for further fattening, the vast majority are destined for slaughter. Slaughter animals are of particular concern, since although, as the European Commission's own Scientific Veterinary Committee points out,[1] road transport is, in general worse for animals than other forms of transporta-tion, the transport conditions for slaughter animals are usually worst of all.

The European Community's legislation on the protection of animals (Council Directive 91/628/EEC) states that, for welfare reasons, the long distance transport of animals, including animals for slaughter, should be reduced as far as possible.

Other animal welfare concerns associated with transportation include the construction of the vehicles, overloading, and the widespread failure of many Member States to enforce the provisions of Community animal trans-port legislation over the past twenty years. Since 1991, monitoring by the Royal Society for the Prevention of Cruelty to Animals and the Nederlandse Vereniging tot Bescherming van Dieren of many live animal shipments have shown that many carriers fail to comply with the legal requirements for food or water, even though the journeys regularly exceed thirty hours. The results of this monitoring are made available to the European Commission and the government ministers of the countries involved.

As the European Commission itself notes, 'It is highly unlikely that the transports being followed happen to be the only ones which fail to follow the rules. It is far more probable that the law is being systematically flouted. Long distance transport in overstocked vehicles, combined with dehydration and starvation, results in very poor welfare and often in high mortality.'[2]

---

[1] Report of the Scientific Veterinary Committee, Animal Welfare Section, on the Transport of Farm Animals, Brussels, 18 May 1992.

[2] Com(93)330 final of 13 July 1993: Communication from the Commission to the Council in accordance with Article 13 of Directive 91/628/EEC – Proposal for a Council Directive amending Directive 91/628/EEC concerning the protection of animals during transport.

In July 1993, the Commission published a proposal to amend Directive 91/628/EEC in respect of farm animal transport. The proposal sought to lay down the maximum travelling times after which food and water must be given, minimum rest periods during journeys were specified and, rules to prevent overloading.

In its response to the Commission's proposal, the European Parliament repeated its call for an eight-hour limit on journeys to slaughter, not least because it is readily enforceable through checks at slaughterhouses. It also called for improved stocking densities and a system for better enforcement.

The Council eventually agreed a compromise text in June 1995. For all farm animals being transported in 'ordinary' vehicles, 24 hours' rest, food and water is mandatory after an 8 hour journey. Journey times are extended if animals travel in a 'special' livestock vehicle. Such vehicles, *inter alia*, must have adequate ventilation (whether a system of mechanical or forced ventilation is required is not yet clear), must provide bedding, carry a supply of food and, in the case of pigs, to carry water and be able to provide drinking facilities on board of the vehicle.

The implementation date for all these new requirements is January 1997 except for those concerning 'special' vehicles which do not have to be complied with until January 1998. It remains to be seen how well these new rules are implemented but it seems that there is already some confusion amongst Member States.

Although Directive 95/29/EC included improved methods for enforcement e.g. registration of transporters and the ability of a Member State to take action against a transporter even if the offences occurred in another Member State, there is still serious concern about either the capability and the willingness of some Member States to enforce transport legislation. Furthermore there is only one Commission Inspector charged with the task of monitoring enforcement and in 1996 the Council have provided no more resources for any increase in Inspectors.

Economic and consumer factors

More live animals travel by road than by any other form of transport. Although it is otherwise economically more viable and practical to transport food animals after slaughter in carcase form, other factors including subsidies, encourage long-distance transport. Large numbers of animals are involved. Approximately two million live pigs are annually exported from the Netherlands to other parts of the Community. The regular transport of live animals from one Member State to another can influence the spread of disease within the Community, particularly if health regulations are not thoroughly fulfilled. This is not without economic consequences.

The treatment of animals during transport appears to be in direct relation to their value. According to the European Commission, it is, for example, relatively rare for serious welfare problems to occur in the transportation of high value breeding animals or horses used in sporting events, whereas animals sent for further fattening or direct to slaughter are the subject of almost all the complaints received by the Commission and EC Member States.

There is strong public feeling on the welfare of animals during transportation. A petition urging an eight-hour maximum time limit for the journeys of animals to slaughter was presented to representatives of the Council of Ministers when the Community's present transport legislation was in preparation. The petition was signed by more than two million people throughout the European Community.

Legislation

Since 1 January 1993, the transport of live animals, for whatever purpose, within, to and from the European Community has been subject to the provisions of Council Directive 91/628/EEC of 19 November 1991 on the protection of animals during transport and amending Directives 90/425/EEC and 91/496/EEC. This measure replaced previous Community legislation introduced in 1977. It works in conjunction with a series of EC veterinary Directives:

- Council Directive 89/662/EEC of 11 December 1989 concerning veterinary checks in intra-community trade with a view to the completion of the internal market

- Council Directive 90/425/EEC of 26 June 1990 concerning veterinary and zootechnical checks applicable in intra-community trade in certain live animals and products with a view to completion of the internal market

- Council Directive 90/675/EEC of 10 December 1990 laying down the principles regarding the organisation of veterinary checks on products entering the Community from third countries

- Council Directive 91/496/EEC of 15 July 1991 laying down the principles governing the organisation of veterinary checks on animals entering the Community from third countries and amending Directives 89/662/EEC, 90/425/EEC and 90/675/EEC.

The transport and veterinary directives also work in conjunction with EC animal identification and disease control measures, including two newly established computerized information systems on the movement of animals within the Community (ANIMO) and the entry of animals/animal products to the Community (SHIFT). The veterinary and health directives are amended from time to time.

An amendment to Council Directive 91/628/EEC of 19 November 1991 on the protection of animals during transport was adopted by the Council in 1995 (95/29/EC). This was required under Directive 91/628/EEC to deal with items which could not be finalised when the main legislation was adopted. The proposed amendment covers space allowances for farm animals in all types of transport, maximum travelling times between breaks for food, water and rest, and the length of rest periods during journeys. The proposal also establishes a procedure for future modification of the legislation in the light of technical progress. The Commission has further undertaken to publish a Directive on Standards for livestock vehicles, conditions for staging points (feeding and watering centres) and detailed provisions for 'special' vehicles.

Live animal transport is also the subject of a Council of Europe Convention. The European Convention for the protection of animals during international transport was opened for signature in 1968. It has since been signed and ratified by all EC Member States. An Additional Protocol, which would allow the accession of the EC to the Convention opened for signature in 1979.

In the meantime, the Parties to the Convention have also agreed a series of Recommendations giving specific guidelines for the transport of horses, pigs, cattle, sheep and goats, and poultry.

Possible EU initiatives

1. Member States must ensure the proper enforcement of Community legislation for the protection of animals during transport.

2. The Member States must ensure that the Commission appoints an adequate number of inspectors to monitor and advise on correct implementation of Community animal transport legislation, and that it has the necessary resources to do so.

3. In the case of animals for further fattening and slaughter, the Community should ensure that the Common Agricultural Policy phases out financial incentives to live export. Such incentives are at variance with the stated aim of Community legislation to reduce long-distance transport of live animals as far as possible.

HUMANE SLAUGHTER

Reasons for concern

The Community's Directive on the protection of animals at the time of slaughter or killing attempts to deal with many of the problems noted by animal welfare and veterinary organisations. Under the legislation, slaughterhouses must be equipped with adequate facilities for unloading animals on arrival, and must provide shelter, food and water if the animals are not to be slaughtered straight away. Equipment used for restraint, stunning and killing must be properly maintained and regularly inspected. Spare equipment must be available in the event of breakdown. The national authorities responsible for implementing slaughter regulations must ensure that persons involved in handling the animals from the moment of arrival to the act of slaughter have the necessary skills to perform their tasks humanely and efficiently. In addition, slaughterhouses in third countries which are licensed to export their products to the Community must handle their animals in conditions which offer guarantees of humane treatment at least equal to those provided for in the new Community legislation. Such premises are already periodically inspected by EC inspectors to ensure compliance with hygiene requirements. To counter the concern that the employment of slaughterhouse workers on a 'piece rate' basis can lead to inhumane slaughter practices in an effort to save time, the Directive requires the completion of the act of slaughter for each animal, before the worker can begin with the next.

Nonetheless, several concerns remain outstanding. The first is the actual practice of preslaughter stunning, particularly by electrical means. Over recent years, much research has been carried out on stunning methods. Much more is now known, for example, about the levels of electrical current required to achieve unconsciousness, the design of captive bolt pistols, and the use of carbon dioxide for stunning pigs. However, the Directive incorporates very few of the improvements recommended by this existing research, particularly in the case of electrical stunning. The Commission is required to report on particular stunning methods and their correct use by the end of 1995. This report is to include recommendations for any amendment of the legislation which the Commission, on the advice of its Scientific Veterinary Committee, thinks appropriate. The report is still awaited.

A second concern is the perennial question of implementation and enforcement. Investigations carried out by the RSPCA and other animal welfare organisations in recent years showed that the previous legislation was poorly enforced in a number of slaughterhouses in certain Member States. The European Commission's own field study on the stunning of slaughter animals[3] revealed the continued use in one Member State of a stunning method banned under EC legislation. It also underlined the general need for improvements.

[3] *Field Study into the International Transport of Animals and Field Study concerning the Stunning of Slaughter Animals*, Commission of the European Communities, 1989.

A third concern, and one of great sensitivity, is the exemption from the requirement to stun food animals before slaughter, which Member States may continue to grant for slaughter in accordance with religious belief. This can clearly be dealt with only through continuing negotiation and with the consent of the authorities of the religious faiths involved. However, animal welfare organisations would welcome the acceptance of some form of prestunning by those communities which have not yet acknowledged a method compatible with their faith.

A final concern is the use of electric goads to move cattle and pigs. This is subject to restrictions under the new legislation. However, animal welfare organisations would prefer to see use of electric goads abandoned altogether, given that they inflict pain, and other ways of moving animals could be employed. Moreover, the misuse of such equipment is always possible and difficult to monitor.

Economic and consumer factors

The slaughter industry has undergone a considerable rationalisation in more than one European country in recent years. The concentration of the industry, for reasons of profitability, in large scale regional units may contribute to the domestic transport of more animals over longer distances. There is already a substantial intracommunity and export trade in live animals for slaughter. However, the more modern slaughterhouses may offer better facilities for the handling of animals. Subsidies are available for the upgrading of slaughterhouses to current hygiene and animal welfare standards through the European Community's structural fund system. The introduction of animal welfare improvements to slaughter facilities leads to less wastage on the carcase due to reduced bruising and other forms of damage. Nonetheless, it is to be expected that any increase in costs not offset by improved carcase condition will be passed on to the consumer.

Legislation

Under Council Directive 74/577/EEC of 18 November 1974 on stunning of animals before slaughter, the European Community requires that animals sent for slaughter should be stunned by one of three approved methods so that they are unconscious at the time of killing. The stunning process must be carried out by a qualified person who possesses the necessary skills and knowledge. Cruelty and unnecessary suffering must be avoided, both in the abattoir and in respect of emergency slaughtering.

With effect from 1 January 1995, this legislation was replaced by Council Directive 93/119/EC of 22 December 1993 on the protection of animals at the time of slaughter or killing. This Directive is both broader and more detailed than the measure it replaces. It lays down rules for the movement, lairaging, restraint, stunning, slaughter and killing of animals bred and kept for the production of meat, skin, fur or other products. It also stipulates methods of killing animals for the purpose of disease control. Although individual Member States retain the right to decide whether to authorise religious slaughter without prestunning in their own territory, the Directive places responsibility for the application and monitoring of religious slaughter provisions with the religious authorities concerned under the overall responsibility of the national official veterinarian. It further requires that animals slaughtered in accordance with religious rites shall be spared any avoidable suffering, pain or excitement during all stages of the slaughter process, and that a mechanical form of restraint be used to prevent injury or bruising when the animal is killed.

The Directive required the Commission to submit a report to the Council of Ministers, by 31 December 1995, on the use of various prestunning methods. The report, which is still awaited, will be based on the advice of the Commission's Scientific Veterinary Committee, and will be accompanied by legislative proposals as appropriate.

The slaughter of certain game species, principally for meat hygiene purposes, is regulated under Council Directive 92/45/EEC.

The humane slaughter of farm animals is also subject to the European Convention for the Protection of Animals for Slaughter. The Convention is enacted through the individual legislation of those Council of Europe Member States which have ratified it and through EC legislation. In 1991, a Multilateral Consultation of Parties to the Convention updated its provisions through a Recommendation on the Slaughter of Animals. This Recommendation was reviewed in 1996.

Possible EU initiatives

1. The Community must ensure that the Commission's veterinary inspectorate has the necessary resources to carry out its role in monitoring the implementation of legislation for the welfare of slaughter animals by the Member States.

2. Member States themselves must make more vigorous efforts than in the past to ensure that the legislation is fully understood and properly applied.

3. Where the review of stunning methods allowed by Directive 93/119/EC, which should have been carried out by 31 December 1995, indicates points which could be improved, these should be acted upon without delay, particularly in relation to electrical stunning.

GENERAL FARM ANIMAL WELFARE

a) General Farm Animal Welfare Principles

Reasons for concern

There is considerable concern over the living conditions of animals on intensive farm units. These can place heavy productive pressure on the animals while restricting their freedom of movement and ability to exercise natural behaviour. Other general concerns include the health and welfare problems which can arise from the application of breeding techniques such as embryo transfer, and the administration of yield and growth promoting substances. The overall animal welfare considerations involved in farming are expressed in the European Convention for the protection of animals kept for farming purposes, which should be implemented through general Community legislation as soon as possible.

Such action was called for by the European Parliament as long ago as 1987 in a Resolution on animal welfare policy in the Community. The Resolution and its accompanying report were based on a series of public hearings on animal welfare organised by the Parliament's Committee on Agriculture, Fisheries and Food. The Parliament wished to see the principles and provisions of the European Convention implemented in Community legislation, in order to ensure that they were fully applied in all Community Member States. The Parliament also considered that such legislation would establish the general welfare principles on which subsequent Community measures dealing with the detailed needs of particular species could be founded. In early 1992, the Commission responded by publishing a proposal for a Directive on the protection of animals kept for farming purposes which would provide exactly this type of general framework. The proposed Directive was approved by the European Parliament in November 1992. However, the Council of Ministers has yet to act.

The Parliament has also stated that full integration of animal welfare considerations within the Common Agricultural Policy should be ensured through amendment of the Treaty of Rome (see Chapter 6 for fuller discussion).

Economic and consumer factors

The Community introduces animal welfare legislation in the agriculture sector in order to ensure that there will be no distortion of competition within the single market. It therefore works to establish common minimum standards in order to ensure the rational development of production. Moreover, a number of Member States already had strong national legislation for the protection of animals on entry to the Community, and would be loath to see these standards undermined. The many petitions and letters to EC and national government institutions attest to the strong interest taken by the public in the welfare of animals.

This interest in animal welfare is sometimes expressed as consumer choice in the shops, when alternatives are available. Buying decisions are certainly influenced by prices, but they are also influenced by other judgements which include opinions on the way foods such as meat, milk and eggs are produced. Labelling of food products to indicate clearly the type of farm production system in which the animals were reared gives consumers the opportunity to make real choices indicating the type of production system they find most acceptable. However, at present, labels are not so clear. They often contain wording designed to give an impression of 'naturalness', and products from intensive farming systems, such as battery eggs, need not be labelled as such at all. Attempts to imply 'naturalness' suggest the importance manufacturers believe consumers attach to this attribute.

As a means of encouraging good animal welfare practice in farming, and at the same time giving clearer information to consumers, animal welfare organisations in some EU countries have devised farm production criteria in support of labelling schemes for meat and other products. The labels indicate that the products come from farms which use the best practical animal-friendly production methods. The schemes involve regular farm inspection and periodic revision of production criteria.

Legislation

The European Convention for the protection of animals kept for farming purposes was drawn up under the auspices of the Council of Europe in the early 1970s. It opened for signature in 1976. It has been ratified by all EC Member States and was ratified by the EC itself in 1988. Like other Council of Europe Conventions, it is dependent for its effect on implementation through EC legislation and the legislation of individual Council of Europe Member States. The Convention is served by its own Standing Committee which has drawn up a series of Recommendations over the intervening years. These Recommendations are listed under the sections dealing with the species to which they relate.

In 1992, the European Commission published a proposal for a Council Directive concerning the protection of animals kept for farming purposes. The purpose of the legislation is to implement the European Convention for the protection of animals kept for farming purposes through a general framework which would also serve as a basis for the introduction of specific measures reflecting Recommendations made under the Convention. The European Parliament approved the proposal in November 1992. Adoption by the Council of Ministers is awaited.

b) Yield and Growth Promoters

Reasons for concern

Various veterinary medical products have an alternative use in livestock farming to increase meat and milk production. The non-therapeutic use of many such products, mainly hormones, antibiotics and beta-agonists, is illegal in the European Community, although by no means unknown, and has featured in a number of Parliamentary reports.

Since 1986, there has been growing concern over the development of a new, non-therapeutic product which is designed to increase the milk yield of dairy cows. In Europe, this product is known as Bovine Somatotropin (BST). In the USA it is called Bovine Growth Hormone (BGH). Based on a naturally occurring growth hormone, the commercial product is manufactured by a recombinant DNA process. It is not yet licensed for use in EC Member States, but was finally approved for use in America by the Food and Drug Administration in February 1994.

From an animal welfare point of view, the use of yield and growth promoters is undesirable first and foremost because of the extra stress it places on animals which are already pushed close to their natural productive limits under intensive agriculture. It can therefore increase the risk of health problems. In the case of BST, the incidence of mastitis in treated dairy cows may, according to some sources, be up to 79% higher than normal. Such increased risk of infection implies an even greater use of antibiotics, at a time when the level of antibiotic use is under scrutiny as a contributing factor to the development of drug-resistant infective bacteria.

The European Commission's Group of Advisers on Ethical Aspects of Biotechnology considered that assurances should be given that BST-treated animals do not suffer pain or discomfort disproportionate to the human good expected from the product. The Commission concluded that fulfilling the necessary safety and animal welfare precautions implies a level of monitoring and control of individual animals equivalent to that required for medical treatment under the care of a veterinary surgeon. Yet BST is intended as a performance enhancer for mass administration to cattle herds. Therefore enforcement of safeguards would require a prohibitively costly control regime at farm level. These factors are among the reasons why the use of BST has not yet been approved by the Community.[4]

Economic and consumer factors

The manufacturers of BST products obviously see considerable potential for profitability. However, milk production in the Community is currently

---

[4]   Communications from the Commission to the Council and to the European Parliament concerning Bovine Somatotropin (BST), July 1993 and October 1994.

covered by a system of quotas aimed at the reduction and prevention of milk product surpluses. The administration of BST can increase dairy cattle productivity by 6–20%. The Commission predicts that its use would lead to greater regional intensification of production, with smaller farmers and milk processors tending to go out of business. It would also have a short term impact on the beef market due to the slaughter of surplus dairy cows. BST use would therefore be contrary to Common Agricultural Policy reform.

Studies carried out in the Community and elsewhere show strong opposition to the use of BST among consumers, with a likely reduction in consumption of both dairy products and beef as a result. Consumers consider milk to be a wholesome, natural, high quality product, and do not wish to see it tampered with.

The use of performance enhancing products of any kind is generally motivated by the financial considerations of the individual producer. Consumers, however, tend to be concerned by the potential health risks associated with residues of such substances in milk and meat.

Under the rules of the General Agreement on Tariffs and Trade (GATT) it may be difficult for the EU to block imports from the USA of dairy products from BST-treated cattle. Importation of these products might lead to the licensing of BST for use in the EU.

Legislation

In 1990, EU Agriculture Ministers imposed a one-year moratorium on the licensing of Bovine Somatotropin (BST). The moratorium was extended for a further two years in 1991, and was subsequently extended again until the end of 1994. In December 1994 the moratorium was linked to the legislation on milk quotas and extended for five years.

However, Member States could permit field trials of BST products although the milk could not be sold to the public. An independent Scientific Committee to evaluate results of field trials would be established and the Commission is due to report to the Council by July 1998.

c)   Genetic Engineering and Farm Animals

Reasons for concern

Genetic engineering means the deliberate modification of the DNA in an organism or micro-organism. It may involve recombinant DNA methods or the exchange of genetic information across the boundaries between species. It is a rapidly expanding area of science with a number of possible commercial applications, including various aspects of agriculture. Its impact on animals so far is chiefly evident in the laboratory, and this aspect of animal welfare concern is referred to under the section on animal experimentation (see p. 94).

Whereas vaccines and new drugs produced by recombinant DNA methods could be beneficial to animal welfare, there is a great deal of concern about the negative effects which accompany other applications of genetic engineering technology. The commercial development of this kind of biotechnology in relation to agriculture has so far focused mainly on applications to plant crops and the production of animal performance enhancers, of which BST is the first to reach the marketing stage. The animal welfare concerns over the use of yield and growth promoters have already been referred to in the preceding pages.

However, work is also being done on the genetic modification of the animals themselves, either to improve productivity through altered growth characteristics, to increase resistance to disease, or to breed animals which can express pharmaceutically useful proteins in their milk.

Early American efforts to produce a pig with more lean meat resulted in an animal that was severely arthritic and prone to infections, and have become a notorious example of what can go wrong at the research stage. Work to produce useful pharmaceuticals in the milk of sheep and cattle is less dramatic, and is already being piloted in the United Kingdom and the Netherlands. Pigs treated with human genes are being bred in the UK on a trial basis for use as organ donors to humans. Genetically modified pigs have also been designed to produce human haemoglobin for use in transfusions. These animals would, in commercial use, essentially be farmed livestock, even if the end product is for medical rather than food use.

Chief among animal welfare concerns for genetically modified animals in livestock farming is the need to ensure that any such animal entering commercial use will not suffer pain or ill health as a result of being transgenic, and that it receives care appropriate to its needs.

Economic and consumer factors

A Directive on the legal protection of biotechnological inventions was rejected by the European Parliament at a second hearing in 1995. In December 1995 a further proposal was published by the Commission. Under this new proposal, genetically modified animals would still be patentable, provided the modification did not result in suffering or physical handicap to the animal without substantial usefulness to man or animals.

However, one change forced on the Commission by the Parliament has been to extend the 'farmer's privilege' to cover the use of livestock, as well as seeds, from genetically modified strains.

Modern livestock used for meat or milk production are already well developed by conventional breeding and farming methods. It is said that to be economically viable, genetically engineered animals must be capable of at least a 10% productivity increase over farm animals improved by normal selective breeding procedures.[5] However, research involving the productive capability of larger animals, such as cattle and pigs, has so far been a source of suffering for at least some of the animals involved, without leading to the production of viable livestock. The rearing of such animals for food production on the most advanced holdings is thought to be at least ten years away. Indeed, in the long term, work to improve the disease resistance of cattle by genetic modification is considered likely to have a more significant economic impact than the improvement of their growth potential.

As far as poultry is concerned, research results have been more forthcoming, and a transgenic broiler chicken carrying a bovine growth gene is understood to be the subject of a recent application to the European Patent Office. The entry of genetically modified farmed fish to the food market may be the most immediate and realistic possibility, however, and is referred to under the section on fish farming (see p. 35).

The effects of consuming food products from genetically modified plants or animals are still largely unknown. Furthermore, consumer attitudes to food products resulting from genetic engineering technology could well be negative. Vegetarians might wish to see labelling of plant foods which contain or were produced using animal genes, while members of certain faiths might be concerned as to whether foods contain genes from animals subject to religious dietary restrictions. One British food retail chain has already begun to label food to indicate production by gene technology. The farming of genetically modified animals to produce pharmaceutically useful products may be viewed more positively.

Legislation

In 1990 the Standing Committee of the European Convention for the protection of animals kept for farming purposes began to consider the impact of biotechnology on farm animal welfare. As a result, a Protocol of Amendment was drawn up to allow the scope of the Convention to be extended to cover the welfare of farm animals produced as a result of genetic modification or new genetic combinations. The Protocol was opened for signature in February 1992. It must be ratified by all the countries which are Party to the farm animals Convention itself, before it

5 *Teknologiske dyr*. Conclusions from consensus conference on genetic engineering and animals, Copenhagen, September 1992, arranged by Teknologinævnet and the Research Committee of the Danish Parliament.

can take effect. The Protocol also refers to the slaughter of animals on the farm, both for emergency purposes and in connection with fur production. The European Community approved the Protocol of Amendment through a Council Decision in December 1992.

In 1993, the Standing Committee of the European Convention for the protection of animals kept for farming purposes was asked to give an opinion on a Recommendation by the Parliamentary Assembly of the Council of Europe on developments in biotechnology and the consequences for agriculture. The Committee supported the proposal, made in the Recommendation, that a European Convention should be drawn up to cover the bioethical aspects of biotechnology in relation to agriculture and food production. In September 1995, the Committee of Ministers of the Council of Europe decided that the question of biotechnology required an in-depth reflection before taking any decision on whether a convention is advisable. Therefore, the Ministers proposed a conference in 1997 dealing with this matter.

Possible EU and Council of Europe initiatives

1. The proposed Council Directive on the protection of animals kept for farming purposes should be adopted as soon as possible. Its implementation, like that of other farm animal welfare measures, must be supported with adequate resources, in particular for monitoring by Commission and national veterinary inspectorates.

2. Labelling of food products to indicate the farm animal production system should be considered by the Community, together with labelling to indicate the use of gene production technology.

3. The Declaration on the protection of animals adopted at Maastricht in 1991 by the European Council refers to the welfare of animals used in agriculture. This statement of intent should be reinforced by the incorporation of animal welfare into the agriculture policy objectives in the Treaty establishing the European Community. The 1996 Intergovernmental Conferences provide an opportunity for this.

4. The EC moratorium on the licensing of BST for administration to dairy cattle should be extended indefinitely.

5. Measures to deal with the illegal use of substances as growth promoters should be strengthened.

6. The Community and its Member States should take an active part in the Council of Europe's work to resolve the ethical problems of biotechnology in relation to agriculture and food production.

CATTLE

a) Veal Production and Fattening of Calves

Reasons for concern

In most of the Community Member States where veal is produced, calves kept for this purpose may still be housed in narrow individual crates or tethered in stalls. They may be fed only on a milk diet which contains insufficient iron and no roughage so that the resulting meat will be pale in colour. The crates are so small that the calves cannot turn around, groom themselves or take up normal resting positions. No straw or other bedding material is provided. The calves are denied contact with other animals. They may have difficulty in walking when removed for slaughter.

Calves reared in other systems may be kept in small groups, but are still often without bedding material and on a restricted diet if kept to produce white veal.

On 1 January 1994, the Community's Directive laying down minimum standards for the protection of calves came into effect. Newly built or rebuilt calf rearing units must comply with this legislation immediately. Older units are expected to conform by the end of the year 2003. However, the legislation still allows calves kept for veal to be housed in individual crates, although it does stipulate minimum dimensions which should ensure that the smallest equipment in present use should be phased out. The new law also requires that each calf should have enough space to lie down, stand up and groom itself without difficulty and should be able to see other calves. However, it still permits veal calves to be fed a milk diet without roughage or iron. Its provisions are therefore inadequate from an animal welfare point of view.

In January 1996, the Commission published a proposal to amend the Directive. This was based on a report from the Scientific Veterinary Committee. Adopted by the Council in January 1997, this proposal prohibits the keeping of calves in individual crates after the age of eight weeks. Slightly improved space allowances for group housed calves have also been proposed. Not yet agreed are further amendments proposed to the Annex of the Directive which would mean calves receiving a balanced diet including adequate roughage and iron. These changes will come into effect for all producers by 31 December 2006.

In 1993, the Standing Committee of the Council of Europe's Convention on farm animals (see 'Legislation' below) adopted a Recommendation setting out special provisions for calves. This did not prohibit the individual penning of calves, but nonetheless set higher standards than the EC legislation. It also states that, since some calf rearing systems in present use are

not designed, constructed or operated in such a way as to fulfil all the biological needs of calves, efforts must be made to develop and apply husbandry systems which minimise the risk of injury and disease, and allow for
all the animals' biological needs to be met, in particular by providing for
appropriate feeding regimes and by avoiding barren environments, areas
which are too restricted, and lack of social contact.

Economic and consumer factors

It is possible that a switch over to more welfare-friendly production systems
would increase production costs, including costs associated with any
additional training of stockmen. However, veal is not, in any case, the
cheapest of meat products available in the shops. So-called white veal is
still in demand in the hotel and restaurant trade, but there is growing consumer interest in farm animal welfare. A market survey in Italy and France
in September 1995 showed consumer concern about veal calf crates (69% in
Italy, 35% in France) and a willingness to buy 'pink' rather than 'white'
veal (81% in France, 70% in Italy).

b) Dairy Cows

Reasons for concern

The welfare concerns aroused by administration of yield and growth promoters such as BST to dairy cattle have already been outlined. The general
drive to productivity has resulted in welfare problems such as metabolic diseases associated with higher milk production levels. Lameness is a serious
welfare problem said to affect some 15–25% of cows each year in the UK
alone. There are various interacting causes underlying these problems,
including high energy diets to produce peak production levels, poor design
of winter accommodation, and the sometimes deficient knowledge and
awareness of farmers themselves.[6]

There are also welfare problems associated with the use of embryo transfer technology. This is particularly so where farmers have bought cheap
heifers to use as recipients of embryo implants which will produce calves
too large to be born naturally. This subjects the cow to caesarian delivery.

Economic and consumer factors

Problems such as lameness are extremely costly in terms of lost production,
veterinary fees, and so on. There is thought to be little consumer awareness
of the welfare problems of dairy cows.

---

[6] *Lameness in Dairy Cows and Farmers' Knowledge, Training and Awareness*, Mill and Ward, Dept
of Veterinary Clinical Science and Animal Husbandry, Liverpool University, The Veterinary
Record, February 1994.

c) Bulls Reared for Beef

Reasons for concern

Welfare problems found among beef cattle in present husbandry systems include lameness due to foot and knee injuries, necrosis of tails (atrophy of the tail which can be caused by cattle kept in limited space treading on each other's tails as they attempt to stand up), inadequate supply of roughage in the diet, lack of exercise, overstocking, and abnormal behaviour, not least in sexual behaviour patterns. Aggression results when bulls are kept in unstable social groups. There is an increasing tendency for fattening cattle, when housed indoors, to be kept on concrete slatted floors which are combined with a liquid slurry disposal system. Beef cattle are subject to a number of potentially painful procedures, such as dehorning, castration, tail docking and nose ringing. The Recommendation concerning cattle, drawn up under the European Convention for the protection of animals kept for farming purposes, bans tail docking and requires that most other procedures should be carried out under anaesthetic by a veterinary surgeon. The Recommendation, like the Convention itself, must be expressed through the national legislation of Council of Europe Member States in order to have effect. There is as yet no Community legislation harmonising the basic elements of the Recommendation which countries also belonging to the EU should apply.

Economic and consumer factors

The rearing of uncastrated male calves to produce a beef animal at about 18 months of age, weighing around 600 kg, has become a more attractive economic proposition since the use of growth hormones was prohibited. From the consumer point of view, there seems to be no taint problem associated with beef from young uncastrated animals.

Legislation

The proposal to amend Council Directive 91/629/EEC of 19 November 1991 laying down minimum standards for the protection of calves was adopted by the Council of Ministers in January 1997 (72/2/EC). Its main provisions have already been described in connection with the reasons for animal welfare concern about calf rearing. There is as yet no Community legislation dealing with the welfare of dairy cows or beef bulls.

The Council of Europe Recommendation concerning cattle, drawn up under the European Convention for the protection of animals kept for farming purposes and adopted in 1988, now contains an additional appendix setting out special provisions for calves. This was adopted by the Standing

Committee of the Convention in June 1993. The Recommendation does not ban the keeping of calves in individual crates. However, it does state that, where possible, calves should be kept in groups. It goes on to say that bedding *must* be provided to calves less than two weeks old, and *should* be provided to older calves. It stipulates that after the first two weeks of age calves shall have access to a palatable, digestible and nutritious diet containing iron and roughage quantities appropriate to their age, weight and biological needs in order to maintain good health and vigour and allow for normal behaviour and development.

It is possible that the Recommendation could be incorporated into Community legislation through the Directive on the protection of animals kept for farming purposes.

Possible EU and Council of Europe initiatives

1. The new Directive on minimum standards for the protection of calves which bans individual crates and introduces higher calf welfare standards, should be implemented as soon as possible.

2. As suggested on p. 16, the Community moratorium on licensing of BST products for administration to dairy cows should be extended indefinitely.

3. Ethical guidelines for the control of embryo transfer should be developed in the framework provided by the European Convention for the protection of animals kept for farming purposes. Such guidelines should be incorporated into future Community law.

4. The Commission should bring forward legislative proposals concerning minimum standards for the welfare of beef and dairy cattle.

PIGS

Reasons for concern

Breeding Sows

Pigs are active, intelligent and inquisitive animals. However, in some commonly used pig breeding systems, the pregnant sow is restrained in a stall, and/or by a tether for most of her four-month pregnancy. Such close confinement causes severe distress. Sleeping and dunging areas are not separated. Normal exercise and nest building are impossible, and indeed it is frequently the case that no bedding or nesting material is provided. Exploratory and social behaviour is denied. As a result, abnormal and repetitive stereotypic behaviour patterns develop. Skeletal abnormalities and skin lesions on the limbs and body are commonplace.

Farrowing crates, in which the sow is housed from the birth of her piglets, are equally restrictive, although they do provide some protection for the piglets by preventing the sow lying on them. However, in the United Kingdom a new farrowing crate has been developed which allows both space for the sow to move and protection for the piglets. It is designed to fit into existing pig breeding accommodation.

In 1990, an expert seminar on the group housing of sows, organised by the European Conference Group on the Protection of Farm Animals, concluded that there was sufficient evidence and practical experience in the group housing of sows to recommend that group housing systems could replace stall systems. Unfortunately, and much to the disappointment of the European Parliament, which had asked for both individual stalls and tethering of sows to be phased out, this was only minimally taken up when the Community adopted a Directive laying down minimum standards for the protection of pigs the following year.

This legislation came into effect on 1 January 1994. While it prohibits the use of tethers in units constructed or converted after 31 December 1995, it allows existing units to continue tethering sows until 31 December 2005. There is no prohibition on the use of individual sow stalls.

However, the Directive requires the Commission to produce a scientifically-based report on intensive pig-rearing systems which comply with the various aspects of pig welfare needs by 1 October 1997. The report is required to take particular account of the welfare of sows reared in varying degrees of confinement and in groups. It is to be accompanied by relevant legislative proposals. It is essential that the Community takes this opportunity to review its legislation and lay down significantly improved standards for the welfare of sows.

Fattening Pigs

Weaning and fattening pigs are kept separately on farms, but certain welfare problems apply to both.

Straw provides comfort and a medium for foraging and rooting behaviour. However, many pig rearing systems provide neither straw nor other bedding material. Floors which are fully slatted, or which have no bedding and may be slippery, can also give rise to foot and leg injuries. Ammonia levels can be very high, especially in weaner accommodation.

Overcrowding of pigs in many systems leads to aggression. The rearing of pigs in such conditions underlies the widespread continuation of the practice of tail-docking, which should be unnecessary if the animals are correctly managed in a suitable environment.

The EC Directive laying down minimum standards for the protection of pigs, which came into force on 1 January 1994, covers the conditions under which weaners and fattening pigs are reared. It stipulates the amount of space to be allowed per pig, and requires all rearing units to comply with these standards by 1 January 1998. It does not, however, require the provision of bedding or foraging material. An annex to the Directive lays down the general conditions which shall apply to the housing and care of all categories of pig. This stipulates that tail docking and tooth clipping should not be carried out as a matter of routine. The castration of male piglets to be fattened for meat must be carried out under anaesthetic by a veterinarian if the animals are more than four weeks old.

The Commission's report on pig-rearing systems, which is required by 1 October 1997 should provide an opportunity to review this legislation and improve general pig welfare standards.

Economic and consumer factors

In the United Kingdom particularly, increased numbers of sows and their piglets are being kept outdoors, in fields with individual huts and straw provided. These pig breeding units do not incur the high building costs of indoor systems, but may not be free of health and welfare problems in wet and muddy conditions. A number of alternatives to close confinement systems are in use, but the many variable factors between them make cost comparisons difficult.

Most large scale pig-rearing units are designed to minimise labour. If straw bedding is provided, the cost of waste management may be higher. There may be no obvious economic benefit to farmers who provide better conditions for their pigs.

However, consumers in various countries are becoming increasingly interested in pig production methods. Products from pigs raised in welfare-friendly systems are now finding a market in Denmark and Germany. Animal welfare societies in Denmark, Germany, and the United Kingdom are involved in devising farm production criteria in support of welfare-friendly labelling schemes for meat products. A system of this sort also operates in Switzerland.

Legislation

Within the Community, Council Directive 91/630/EEC of 19 November 1991 laying down minimum standards for the protection of pigs came into effect on 1 January 1994. In addition to the provisions already described, it establishes a procedure by which the Commission can amend the general conditions stipulated in the Annex to the legislation. It also requires Member State government agencies to inspect a representative sample of pig farms in their national territory three times a year and send two-yearly reports to the Commission.

Animals imported from non-EC countries must be accompanied by a certificate stating that they have been reared in conditions at least equivalent to those demanded by Community welfare legislation.

To some extent, the Community legislation follows the provisions of the Recommendation concerning pigs adopted by the Council of Europe in 1986. This was drawn up under the European Convention for the protection of animals kept for farming purposes. It deals in some detail with stock-manship and inspection by the farmer, buildings and equipment, manage-ment, physical procedures such as tail docking and castration, and special provisions for the various categories of pig (breeding boars, sows, piglets, pigs kept for fattening or until maturity as breeding animals). It also recom-mends that research be done into the development of housing systems which allow for the behavioural needs of pigs, and in which sows are not tethered or closely confined.

In the United Kingdom, the 1991 Welfare of Pigs Regulations provide for both individual sow stalls and tethers to be phased out by 1999.

Possible EU initiatives

1. The Community could bring forward the date established for considera-tion of the Commission's report on pig-rearing systems.

2. The Community should revise its minimum standards for the protection of pigs to ban the keeping of breeding sows in individual stalls.

3. The Community should ensure that, in revising its legislation, full account is taken of the behavioural, as well as the physiological, needs of all pigs.

LAYING HENS

Reasons for concern

Around 90% of the more than 250 million laying hens kept in EU Member States are housed in battery cages. These cages are made of thin wire mesh. The cage floors slope and are also constructed of wire mesh. One building may contain tens of thousands of birds stacked in cages six tiers high, although two to three tiers is more common. The EC Directive on the protection of laying hens in battery cages, in force since 1988, allows each bird a minimum living space of 450 cm^2 – an area smaller than the size of an A4 page. These battery cage systems provide a barren environment for the birds. Research shows that hens need a nest box in which to lay their eggs, a perch, material in which to dust bathe and scratch, and sufficient room to flap their wings and move around without the risk of attack from other birds. Welfare and health problems arising from the keeping of hens in battery cages include stereotyped behaviour, poor feather cover and bone weakness caused by inability to move normally. Osteoporosis, as the condition of having weak and brittle bones is known, is a major problem. Up to 30% of battery hens may have broken bones by the time they are slaughtered. Many birds in battery cages also have ulcerated feet and long claws which get caught and torn off in the wire mesh cage floors.

A further welfare concern, which is associated with both the battery cage system and some alternative colony systems, is beak-trimming. This operation is carried out as a matter of routine to prevent feather pecking and cannibalism in systems where birds are kept closely confined together. It is known to cause pain which persists after the operation, and should be phased out in parallel with the introduction of housing systems which do not give rise to the welfare problems that beak-trimming is used to prevent. Danish research indicates that feather pecking may be a misdirected behaviour which does not occur if chicks have material in which to scratch and peck, as they naturally would, from their first days of life.

Non-battery systems for the keeping of laying hens, which are defined in Community marketing legislation for labelling purposes, include percheries, deep litter systems, semi-intensive housing and free range. In perchery and deep litter systems, the birds are reared indoors, but do have access to either a perch or floor material in which to scratch. Semi-intensive and free range housing both provide perches and/or litter and nest boxes, together with free daytime access to an open-air run. However, EC legislation stipulates four times as much ground space for free range hens as for semi-intensive hens. The maximum stocking densities specified for indoor and semi-intensive systems are considered to be too high, with consequent welfare problems. However, it is generally considered that these alternative colony and free range systems, if well designed and run, can better fulfil the needs of hens.

All battery egg production units had to conform to the present Community legislation by 1 January 1995. The Commission was also required to submit a report on scientific developments concerning the welfare of hens kept in different production systems by 1 January 1993, together with appropriate proposals for amending the Directive on laying hens in battery cages. Although the Scientific Veterinary Committee prepared an initial report in 1992, the Commission postponed any action until 1996. A further report from the SVC was published at the end of 1996. The Commission proposals to amend the Directive are awaited.

Economic and consumer factors

The battery cage is currently the cheapest method of egg production. However, modification of the cage size requirements in relation to the number of birds, together with other welfare improvements, will change the cost relationship to other systems of egg production. In a few Member States, some movement towards colony systems, as a result of consumer demand, is already indicated. Eggs from all systems which conform to the specifications of EC marketing regulations may be labelled to show the production system. Eggs from free range systems in particular can often be marketed as a premium item at an enhanced price, although some producers do not think the higher production costs will necessarily be met with commensurate returns.

Most consumers tend to buy on the basis of price, but there is increasing interest in buying eggs from non-battery systems. This is recognised in many supermarkets, which now regularly stock free range eggs.

Legislation

The welfare of battery hens is provided for under Council Directive 88/166/EEC of 7 March 1988 complying with the judgment of the Court of Justice in Case 131/86 (annulment of Council Directive 86/113/EEC of 25 March 1986) laying down minimum standards for the protection of laying hens kept in battery cages. This Directive incorporates the original Directive on battery hen welfare which was modified on the instructions of the Court of Justice following a procedural complaint by the British Government. New battery cage equipment has been required to comply with the Directive since January 1988. All battery cage equipment must conform to the standards of the Directive by 1 January 1995. Under this legislation, all hens in battery cages must have at least 450 cm^2 available floor area and access to a feeding trough 10 cm in length. The cage must be at least 40 cm high over 65% of its area and no lower than 35 cm at its lowest point. The cage floor must support at least three claws on each foot and not slope more than 14%.

The Directive required the Commission to report to the Council of Ministers by 1 January 1993 on scientific developments in the field of alternative rearing systems for laying hens. The Commission released a report of its Scientific Veterinary Committee in 1992 but this was updated in 1996. At the time of writing, proposals are expected from the Commission with amendments to the Directive.

Categories of egg production other than the battery cage are defined in an annex to Commission Regulation (EEC) No 1274/91 of 15 May 1991 introducing detailed rules for implementing Regulation (EEC) No 1907/90 on certain marketing standards for eggs. These basic Regulations were further modified in 1995 (786/95) to allow eggs from battery cages as well as free range, semi-intensive, deep litter and perchery systems to be labelled as such. The systems are defined for marketing, rather than welfare purposes.

A Recommendation concerning poultry of the species *Gallus gallus* kept to produce eggs was adopted by the Standing Committee of the European Convention for the protection of animals kept for farming purposes in November 1986. The Recommendation was updated in 1995 and became part of an extended Recommendation concerning domestic fowl. This deals with the keeping of *Gallus gallus* for both egg and meat production.

Possible EU initiatives

1. The Community should lay down welfare requirements to be met by all production systems for laying hens, and should set a deadline for phasing out the present battery cage.

2. In the meantime, space allowances in battery cage systems should be increased.

POULTRY KEPT FOR MEAT

Reasons for concern

Chickens, turkeys, ducks and geese are all kept for meat. Broiler hens and turkeys are the most common intensively reared species, although ducks and geese are also to be found in such systems. They are often kept in over-crowded conditions where normal behaviour patterns are restricted and boredom and aggression can result. Poor quality litter, in which ammonia has been allowed to build up, leads to breast blisters and hock burns as a result of the birds having to squat for long periods of time. The rapid growth rate and high stocking densities, particularly in broilers, cause muscle and skeletal abnormalities, arthritis and ulcerated feet. At the end of the fattening period (37–40 days) many broilers are in considerable pain.

Four systems of keeping poultry are defined under Community regulations for the marketing and labelling of poultry meat. These are extensive indoor (barn reared), free range, traditional free range, and free range – total freedom. The similarity of the labelling terms is confusing to the consumer. Only poultry reared in accordance with the stocking densities, slaughter age, and outdoor access provisions of these regulations can use the Community labelling terms.

Catching, crating and transportation of the birds for slaughter causes damage and considerable suffering. There is an urgent need for reform of all stages of the poultry production process, and of the Community's labelling regulations.

Pâté de Foie Gras

Pâté de foie gras is made from goose or duck livers. It is produced by force-feeding fully grown birds with cooked maize mash. When this is done manually, a funnel is pushed down the bird's throat, and the mash is poured in and pushed down. The food exceeds what the bird would normally eat. The bird's body becomes distended and the liver becomes abnormally large and fatty. The process is said to exploit the bird's natural capacity to store fat reserves in preparation for migration. Modern mechanical force-feeding methods, in which a metal tube attached to a machine is passed down the throat, allow greater numbers of birds to be handled.

The birds are force-fed at least twice a day for sixteen days. They may be reared indoors or outdoors. Generally large numbers are kept together in cages or in a fenced area of ground. Insertion of the feeding funnel or tube is, at the least, a source of discomfort, and may also be stressful. Throat inflammation and subsequent infection are a risk. Towards the end of the sixteen days, the birds may suffer discomfort due to pressure of the enlarged liver on other internal organs. The livers can be anywhere between four and eight times normal size.

One limited experiment, conducted on the initiative of a former French Member of the European Parliament, suggested that foie gras could be produced without force feeding, although the livers would be smaller. No further trials have yet been conducted.

Farmed Game Birds

Game birds such as quail, pheasant, partridge and guinea fowl are raised both for slaughter, when the end product is meat, and as quarry for commercial shoots. Intensive rearing of these birds for either purpose gives rise to welfare concerns similar to those for more traditional poultry species. In the case of birds which are reared intensively indoors and then released for shooting, there are additional problems relating to the birds' restricted ability to react and function as wild birds normally would. The rearing of birds for this purpose is referred to in the section on Field Sports (see p. 117).

Farming of Ratites (Ostriches, Rheas and Emus)

The ostrich is the most common of the farmed ratites. It has been farmed in South Africa since the 1860s, originally to meet demand for ostrich feathers. However, in the long term, the future of the ostrich farming industry will primarily be meat production, supplemented by sales of skins and feathers.

Farmed ostriches have been selectively bred over between ten and twenty generations, but are still largely thought of as wild animals. The industry has developed since the early 1980s in Namibia, Zimbabwe, Australia, Israel and the USA. European interest in ostrich farming dates from around 1989. By June 1993, farmers in the United Kingdom had acquired around 300 birds, mostly chicks and juveniles. By January 1994, Denmark had imported 90 birds from suppliers in other EU Member States. Other countries where there is known to be interest in ostrich farming include Germany, Holland, Portugal, Italy, Sweden and Finland.

Keeping of ratites in Europe raises a number of serious animal welfare concerns. Morbidity and mortality figures are much higher than for domesticated farm animal species. One of the major problems is the northern European climate. Shelter from wet weather is particularly important, as ostriches lack preen glands and their feathers lack barbs, so that their plumage can become waterlogged. There is also a lack of experience of keeping these birds, other than in zoos. These points, together with the fact that ostriches are already subject to the development of intensive farming methods in the USA, make it essential that proper welfare standards should be set in Europe straight away. These should cover feeding and watering regimes, health care, shelter and enclosure size, handling, transportation and slaughter. There can be few, if any, slaughterhouses equipped to deal with ostriches humanely.

The harvesting of feathers must also be considered. The process of plucking feathers from live birds causes discomfort, pain and distress. Removal of larger feathers can cause bleeding and adds to the risk of infection. Removal of feathers by clipping the non-growing shafts is painless, but removal of too many affects the bird's temperature control and could cause stress. Feather plucking from live birds should not take place, and clipping should be controlled.[7]

Economic and consumer factors

Chicken was once a luxury food, but modern intensive production methods have reduced the cost of both this and turkey, so that these are now the cheapest available kinds of meat. Demand for turkey was seasonal, focusing on Christmas and Easter, when the largest sales are still likely, but turkey meat in various forms is now consumed all the year round. Sales of duck and goose are still largely seasonal. Pheasant, pigeon, partridge, guinea fowl and quail are now supermarket products.

As far as pâté de foie gras is concerned, France is the world's largest producer and consumer, with production concentrated in the Périgord, Strasbourg and Gascogne areas. Belgium is also a foie gras producer. Imports to the Community come from Hungary, Israel, Poland, Bulgaria, the Czech Republic and Slovakia. Pâté de foie gras is consumed in most EU countries. It is generally viewed as a luxury delicacy and is extremely expensive. It is defined under Community regulations for the marketing of

---

[7] *Welfare Standards for the Humane Farming of Ostriches in the United Kingdom*, 1993. Compiled for the Royal Society for the Prevention of Cruelty to Animals by Dr Brian Bertram.

poultry meat as the livers of domestic geese and Muscovy ducks. Under the regulations, duck livers are required to weigh at least 250 g, while goose livers must weigh a minimum of 400 g. The liver of a goose which has not been force fed weighs around 120 g.

Ostriches will typically be slaughtered for meat at the age of 14 months. It is not yet known what the demand for the meat will be in Europe. However, given the rapid growth of interest in a number of countries, ostrich farming will certainly be an internationally competitive industry.

Legislation

There is currently no specific Community legislation setting welfare standards for the keeping of poultry for meat. However, the slaughter of meat poultry, including farmed quail, partridge and pheasant, is regulated under Council Directive 93/119/EC of 22 December 1993.

The marketing of meat from chickens, guinea fowl, turkeys, Muscovy duck and domestic geese is regulated under Council Regulation (EEC) No 1906/90 of 26 June 1990 on certain marketing standards for poultrymeat, and Commission Regulation (EEC) No 1538/91 of 5 June 1991 introducing detailed rules for implementing Regulation (EEC) No 1906/90 on certain marketing standards for poultry. Pâté de foie gras is defined as a product under Commission Regulation (EEC) No 1538/91 of 5 June 1991 introducing detailed rules for implementing Regulation (EEC) No 1906/90 on certain marketing standards for poultry. This implementing Regulation also defines the labelling terms used to indicate certain types of poultry rearing systems.

Intracommunity trade in poultry and eggs for incubation is covered by a Regulation which came into effect on 1 January 1994. This includes trade in ostriches between Community Member States. The importation of ostriches and their eggs from outside the Community is subject to national quarantine laws and Community health controls. In the UK, a licence to import and keep ostriches outside zoos must also be obtained under the Dangerous Wild Animals Act of 1976. Conditions for the keeping of the birds are attached to the licences.

Within the Council of Europe, the Standing Committee of the European Convention for the protection of animals kept for farming purposes has agreed a Recommendation on domestic fowl (*Gallus gallus*) to take into account the keeping of chickens for meat. The Recommendation is very disappointing as it will have little effect on the present serious welfare problems. Other Recommendations for poultry of other species are soon to be decided. These will cover ratites, ducks, turkeys, guinea fowl, quail, partridges, pheasants and pigeons.

There may be implications for the continued force-feeding of geese and ducks to produce pâté de foie gras in the European Convention for the protection of animals kept for farming purposes, which refers to methods of feeding animals. Article 6 of the Convention states:

> No animal shall be provided with food or liquid in a manner ... which may cause unnecessary suffering or injury.

This provision also features in the Community's draft Directive concerning the protection of animals kept for farming purposes. The proposed Directive is designed to implement the European Convention in Community law. It has been approved by the European Parliament and is awaiting final adoption by Agriculture Ministers.

EU Member States whose national legislation effectively prohibits force feeding include Denmark, Germany, and the United Kingdom.

Possible EU and Council of Europe initiatives

1. The work of the Standing Committee of the European Convention for the protection of animals kept for farming purposes to establish welfare standards for the keeping of all meat poultry species should be supported by Council of Europe Member States and by the EU, which is a party to the Convention. Research to develop poultry housing systems which meet the welfare needs of the birds should be encouraged as a priority.

2. Welfare standards for poultry kept for meat should be incorporated into Community legislation at the earliest possible date.

3. Community labelling criteria for indicating methods of farm production should be revised in line with welfare standards. The labelling terminology should also be revised so that it is less confusing for the consumer.

4. The EU should reconsider a ban on the force-feeding of birds, given that more information is available than when the subject was last taken up in a European Parliament report in 1982/83.

FARMED DEER

Reasons for concern

Red deer and, to a more limited extent, fallow deer are the two species generally found on farms. Deer are highly strung, nervous animals which can be easily excited or frightened. They have different behavioural characteristics from other farmed animals. Red deer can be relatively quickly 'tamed', but because of their temperament and athleticism they require very careful handling by properly trained stockmen. Fallow deer are considered less tractable. If the deer are not housed during the winter, they need access to shelter and suitable food. Hinds about to calve tend to seek solitude in natural cover. The practice of cutting off the growing antler (velveting) is prohibited in at least two Member States, but may still be permitted in others.

Of particular animal welfare concern are the transportation and slaughter methods used for deer. A number of animal welfare organisations support the field shooting of farmed deer by trained marksmen as the slaughter method of choice. However, deer are also shot, on the farm, in a handling system or small pen. Otherwise, they may be transported to abattoirs where slaughter is usually carried out using a captive bolt pistol whilst the animal is restrained in a crate or other arrangement.

Transportation of deer, like all other aspects of their treatment, requires extreme care, together with specialist skill and knowledge.

Park deer – basically wild animals, although with very similar conditions of life to those on farms – are usually shot in small numbers throughout the year.

Economic and consumer factors

Antler velvet has been sold to China where it features in traditional medicine recipes, but the main product obtained from wild or farmed deer is venison. The sale of venison is a growth area in meat marketing with demand influenced by its competitive price (two-thirds that of the equivalent quantity of beef) and the fact that it is a lean meat, low in cholesterol. Meat from wild deer is generally sold to butchers and restaurants, and is regarded by some as a superior product, while meat from farmed deer is usually sold to supermarkets, which need a guaranteed supply. However, on the markets of countries such as Denmark and the UK, venison is not fully established, and therefore the economics of production have yet to stabilise. The market is better established in Belgium, France and Germany, where venison is less likely to be viewed as a luxury product.

Deer farming has developed considerably over the last twenty years, as farmers wanting to diversify their activities have turned to deer production. During this period, the main financial incentive has been the production of breeding animals for the expanding industry. Deer farming is a highly specialised business requiring high input in terms of buildings, fencing and handling facilities. Disease problems include tuberculosis and, more rarely, anthrax and foot and mouth.[8]

---

[8] Sources: *Management, Welfare and Conservation of Park Deer*, 1992, Proceedings of the 2nd deer park symposium, published by Universities Federation for Animal Welfare. *Code of Recommendations for the Welfare of Farmed Deer*, 1989, UK Ministry of Agriculture, Fisheries and Food.

Legislation

The slaughter of wild game species is covered under Council Directive 92/45/EEC. The slaughter of farmed deer is subject to the provisions of Council Directive 93/119/EEC of 22 December 1993 on the protection of animals at the time of slaughter or killing.

The transport of deer is subject to Council Directive 91/628/EEC of 19 November 1991 on the protection of animals during transport. However, no special provisions are made.

Possible EU and Council of Europe initiatives

1. In view of the specialised requirements of deer farming, the EU should consider introducing Community legislation to ensure good standards of care and welfare on the farm, in transportation, and at slaughter.

2. The elaboration of a Recommendation on farmed deer could be considered by the Standing Committee of the European Convention for the protection of animals kept for farming purposes.

SHEEP AND GOATS

Reasons for concern

There are three basic areas of concern for the welfare of sheep. The first is the question of ensuring that they are kept in accordance with good health and welfare standards. General principles of sheep welfare are set out in a Recommendation drawn up under the European Convention for the Protection of Animals kept for farming purposes, and it is hoped that the Community and Member States will apply these through legislation. The second concern is the recent application of embryo transfer and other new techniques to sheep breeding. The third and most immediate is the welfare of sheep during long distance transportation. Recent work by researchers from the University of Bristol indicates that lambs show signs of dehydration and stress after nine hours' travelling.

Goats have been domesticated longer than any other farm animal, yet are the least changed in comparison to the wild animals from which they derive. They too are now the subject of a Recommendation under the European Convention for the Protection of Animals kept for farming purposes. This was drawn up in 1992 in view of the increasing interest in developing goat keeping. Once known as the poor man's cow and kept in small numbers for domestic use in many European countries, goats are now also kept in larger flocks on a more commercial basis. This presents different animal management problems, and so it was felt that welfare standards should be established.

Economic and consumer factors

Sheep are kept for their meat, wool and skins. Lambs in particular feature in significant numbers in the intracommunity trade in live animals, yet it is only recently that research into their welfare during transportation has been undertaken. Most of the animals involved are sent for slaughter.

Goats are kept for meat, milk, wool and skins. The milk, which can be made into yoghurt and hard and soft cheeses, is the principal product. Goat milk products have moved from health food shops and delicatessens on to the supermarket shelves in recent years.

Legislation

There is currently no Community legislation laying down welfare standards for the farming of sheep or goats. However, the Standing Committee of the European Convention for the protection of animals kept for farming purposes adopted a Recommendation concerning sheep and a Recommendation concerning goats in November 1992. The principles of the European Convention are to be put into Community legislation through the proposed Directive on the protection of animals kept for farming purposes. This measure has been approved, subject to minor amendments, by the European Parliament. Its adoption by the Council of Ministers is awaited. The new Directive also provides a mechanism for incorporating Recommendations made under the Convention, such as those on sheep and goats, into Community legislation.

The transportation of sheep and goats is covered by Council Directive 91/628/EEC of 19 November 1991 on the protection of animals during transport, which took effect on 1 January 1993. Improved conditions for stocking densities, food water and rest intervals were introduced in an amendment to the Directive (95/29/EC) agreed in June 1995.

The slaughter of sheep and goats is included in the provisions of Council Directive 93/119/EC of 22 December 1993 on the protection of animals at the time of slaughter or killing.

Sheep and goat food products are subject to Community marketing and health rules.

Possible EU initiatives

1. The European Convention Recommendations concerning sheep and goats should be incorporated into Community legislation.

COMMERCIAL RABBIT PRODUCTION

Reasons for concern

Animal welfare concerns over the conditions in which rabbits are reared include the use of cages with inadequate space and unsuitable wire mesh flooring. There is also concern as to the transportation and slaughter of rabbits.

Although small-scale rabbit breeding has a long tradition in Europe, as a commercial industry, rabbit meat production is relatively new and there is little scientific information about the effects of intensive rearing systems.

Economic and consumer factors

Within the EU, commercial rabbit production takes place in Denmark, France, Germany, Italy, Portugal, Spain and the United Kingdom. It is also undertaken in several East European countries, Central America, the USA, parts of Africa, the Republic of Korea and China. China produces a large percentage of the rabbit meat consumed within the EU.

Consumption of rabbit meat varies widely from one EU Member State to another. In the United Kingdom it remains low following the introduction of myxomatosis to wild rabbits in the 1950s. However, rabbits have strong potential as a meat source, since their food conversion rate is better than that of most bovines. Indeed, the rabbit's biological characteristics make it the best producer of animal protein after chickens and turkeys. However, on general sale, the meat is expensive in comparison to poultry. Rabbits are commonly found in backyard rearing systems, where they are a useful supplement to diet and income in rural areas. However, commercial production costs are relatively high, and little work has been done to develop optimal rearing systems, although research into and experience of small- and large-scale rabbit production by the *Institut national de la recherche agronomique* in France has been published by the Food and Agriculture Organisation of the United Nations.[9]

Rabbit skins are a secondary product of the industry. These may be tanned and used for garments, linings and gloves. The hair is recovered from poorer quality skins. Much of the processing is done in Asian countries with low labour costs. The dressed skins are later re-exported back to Europe. The wool of Angora rabbits is used in textiles. EU producers include Belgium, France, Germany, Spain and the United Kingdom. The Rex rabbit is raised for its fur. These two are the only rabbit species not raised primarily for meat.

---

[9]   *The Rabbit: husbandry, health and production* by Lebas, Coudert, Rouvier and de Rochambeau, Food and Agriculture Organisation of the United Nations, 1986.

Legislation

There is currently no Community legislation laying down welfare standards for commercial rabbit production, although there is legislation concerning the marketing of rabbit meat. Rabbits are covered by Council Directive 91/628/EEC of 19 November 1991 on the protection of animals during transport. This legislation took effect on 1 January 1993. Some additional conditions for rabbits are specified under Chapter II of the Annex to the Directive.

The slaughter of rabbits is included in the provisions of Council Directive 93/119/EC of 22 December 1993 on the protection of animals at the time of slaughter or killing.

Although there is no specific recommendation on rabbit welfare, the keeping of farmed rabbits is covered by the general principles of the European Convention for the protection of animals kept for farming purposes. The principles of this Convention are to be put into Community legislation through the proposed Directive on the protection of animals kept for farming purposes. This measure has been approved, subject to minor amendments, by the European Parliament. Its adoption by the Council of Ministers is awaited.

Possible EU and Council of Europe initiatives

1. Further research into rabbit raising systems, together with their handling during transport and slaughter, would be helpful to the establishment of good welfare standards.

2. Given that there are, in the light of present knowledge, established codes of practice for the keeping of livestock rabbits, it should be possible, and would be desirable, for the Standing Committee of the European Convention for the protection of animals kept for farming purposes to draft a Recommendation, which could serve as a basis for future Community legislation.

FISH FARMING

Reasons for concern

Fish farming, or aquaculture, is a fast growing industry. Trout and salmon species are the most commonly farmed species followed by carp and other cyprinids. Young eels are caught and 'fattened' in Denmark, among other countries. Significant numbers of a wide variety of other species are farmed including catfish, sea bream, sea bass, turbot, tench and sturgeon. The concerns associated with fish farming are: problems with handling the fish, killing methods, aggression and cannibalism, poor stockmanship and with the effect on the surrounding environment, including other animals and fish. Other problems include pollution due to faeces and waste food, and the higher disease and infestation levels to which farmed fish are subject due to high stocking densities. The use of wrasse as cleaning fish to control parasites, instead of introducing chemicals, has been tried, but is problematic, as the territorial nature of wrasse leads to behavioural problems when they are reared intensively. At present they are also taken from the wild, so depleting natural populations.

The methods of handling live salmon and trout, and of slaughter, are major sources of concern. Slaughter of commercial quantities of eels for smoking usually involve stripping off the live animals' natural slime by immersing them in either dry common salt, saturated saline solution or soda. This simultaneously kills the animals but clearly causes suffering and has been condemned by the Danish Veterinary Advisory Council. An alternative method of handling eels, which is also commonly applied to catfish, is to deep freeze them. However, although this appears to be less cruel than immersion in chemicals, death is still quite slow. Research undertaken by the University of Utrecht in the Netherlands concludes that fish generally are capable of suffering pain and stress, and therefore deserve a place in animal welfare legislation.

On the environmental level, escaped farm fish varieties can have a detrimental effect on native trout and salmon populations. In Norway, which has long experience of fish farming, around two million small salmon have escaped from fish farms into rivers over the last few years. In Scotland, 13 west coast rivers contain salmon originally from fish farms. The farm-bred fish differ genetically from wild salmon, and also breed and behave differently. There are fears that they could compete for food more successfully than the native salmon, which they might ultimately replace and to which they might spread disease.

The concentration of fish on fish farms attracts other animals. Seals, otters and mink, together with cormorants, herons, goosanders and other birds, may be shot under licence by fish farmers. However, as far as protected species of birds are concerned, there is some requirement under the Directive on the conservation of wild birds that steps to prevent predation, such as use of protective netting, should be taken, and that killing should only be a last resort if preventive measures fail. A broadly similar provision with regard to other wildlife is contained in the Council Directive on the conservation of natural habitats and of wild fauna and flora.

In recent years, genetic engineering research has begun to be applied to the problems of fish farming. A new genetically engineered vaccine against a common bacterial infection, furunculosis, has been developed in Ireland. The vaccine could significantly reduce use of antibiotics. Elsewhere, particularly in America, work has focused on the development of transgenic fish, which are genetically modified to carry additional growth genes. Further research is being conducted into the introduction of disease-resistant characteristics.

Economic and consumer factors

Fifteen per cent of world fish production takes place on fish farms. This is expected to exceed 20% by the year 2000. The importance of fish as food is the impetus behind the expected growth of the industry and the research to create transgenic fish. The farming of salmon and trout has been highly profitable, but output reduced when problems with chemical residues first became apparent. Chemicals used include colorants such as canthaxantin, which makes the flesh look pink, in addition to the parasite and disease controlling substances. Production costs are raised by the methods needed to remove these chemicals from both the water and the fish prior to slaughter and sale. Indeed, disease and pollution are both strong limiting factors on the industry's growth.

Consumers may still perceive salmon and trout as luxury foods, but supermarket prices of frozen trout are now quite low in many European countries. Frozen salmon is also relatively cheap. The main market for smoked eel is in Denmark, Germany and the Netherlands.

Legislation

Community legislation on aquaculture deals with health and marketing rules in connection with farmed fish as food products. It does not extend to the welfare of the fish.

Within the Council of Europe, the Standing Committee of the European Convention for the protection of animals kept for farming purposes has begun to consider the possibility of drafting a Recommendation on farmed fish.

Possible EU and Council of Europe initiatives

1. Ideally, the work of the Standing Committee of the European Convention for the protection of animals kept for farming purposes should lead to the drafting of a Recommendation concerning farmed fish, which could provide a basis for subsequent Community legislation.

2. The European Union and Member States should ensure that full attention is paid to the environmental impact of fish farms. This should include research into non-lethal ways of discouraging predation by mammals and birds.

ANIMALS FARMED FOR FUR

Reasons for concern

Among the foremost reasons for concern over the farming of fur bearing animals is the question of whether the species involved can be kept on farms in conditions which are compatible with their behavioural and physical needs. This question arises because most of the animals concerned do not come from long-domesticated species. For example, the two most commonly farmed species, mink and fox, have only been captive-bred for some 60 generations. In 1989, the Farm Animal Welfare Council, which advises the UK Ministry of Agriculture, stated that it was particularly concerned that these essentially wild animals are kept in small, barren cages which do not provide appropriate comfort or shelter, and do not allow the animals freedom to display most normal patterns of behaviour. Fur animals, in common with most other intensively farmed animals, exhibit stereotypic behaviour, and research indicates that this is particularly obvious in foxes. All farmed species are typically kept in batteries of wire cages (mostly with wire floors) in long sheds. Nest boxes are usually only provided to breeding females. Mink, which use water extensively in the wild, generally have no access to it in captivity, other than for drinking. Species which are solitary in the wild, except when breeding, are kept in individual cages but in close proximity to other animals. Large farms keep many thousands of animals, which can mean that inspection is cursory.

While most EU Member States have legislation dealing with the environmental and health aspects of fur farming (covering location, import of potentially destructive or disease carrying species, etc), there is little or no national legislation specifying standards for the welfare of fur animals kept on farms, although there is a Council of Europe Recommendation concerning fur animals, which was formulated under the European Convention on the Protection of Animals kept for Farming Purposes. This Convention has been ratified by the European Union and by all its Member States individually.

Economic and consumer factors

Farmed fur production has seen both expansion and depression in the last twenty years. In 1973/74, 16 million mink skins were produced worldwide. This rose to 39 million mink pelts in 1989 but fell to 26 million in 1990. Fox pelt production in 1986 was 4.3 million, in 1990 it was 2.6 million.

Although demand for mink expanded in Japan during the 1980s, retail fur sales generally in the United States, United Kingdom, Germany, France and the Netherlands began to contract. They were affected by growing public distaste for wearing fur, due to the cruelty of trapping and the ethical questionability of keeping essentially wild animals in restricted farm conditions.

Moreover, trends in public taste and modern life styles in western Europe had tended to move away from fur products, which are, in any case, mostly luxury items. Over-production in relation to the falling demand meant that by 1990, sales had stagnated to the extent that 40% of pelts produced had to be placed in cold storage. The largest market for furs within the EU today is Italy.

However, there are still fur farms in all EU Member States except Luxembourg. Mink, fox, polecat, raccoon dog, coypu and chinchilla are kept. The largest producers are Denmark, Finland and Sweden. In 1990, Finland supplied 65% of the farmed fox pelts on the world market. Denmark, Sweden, Finland and Norway together claim to market around 40% of the world's production of furs. The Copenhagen-based marketing organisation handling their furs now also sells farmed fur from Ireland, the Netherlands, the United Kingdom and Iceland.

Within the EU, fabrication of skins into garments is carried out in Belgium, Finland, France, Germany, Greece, Italy, Sweden and the United Kingdom. Greece is one of the world's most important manufacturers of fur garments. Her industry, which has received EC funding, is concentrated in the town of Kastoria, near the Albanian border.[10]

Legislation

In October 1990 the Standing Committee of the European Convention on the Protection of Animals kept for Farming Purposes adopted a Recommendation concerning Fur Animals. The Recommendation took effect in November 1991, but its implementation is dependent on enactment through the national laws of countries which are parties to the Convention. The Recommendation requires that animals born in the wild shall not be kept on fur farms, and that no animal should be farmed for its fur if the conditions of the Recommendation cannot be met or if the animal belongs to a species which cannot adapt to captivity without welfare problems. The Recommendation states general conditions for the keeping of animals for fur and lists special provisions for mink, polecats, foxes, coypu and chinchilla. It also lists methods for the humane killing of animals farmed for their fur. The Recommendation was discussed in 1996 with a view to updating the text. However few changes are anticipated.

Permitted methods and conditions for the slaughter of animals farmed for their fur are laid down in Annex F of Council Directive 93/119/EC of 22 December 1993 on the protection of animals at the time of slaughter or killing. The Directive came into force on 1 January 1995.

---

[10] *Study into the Legal, Technical and Animal Welfare Aspects of Fur Farming*, Commission of the European Communities, 1991.

Possible EU initiatives

1. Community legislation should be introduced to lay down minimum standards for the keeping of animals farmed for their fur, either through the proposed Council Directive concerning the protection of animals kept for farming purposes, or as a separate item of legislation.

Chapter 2

Wild Animals

INTERNATIONAL WILDLIFE TRADE

Reasons for concern

The trade in wild animals and wildlife products is of concern for several reasons. The most obvious is the threat it poses to the survival of individual species in the wild. However, there is also considerable cruelty entailed in the capture of the animals, the killing methods used, or, in the case of animals to be sold alive, the transportation conditions to which they are subjected, and the conditions in which they may be kept at holding centres or on arrival at their final destination in Europe and elsewhere. Moreover, importation of exotic species can constitute a disease risk to native species, although some authorised imports are subject to health controls.

Tropical fish, reptiles, birds and mammals are all traded and are equally subject to the general concerns outlined above. Many species are not yet covered by conservation legislation, and may only become so when their numbers are already heavily depleted. When information on the population status of a species is lacking, the decision whether to allow trade should err on the side of caution, but mostly does not. Furthermore, legislative controls on the trade in wild animals and animal products are sometimes weak and often evaded. Poaching and illegal trade continue to affect even those animals, such as the African elephant, which are given strict protection under national laws and international agreement. European Union Member States have been strongly criticised for failing to coordinate their efforts to stop illegal wildlife trade, despite the fact that all 15 are bound by a common Regulation through which they implement the Convention on International Trade in Endangered Species. The failure to enforce this legislation adequately by individual countries – particularly Greece – continues to be of concern. Laxity in one or two countries undermines the whole EU control system.

The trade in wild caught birds gives a prime example of the problems. More than one million wild caught birds are imported annually to the European Community, where France is the largest single importer. Collectively, the EU features as one of the largest importers in the world, alongside Japan and, until recently, the United States. The annual world

41

trade is believed to exceed five million birds. Two thousand six hundred bird species have been recorded in trade over the last 20 years. The UK Ministry of Agriculture is the only government body in the EU to keep comprehensive import records. Its published statistics for the years 1988–92 show that, on average, 13% of wild birds imported to the UK are either dead on arrival or die later during quarantine. An independent study showed a death rate of 26.7% for birds imported to Denmark during 1989–90.[11] Other studies indicate that 40–50% of captured wild birds die before they can even be exported from their country of origin, due to crude trapping methods and the poor conditions, inductive of stress and disease, in which they are locally transported and held.

Economic and consumer factors

Trade, legal or illegal, is driven by consumer demand and has increased to its present scale in parallel with the development of modern transport. Traffic generally flows from Africa, Asia and South America to Europe, Japan and the USA, and from Africa, India and South East Asia to China and Taiwan. The various categories of wildlife trade and the species involved are too numerous to list here, but the following examples should give an indication of the scale and scope.

Importation for the Pet Trade

Tropical birds and fish are often taken for sale as exotic pets, to private breeders and to collectors. There is a disturbing growth of interest in the keeping of reptiles as pets. Red-eared terrapins are still legally exported by the USA to 29 countries, despite the obvious decline of the species in its native land. In 1994 the overall trade was estimated at 4–7 million terrapins annually. Arriving as babies, between 78% and 99% die of natural causes in their first year as pets. Those which reach adulthood become unmanageable and may sometimes be dumped in local ponds. They do not usually survive in the wild in the cold north European climate, but are a threat to local wildlife in warmer areas. Within the EU, France and Germany have already banned imports of red-eared terrapin, but the UK imports some 40,000 a year. The Commission is proposing to impose some controls under new EC wildlife trade rules.

Although the individual trapper will only make US$1–10 for each bird sold, it is estimated that trappers in neotropical countries earned US$33 million for parrots exported between 1982 and 1986, with middle-men earning US$114 million. The gross retail value of the birds in import-

[11] *The Effect of Transport Conditions on Mortality in Tropical Birds imported for the Pet Trade*, M. Jensen, Institute of Population Biology, University of Copenhagen.

ing countries was an estimated US$1.6 billion.[12] That represents a fifty-fold increase in the value of the birds between the first and last trade levels, and shows clearly that the income to the numerous exporting countries is negligible in comparison with the trade's value at the consumer end. Further restrictions on the import of wild birds would not, as bird fanciers fear, prevent the keeping of many species as pets or for exhibition, since those which thrive in captivity can already be bred in captivity, given the appropriate care and conditions. More than one hundred of the world's 333 parrot species are already regularly captive bred.

Increased information on the effects of the trade in tropical fish is focusing more attention on these animals than hitherto. Relatively cheap and apparently plentiful, aquarium fish are typically kept by private individuals in Europe and the USA. Within the EC, Germany is believed to have the largest number of ornamental fish in captivity. Few records are kept of live fish imports and few data are demanded of importers other than for the most strictly protected species. It is thought that approximately 35 million freshwater fish are imported to the UK annually. Around two-thirds of tropical species come from commercial farms in the Far East.

Some freshwater species, particularly South American, continue to be taken in the wild. Shoals are netted, particularly in the breeding season. Unwanted species are thrown away. Sometimes a stop net is placed downstream and a fish narcotic or poison is introduced upstream. The commercially valuable species are taken from the net and placed in fresh water to recover.

Narcotics are commonly used in lakes, and by the 1990s this had led to the decline of commercially prized species in Malaysia and Sri Lanka except in the most inaccessible areas. Larger or rarer species are caught individually and handled in accordance with their value. Mortality rates between capture and export are high, reaching 80% for some of the most fragile species. A further 10–15% of fish are likely to die between export and final destination. The fish may also be treated with hormones before export to induce display of their attractive breeding colours. This practice renders the fish sterile and thereby ensures continuing demand. The commercial farming of ornamental freshwater fish involves lower mortality rates than capture from the wild, but may result in physical changes to the species due to inbreeding, while escaped farmed fish affect the indigenous fish of the area.

Almost all imported marine species are taken from the wild in tropical waters. Collectors are known to use explosives to stun fish with the result that sensitive areas of coral reef are simultaneously destroyed. More

---

[12] *Perceptions, Conservation and Management of Wild Birds in Trade*, Thomsen, Edwards and Mulliken, Traffic International, 1992.

common today is the use of a potent poison, natrium cyanide, which actually kills 75% of the target fish. The rest sustain liver damage which only shows up when the fish die a month or so after purchase from shops.[13]

Fish are generally transported in polythene bags. Those with sharp or poisonous spines may be injured by use of corks to cap their spines during transit. The sensitivity of tropical species to temperature means that transit delays can be fatal, while acclimatisation is necessary on arrival.

Luxury, Souvenir and Craft Products

Animal products such as caiman or crocodile skins, which are mostly obtained through ranching, and snake skins and spotted cat furs, which are mostly obtained in the wild, fulfil a luxury market, both within the framework of permitted trade and outside it. Rhinoceros horn has, until very recently, still been made into dagger handles in Yemen, despite an international trade ban on products from all rhino species. Ivory obtained from the African elephant has been a significant trade item. However, despite continued poaching, its availability has declined since the animal was given the strictest level of international protection in 1989. Ivory dealers in South East Asia are now focusing on ivory from the equally protected but even less numerous Asian elephant, of which only the males, though not all of them, produce tusks. Ivory carvers are experimenting with bone substitutes. Despite decline since 1989 in world ivory demand, and thus prices, worked ivory on sale in Asia remains so expensive that it is generally sold to foreigners. Indeed tourist souvenir demand is a notable factor in the wildlife product trade in many countries, although tourists may not always realise that if the product comes from an internationally protected species, they risk confiscation of their souvenirs on return home.

Scientific Research

Non-human primates in Africa and Asia are trapped for export. The majority will be supplied to scientific research laboratories worldwide. For example, the UK imported 1,985 in 1995, many of which would typically have been shipped on to other countries. This aspect of wildlife trade is referred to more fully under the section on experimental animals (see p. 91).

Traditional Medicinal Uses

Japan, China, Taiwan and South Korea are among the Far Eastern countries which import wild animal products for use as remedies in traditional medicine. Rhinoceros horn from African and Asian species is one of the most

---

[13]   Danmarks Aquarium.

sought-after items. Asiatic rhino horn can fetch a wholesale price several times greater than its weight in gold in Taiwan, with mainland China also a major buyer. The gall bladders, bile and paws of bears are valued both for their alleged medicinal properties and as health foods. Japan and China both hold captive bears for these purposes as well as importing body parts. These products also fetch exorbitant prices. All bear species are now covered by the Convention on International Trade in Endangered Species, but strictly protected Asiatic species still find their way into the traditional medicine market, while pressure has extended to less threatened species in more distant countries. Chinese raw medicine traders supplying communities all over the Far East also prize deer velvet and tortoise shells, along with tiger bones, which Indian poachers sell illegally at US$50 per kg. The Chinese traditional medicinal market is actually the main threat to the survival of all rhino and all tiger species. Other animals caught up in the same trade include bush tailed porcupine, gecko, pangolin, monitor lizard, cobra, python, green snake, flying fox and the pygmy slow loris.

Exhibition Purposes

Non-human primate species are among those still trapped for sale to menageries, circuses or safari parks. Animals of many species may be traded worldwide for exhibition or conservation work in zoos. Zoos account for around 1% of animal trade transactions, and in view of their role in conservation are discussed separately (see p. 103). Circuses involve other welfare concerns besides trade. These are also considered in a separate section (see p. 106).

Possibilities for Change

Public attitudes towards the consumption of wildlife products can and do change, particularly when information is provided, with the result that public opinion in the western nations has supported legislation and international pressure to increase the protection of particular species. Just such public pressure has led more than 100 airlines worldwide to cease carriage of wild caught birds since 1991. This has in turn affected imports. Public pressure also supported the ban on ivory trading. However, much also depends on the will and ability of people in the exporting countries to protect and coexist with their wildlife.

Legislation

The most important single instrument for the control of wildlife trade is the Convention on International Trade in Endangered Species (CITES). The

Convention was drafted in 1973 and is implemented through the national legislation of the Parties. Currently 130 countries are Parties to the Convention. The Convention divides the species it covers into three categories: Appendix I lists species which are essentially barred from commercial trade, Appendix II lists those which can be traded subject to quotas and conditions, and Appendix III lists species for which individual countries have notified their own trade restrictions.

The European Union implements CITES as a bloc through Council Regulation 3626/82 (EEC) of December 1982. This took effect in 1984 and has been supplemented and amended by a series of minor regulations since then. It is both stricter and broader in its coverage than the Convention itself. The import of raw and worked African elephant ivory to the Community was banned by a Commission Regulation in 1989, just prior to the introduction of an international ivory trade ban under CITES. Transport conditions for live wild animals to, within and from the EU have been regulated under Council Directive 91/628/EEC on the protection of animals during transport since January 1993.

Partly in view of the general abolition, in 1993, of border checks for trade between EC Member States, and partly in response to criticism of the structure and enforcement of Council Regulation 3626/82, the Commission published a proposal for a new EC Regulation to improve implementation of CITES in 1991. The proposal is intended to be still more comprehensive than the Regulation it will replace, stating more clearly the obligation of animal owners and traders to provide adequate care for the animals they hold. In June 1993 the European Parliament approved the proposal, together with amendments which would further strengthen enforcement of trade controls. They would also ban importation to the EC of species which may not yet be internationally classified as endangered, but which are too vulnerable to survive transportation, quarantine and captivity. This to some extent takes up the concern expressed in a previous European Parliament report, adopted in 1991, which urged a ban on the commercial importation of wild caught birds. The Commission issued a revised version of its proposal, taking into account only a few of the points raised by the European Parliament. After long deliberations, the Council of Ministers agreed a common position in February 1996 which considerably simplified the Regulation and, hopefully, making it easier to enforce. A second hearing in the European Parliament took place in September 1996.

The transportation of pets, wild animals and zoo animals was under consideration by a working group established by the European Commission. No further legislative proposals are anticipated. Council Directive 91/628/EEC on the protection of animals during transport provides for the possibility of introducing special additional conditions for the transportation of animals such as wild birds.

Possible EU initiatives

1. The Community may adopt the new EC Regulation laying down provisions with regard to possession of and trade in specimens of species of wild fauna and flora in the course of 1996 so that it may take effect from 1 April 1997. It is hoped the final text will include provisions to exclude animals from trade with Europe whenever there is doubt as to their conservation status or welfare during transport and captivity. Such an approach reflects the spirit of CITES and has already been applied in the 1992 USA law restricting wild bird imports.

2. Active enforcement of the new EC Regulation, and of the relevant transport legislation, by the Community and all Member States is vital. In view of the concern caused by the abolition of border checks for intra-community trade and the poor implementation record of certain Member States, it is suggested that the working of the new Regulation should be reviewed within three to five years.

3. Given that many of the conservation and welfare problems referred to are found outside the territory of the Community in the exporting countries, the EU should use its influence to encourage countries which have not yet become Parties to CITES to join in the work of the Convention and to develop wildlife protection initiatives.

4. The EU and Member States should also work to encourage effective implementation of wildlife protection and trade controls in those countries which are already Parties to CITES.

5. The EU should support international pressure through CITES, such as that exerted on China and Taiwan to register their stocks of rhino horn and tiger bone with a view to ending trade in these items.

6. Council Directive 91/628/EEC on the protection of animals during transport provides for the possibility of drawing up additional special legislation for the protection of wild birds in transit. In view of the movement of captive bred specimens of wild species within, to and from the Community, such legislation would be desirable.

PROTECTION OF WILDLIFE AND HABITATS IN EUROPE

Reasons for concern

Farming methods, field sports, and the use of traps, snares and poisons to prevent crop damage or transmission of disease to livestock all have a direct impact on wild animals. This impact is compounded by the threat to wildlife habitats from pollution, degradation and destruction due to the development of transport, industry and tourism. There is now a basic core of European Community legislation designed to protect wild animals and their habitats – both marine and on land – from disturbance and other negative effects of human activity, but problems, such as the following, remain.

Snares and Traps

With the exception of the leghold trap, the use of cruel and non-selective methods of catching animals is not totally banned by Community legislation. The 1992 Directive on the conservation of habitats and wild flora and fauna only forbids use of such methods for permitted taking of the species it lists, or where a strictly protected species might be put at risk. While such methods remain in use at all, animals such as foxes and rabbits will suffer an inhumane death, and protected species, along with domestic pets, will continue to be caught incidentally.

Pollution from Lead Shot

Large numbers of wildfowl and wading birds suffer from poisoning due to swallowing lead shot, which is present in the environment due to the activities of anglers and wildfowlers. The lead is taken up along with the gravelly substances used by birds to break up food in the gizzard. It is broken down by the bird's digestive system to form toxic salts in the bloodstream. In the United Kingdom, legislation has already been introduced requiring the replacement with non-toxic alternatives of certain sizes of anglers' weights. The sizes affected are those small enough to be swallowed and large enough to lodge in a bird's gizzard. In 1991, the Standing Committee of the European Convention on the conservation of European wildlife and natural habitats adopted a Recommendation on the use of non-toxic shot in wetlands, which took into account the results of studies by the International Waterfowl and Wetlands Research Bureau. The Recommendation urges a ban on the use of lead shot in wetlands before the end of 1996. The ban would be coupled with the phasing in of non-toxic alternative shot and training programmes for hunters. So far Denmark, the Netherlands, Finland and Sweden are EU Member States which have progressively restricted lead shot use on wetlands by wild bird hunters, while the UK is in the process of introducing voluntary restraints.

Impact of Industrial Fishing on Sea Birds and Other Marine Wildlife

Twice in recent years many thousands of dead seabirds have been washed up along British North Sea coasts. The birds appear to have starved to death, and it is thought that so-called industrial fishing for sand eels and small fish species, for processing into fertilisers and animal feedstuffs, may be to blame. Birds may not be the only larger marine species affected. The British Government has obtained the support of other EC Member State governments for a study of the subject. The European Parliament adopted a Report critical of the effects of industrial fishing on stocks of the larger fish species which are the target of the conventional fishing industry in April 1994. The impact of other fisheries activities on wildlife is referred to in the sections on Dolphins and Porpoises (p. 62) and Seals and Walrus (p. 68).

Enforcement of Legislation

Enforcement of the Community's oldest piece of wildlife protection law, the Directive on the conservation of wild birds, has been widely and justifiably criticised. The Community's Court of Justice has so far given judgment in eleven cases against seven Member States for failure to implement the Directive properly. Two further cases are awaiting final judgment, and proceedings have recently begun in two more. The judgments show that in most cases, Member States had failed to update their hunting and nature protection laws to comply with the more stringent demands of EC legislation. In some instances, development had been allowed to encroach into protected areas of bird habitat. The Court has also judged that certain Member States have too freely given dispensations for the killing of birds under Article 9 of the Directive, which allows control of birds in the interests of public health and safety, air safety, prevention of serious damage to crops, livestock, forests, fisheries and water, and the protection of flora and fauna. Dispensations to control by killing should, says the Court, be given *only* if specifically authorised and strictly regulated, when no other solution is available. Failure to enforce the law banning the shooting of migratory birds en route to their nesting grounds has been the subject of further Court action.

In a 1988 report on the implementation of the Directive on the conservation of wild birds, the European Parliament identified two more enforcement failures:

- methods of hunting and trapping, such as nets, snares, traps, and poisons, all banned because of their cruelty and/or non-selective nature, were still in use in several Member States;

- illegal trade in birds and bird products continued in some Member States.

In response to French political pressure, in March 1994 the Commission proposed an amendment to the Directive on the conservation of wild birds in the form of an annex specifying the limits within which Member States may use their discretion in fixing the end of the hunting season for migratory species. Member States already fix the opening and closure of hunting seasons according to their own local conditions, but must do so within the limits of the principles set down by the Directive. There are fears that if it is adopted in its present form, the proposal will allow the shooting of birds returning north to breed. Spring shooting of returning migrants, such as turtle doves, which are still illegally shot in France, is currently forbidden by the Directive. The European Parliament was asked to consider the Commission's proposal under the urgency procedure but rejected this request in order to allow time for a full debate. In its report's latest reading, eventually adopted in February 1996, the Parliament rejected much of the proposal and advocated a strict cut-off date for hunting.

Given the experience with the wild birds Directive, there is obvious anxiety as to how adequately the Council Directive 92/43/EEC of 21 May 1992 on the conservation of natural habitats and of wild fauna and flora will be implemented and enforced as it should have come into force in mid-1994. Some Member States have not yet implemented this Directive.

Economic and consumer factors

Community legislation recognises the need to balance the requirements of man with those of wild animals. That such a balance is not always sought is illustrated by the failure, in recent years, to give real consideration to the effect of road transport development projects through the last remaining bear habitats in Spain and France, despite the obligation to carry out environmental impact assessments. Both projects attracted widespread public criticism, with protests leading to legal action to change the plans. They are but two examples of the problem of ensuring habitat protection.

As far as agriculture is concerned, the Community has taken some limited steps to support less intensive and more environmentally sensitive forms of farming. Recent modification of the set-aside rules may be helpful to wild birds. The system of environmentally sensitive areas is being exploited in some Member States to help maintain wildlife-friendly habitat and reduce farming pressures. However, the potential for conflict between wildlife and farmers is shown, perhaps at its most extreme, in Member States where larger predatory mammals, such as bears and wolves, are viewed as a threat to livestock. Compensation schemes covering livestock loss have been established in some areas to prevent poisoning and trapping as a result of alleged predation, alongside complementary moves to increase the level of natural prey species. In some countries there continues to be a problem with the accidental or deliberate killing of birds or prey.

Recreation brings large numbers of people into the countryside. There are, for example, some seven million hunters in EU Member States, in addition to the two million or so bird watchers, and the uncounted others who visit nature reserves or simply go for walks. Visits to nature reserves are increasingly undertaken by schools as part of their teaching programme. In general, there is strong public awareness of the natural environment today, coupled with broad concern that it should be safeguarded.

Legislation

The two main pieces of legislation for the protection of European wildlife are Council Directive 92/43/EEC of 21 May 1992 on the conservation of natural habitats and of wild fauna and flora, which came into effect in 1994, and Council Directive 79/409/EEC of 2 April 1979 on the conservation of wild birds, which came into force in 1981. Both texts recognise the common responsibility and need for cooperation between Member States implied by the fact that many wild animal species are distributed across national boundaries and many are migratory.

The first objective of the Directive on the conservation of wild birds is to ensure that all wild birds in the European territory of the Community are given basic protection from trapping and killing, and that all large scale or non-selective methods of killing and capturing birds, together with the exploitation, sale or commercialisation of most species, are prohibited. The second objective is to ensure the preservation, maintenance and re-establishment of sufficient diversity and area of habitat for all species, with special habitat conservation measures for particularly vulnerable species and migratory species. The capture of birds for scientific research and reintroduction of species may be authorised. Hunting of certain species is permitted and provision is made for killing birds in the interests of public health and safety, air safety, prevention of serious damage to crops, livestock, fisheries and water. However, this may only be done, with specific authorisation, when there is no other satisfactory solution to the problem.

A Commission proposal for amendment of the Directive on the conservation of wild birds was presented to the Council of Ministers in March 1994. This specifies, or rather respecifies, the extent of Member States' discretion in fixing the end of the hunting season for migratory species. The European Parliament, at the first hearing, adopted a report which rejected the Commission's proposal and advocated a specific cut-off date for hunting. The common position is expected.

The Directive on the conservation of natural habitats and of wild fauna and flora will complement the Directive on birds by setting similar objectives for land, aquatic and marine animals in the territory and waters of EU Member States. It is designed to contribute to ensuring biodiversity in the Community. It aims to set up, by the end of the century, a coherent European ecological network of special areas of conservation under the title Natura

2000, and requires that these wildlife habitats must be protected from the effects of pollution and development. It lists:

- Special Areas of Conservation (natural habitat types of Community interest to be designated by Member States);

- animal and plant species whose habitat should be designated a Special Area of Conservation;

- animal and plant species in need of strict protection;

- animal and plant species which may be taken in the wild and exploited subject to management plans;

- methods of capture and killing which are prohibited. Capture or killing by any method from an aircraft or moving motor vehicle is prohibited.

In addition, the Directive bans the use of certain cruel and/or non-selective hunting and trapping methods, although these provisions only deal with use of such methods for species which may be managed or controlled under the Directive, and in situations where protected strictly species may be put at risk. It also requires that permitted hunting should not disturb areas frequented by protected species, particularly during the breeding season. Furthermore, permitted hunting must be regulated so that it is compatible with a favourable conservation status for the species taken.

The provisions of the Directive on the conservation of wild birds and the Directive on the conservation of natural habitats and of wild fauna and flora prohibiting possession and sale of protected species and governing the sale of those species which may legally be taken are likely to be repealed, as the Commission proposes that these aspects will instead be dealt with under the new European Parliament and Council Regulation laying down provisions with regard to possession of and trade in specimens of species of wild fauna and flora. The Convention on International Trade in Endangered Species (CITES), implemented through Council Regulation 3626/82 of 3 December 1982 until the new wildlife trade regulation takes effect, also applies to certain wild animals and birds found in the territory of EU Member States.

The use of the leghold trap in the Community is specifically banned under all circumstances, with effect from 1 January 1995, by Council Regulation (EEC) 3254/91 of 4 November 1991 (see Animals Trapped for Fur, p. 80).

Data on wildlife are gathered under the EC's CORINE information gathering programme, established in 1985. Priority environmental action by the Community is financed under the LIFE scheme set up in 1992. Environmental impact assessments of industrial, transport and other development must be carried out under Council Directive 85/337/EEC of 1985.

The EU also participates in the work of four international Conventions relevant to wildlife and habitat protection. These are:

- The Convention on the conservation of European wildlife and habitats, known as the Bern Convention, which dates from 1979. The aim of the Convention is the conservation of wild fauna and flora and habitats, especially where the cooperation of several countries is required. The Convention is open to membership by North African States as well as European countries. It has been signed by all EU Member States and by the Community itself. The Convention prohibits the deliberate capture of animals listed for strict protection. It also prohibits the use of indiscriminate capture methods for generally protected animals. For example, trapping as a means of catching mammals and snaring as a means of catching birds are both prohibited.

- The Convention on the Protection of the Mediterranean Sea against Pollution, also known as the Barcelona Convention. A Protocol allows this Convention to deal with fisheries-related questions also. It is open to signature by Mediterranean border States. Mediterranean Action Plans agreed under this Convention for the protection of the monk seal, marine turtles and small cetaceans are to run until 1995. The action plans receive Community funding.

- The Convention on the Conservation of Migratory Species of Wild Animals, also known as the Bonn Convention. This Convention dates from 1979 and is open to signature on a worldwide basis. It was ratified by the EC in 1983 and is reflected in Community wildlife protection legislation. Parties to the Convention aim to take the appropriate and necessary steps to ensure conservation of migratory species and their habitats. The taking, hunting, fishing, capture, harassing or deliberate killing of species listed in Appendix I of the Convention is prohibited other than in exceptional circumstances. Species listed in Appendix II are subject to conservation and management agreements.

    Under Article IV of the Bonn Convention, an Agreement on the Conservation of Small Cetaceans of the Baltic and North Seas has been ratified by Sweden, UK, the Netherlands, Germany, Denmark and Belgium and came into force in March 1994. A similar Agreement on the Conservation of Small Cetaceans in the Mediterranean and Black Seas is in preparation jointly with the Bern and Barcelona Conventions. An Agreement on the Conservation of Bats in Europe entered into force on 16 January 1994. These Agreements outline specific policies for the protection and management of the species in question and complement the work which EU countries will have to carry out under the Directive on the conservation of natural habitats and of wild fauna and flora.

- The Convention on Biological Diversity, agreed at the Earth Summit in Rio de Janeiro in June 1992, has been signed by the Community.

Possible EU initiatives

1. The Member States must actively enforce the wildlife protection legislation to which they have agreed as a Community.

2. The Community should set up a system of inspection to ensure implementation of nature protection legislation. This has been suggested by the European Parliament in its reports on implementation of the Directive on the conservation of wild birds and other nature protection issues. The Community now has a European Environment Agency through which this activity might be undertaken.

3. With regard to protection of migratory birds, the European Parliament's 1988 report on implementation of the wild birds Directive suggested that the Community should encourage North African countries with which it has trade agreements to ban hunting in resting grounds and to prevent intensive exploitation in wintering areas. The Parliament repeated this demand in a further report on the protection of wild birds in February 1994.[14] As a means of fulfilling this demand, countries which have not already become parties to the Bern, Bonn and Barcelona Conventions and the Ascobans agreement could be urged to do so.

4. Cyprus and Malta both have a long history of intensive bird trapping and hunting, including shooting during spring migration, which has only recently been restricted. Both are seeking to join the Community. The Community should ensure that these countries apply wildlife protection legislation at least equal to its own before their accession is accepted.

5. All Community Member States should implement the Bern Convention Recommendation on non-toxic shot. This could be viewed as part of their obligations under the EC Directives on the conservation of natural habitats and of wild fauna and flora and the conservation of wild birds.

COMMERCIAL WHALING

Reasons for concern

Commercial whaling was suspended in 1986 as a result of a moratorium agreed between the majority of the countries represented on the International

---

[14] *European Parliament Report and Resolution (A2-181/88) on the Implementation of the Directive on the Conservation of Wild Birds in the European Community,* by Hemmo Muntingh MEP, and *Report and Resolution (A3-0002/94) on the Protection and Conservation of Wild Bird Species in the European Union* by Jean-Pierre Raffin MEP.

Whaling Commission (IWC). However, Japan, Norway and Iceland continued to kill large numbers of minke whales under a provision allowing capture for the purposes of scientific research. Norway, which lodged a formal objection to the moratorium has now recommenced commercial whaling. All whaling is of concern for two reasons. First, it is impossible to kill whales humanely in the conditions of hunting at sea. The definition of humane killing used by the International Whaling Commission's working group on humane killing techniques is that death should take place 'without pain, stress or distress perceptible to the animal'. Despite forty years of research no killing method applicable at sea, including the explosive harpoon in current use, approaches this definition. One gauge of the cruelty involved in killing whales is the length of time it takes before death or unconsciousness occurs. In 1992, despite opposition from the International Whaling Commission, Norway took 95 minke whales for scientific reasons. Of these, 42% lived for up to ten minutes after harpooning, while 8% lived longer. One of the whales took as long as 30 minutes to die. Whale killing for scientific reasons is no less cruel than commercial hunting and today is widely condemned as unnecessary, given that benign research methods are now in general use.

The second reason for concern is, that commercial whaling has already driven many of the great whales to the brink of extinction. Too little is known about the populations of even the most numerous whale species, or about the effects of threats from general fishing and marine pollution, to allow confidence that even limited resumption of commercial hunting would not further threaten their destruction.

Moreover, no system of inspection has been agreed to verify compliance with quotas given under the IWC's recently formulated Revised Management Procedure, should this be implemented. Past experience of inspection schemes is not encouraging. Evidence from the former USSR's fisheries ministry shows that the IWC's international observer scheme set up in 1971 failed to ensure the protection of blue and southern right whales, and that catches of all species were under-reported.

Norway has begun to take minke whales again in the North East Atlantic, claiming to use the Revised Management Procedure calculation methods as a basis for catching 300 whales, mainly for commercial purposes. However, no IWC agreement has yet been reached for commercial whaling to restart and Norway has been asked to stop by the IWC. The quota of minke whales that Norway allocated itself in 1996 was almost double that agreed in 1994.

The area in which commercial whaling could take place, were it to be allowed, is now considerably restricted, since the IWC has declared both the Indian Ocean and Antarctic waters to be whale sanctuaries. The sanctuary status of these waters is subject to review every ten years. Technically, whaling for scientific reasons could take place within the waters of the whale sanctuaries. Japan continues to kill some 300 minke whales annually in the Antarctic, despite it being declared a sanctuary and has started another scientific hunt in the North Pacific Ocean. While illegal whaling activities, which have involved South Korean ships, should reduce now that South Korea has joined the Convention on International Trade in Endangered Species (CITES), which protects most large whales, there still remains the problem that demand for whale meat in Japan and South Korea will lead, if not to illegal whaling, then certainly to yet more pressure on dolphins and other small cetacean species. These are not protected by the IWC moratorium on the commercial hunting of large whales, and are not fully protected under CITES either.

Economic and consumer factors

The main commercial market for whale products today is Japan. Whalemeat is also on sale in restaurants in South Korea, itself a former whaling nation. At present, whalemeat prices are unusually high in Japan, and will rise higher, due to the limited supply. Dolphin meat is often marketed as whale meat in Japan.

In 1993 Norway resumed commercial whaling. She had previously objected to the IWC declaration of North East Atlantic minke whales as a protected stock and to the moratorium, and has therefore now taken up her legal option to hunt these whales commercially. Norway has always continued to take whales under scientific quotas. The European Union is closed to whale products under Community legislation which bans the exploitation of all whale species and prohibits imports.

Economic Sanctions against Whaling Countries

The possibility of the USA imposing official sanctions, in the form of a fish product embargo, on Norway remains open as a means of pressing for an end to whaling. In the meantime, consumer pressure has led some American companies voluntarily to boycott Norwegian goods and produce. Consumer pressure in Australia has had similar results.

Subsistence Use

Limited numbers of whales are taken by indigenous and coastal peoples from St Vincent and The Grenadines, Greenland, Alaska and Russia for their own subsistence use under a quota system established by the International Whaling Commission.

Interaction with Commercial Fisheries

Minke whales have been presented by the Norwegians as increasing in numbers and therefore a threat to commercial fisheries in the North East

Atlantic. However, there is no evidence to suggest that reducing whale numbers would lead to increased fish catches. In the Antarctic, the Japanese, who have alleged that minke numbers threaten the blue whale, are among the nations interested in harvesting krill, the principal food of Antarctic baleen whales. Conversely, growing evidence of the deaths of whales and other marine mammals due to entanglement in driftnets has led to a United Nations Resolution which enacted a moratorium on large scale ocean use of these fishing nets from January 1993.

Non-Consumptive Use of Whales: Whale Watching and Cultural Valuation

In response to rapidly growing general public interest in whales as living animals, recreational whale watching has developed into a multi-million dollar industry in the USA since 1971. There are now 37 countries providing facilities for 4 million people a year to go whale watching. In 1992, 6,000 visitors from 26 countries took whale watching trips from one Norwegian port alone. However, the industry is said to be growing most rapidly in Japan, where it has considerable tourist potential, and where whale watching as recreation supports whale watching for scientific and educational purposes. Nonetheless, both Norwegian and Japanese governments have hitherto continued to put greater emphasis on resumed whale catching. The issue of whale watching has been raised at IWC meetings since the mid-1970s. In 1993, the British Government put forward a paper recognising the scientific and educational value of whale watching and urging the IWC to guide its development and in 1996 the IWC Scientific Committee agreed guidelines in whale watching.

Whales have been of aesthetic value and cultural significance to mankind since ancient times. They have been depicted in art and have featured in myths and literature throughout the world for thousands of years.

Legislation

Whaling for commercial or scientific purposes is controlled under the International Convention for the Regulation of Whaling which came into force in November 1948. Countries which are parties to the Convention are represented on the International Whaling Commission (IWC) which meets annually. In 1982, the IWC agreed to impose a moratorium on commercial whaling, which took effect from the 1985/86 season. This moratorium was reviewed in 1990 and still stands, as there is currently no agreement on how or whether to implement the recently devised Revised Management Procedure for allocating commercial catch quotas. Norway, the former USSR and Japan originally lodged objections to the moratorium and so technically were not bound by it. Japan and the Russian Federation have since withdrawn their objections, while Iceland, which had earlier accepted the moratorium, left the IWC in 1993. Canada is another former whaling nation which has left the IWC.

In addition to the moratorium on commercial whaling, the IWC has acted to protect whales by declaring the Indian Ocean and Antarctic waters to be whale sanctuaries. Both are subject to review at ten-year intervals, and will be voted on again in 2003 and 2004 respectively. The Antarctic sanctuary, which was only declared in 1994, is circumpolar. It adjoins the Indian Ocean sanctuary on one side, and otherwise extends to latitude 40° south except for a small area where it dips to 60° to accommodate the territorial waters of Chile.

Within the EU, the Commission was authorised by the Council of Ministers in July 1992 to seek negotiation on Community accession to the International Convention for the Regulation of Whaling. A proposal for EC participation in the Convention was first put forward by the Commission in 1979, but was not pursued because of objections by Denmark. However, the Commission attends IWC meetings as an observer. EU Member States which are party to the International Convention for the Regulation of Whaling are Denmark, France, Germany, Ireland, the Netherlands, Spain, the United Kingdom, Finland, Sweden and Austria.

All large whale species, except the West Greenland minke population, are banned from commercial exploitation under the Convention on International Trade in Endangered Species (CITES). The West Greenland minke whales are listed on Appendix II of the Convention which would allow licensed exploitation. Japan and Norway both maintain reservations to the CITES trade ban on products from the great whales.

The commercial importation of *all* whales or whale products to the European Community was first banned under Council Regulation (EEC) 348/81 on common rules for imports of whales or other cetacean products. Subsequently, all commercial handling of whales and whale products, including import and export, was banned under Council Regulation 3626/82 of 3 December 1982 on the implementation within the Community of the Convention on International Trade in Endangered Species of Wild Fauna and Flora. The Commission proposes that the EC ban on commercial exploitation of whales should continue when Regulation 3626/82 is replaced by the new European Parliament and Council Regulation laying down provisions with regard to possession of and trade in specimens of species of wild fauna and flora. This new Regulation will repeal Regulation 3626/82 but will keep in place 348/81.

Additionally, all whale species are listed on Annex IV of Council Directive 92/43/EEC of 21 May 1992 on the conservation of natural habitats and of wild fauna and flora. This means they are strictly protected from all deliberate disturbance, capture or killing within Community waters. Norway asked for a derogation from this provision for fin, sei and minke whale during her negotiations for EU membership, but her request was refused.

The exploitation of krill, which is the main food source of several species of baleen whale, is regulated under the Convention on the Conservation of Antarctic Marine Living Resources (1982), to which several EU Member States are Parties. EU participation in the Antarctic Treaty system has been under negotiation.

The 1992 Earth Summit in Rio de Janeiro endorsed the UN Convention on the Law of the Sea, confirming that as large whales are highly migratory, their conservation must be under full international control, and that the IWC is the correct forum for decision making and stated that, therefore, no individual country would have the unilateral right to decide to kill whales.

Possible EU initiatives

1. It should be ensured through Community legislation, that the EU remains closed as a market for whale products, and that it takes all steps necessary to ensure the protection of whales and their habitat in the territorial waters of its Member States.

2. EU Member States should support, and urge other countries to support, a UN Resolution endorsing the whale sanctuary status for Indian Ocean and Antarctic waters, in order to exert full international pressure for the whale sanctuaries to be respected.

3. EU Member States belonging to the IWC should support further consideration of the development of whale watching, and, most importantly, should call on the IWC to extend its activities to include the management and protection of small cetaceans.

4. The EU and its Member States should work to ensure that CITES accords the same full protection to all cetaceans as Community legislation.

5. The possibility of Community accession to the International Convention on the Regulation of Whaling must not be permitted to negate the voting role of the majority of individual EU Member States which have consistently opposed resumption of commercial whaling.

FAEROESE PILOT WHALE HUNT

Reasons for concern

The long-finned pilot whale (*Globicephala melas*) is found in the Skagerrak and North Sea, where it is the fourth most common cetacean species. It is also found in the temperate parts of the North Atlantic and the southern oceans. Pilot whales swim in schools consisting of mainly females and their offspring. The males migrate between schools to mate. Pilot whale numbers are unknown, and in 1989, the Small Cetaceans Sub-committee of the International Whaling Commission stated that the conservation status of the species could not be confidently assessed. It has, however, long been clear that pilot whales are contaminated and affected by pollution from mercury and PCBs. Unknown numbers of pilot whales are also caught and drowned incidentally to ordinary fishing operations. The Faeroese pilot whale hunt is of concern, not only because it compounds these conservation problems, but also because it is in itself a cruel and indiscriminate drive which also takes other species, some of which are internationally protected. For example, in September 1988, three bottle nosed whales were killed. In the same year, 627 other non-target small whales, including one orca and 540 Atlantic white-sided dolphins were killed during the pilot whale hunt. The number of pilot whales taken was 1,690.

The cruelty of the Faeroese pilot whale hunt is well documented. Pilot whales sighted near the islands are herded towards the shore by men in small boats. After some hours, the whales are eventually forced into bays where they either become stranded or are grounded by the hunters using gaffs (steel hooks weighing 2.5 kg) and ropes to pull them up the beach. The beached whales are then killed. Alternatively, the whales may be hooked and killed from boats. Hunters kill beached whales in shallow water by using a 15 cm long knife to cut the carotid arteries near the spine. It is not possible to restrain the animals, which thrash around. It is therefore very difficult to cut the carotid arteries, so multiple wounds may be inflicted by hook and knife. From the infliction of the first wound with the gaff it may take up to twenty minutes before the whale is unconscious or dead. To kill an entire herd takes several hours. Hundreds of people participate and spectators including children watch from the beaches.

Economic and consumer factors

Records of the Faeroese pilot whale hunt date back to 1584. Until the late 1960s, the meat played an essential role in the survival of the Faeroese people. However, the 1970s brought rapid expansion to the fishing industry and new wealth to the Islands. Today the Faeroese standard of living is as high as that of other European countries, although the fisheries industry is no longer so profitable, due to a combination of over expansion and world-wide fishery problems, and the economy has suffered recent budgetary problems resolved in part by subsidies from Denmark.[15]

---

[15]   The Faroe Islands are self-governing, although represented in the Danish Parliament and subject to Denmark on foreign policy and defence. They are no longer part of the EC, although they are party to reciprocal fisheries agreements with the Community.

Today's reduced demand for whale products is now said to account for less than 10% of the Faeroese' protein intake, and much of the meat and blubber is unused. Since 1977, the Faeroese hygiene and health authority has advised people not to eat the kidneys and liver of pilot whales because of mercury contamination.

Legislation

The Faeroese hunt is governed by local regulations dating back to 1832. These were revised to some extent after the International Whaling Commission (IWC) recommended in 1986 that use of the metal whaling hook (gaff) and killing from boats should be minimised, and that whaling should be restricted to those bays where it could be carried out most humanely.

However, the Faeroese regulations licensed more bays than had previously been in use, although stating that whales must be driven to an authorised whale bay where there is the greatest possibility for a quick and neat kill. The revised regulations do not in practice alter the killing time or the methods. Killing from boats is not specifically forbidden.

Within the International Whaling Commission, the Faroe Islands are represented by Denmark. In 1992, the IWC adopted a resolution urging the Danish Government to inform the IWC of methods used to kill long-finned pilot whales and to participate fully in the IWC's action plan on humane killing. In 1993 a further resolution was adopted, expressing concern over the adequacy and implementation of Faeroese legislation.

The long-finned pilot whale is listed on Appendix II of the Convention on International Trade in Endangered Species of Wild Fauna and Flora, which allows exploitation.

Within the EU, commercial exploitation of the pilot whale is banned under Council Regulation 3626/82 of 3 December 1982 on the implementation within the Community of the Convention on International Trade in Endangered Species of Wild Fauna and Flora. The Commission proposes that this ban should continue when Regulation 3626/82 is replaced by the new European Parliament and Council Regulation (EC) laying down provisions with regard to possession of and trade in specimens of species of wild fauna and flora.

Additionally, all whale species, including the pilot whale, are listed on Annex IV of Council Directive 92/43/EEC of 21 May 1992 on the conservation of natural habitats and of wild fauna and flora. This means they are strictly protected from all deliberate disturbance, capture or killing within Community waters.

The pilot whale is given general protection under the Convention on the Conservation of European Wildlife and Natural Habitats (Bern Convention), which also requires that indiscriminate killing methods should not be used. It is also protected under the Ascobans agreement so killing in the North and Baltic Seas is prohibited. This agreement does not extend to the Faeroese.

Possible EU initiatives

1. The EU and its individual Member States should support the establishment of a framework under which the International Whaling Commission can address matters concerning small cetaceans, in accordance with the IWC Resolution adopted in 1993.

2. The EU and Member States, particularly Denmark, should ensure that information is provided to the IWC on the Faeroese pilot whale hunt, in accordance with the 1993 and 1995 IWC Resolutions which expressed concern over the adequacy and implementation of Faeroese legislation relevant to the hunt and encouraged the prohibition of the gaff.

3. The EU and Member States, including Denmark, should work to encourage the Faeroese to end the pilot whale hunt, since it is no longer necessary for food and cannot be conducted without cruelty.

DOLPHINS AND PORPOISES

Reasons for concern

The welfare and protection of dolphins and porpoises is not only a European but a world problem. Large scale ocean fisheries cause suffering and death, not only of dolphins but also of other marine mammals and birds. Dolphins and porpoises which frequent coastal areas are vulnerable to entanglement in passive fishing nets and traps, where they drown. Inshore species such as the bottlenose dolphin and harbour porpoise are thought to be especially vulnerable to coastal pollution, including the discharge of heavy metals and other toxins from industrial effluent and sewage. A further threat is disturbance in breeding and feeding areas from leisure sailing and commercial navigation.

Incidental Killing in Fisheries

In 1990 it was estimated by Danish environmental ministry research that between 2,000 and 3,000 harbour porpoises drowned in the nets of Denmark's coastal cod, plaice, lumpfish and turbot fisheries every year.[16] Further surveys of Danish fishing operations in the North Sea, conducted in

---

[16] *Health Status and Bycatch of Harbour Porpoises in Danish Waters*, Danmarks Miljøundersøgelser, 1990.

1992 and 1993, show that the incidental take of harbour porpoises in cod and turbot fisheries in those waters amounts to 4,529 annually.[17] Around British coasts, a decline of common dolphin, harbour porpoise and bottlenose dolphin populations is indicated over the last 50 years. A report to the IWC in 1995 showed that some 2,200 harbour porpoises were caught by gill net fishing in the Baltic Sea and that these catches were not sustainable.

In the Mediterranean, it is estimated that some 7,000 cetaceans, over half of which are believed to be striped dolphins, are caught in fishing gear each year. The striped dolphins of the Mediterranean were also substantially affected in 1990 and 1991 by a virus similar to that found in North Sea seal populations two years earlier. Researchers at the University of Barcelona considered the dolphins' vulnerability to the virus might be linked to the presence of toxic chemicals such as PCBs.

Squid and tuna fisheries using drift-nets and purse seine nets are operated by several countries. These fisheries result in the entanglement and drowning of large numbers of dolphins and other marine species. The EU now limits vessels belonging to its own Member States, and all vessels operating within its territorial waters, to use of drift-nets no more than 2.5 km long. However, an exemption was given to certain Member States to allow them to continue using drift-nets up to 5 km long in the North East Atlantic tuna fishery until the end of 1993, while drift-nets up to 21 km long were allowed to continue in use in the Baltic. France and Ireland asked for the North East Atlantic exemption to be extended, claiming that no significant environmental damage was done. However it is understood that some 1,700 dolphins were caught in French drift-nets in this fishery in the course of 1993. In view of the environmental impact, the need to conserve fish stocks and the difficulties of monitoring drift-net use, the European Commission has proposed that the Community phases out drift-nets altogether in the North East Atlantic and Baltic fisheries by the end of 1997. In 1994, the Council asked the Parliament for an opinion. In September 1994, the Parliament voted for a total ban on drift-nets by the end of the year. No decision has yet been reached by the Council.

Concern has also focused on the large-scale Japanese, Taiwanese and South Korean drift-net fisheries. These have taken vast quantities of non-target fish species while trapping seabirds, turtles and seals in addition to dolphins and other cetaceans. The Japanese drift-net squid fishery in the North Pacific captured an estimated 26,000 cetaceans in 1990. Japan, Taiwan and South Korea stopped large scale ocean drift-netting at the end of 1992, under pressure from the United Nations and the United States of America. Nonetheless, even in a reduced form these and other large-scale fisheries still prove damaging to dolphins and other marine mammals.

[17] *Garnfiskeri og marsvin*, Danmarks Fiskeri- og Havundersøgelser, 1994.

A further problem arising from drift-net fisheries is caused by lost or discarded nets, which are made of synthetic materials and so do not degrade. These continue to ensnare marine mammals and birds until they eventually sink under the weight.

Due to restrictions imposed under American legislation, the number of dolphins has continued to decline to about 4,000 a year killed in the yellowfin tuna fishery of the Eastern Tropical Pacific. This fishery has, since the 1950s, increased its catches by using purse seine nets deliberately set around the dolphin schools under which shoals of tuna are known to gather. The dolphins are frequently unable to escape before the net is closed, and drown in thousands every year. EC legislation now regulates the use of purse seine nets by vessels belonging to its own Member States to prevent the encirclement of dolphins during purse seine fishing operations. American attempts to enforce a reduction in dolphin kills through an import embargo on tuna obtained by countries which exceed agreed levels for incidental capture of dolphins have fallen foul of GATT rules.

Deliberate Catches and Commercial Exploitation

Illegal deliberate catching of dolphins is still reported in the Mediterranean and Atlantic area, involving Italian, Spanish, French and Portuguese fishermen. Some of the dolphins are taken for food but most are taken because they are seen as competitors for fish resources. Historically, the common dolphin, harbour porpoise and bottlenose dolphin have been exploited commercially in the Black Sea by Turkey, Bulgaria, Romania and the former USSR. Although this fishery had ceased by 1983, there is pressure in Turkey for its reopening.[18]

The taking of dolphins for food is carried out extensively by Japanese fishermen using extremely cruel methods. It is estimated that up to 50,000 dolphins are killed each year in coastal waters, while thousands more are taken offshore. Initially the catch focused on striped dolphins, but as the numbers of this species declined, hunting switched to Dall's porpoises. Hunters use hand harpoons consisting of a barbed metal blade attached to a line and float. The harpoon's wooden handle detaches on impact. The animal is not killed outright, but remains wounded and drowning in the sea until it, and others harpooned in the same area, are hauled into boats by fishermen using metal hooks. Some hunters deliver an electric shock to the dolphin via a cable attached to the harpoon head, but this is said to reduce the quality of the meat by softening it. There are also coastal drive hunts in which bottlenose dolphins are herded into bays where they are slaughtered with knives.[19]

[18] *Dolphins, Porpoises and Whales of the World*, The IUCN Red Data Book, 1991.
[19] *The Global War against Small Cetaceans*, Environmental Investigation Agency, 1990.

Finally, there is a very small international trade in live captive dolphins, mainly bottlenose, for display and entertainment shows in dolphinaria.

Economic and consumer factors

Food use of dolphins in Italy is very small and restricted to the Liguria area where traditional salted and smoked dolphin fillets called *musciame* are reported to be sold in shops and restaurants. Spanish fishermen catch dolphins for use as bait in prawn, crab and shrimp operations. Dolphin meat is also used as food by the fishermen and has been found in snack bars around the Mediterranean coast. It is also reportedly sold along the Biscay coast for use as fish meal. All these activities are illegal under both national and EC legislation, which bans the commercial exploitation of cetacean species.

The meat obtained from Japanese dolphin hunting activities is mostly labelled for supermarket sale as 'whale meat'. Dolphin catches are said to have increased as whale catches reduced following the 1986 moratorium on commercial whaling. Dolphin meat as such is eaten by very few Japanese. However, Japan also represents a market for oil and meal derived from dolphins, and would be the major market if the Turkish dolphin fishery were to recommence.

American national legislation has set quotas for 'acceptable' levels of dolphin by-catches in the Eastern Tropical Pacific tuna fishery, backed up by the threat of an embargo on access to the US market for tuna exported by countries whose boats exceed their allotted limit of dolphin kills. The aim of the legislation was to reduce the incidental dolphin kill to zero. However, there has now been agreement in the IATTC on acceptable mortality levels and to avoid a further confrontation under GATT there is a proposal to amend this legislation to take these new levels into account.

On a general commercial level, the huge catches and lower running costs made possible by drift-nets, purse seines and modern technology are offset by higher capital costs and the destruction of fisheries resources through overfishing. This also adversely affects the economy of small-scale fishing communities.

Legislation

In 1989, 1990 and 1991 the UN General Assembly adopted Resolutions calling for a worldwide ban on high seas drift-netting from December 1992. Since then, all large-scale drift-netting has stopped although reports indicate that some illegal drift-netting continues.

As far as the EU is concerned, Council Regulation (EEC) 345/92 of 27 January 1992 amending for the 11th time Regulation 3094/86 laying down certain technical measures for the conservation of fishery resources bans the use of drift-nets over 2.5 km long in Community waters or by Community vessels anywhere in the world. Vessels which had been using drift-nets in the North East Atlantic albacore tuna fishery for more than two years were allowed to continue using drift-nets up to 5 km long until the end of December 1993, provided that the nets were submerged 2 metres below the surface. This derogation could only be extended if fishery monitoring showed that no environmental damage would be caused by its continuation. The Commission has started proceedings against Italy for non-enforcement of the 2.5 km drift-net ban in the Mediterranean. The USA has also threatened sanctions against Italy under its own legislation.

On 8 April 1994, the Commission proposed that drift-nets up to 5 km long could continue in use in the North East Atlantic, and drift-nets up to 21 km long in the Baltic, until the end of 1994, provided this was restricted to boats which had been fishing the area under the existing derogation in 1992/93. The proposal went on to state certain restrictions to be introduced over the next three years in the North East Atlantic and Baltic so that drift-net use in these waters would be phased out altogether by 31 December 1997. This proposed Council Regulation (EC) amending for the 16th time Regulation (EEC) No 3094/86 laying down certain technical measures for the conservation of fishery resources also contains a number of new inspection and monitoring requirements to be implemented during the interim period. It was proposed that the new measure would come into force in June 1994. The proposal was not able to be examined by the Parliament before the end of 1994 and it then voted for a complete ban on all drift-netting. No Council decision has yet been made.

Council Regulation (EEC) 3034/92 of 19 October 1992 amending for the 14th time Regulation 3094/86 laying down certain technical measures for the conservation of fishery resources bans use of purse seine nets for tuna or other fisheries where this could result in the catching or killing of marine mammals. The ban applies to EC registered vessels operating in any waters.

The marine dolphin and porpoise species mentioned in this section are listed on Appendix II of CITES, which means that some international trade is allowed. However, within the EU, commercial exploitation of dolphin and all other cetacean species is banned under Council Regulation 3626/82 of 3 December 1982 on the implementation within the Community of the Convention on International Trade in Endangered Species of Wild Fauna and Flora. The Commission proposes that this Community ban should continue when Regulation 3626/82 is replaced by the new European Parliament and Council Regulation laying down provisions with regard to possession of and trade in specimens of species of wild fauna and flora.

Additionally, all cetaceans are listed on Annex IV of Council Directive 92/43/EEC of 21 May 1992 on the conservation of natural habitats and of wild fauna and flora. This means they must be strictly protected from all deliberate disturbance, capture or killing within Community waters. The bottlenose dolphin (*Tursiops trunchata*) and harbour porpoise (*Phocoena phocoena*) are also listed on Annex II of the Directive, which means that crucial areas of their habitat should be designated as special areas of conservation.

The Agreement on the Conservation of Small Cetaceans of the Baltic and North Seas (ASCOBANS), concluded under Article 4 of the Bonn Convention on the Conservation of Migratory Species, came into force in March 1994. It has been ratified by Belgium, Denmark, Germany, the Netherlands, Sweden, the UK and the European Community. The Agreement requires parties to apply conservation, research and management measures in their territorial waters, including modification of fishing techniques to reduce the incidental capture of dolphins and other cetacean species. Each country must also set up a national coordinating authority for these activities. The Agreement is likely to be extended into the Irish Sea, and possibly Irish Atlantic waters. The first meeting of parties was held in 1995 and a second meeting planned for 1997.

A Joint Agreement on the Conservation of Cetaceans in the Mediterranean and Black Seas is in preparation under the Bonn, Bern and Barcelona Conventions (see p. 53). Its requirements will be similar to those of ASCOBANS.

Possible EU initiatives

1. Implementation of Council Directive 92/43/EEC of 21 May 1992 on the conservation of natural habitats and of wild fauna and flora is extremely important, implying as it does that steps must be taken to deal with pollution, disturbance, and fisheries problems.

2. The Community should adopt the proposal to end drift-netting altogether, by the end of 1997, in Member State waters and by Member State vessels in any waters. Although delayed, the proposed legislation should grant no further derogation for use of drift-nets by certain Member States.

3. Present Community fisheries legislation does not address the prevention of cetacean entanglement in fishing gear in coastal areas. The Community and Member States should assess the problems and possible solutions.

4. The EU and its Member States should participate fully in the work of the two Agreements on the conservation of cetaceans drawn up under the Bern and Bonn Conventions, since this is complementary to the implementation of Council Directive 92/43/EEC and relevant to the fisheries problems.

5. The EU and its Member States should support the establishment of a framework under which the International Whaling Commission can

address matters concerning small cetaceans, in accordance with the IWC Resolution adopted in 1993.

SEALS AND WALRUS

a) Hooded and Harp Seals (*Cystophora cristata and Phoca groenlandica*)

Reasons for concern

Annual hunts of hooded and harp seals are still carried out by Canadian, Norwegian, Greenland and Russian sealers. The seals are hunted around the White Sea, and the coasts of Greenland, Jan Mayen Island, Labrador and Newfoundland. The hunts are a source of concern principally because of the extreme cruelty involved, but also because of the need to monitor the impact of exploitation on the biology and population of both species. Annual quotas are proposed nationally for the number of seals to be taken. Except in Greenland, the hunt focuses on the breeding grounds. Seal hunting on Norway's coastal ice recommenced in March 1996 after a seven year break.

Among harp seals, pups between three and ten days old, known as 'whitecoats' have been the main object of commercial exploitation because of their white, translucent fur. Around the age of fourteen days, the pups start to moult and develop a soft, thick, grey spotted coat. Pups at this stage are known as 'beaters' and may also be taken for their fur, which is more highly prized than the eventual adult pelt. In the case of hooded seals, the blueish pelts of the pups, which are known as 'bluebacks', have also been of most commercial value. Pups of both species are clubbed to death. Harp seal 'beaters' which have left the ice are shot.

Regulations introduced in Norway to reduce the cruelty are known to have been routinely ignored by sealers. Sealing and fisheries interests in Norway and Canada have sought to justify hunting on the grounds that large seal populations threaten cod fisheries, both through consumption and the transmission of parasites. However, such arguments have been strongly disputed as ill-founded.

Economic and consumer factors

Seals of both species have been hunted commercially for more than a century, chiefly for the pelts of their pups. In Canada, 32,000 whitecoat and beater pups were taken annually between 1983 and 1989, representing 79% of the average annual catch of 45,000 harp seals. Both hooded and harp seals are also hunted for leather and blubber oil, although the leather obtained from adult hooded seals is less resilient and more porous than that of harp seals. Canada's annual quota system allows some 186,000 hooded and 8,000 harp seals to be taken, but until recently far fewer have actually been killed in Newfoundland and Labrador, due to the collapse of demand for seal pelts. In the 1993 season, only 27,000 seals were killed. However, a new market appears to have opened up for Canadian seal products in China, which uses seal penises and other organs, together with seal oils, to make traditional medicines and aphrodisiacs. This, together with the disputed argument that seals threaten commercial fish stocks, led Canada to increase the 1996 quota to 250,000 seals.

In Europe, the edible oil obtained from seals was used in products ranging from margarine to cosmetics, but has been superseded by vegetable-based or other alternatives. The pelts of beaters and adult harp and hooded seals remain saleable to the fur and leather goods industry, but the market has virtually collapsed, as the introduction in 1983 of an EC import ban on whitecoat and blueback pelts, combined with public revulsion at the cruelty involved in the hunt, has had an impact also on demand for pelts from older seals. With demand for the products beginning to fall, the Canadian Government introduced subsidies to land-based sealers in 1983. In 1994, the Canadian and Newfoundland governments started to pay a subsidy for seal meat. In 1991, sealing in Norway attracted NKr 12.9 million in subsidies, while earning NKr 1 million in sales and employing some forty people part time.

Inuit peoples in Canada and Greenland take adult seals for meat. Pelts from the Greenland hunt, which does not involve pups, are exported through Denmark.

Some additional revenue to sealing communities in Canada comes from tourism based on seal watching. This takes place in February/March when the whitecoat and blueback pups are to be found on the ice.

Legislation

Canada banned large vessel commercial hunting of hooded and harp seals in 1987, but continues to set annual catch quotas for land-based or small boat sealers under its Seal Protection Regulations, for what is still the world's largest seal hunt. In the early 1990s Norway introduced a ban, renewable annually, on the taking of whitecoats by Norwegian sealers.

Since 1983, the European Community has banned the import of skins and products obtained from whitecoat and blueback pups. The original ban, introduced under Council Directive 83/129/EEC of 28 March 1983 concerning the importation into Member States of skins of certain seal pups and products derived therefrom, was renewed provisionally in 1985 and indefinitely in 1989.

Possible EU initiatives

1. The import ban on whitecoat and blueback skins and products derived from them should remain in force, and should, ideally, be extended to cover harp seal 'beaters'.

b) Cape or South African Fur Seals (*Arctocephalus pusillus*)

Reasons for concern

The Cape fur seal has been hunted off the coasts of South Africa and Namibia. Concern is based both on the cruelty involved in the hunt and on the need to monitor the status of the species. The hunt targets pups and adult bulls. Between 25% and 50% of pups born annually are taken. The pups are clubbed to death. The bulls are shot.

In addition to the authorised hunt, an unknown number of seals are caught incidentally by pelagic purse seine pilchard and anchovy fisheries. Seals feeding in the vicinity of fishing operations are shot by fishermen.

Economic and consumer factors

Pelts from both pups and bulls are used in the fur market, with the pup pelts being the most valued. The blubber is processed to obtain oil. Meat from the bulls is also used as pet food. Seal penises are sold to traders from the Far East where customers believe they have aphrodisiac properties. From the end of the 1970s, most sealing has been carried out by private, rather than State-run, groups on a concession basis.

Public pressure led the South African government to postpone the seal hunt for the 1990 season, when it had planned to set a quota of 30,500 seals. In 1991 it again postponed the hunt, and it has not resumed. A report on the seals was commissioned. This concluded that the impact of the seal population on rare and vulnerable birds was a matter of concern, but that this could be dealt with by shooting individual seals at specific sites, with no more than 100 seals killed each year. Both this report and a further report commissioned by the government concurred that there was no reason to cull seals in order to reduce conflict with fisheries. The reports went on to say that fisheries fluctuations were so complex in origin that it would actually be impossible to assess whether a seal cull had made any difference.

In Namibia, the seal hunt has continued and annual quotas are set by the governments. For 1992 the quota was set at 40,000 pups and 2,200 adult bulls, for 1994 – 43,000 pups and 12,000 adult bulls.

Ecotourism has been suggested as a way of providing revenue from seal watching, rather than seal killing.

Legislation

South African sealing is controlled through the Sea Birds and Seal Protection Act 1973. Permits issued under this Act specify killing methods, age groups, season and area.

Within the EU, the Commission proposes to add all hitherto unprotected species of southern fur seal, including the Cape fur seal, to Annex B of the new European Parliament and Council Regulation laying down provisions with regard to the possession of and trade in specimens of species of wild fauna and flora.

Possible EU initiatives

1. The addition of the Cape fur seal to Annex B of the proposed European Parliament and Council Regulation laying down provisions with regard to possession of and trade in specimens of species of wild fauna and flora should be supported.

2. The EU should work to encourage alternative, environmentally- and animal-friendly forms of economic activity in the relevant countries.

c) Grey and Common Seals (*Halichoerus grypus* and *Phoca vitulina*)

Reasons for concern

The grey seal is found on both sides of the Atlantic and in the Baltic. In the North East Atlantic, it chiefly breeds on British coasts from the Shetlands to the Scillies, where 40–45% of the world population is to be found. The number of grey seals around the UK was estimated to be 102,000 in 1992. Small groups are found along the Irish, French and Spanish coasts. The Baltic population of grey seals has been in decline for around fifty years.

The common seal is found on both sides of the Atlantic and in the Pacific. In European waters it breeds on land around Iceland, the British Isles, and the coasts of the Netherlands, Germany, Denmark and Norway. The 26,000 common seals estimated to be distributed around the British coasts in 1992 represent 40% of the European population, and 5% of the world population.

Concern for both species is based on the continuation of hunting, killing for fisheries protection, and the effects of habitat disturbance. Both species, but particularly the common seal, have been hunted throughout their range. Canada still sets annual catch quotas for land-based sealers. The common seal has been radically reduced or eliminated in some localities.

Within European countries, fishermen are allowed to shoot seals of either species if they are near fishing gear. Both species are sensitive to disturbance from human activity and may desert breeding areas. Furthermore, because they live and breed in the relatively closed waters of bays and estuaries, they are prone to the effects of environmental pollution.

In 1988, a viral illness spread rapidly through populations of both species in the North Sea, Wadden Sea, Orkneys, Shetlands and Ireland. More than 10,000 seals succumbed. The virus was thought to be similar to the canine distemper virus, and the outbreak was linked to a possible breakdown in the seals' immune system due to pollution. High concentrations of mercury and organo-chlorine compounds have been found in common seals around the Netherlands and Wadden Sea. Research into the effects of pollution on the seals continues and has been funded by the EC.

Economic and consumer factors

Grey seal pups produce a low quality fur. Skins from the adults are used for leather. Common seal pups yield a high quality fur. The blubber is processed for oil, which, together with the meat, is mostly used by Inuit populations. Common seal products are used by Inuits to make trinket and handcraft objects. The meat has been used as food on mink and fox farms in Alaska.

The common seal is frequently kept in aquaria and is the most widely used seal in experimental research.

Both common and grey seals are regarded as a tourist attraction in some areas. However, both species are killed because of alleged or potential damage to salmon and other fisheries, and fish farms. The grey seal is also regarded as the major host of the cod-worm parasite.

Legislation

The United Kingdom has allowed so-called surplus stocks to be taken under licence for commercial reasons and fisheries protection. One thousand to one thousand five hundred seals, mostly pups, were shot annually in the last decade. Fisheries protection is now the principal reason for seal shooting. Most European countries give general protection to these seal species but allow fishermen to shoot them in the vicinity of nets or fish farms. Hunting is prohibited in Greenland during the summer.

The grey and common seal are both listed on Annex II of Council Directive 92/43/EEC on the conservation of natural habitats and of wild fauna and flora. This means that their habitat (i.e. land and sea of certain coastal areas) requires designation as a special area of conservation. The seals themselves are otherwise covered by Annex V of the same Directive, which allows them to be subject to management measures. This legislation came into force in July 1994, and takes account of the 1988 Bern Convention Recommendation on protection of the common seal.

Possible EU initiatives

1. Implementation of the habitat protection required under Council Directive 92/43/EEC is vital and should be monitored. Management provisions should also be monitored.

2. Efforts should be made by the Community and the Member States to ensure that methods other than killing are used wherever possible in connection with fisheries protection. Further research to assess the effects of seal predation on fisheries, as well as further work on the influence of pollution would be useful.

d) Mediterranean Monk Seal (*Monachus monachus*)

Reasons for concern

Despite its highly protected status, the Mediterranean monk seal is still in decline. It continues to be threatened by fishing activities and disturbance of its habitat.

Economic and consumer factors

None of current relevance.

Legislation

Internationally, all monk seal species are listed on Appendix I of the Convention on International Trade in Endangered Species, and therefore barred from commercial exploitation. It is therefore also strictly protected under Council Regulation 3626/82 on the implementation of CITES within the Community. The same level of strict protection will be continued under the new European Parliament and Council Regulation laying down provisions with regard to the possession of and trade in specimens of species of wild fauna and flora. Additionally, the Mediterranean monk seal is listed on Annex IV of Council Directive 92/43/EEC on the conservation of natural habitats and of wild fauna and flora. This means it is accorded strict protection under this legislation also. It is moreover a priority species on Annex II of Council Directive 92/43/EEC, which means that its habitat should be designated as a special area of conservation.

The European Community supports the Mediterranean Action Plan for the monk seal drawn up under the Convention on the Protection of the Mediterranean Sea Against Pollutants (Barcelona Convention). Protection of the monk seal is a priority.

Possible EU initiatives

1. Work to ensure the full protection of the monk seal should continue. The quality of the implementation of measures under Council Directive 92/43/EEC on the conservation of natural habitats and of wild fauna and flora is vital.

e) Walrus (*Odobenus rosmarus*)

Reasons for concern

The Atlantic walrus is found on Spitzbergen, in the Barents Sea, on the east and west coasts of Greenland, and in the eastern Canadian Arctic. The Pacific walrus is located around the eastern Arctic coasts of the former Soviet Union and Alaska. Concern for the walrus has revived following an apparently substantial increase in kills purely to obtain its ivory tusks.

Economic and consumer factors

The walrus was substantially hunted for ivory in the 19th and early 20th centuries. Following a radical decline in numbers, controls were introduced by all countries of origin, limiting the taking of walruses to local subsistence hunters. However, the former Soviet Union continued to allow 2,000 animals to be taken annually, while in Alaska no limit was imposed on the number of animals that local hunters could take.

Traditionally, the walrus has been killed for its meat, only 35% of which is fit for human consumption. The rest is fed to dogs. Ivory from the tusks, which both males and females produce, is locally made into craft items including amulets.

Since the introduction in 1989 of an international ban on trade in ivory from the African elephant, and with Asian elephant ivory previously banned from trade, there has been renewed interest in walrus ivory as a substitute. In 1989, there were an estimated 250,000 walruses in the Bering Sea area and some 30,000–40,000 in the North Atlantic. This was fewer in total than the contemporaneous estimate for the African elephant population, which was accorded international protection.

Legislation

Internationally, the walrus is listed on Appendix III of the Convention on International Trade in Endangered Species at Canada's request. The Commission proposes to list the walrus on Annex B of the new European Parliament and Council Regulation laying down provisions with regard to the possession of and trade in specimens and species of wild fauna and flora.

Possible EU initiatives

1. Trade in walrus ivory should be monitored and limited through the new European Parliament and Council Regulation on wildlife trade.

2. The EU and its Member States could ask for or support the introduction of increased international controls through CITES.

MARINE TURTLES

Reasons for concern

Six of the seven known turtle species have substantially declined in numbers. Two of these species, the loggerhead (*Caretta caretta*) and the green turtle (*Chelonia mydas*) nest almost exclusively in localised areas of the Mediterranean. Three others, the leatherback (*Dermochelys coriacea*), the Hawksbill (*Eretmochelys imbricata*) and Kemp's ridley (*Lepidochelys kempii*) visit Mediterranean and European Atlantic waters.

Captured turtles are commonly kept alive until sale, when they are killed by decapitation or the throat being cut.

The welfare and conservation of turtles is principally threatened through habitat destruction and fishing. For example, tourist developments disturb nesting beaches, whilst nesting and feeding areas are affected by pollution in the form of seaborne plastic waste, tar, heavy metals and pesticide residues. Turtles are taken by fishermen both accidentally and deliberately.

Economic and consumer factors

In India, a much-criticised proposal to build an industrial fishing facility close to one of the three main breeding sites of the Olive ridley turtle illustrates the potential for conflict between economic and habitat protection considerations. Closer to home, the major threat to the Mediterranean nesting sites of the loggerhead and green turtles is the development of mass tourism. This important source of revenue to local people has developed rapidly since the mid-1970s in the best known turtle nesting areas of Greece, Turkey and Cyprus.

Marine turtles are still taken by Mediterranean fishermen, principally from Egypt, Malta, south Italy and Morocco. Tunisian fishermen harvest turtles taken incidentally to their main trawling operations. The meat is an important source of cheap food for the poorer sections of the population in both Tunisia and Egypt. Turtles are also incidentally captured in drift and seine net fisheries. These fishing methods, together with a move towards the use of smaller hooks for taking swordfish by long-line, account for an estimated annual loss of 10,000 turtles.

The carapaces of turtles taken in the Mediterranean are decorated and sold to tourists. Worldwide, the trade in products obtained from the Hawksbill, Olive ridley and green turtles is generally declining, and is carried on mainly by countries which are not yet Parties to the Convention on International Trade in Endangered Species. For example, there is still some demand for turtle shells in Chinese traditional medicine. The more worldwide use of shell products, mostly from the Olive ridley, for items such as spectacle frames has largely been replaced by alternative non-allergenic substances.

In December 1992, Japan agreed to end commercial exploitation of marine turtles and has since instituted a compensation scheme for former turtle fishermen. The major remaining turtle fishery today is carried out in Indonesian waters.

Legislation

At present the EU prohibits trade in marine turtles under Council Regulation 3626/82 of 3 December 1982 on the implementation in the Community of the Convention on International Trade in Endangered Species. Marine turtles would still be barred from trade in the Community when this legislation is replaced by the new European Parliament and Council Regulation laying down provisions with regard to the possession of and trade in specimens and species of wild fauna and flora.

Council Directive 92/43/EEC of 21 May 1992 on the conservation of natural habitats and of wild fauna and flora lists loggerhead turtles, green turtles, Kemp's ridley and the hawksbill turtle in Annex IV. This means that they are strictly protected in Community waters. The loggerhead turtle is also listed in Annex II as a species whose habitat should be designated as a special area of conservation, and is designated as a species for which the Community has a particular responsibility.

Under Council Directive 92/43/EEC, Community Member States must prohibit all deliberate capture or killing in the wild of the four turtle species covered by the legislation. They must also prohibit the deliberate disturbance of the turtles, especially during breeding, rearing, hibernation and migration. The deliberate destruction or taking of their eggs in the wild must be banned, and so must the deterioration or destruction of breeding sites and resting places.

Internationally, marine turtles are accorded full protection under the following Conventions:

- the African Convention on the Conservation of Nature and Natural Resources (from 1968);

- the Convention on International Trade in Endangered Species (CITES);

- the Convention on the Conservation of Migratory Species (Bonn);
- the Convention on the Protection of the Mediterranean Sea against Pollution (Barcelona);
- the Convention on the Conservation of European Wildlife and Habitats (Bern).

The EC is a Party to the Bonn, Bern and Barcelona Conventions.

Possible EU initiatives

1. Most urgent is the protection of habitats from disturbance and destruction through development. The steps required under Council Directive 92/43/EEC should be taken without delay. As long ago as 1988, the European Parliament adopted a Report and Resolution which called on the Commission to cooperate with Greece in the creation and funding of marine nature reserves in key nesting areas. At the same time, far more effective efforts are needed to enforce existing protective legislation at national level.

2. The European Parliament also called for the development of a turtle protection strategy in European waters to be implemented with Community funding in cooperation with turtle protection organisations and the governments of Greece, Spain, Italy and France. This is partly covered by the Mediterranean Action Plan formulated under the Barcelona Convention, in which the EC participates, which makes turtle protection a priority target to be achieved by 1995. In addition to relevant measures to fulfil this work under Council Directive 92/43/EEC, the Community should assess and take steps to minimise the incidental capture of turtles during fishing activities.

3. The EU should work to enforce the trade ban on marine turtles through its own legislation and through CITES. It should urge non-Member Mediterranean countries to comply with the provisions of CITES and of the Bern Convention, which demands protective measures similar to those under Council Directive 92/43/EEC.

IMPORT OF FROGS' LEGS

Reasons for concern

Frogs' legs are imported to EU Member States as food for the table. The trade is of concern both for its extreme cruelty to the frogs and for the threat it represents to the conservation of frog species in the exporting countries. There are also potential adverse environmental consequences. For example, the reduction in frog numbers in India, prior to the introduction of an export ban in 1987, is believed to have resulted in the proliferation of pests, such as small crabs which damage rice crops, and insects, most notably mosquitoes. Frog farming is reportedly being tried in Italy and has been tried in France. The escape of imported frogs from farms is viewed as a possible threat to the survival of native European species.

The frogs imported to Europe today mostly come from Indonesia, but are also obtained from Turkey, China and Bangladesh. They are caught in large numbers, often at night by children using lamps and nets, and taken in sackloads to freezer factories, where some may be dead and putrefying on arrival. Those still living will be sliced in half across the belly while fully conscious. The torso is discarded, and the leg section rinsed and frozen. Frogs' legs weigh around 40–50 g per pair. Therefore 1 kg represents 20–25 frogs.

The most sought after species in Indonesia are reportedly the smaller forest frogs, which lay fewer eggs than the larger paddyfield frogs. German proposals to control the trade by having 16 Asian frog species listed on Appendix II of the Convention on International Trade in Endangered Species in 1992 were withdrawn due to lack of supportive population data. Germany first tried to have Asian frogs brought under the control of the Convention in 1985. Such action, would, however, be difficult to monitor and enforce as it is almost impossible to identify the frog species contained in imported frozen packages without costly biochemical analysis. An outright import ban appears the best solution to the problem for conservation as well as welfare reasons.

Economic and consumer factors

In 1990, the EC imported 6,202 tonnes of frogs' legs, equivalent to 120–150 million frogs, of which 4,683 tonnes came from Indonesia. The rest came from Turkey, China and Bangladesh. France consumed 42% of these imports, Belgium and Luxembourg took 44% between them, and the remainder went to Italy. Since India introduced a frog leg export ban in 1987, Indonesia has replaced her as the largest supplier. Before the Indian ban, 7,000 tonnes were imported annually to the EC from India and Bangladesh alone, while Indonesia's contribution was relatively modest.

Frogs' legs can be found on sale, at least as a restaurant delicacy, in most EU countries. Today, frogs' legs sell relatively cheaply in France at FF26 per half kilo. In the past, they were mainly a regional delicacy, with families hunting sufficient quantities for dinner. Hunting, coupled with pollution, led to the decline of French frog populations, and almost all native species are now protected. In the 1950s, French fish markets began to sell live frogs from Yugoslavia, Turkey and Egypt. With the introduction of frozen foods, French consumption of frogs' legs is reported to have multiplied tenfold. They can even be found on the menu in school and factory canteens.

The farming of frogs for the table is being tried in a number of countries, including the USA, Brazil and Italy. It has also been tried in France. However, there is a problem in fulfilling the frogs' need for live prey.

The economics of the frog export trade result in a net cost to countries which allow their native frog populations to be depleted. When the Indian frog trade was at its height, India earned £5.5 million in foreign exchange from frog leg exports, but spent £13 million on importing pesticides to control the rising numbers of insects.[20]

Legislation

At present, two frog species, *Rana tigrina* and *Rana hexadactyla*, are listed on Appendix II of the Convention on International Trade in Endangered Species (CITES). These do not appear to be in trade within the EC, which implements CITES through Council Regulation (EEC) 3626/82 of 3 December 1982 on the implementation in the Community of the Convention on International Trade in Endangered Species of Wild Fauna and Flora. The Commission intends to list seven true frog species on Annex A and 12 on Annex B of the new European Parliament and Council Regulation laying down provisions with regard to possession of and trade in specimens of species of wild fauna and flora. This measure is destined to replace Council Regulation (EEC) 3626/82, possibly by the end of 1994.

European frogs are protected to a considerable extent under EU Member States' national legislation. Several species are also listed for strict protection on Annex IV of Council Directive 92/43/EEC of 21 May 1992 on the conservation of natural habitats and of wild fauna and flora.

Possible EU initiatives

1. The Community should adopt the Commission's listing of frog species in its new wildlife trade legislation as a first step.

2. In view of the cruelty involved and the environmental concerns posed by the trade in frogs' legs, the Community should also consider banning the importation of these products and the commercial importation of the live animals.

---

[20] *New Scientist*, 10 April 1993; *Traffic Bulletin*, Vol. 13 No. 1 and Vol. 14 No. 1; Compassion in World Farming; *Dyrevennen*, Issue No 3/85.

ANIMALS TRAPPED FOR FUR

Reasons for concern

The device most commonly used to capture wild animals for their fur is the leghold trap. Versions of the trap may be set on land or underwater. It is designed to immobilise an animal by trapping its leg between two jaw clamps. In the process it causes injuries ranging from lacerations and bruising to broken bones.

Other devices in regular use are the conibear trap, which is designed to break an animal's neck or back, and the snare (essentially a wire loop which tightens around foot, neck or body). None of these devices works predictably. All three devices are non-selective, in that they may take animals which are not the trapper's target. They therefore cause needless suffering to thousands of discarded animals and pose a threat to protected species. In Canada it is estimated that the number of 'trash' or non-target animals amounts to more than 50% of those taken.

Worldwide, 10 to 15 million animals are trapped every year. Although its use is banned in the European Union and in over 60 countries around the world, the leghold trap is still widely employed by fur trappers in the former Soviet Union, the USA and Canada. In the USA, 5,576,132 animals were recorded as trapped in the 1989/90 season. In Canada, 990,775 were recorded for the same period, although in previous years the annual total of animals trapped in Canada has reached 2.6 million. The overwhelming majority of these animals are taken in leghold traps. As the trap immobilises, rather than kills, the trapper usually clubs the animal to death, but may also pin it down with one foot and stand with his weight on the animal's chest for several minutes. Due to the length of trap lines in remote areas, it may be some days before a trapper returns to check his traps. In the meantime, trapped animals have been found to starve to death, to become prey to other animals, or in some cases to chew off a trapped foot in a desperate effort to escape.

A Regulation banning the use of the leghold trap throughout the Community came into force on 1 January 1995. This Regulation also included a ban on the import to the Community of fur products derived from 13 commonly trapped wild animal species with effect from 1 January 1995. However, the Commission deferred the import ban until 31 December 1995. A country may avoid the import ban altogether if it can satisfy the Commission that it has either banned the leghold trap or that it uses trapping methods which meet internationally agreed humane trapping standards.

There are at present no internationally agreed humane trapping standards, although the International Standards Organisation (ISO) set up a Technical Committee to examine the matter in 1987. The Committee was established at Canada's request, motivated by discussion, at the 1983 meeting of parties to the Convention on International Trade in Endangered Species, of a proposal to ban trade in animal products obtained by cruel methods. The recommendations drafted by the ISO Technical Committee have aroused concern that they might perpetuate the use of the leghold trap, despite its widely acknowledged cruelty and non-selective nature. There have been fears that countries might manage to avoid the import ban provided for by the EC Regulation on the leghold trap without changing their trapping practices.

In February 1994, draft trapping standards were put before the ISO Technical Committee on Animal (Mammal) Traps. The twelve countries involved agreed that the title of the draft standards and the Committee's remit should no longer include the word 'humane'. No agreement was reached on performance criteria on either killing or restraining traps. Submersion (or drowning) traps were opposed in principle by the representatives from Europe. The draft standards were referred to a new Working Group which met in June and October 1994. The Working Group also failed to agree performance criteria and this deadlock was not broken at a meeting of the full Committee in September 1995. In general terms, the fur-trapping countries – USA, Canada and Russia – wish to allow restraining traps which cause considerable injury and killing traps which take several minutes to kill. The European countries want more restrictive criteria. The ISO Committee has agreed to discontinue attempts to reach agreement on performance criteria and only concentrate on a standard for trap testing methodology.

In early 1995, Canada initiated a complaint against the European Community under the General Agreement on Tariffs and Trade regarding the possible introduction of the import ban on 1 January 1996. This threat plus increasing pressure from the USA led the Commission to propose in December 1995 an amendment to Regulation 3254/91. This was in spite of a European Parliament's Resolution in November 1995 which insisted that the Regulation be fully implemented. The proposed amendment would, if adopted by the Council, postpone the introduction of an import ban indefinitely. At the same time negotiations began to try to obtain a multilateral agreement on humane trapping standards between the EU, USA, Canada and Russia. In December 1996, the Council of Environment Ministers rejected a draft agreement reached between the Commission, Canada and Russia. Discussions continue.

Economic and consumer factors

In the 1980s, when the market for fur was at its peak, pelts obtained through trapping were worth around $40 million annually to Canada, where there were, at that time, an estimated 100,000 trappers (0.4% of the national population). For most of them, trapping is a part-time or occasional activity by which they may supplement their income. Although it is often stated that native peoples depend on trapping, a study of the Northwest Territories showed that only 5% of the local population actually listed their occupation as trapper.

In the United States, it was estimated by the national Census Bureau in 1981 that there were less than 2,000 professional hunters and trappers, although many more people are involved on a weekend or part-time basis. Part-time and occasional trappers are not always licensed and make very little money from the activity, which would therefore appear, for them, to be recreational as much as commercial. No more than 5% of trappers come from the native population, and they are mostly active in Alaska. They provide only a very small proportion of the number of fur pelts obtained through trapping.

The Russian Federation and other republics of the former Soviet Union are both a major market for and suppliers of fur. Although sable, which is difficult to rear in captivity, had begun to be farmed in the USSR by 1990, 85% of pelts from this animal are still obtained through trapping. Sable is not farmed elsewhere and is unlikely to be.

The market for fur obtained from either farming or trapping has undergone a considerable overall decline since the mid-1980s. The USA, Canada and the former members of the Soviet Union are the countries most likely to be affected by Community legislation banning certain fur imports on the basis of leghold trap use and inhumane trapping standards.

Legislation

The EU bans use of the leghold trap under all circumstances in its own territory and provides for a ban on the importation of fur and fur products derived from thirteen listed species under Council Regulation (EEC) No 3254/91 of 4 November 1991 prohibiting the use of leghold traps in the Community and the introduction into the Community of pelts and manufactured goods of certain wild animal species originating in countries which catch them by means of leghold traps or trapping methods which do not meet international humane trapping standards. To avoid the import ban, countries must satisfy the Commission that they have either prohibited use of the leghold trap or adopted trapping standards which meet internationally agreed humane trapping standards. The species to which the import ban would apply are: beaver, otter, coyote, wolf, lynx, bobcat, sable, raccoon, musk rat, fisher, badger, marten and ermine.

Some of the species listed under Council Regulation (EEC) No 3254/91, or their European relatives, also figure in the listings of the Convention on International Trade in Endangered Species, and therefore in Community legislation implementing the Convention, which subjects them to trade controls. Some species listed under Council Regulation (EEC) No 3254/94 which are also found in Europe, together with European relatives of some other species covered by the Regulation, are also listed for varying degrees of protection under Council Directive 92/43/EEC on the conservation of natural habitats and of wild fauna and flora. This Directive bans the use of non-selective traps for the taking of any species for which it allows management measures.

Possible EU initiatives

1. The EU should not allow the potential for increased animal protection offered by the Community fur import ban to be circumvented on the basis of standards which allow the continued use of traps which are non-selective and cause an unacceptable level of pain and distress. Such trapping methods are already prohibited under the Community's own nature protection legislation.

2. The EU should implement Regulation 3254/91.

Chapter 3

Companion Animals

GENERAL WELFARE OF COMPANION ANIMALS

Reasons for concern

General principles for the welfare and protection of animals kept by man for companionship and enjoyment are set down in the provisions of the European Convention for the Protection of Pet Animals. Drawn up at the request of the Parliamentary Assembly of the Council of Europe, the Convention deals with the care of pet animals of all kinds, the humane control of dog and cat populations, and control of the trade in pet animals. Among the motivations for drafting the Convention was the growing concern over the importation of exotic species obtained in the wild. The Convention therefore states that the keeping of wild animals as pets should be discouraged and that any animal which cannot adapt to captivity shall not be kept. The Convention has been open for signature since 1987 and has been ratified by 12 Council of Europe Member States.

The importation of wild animals for the pet trade is referred to on p. 42 of the section on International Wildlife Trade. Other concerns connected with the welfare of pet animals are listed below.

a) Dog Registration and Control

Animal welfare organisations give a high priority to encouraging responsible pet ownership and proper pet care. Through the animal homes and shelters which they run, they have first-hand knowledge of the health and welfare problems suffered by animals allowed to stray or simply abandoned by their owners. Thousands of unwanted dogs are humanely destroyed each year because their previous owners, or alternative new homes, cannot be found, and the dogs cannot be kept indefinitely in most shelter accommodation. A survey conducted by Eurogroup for Animal Welfare in 1990 indicated that there were more than 30 million pet dogs in the EU, around 2.25 million of which were straying or abandoned at any one time.

The proliferation of stray dogs in rural areas also poses a conservation problem in countries such as Italy, Spain and Portugal, where feral dogs have a detrimental effect on the wolf population, through both hybridisation and competition for food. Wolves are also blamed, and killed, for predation on farm livestock, which is often caused by feral dogs.

In recognition of the public health, environmental and animal welfare problems associated with stray and abandoned dogs, the European Convention for the Protection of Pet Animals calls for dogs to be registered as one of a series of measures to reduce the number of strays. The majority of EU Member States operate some kind of dog registration system. However, the systems vary from country to country, as does their effectiveness. In countries where compulsory registration is enforced, the stray dog problem is small, and the number of dogs humanely destroyed is reduced. In France, where registration is linked to vaccination against rabies, a registered dog which strays can be returned to its owner rather than automatically put down. In the United Kingdom, the gradual spread of voluntary microchip identification, using a system nationally recognised by veterinarians, local authorities and animal welfare organisations, is beginning to have a positive impact. The microchip, which is encased in plastic and is about the size of a large rice grain, is implanted under the loose skin at the back of the neck without discomfort to the animal. The individual identity number on the chip can be read by scanner. Details of the dog and its owner are listed on a central computerized register from which information can easily be retrieved. The microchip is beginning to supersede the system of tattooed identity numbers which has been in use in several European countries for a number of years, and can be used for cats, horses and other animals as well as dogs.

At present, the ability of pet owners to take their dogs or cats with them on visits to other EU Member States is restricted by varying health certificate and vaccination requirements, with the containment of rabies being the most serious disease concern. Animals of these species entering the United Kingdom or the Republic of Ireland must still spend six months in quarantine, unless they are part of a recently instituted EC system of rigorous alternative health controls for animals traded between registered commercial holdings. Should the free movement of privately owned pet dogs and cats between EU Member States ever be permitted under some form of harmonised health control, the animals would have to be identified by permanent marking or microchip, accompanied by proof of vaccination, and registered with national authorities in a system which was compatible with, or at least linked to, registration systems used in other Member States.

Economic and consumer factors

The annual cost of keeping, destroying, or rehoming stray dogs in the United Kingdom, added to the cost of dealing with the road accidents and injuries to livestock they cause, has been estimated as £70 million by the London School of Economics. If dogs, and details of their owners, are registered, it is easier for local authorities to locate the owners of strays, or for the owner to relocate a missing animal, and for other people to obtain redress if an animal causes damage or injury. In the last two years, at least three EU Member States have introduced special compulsory registration systems, accompanied by requirements for neutering and leashing and muzzling in public places, for dogs which are classed as dangerous to the public. These laws are mainly focused on the pit bull terrier type of dog, but encompass measures to curb incidents involving other large dogs also. Pet ownership is a pleasure to many people and considered as a right, but failure to fulfil the accompanying obligation to take care of the animal responsibly is quite costly to society as a whole.

b) Feral Cats

Domestic cats which have strayed or been abandoned may form feral groups which base their territories around human habitation and food sources including warehouses, hotels, factories and hospitals. They may be welcomed and fed by local people, or they may be viewed as a serious nuisance. Depending on the circumstances, in some areas the cats are collected, and, if healthy, neutered and returned to the colony. Elsewhere they are caught and killed for the public health risk they can represent. Humane methods of capture and destruction should be used, but there is concern that this is not always the case.

Just as feral dogs are viewed as a threat to wolves, feral cats are regarded as a problem for the conservation of the true wild cat (*Felis silvestris*) which is listed as a protected species under Community legislation for the protection of wildlife and habitats.

Economic and consumer factors

Cat owners may now also register their pets with voluntary schemes in some countries. In France it has been compulsory since 1992 to identify, vaccinate and register pet cats in the same way as dogs. The cost of dealing with feral cats is not known, but is almost certainly less than the cost of dealing with stray and feral dogs.

c) Mutilation of Pedigree Dogs

Pedigree dogs are not only selectively bred to conform to the recognised standards of their breed. They may also be required to undergo a form of mutilation. This has involved both ear cropping and tail docking, although today ear cropping is widely prohibited leaving tail docking as the most common 'cosmetic' procedure still carried out. Dog breeds which are typically docked include the poodle, boxer, dobermann and rottweiler. Other breeds used as gun dogs may also have their tails docked to prevent injury in the field, although the necessity of this is disputed. The operation has been, and in some countries may still be, carried out on young puppies without anaesthesia, often by the dog breeder. It undoubtedly causes pain and can result in later health problems for the dog. That it still continues is largely due to the requirements of breed societies in connection with competitive exhibitions.

A number of countries have now introduced legislation banning tail docking for other than medical reasons and prohibiting anyone other than a veterinary surgeon from carrying it out. However, on the European mainland, it is possible for dog breeders and owners to circumvent these national bans by taking their animals to neighbouring countries, such as Belgium, Germany or Poland, which still allow tail docking to be routinely performed. The operation is, along with other procedures undertaken for non-therapeutic reasons, banned under the European Convention for the Protection of Pet Animals, which has now been ratified by some 12 countries. However, at the time the Convention was drawn up, it was agreed that the ban on tail docking was desirable, but that it should remain optional. Therefore countries ratifying the Convention were allowed to exempt themselves from that particular provision. Belgium, Finland, Germany and Portugal have all taken advantage of this exemption. Former Eastern bloc countries, which are eligible to sign the Convention because they are Members of the Council of Europe, have yet to do so. Clearly, from the point of view of effectiveness, it would be preferable for all EU and Council of Europe Member States to ratify the Convention in full. In the meantime, some countries have taken action to prevent the undermining of their national legislation, while others are considering doing so. In Norway and Sweden, the incentive to continue tail docking is removed, since dogs with docked tails cannot be entered for shows. In the Netherlands, the law requires the owner of a dog with a docked tail to be able to demonstrate that the operation was carried out for veterinary medical reasons.

Economic and consumer factors

The incentive to continue tail docking of dogs is essentially financial, since a successful show dog or bitch has considerable breeding value to its owner. However, as more countries have moved to ban tail docking, and show judging criteria are modified to allow dogs with full tails to compete on an equal basis, the practice should decrease.

d) Sale of Pet Animals and Award of Animals as Prizes

Pet animals are most often purchased in shops or direct from the breeder, but may also be found on sale in street markets in some places. They may also be given as prizes. It is a matter of concern that shops and commercial breeders should be licensed on the basis of inspection to ensure that the premises and conditions in which the animals are kept are suitable from the animal welfare, as well as the public health, point of view, and that proper care is provided. Among present problems are the display of animals in unsuitable cages or containers and the sale of young animals which have been weaned earlier than is desirable for their health and welfare. The wish to present animals to the buying public in the most appealing way is the commercial factor underlying these last two points.

Formal registration of all premises breeding, trading or boarding animals commercially, and of animal sanctuaries, is required by the European Convention for the Protection of Pet Animals. The sale of animals in street markets should be prohibited, as should the award of animals as competition prizes in fairgrounds or under other circumstances, since in these cases the welfare of the animals cannot be guaranteed.

Economic and consumer factors

The trade in pet animals is extensive and can be extremely lucrative for importers, as well as profitable for shopkeepers and pedigree animal breeders selling direct to the public. Pet ownership is a source of pleasure and companionship to a great many people.

Legislation

There is no Community legislation dealing with the welfare of pet animals at present. Council Directive 91/628/EEC on the protection of animals during transport does not cover pet animals travelling with their owners for non-profit-making purposes, but does cover transportation of pet animals commercially. It also provides for the possibility of introducing special additional conditions for the transport of various categories of animal.

The basic principles of pet animal welfare are laid down in the European Convention for the protection of pet animals. Drawn up under the auspices of the Council of Europe, the Convention was opened for signature in November 1987. It officially entered into force in 1992. Implementation of the Convention depends on legislative action by individual Council of Europe Member States. By the end of 1996, the Convention had been ratified by Belgium, Cyprus, Denmark, Finland, France, Germany, Greece, Luxembourg, Norway, Portugal, Sweden and Switzerland. Countries which ratify the Convention may take out reservations in respect of Articles 6 and 10.1.a. Article 6 stipulates that no pet animal shall be sold to persons under the age of 16 without the consent of their parents or legal guardians. Some European countries still operate a lower age limit of 14. Article 10.1.a deals with the docking of tails, principally of dogs. A number of Council of

Europe member countries have introduced bans on tail docking other than for veterinary medical reasons. However, in the case of Denmark, the law still allows five hunting breeds to be tail docked. In mainland European countries other than the Netherlands, Norway and Sweden, there is nothing to prevent dog breeders circumventing a ban in their own country by having their animals' tails docked in a neighbouring country which still allows this procedure for non-therapeutic purposes. Belgium, Finland, France, Germany and Portugal have maintained formal reservations to Article 10.1.a, and therefore still allow tail docking.

Finland and Germany also maintain reservations on Article 6, and allow sale of animals to persons younger than 16.

With the exception of tail docking, surgical operations such as ear cropping, devocalisation and the removal of claws or fangs are fully prohibited unless they are necessary for veterinary medical reasons.

Apart from these points, the Convention deals with general principles for the proper keeping and breeding of pet animals, their training, sale, housing in boarding establishments or sanctuaries, use in advertising, entertainment, exhibitions, competitions or similar events, humane killing, and control measures for strays. Information and education programmes on pet care and ownership are encouraged.

The Convention applies to the keeping of any animal as a pet. However, it forbids the keeping as pets of wild animals which cannot adapt to captivity.

Under the Convention on the conservation of European wildlife and habitats (Bern Convention), Recommendations have been drawn up on the protection of the wolf and of the wild cat. These refer to the problems posed by feral dogs and cats for the conservation of these two species.

Possible EU, Council of Europe or other initiatives

1. All EU and Council of Europe Member States which have not yet done so should ratify the European Convention for the Protection of Pet Animals in full as soon as possible, ensuring that tail docking is prohibited for other than curative purposes and that other provisions of the Convention are fully implemented in national legislation.

2. Those countries which have ratified the European Convention for the Protection of Pet Animals with the exception of the provisions on tail docking and sale of animals to children under 16 are urged to withdraw their reservations and comply with these aspects of the Convention.

Chapter 4

Animal Experimentation

ANIMALS USED FOR EXPERIMENTAL AND OTHER SCIENTIFIC PURPOSES

a) General Issues

Reasons for concern

Implementation of Community Legislation

Council Directive 86/609/EEC lays down conditions for the use of animals for experimental and other scientific purposes. It applies to experiments undertaken for the purposes of developing, manufacturing and testing the safety and effectiveness of drugs, foodstuffs and other substances or products, and to experiments undertaken for the protection of the environment from the point of view of the health and welfare of man and animals. Although it does not apply to experiments carried out in connection with fundamental research and education, a Council Resolution adopted at the same time as the Directive urges Community Member States to apply equally strict national provisions to these areas.

Although transposition of Directive 86/609/EEC should have been completed by November 1989, several Member States have been slow to implement and introduce some of its provisions. In some cases it was clear that the basic administrative structures for implementation were either absent or inadequately resourced. Eurogroup has worked with national governments and other relevant organisations to improve understanding of the aims of the Directive, to improve communication between laboratory and government officials, and to develop training courses for all levels of laboratory staff in Italy, Portugal, Spain, Belgium, Ireland and Greece.

According to Directive 86/609/EEC, persons carrying out or taking part in experiments, and persons taking care of the animals involved, must have appropriate education and training. Despite ongoing discussions, there are as yet no agreed Community guidelines or requirements for competence in working with animals to which the various grades of laboratory staff should conform. Implementation of a proper system of training courses as a basis for licensing staff to work with laboratory animals should be a priority. Directive 86/609/EEC also requires the collection and publication of

90

statistical information on the numbers and species of animals used in experiments, and the purposes for which they are used. This is also the subject of ongoing deliberations. As a result, the Commission and Member States have agreed on a common system of tables which still has to be adopted officially.

Import from Third Countries of Non-Human Primates for Research

Primates are highly intelligent social animals. They are used in a wide variety of biological and medical research programmes, including the development and safety testing of medicines and vaccines. A significant proportion of the test procedures involving primates are required under laws or regulations. Chimpanzees and pig-tailed macaques are both used as models for AIDS research, although there is disagreement among researchers as to the suitability of either species for this work. The use of non-human primates in research generally is questioned by many people on ethical, welfare and conservation grounds. While primates continue to be used in research, it is imperative that their welfare and conditions of housing and care be improved.

At least 20 species of non-human primate are used worldwide in a variety of biomedical research programmes and in toxicity testing. According to the EUPREN UK Working Party on Primate Supply, in 1994 the UK bred around 48% of the primates it used in research (compared with 24% in 1991 and 24% in 1992). The total number of primates imported into the UK has gone down in the past few years (according to the UK Home Office figures, 2,835 primates were imported into the UK in 1990 as compared with 1,985 in 1995). Primate breeding centres also exist in France, Germany and the Netherlands. However, most of the animals, of certain species particularly, are still caught in the wild or imported from captive breeding centres in the countries of origin. The USA, Japan, Russia and Taiwan are all substantial buyers of non-human primates. Within the EU, the UK, France and the Netherlands are the biggest importers, although some of the animals involved are in transit to final destinations elsewhere.

Since 1993, a UK-based animal welfare organisation has been campaigning against airlines which transport wild-caught primates intended for research purposes into the UK, with the hope that this would prevent their use. The campaign has been partially successful, in that the number of wild-caught primates imported has gone down, however the campaign appears to have had little impact on total imports of primates into the EU.

Wild-caught animals come from a range of Asian, African and South American countries. Methods of trapping and handling are often cruel. Animals, which, by reason of age or disease, are unsuitable for export, may be killed indiscriminately. Whole family groups will often be destroyed. Holding conditions for the trapped animals, which are distressed and succumb readily to disease, are often cramped and overcrowded. Shipment is a further source of suffering and may fail to comply with international rules established by the Convention on International Trade in Endangered Species (CITES) and the International Air Transport Association (IATA). It has been estimated that up to 80% of the animals trapped die before reaching the laboratory.

Capture of primates in the wild for laboratory supply significantly contributes to the decline of several species, many of which are already threatened by the destruction of their habitat. Although species such as chimpanzees are strictly protected under both the Convention on International Trade in Endangered Species and Community wildlife trade legislation, wild animals otherwise barred from trade may still be imported for 'essential biomedical research'. Council Directive 86/609/EEC limits the use of wild animals in research mainly to work aimed at preservation of the species in question, but still allows use of wild animals for 'essential biomedical purposes' where no other suitable species is available.

Housing of Laboratory Animals

Guidelines for the accommodation and care of laboratory animals drawn up under the European Convention for the Protection of Vertebrate Animals used for Experimental and Other Scientific Purposes, and incorporated in Directive 86/609/EEC, were drafted some ten years ago. Since then, scientific knowledge and experience have advanced. There is now increased concern over the restricted space, the lack of possibilities for carrying out normal behaviour, including social interaction, and the barren environment which represent the conditions of daily life for all laboratory animal species, including breeding stock. Further investigation into ways of improving the living conditions of experimental animals, with a view to updating the guidelines on laboratory animal accommodation at an early date, is needed.

Replacement, Reduction and Refinement of the Use of Animals in Research

In 1991, the Commission announced the establishment of the European Centre for the Validation of Alternative Methods (ECVAM), in response to the European Parliament's demands for more action to ensure the development and acceptance into legislation of non-animal alternative test methods. The role of ECVAM is to focus and coordinate the development and validation of such methods, and to act as a centre for information on progress. It is of foremost concern that the work of ECVAM should be well supported and adequately funded.

ECVAM has given priority to alternatives for cosmetics testing. Products involving animal testing for marketing as cosmetics after 1 January 1998 will be banned from sale in the Community, provided that scientifically recognised alternative safety test methods are available. Some areas have already been identified as promising, and it is to be hoped that ECVAM's achievements will be incorporated into Community regulations by 1997. Apart from coordinating the validation of alternative test methods at the EU level and undertaking experimental studies with research groups in the Member States, other projects of ECVAM include the scientific, ethical and legal aspects of the use of transgenic animals and the use of human volunteers in assessing the safety and efficacy of cosmetic products.

A target set by the European Commission's Fifth Environmental Action Programme was to achieve a 50% reduction in animal experimentation by the year 2000. While the replacement of experiments using animals with non-animal tests is the ideal, the potential for reducing the number of animals used in research, and the extent of their suffering, through refinement of test methods should also be encouraged. Harmonization of test requirements and chemical classification systems, both within the Community and at wider international level, together with mutual recognition of test data, has a major part to play in reducing the need for testing.

Economic and consumer factors

Consumers demand safe products. At the same time, there is considerable consumer resistance towards the use of animals for product development and testing. Many companies manufacturing and retailing cosmetics and household products today acknowledge this unease over animal testing, and are keen to increase the attractiveness of their goods by indicating that they are produced without animal experimentation. This means, for example, that a product may contain only recognised ingredients of long-established safety. Some manufacturers have a policy of not using substances tested on animals after a certain date. These cut-off dates vary from one company to another. The best policy is where an absolute fixed date is used. Some companies say their products have not been tested on animals within the last five years. This accommodates innovation based on animal-tested substances by allowing the cut-off date to roll forward.

Until scientifically recognised alternative tests are available and incorporated in legislation on test requirements, the banning of animal tests would limit product innovation, thus also limiting the market potential and profitability of a number of industries. Animals are widely used for safety and efficacy assessment of cosmetics, household cleaners, pesticides and a range of other chemicals and products which might pollute the environment or endanger health.

However, it is costly to breed, maintain and use animals for testing, and this should in itself be an incentive to switch over to non-animal test methods where these are available and recognised in the relevant legislation. Harmonisation of national and international test requirements and mutual recognition of test results should reduce costs at the same time as reducing duplication of testing.

b) Genetic Manipulation of Animals in Research

Genetic 'manipulation' or 'engineering' involves the deliberate modification of the genome – the material responsible for inherited characteristics. It may involve the transfer of DNA or genes from one species to another. The crossing of boundaries between species and the interference with the integrity – the biological identity – of the animal implied by genetic manipulation have evoked strong moral objections to genetic engineering in principle.

Animal welfare concerns about genetic engineering in practice fall into two areas. First, an increase in the number of animals used in experiments could result from the need to assess the risks posed by products and processes involving genetic manipulation of micro-organisms. Second, the production and use of genetically modified animals could in itself involve suffering. Such animals can include farm animals with altered growth characteristics, farm animals which secrete the raw material for useful pharmaceutical products in their milk, and animals designed for use as laboratory models in the study of disease. One now famous example of this last category is the Harvard University Oncomouse, which is designed to develop tumours so that it can be used as a model for the study of cancer. Animals may also suffer simply because they are genetically modified, as the desired result may be accompanied by painful physical side effects.

Eurogroup is therefore concerned that all research projects involving genetically modified animals should be submitted to a proper ethical evaluation before they are permitted. The welfare of the animal should be an essential part of such an evaluation. Before any genetically modified organism is released into the environment, the welfare implications should be assessed. This means that the welfare of the animal and its progeny should be assured and that other animals in the environment are not put at risk.

Patenting of Genetically Modified Animals

The development of genetic engineering has led to a number of applications for the protection of biotechnological 'inventions' under patent law. Present patent rules in Europe are established under both national law and a small number of international conventions, including the Convention on the Grant of European Patents. The Munich-based European Patent Office (EPO), which administers the Convention, is currently considering a number of appeals against its decision to grant a patent for Harvard's Oncomouse. A public hearing was held at the EPO in September 1995 to examine opposition to the granting of this patent, but it did not result in any decision being taken. The EC is close to finalising its own Directive on the legal protection of biotechnological inventions. This will harmonise the granting of patents for biotechnological processes and products, including transgenic animals, by EC Member States.

It is a matter of concern that the financial incentives involved in developing patentable genetically modified animals could outweigh welfare considerations for the animals concerned. Animal welfare organisations do not accept that any animal should be the object of a patent, but, like the European Patent Office, those involved in making the EC law have accepted that animals are, in principle, patentable.

However, although the EC legislation does not prohibit the patenting of genetically modified animals as such, it would prohibit the patenting of genetic engineering procedures causing suffering or physical handicap to the animal involved, or to its progeny, without being of substantial use to man or animals. The animal resulting from such a procedure could not be patented either.

A similar 'cost-benefit' approach is part of the evaluation used by the EPO when considering animal patent applications under the Convention. It was a factor in the refusal to grant a French company's patent request for a genetically modified mouse designed for the study of hair loss.

The welfare of genetically modified animals in agriculture is referred to under the section on General Farm Animal Welfare (see p. 13).

Economic and consumer factors

By early 1993 assessment of the biotechnology industry indicated that two-thirds of all companies involved were focused on therapeutic or diagnostic applications. Only some 10% were applying biotechnology to food and agriculture. Applications in the chemical industry and for cleaning up the environment (i.e. bacteria used to break down oil slicks and enzymes used to curb phosphor emissions) accounted for 8% of the industry. Commercial control of biotechnological inventions for whatever purpose will be concentrated in the hands of the larger industrial concerns.

The use of livestock to produce pharmaceutically useful substances is considered to be potentially profitable for the manufacturers of the end products. It is also thought that the retail price of such products will come down considerably.

Legislation

General Conditions for Laboratory Use of Animals

Conditions for the use of animals in all experimental situations are set out in Council Directive 86/609/EEC of 24 November 1986 on the approximation of laws, regulations and administrative provisions of the Member States regarding the protection of animals used for experimental and other scientific purposes. The purpose of the Directive is to ensure harmonisation of legislation between Community Member States. Such harmonisation has two aims. The first is to ensure that disparities between national measures do not distort the trade conditions of the internal market. The second is to ensure that the number of animals used in experimentation is reduced to a minimum, that the animals are adequately cared for, and that no pain, suffering, distress or lasting harm are inflicted unnecessarily. The Directive states that where pain, suffering, distress or lasting harm are unavoidable, these shall be kept to a minimum. The Directive covers use of animals in experiments for:

- the development, manufacture, quality, effectiveness and safety testing of drugs, foodstuffs and other substances or products;

- the avoidance, prevention, diagnosis or treatment of disease in man, animals or plants;

- the assessment, detection, regulation or modification of physiological conditions in man, animals or plants;

- the protection of the natural environment in the interests of the health or welfare of man or animal.

The Directive states that the Commission and Member States should encourage research into the development and validation of alternative techniques involving the use of fewer animals and less painful procedures. It further states that an experiment shall not be performed if a scientifically satisfactory method of obtaining the desired result without using an animal is reasonably and practically available.

A supplementary Council Resolution of 24 November 1986 urges Member States to apply national provisions at least as strict as those of the Directive to the use of animals in fundamental scientific research and education and training. These areas are not covered by the Directive.

Commission Decision 90/67/EEC of 9 February 1990 set up an Advisory Committee on the Protection of Animals used for Experimental and Other Scientific Purposes. This Committee's establishment is required by Council Directive 86/609/EEC. Each Member State is represented by two officials from the national authority responsible for implementing the Directive. The Committee's task is to assist the Commission on questions related to the implementation of the Directive, such as the exchange of information between Member States and the mutual recognition of test data, with a view to avoiding unnecessary duplication of experiments.

Council Directive 86/609/EEC and ancillary measures broadly reflect the provisions of the European Convention for the Protection of Vertebrate

Animals used for Experimental and Other Scientific Purposes. The Convention was prepared under the auspices of the Council of Europe and opened for signature on 18 March 1986. It was ratified by the Community in 1987 and entered into force in 1991. To have effect, the Convention must be implemented through the legislation of the individual countries which have ratified it and by the Community.

In 1992 a Multilateral Consultation of Parties to the Convention agreed that its scope included research work involving the breeding of genetically modified animals and their laboratory use. The Parties to the Convention are currently looking at improvements to laboratory animal housing and the development of guidelines for the training of laboratory staff in the ethical and practical aspects of working with animals.

A series of Community measures applying the principles of Good Laboratory Practice recommended by the Organisation for Economic Cooperation and Development (OECD) may play a part in determining and severely limiting the framework of conditions for the housing and care of laboratory animals.

The transfer of certain animals, such as non-human primates, for laboratory use between registered breeding units in EU Member States is provided for by the health check provisions of the so-called 'Balai' measure, Council Directive 92/65/EEC.

Use of Wild Animals in Experimentation

Council Directive 86/609/EEC prohibits experiments on animals taken from the wild except where the aims of the experiment cannot be met by using any other animal. The Directive also prohibits experiments using animals considered as endangered and listed in Appendix I of the Convention on International Trade in Endangered Species (CITES), or in the corresponding annex of Community legislation implementing the Convention. Exceptions are permitted only for research aimed at preservation of the animal species in question or for 'essential biomedical purposes' where the particular species is the only one suitable.

Council Regulation 3626/82 (EEC) on the implementation in the Community of the Convention on International Trade in Endangered Species allows the import and export of otherwise strictly protected species for research. The proposed Regulation which will update and replace Council Regulation 3626/82 would also allow the import of highly protected species for 'essential biomedical purposes'.

The shipment of all laboratory animals from, to and within the Community is covered by Council Directive 91/628/EEC of 19 November 1991 on the protection of animals during transport. This gives legal force, at least as far as EU countries are concerned, to the transport guidelines for wild animals established by CITES and IATA.

Development of Alternative Non-Animal Test Methods

A Communication from the Commission to the Council and the European Parliament (SEC{91}final of 29 October 1991) set out the objectives and initial costs of establishing the European Centre for the Validation of Alternative Methods (ECVAM). The primary objective of ECVAM is to coordinate the validation of alternative methods which either replace or reduce the use of animals, or refine test methods to inflict less suffering. ECVAM is also expected to act as a focal point for the exchange of information on the development of alternative test methods, setting up and maintaining a database with user services, and to promote dialogue between legislators, industry, scientists, consumer organisations and animal welfare. These interests are represented on a Scientific Advisory Committee which assists ECVAM in setting priorities for its annual work programme. Eurogroup for Animal Welfare is represented on this Committee.

ECVAM is located within the Commission's Joint Research Centre at Ispra in Italy. Its first project was the evaluation of potential non-animal alternatives to the eye and skin irritation tests currently used in the safety assessment of products such as cosmetics. ECVAM's studies on alternative methods for the period 1995–8 include the skin corrosivity test, the embryotoxicity test, vaccine production and human volunteers studies.

Use of Animals to Test Cosmetic Products

Council Directive 93/35/EEC of 23 June 1993 amending for the sixth time Directive 76/768/EEC on the approximation of the laws of the Member States relating to cosmetic products provides for a ban on the sale of products containing ingredients or combinations of ingredients tested on animals after 1 January 1998 in order to meet marketing requirements laid down by Directive 76/768/EEC. However, the ban may be postponed for two or more years in cases where alternative test methods have not yet been scientifically validated. The decision to postpone the ban will be proposed by the Commission, acting in consultation with a Committee of Member State representatives established under Council Directive 76/768/EEC and on the advice of its own Scientific Committee on Cosmetology. In November 1996 the Commission put forward a draft proposal that the ban should apply to finished products only. A decision on banning the testing of ingredients on animals would be postponed until 2000. No final decision has yet been taken.

Although the European Parliament will not be involved in any decision to defer the animal test ban, the Commission is obliged by Council Directive 93/35/EEC to present an annual report to the Parliament and the Council of Ministers on progress in the development, validation and legal acceptance of alternative methods to those involving experiments on animals. The Member States must collect and provide the Commission with data on the number and type of animals used for testing of cosmetics. In July 1996, the Commission published its 1995 Report on Development, Validation and Legal Acceptance of Alternative Methods to Animal Experiments in the Field of Cosmetic Products. Validation of alternatives has turned out to be more time-consuming than expected. Some areas have been identified as promising, notably phototoxicity, skin penetration and skin corrosivity. The data forwarded by Member States to the Commission for 1995 fail to be comprehensive and lack precision. Only three Member States (Austria, France and the UK) have communicated figures relating to the number of animals use, while pointing out however that these figures might not be entirely reliable. Furthermore, eight Member States have declared that animal tests for finished cosmetic products have not been carried out on their territory (Italy, Greece, Belgium, Ireland, Sweden, Finland, Luxembourg and Germany) and six Member States have declared that animal tests for cosmetic ingredients have not been carried out on their territory (Greece, the Netherlands, Ireland, Sweden, Finland, Luxembourg).

A further provision of Council Directive 93/35/EEC requires that any reference to animal testing on package labels must state clearly whether the tests carried out involved the finished product and/or its ingredients.

Animal Testing in Classification, Packaging and Labelling of Dangerous Substances

Council Directive 92/32/EEC of 30 April 1992 amending for the seventh time Directive 67/548/EEC on the approximation of laws, regulations and administrative provisions relating to the classification, packaging and labelling of dangerous substances seeks to avoid duplication of testing by doing away with the need to renotify the same substance in each Community Member State where it is to be marketed. A further modification to the basic Directive also recognises the Fixed Dose Procedure as an alternative to the classical LD50 test for toxicity. The Fixed Dose Procedure uses fewer animals and involves less suffering because it does not require their death. The experiment can be stopped as soon as symptoms can be observed. However, the classical LD50 continues to be used, partly because of the attitudes of regulators towards new test methods, and partly because regulatory authorities outside the EU may still require it for substances destined for use in their countries.

Genetic Manipulation of Animals and Patenting

The welfare of genetically modified animals in the laboratory is covered under Council Directive 86/609/EEC of 24 November 1986 on the approximation of laws, regulations and administrative provisions of the Member States regarding the protection of animals used for experimental and other scientific purposes and under the European Convention for the Protection of Vertebrate Animals used for Experimental and Other Scientific Purposes. From the environmental safety point of view, the deliberate release into the environment of genetically modified organisms is covered by Council Directive 90/220/EEC.

A common position on the European Parliament and Council Directive on the legal protection of biotechnological inventions was agreed by the Council of Ministers in February 1994, although Denmark, Spain and Luxembourg voted against it. The text agreed by Ministers was referred back to the European Parliament, which wished to amend references to the patenting of the human body and to the 'farmer's privilege' in relation to livestock. The Parliament asked the Council of Ministers to institute the conciliation procedure to resolve these points. The first conciliation meeting, held in November 1994, ended in deadlock as the Council refused to offer all the legal guarantees that the Parliament was seeking: the non-patentability of parts of the human body, the exclusion from patentability of innovations that go against the public order or public morality, and more precisely those that cause suffering or handicap to animals. In May 1995, the Parliament rejected the compromise text proposed by the Council, which meant that the proposal submitted was lost. In December 1995, the Commission made a new proposal on patenting, which permits the patenting of processes for modifying animal genetics on condition that the usefulness of the invention exceeds the suffering inflicted on the animal. This proposal will probably be voted by Parliament by the end of 1996 and should finally be adopted by Ministers by the end of 1997.

The 'patenting' of genetically modified, or transgenic, animals is also approached under the Convention on the Grant of European Patents, to which most Community Member States are signatories. By the spring of 1994, a number of animal patent applications under the Convention were being considered but none had been granted, except that for the Harvard Oncomouse, which is being reconsidered in the light of several formal objections.

National legislation governing the exploitation of biotechnological inventions, together with Community safety legislation, applies to their commercial use, regardless of whether they are patented or not.

Possible EU and Council of Europe initiatives

1. It is essential that Council Directive 86/609/EEC of 24 November 1986 on the approximation of laws, regulations and administrative provisions of the Member States regarding the protection of animals used for experimental and other scientific purposes be fully implemented and enforced by all Member States.

2. The Council of Ministers' Resolution on a Community programme of policy and action in relation to the environment and sustainable development, agreed at the end of 1992, contains a target set by the Commission for a 50% reduction in the number of vertebrate animals used for experimental purposes by the year 2000. This target is endorsed by the European Parliament. A strategy should be developed, and all efforts made, to meet it.

3. The European Centre for the Validation of Alternative Methods has a vital role to play in developing non-animal test methods and must be adequately supported, both financially and in terms of the emphasis which should be given to implementing its decisions, both within the Community and at wider international level.

4. There is conflict in practice between the requirements of Community legislation controlling animal use (Council Directive 86/609/EEC) and other measures which require it (such as legislation on chemical testing). Council Directive 86/609/EEC requires that animal experiments be avoided where alternatives are available. Otherwise, preference should be given to tests which give the desired result by using the lowest number of animals and causing the least pain and distress. This should mean, for example, that the Fixed Dose Procedure is used in preference to the classical LD50 test, but in practice this is not necessarily the case. This conflict should be acknowledged, and efforts should be made to reduce it by ensuring that the principles of Directive 86/609/EEC are adhered to, and by working for the acceptance of tests which use either fewer or no animals at wider international level.

5. Support and encouragement should be given by the Commission and Member States, and by all Council of Europe Member States, to the work of the Multilateral Consultation of Parties to the European Convention for the Protection of Vertebrate Animals used for Experimental and Other Scientific Purposes on the development of improved housing requirements for laboratory animals and guidelines for the training of laboratory staff in ethical and welfare aspects of working with animals. Improvements should be incorporated in Community legislation.

6. Action should be taken to develop and implement a Community policy on the use of non-human primates. This should aim to ban the use of wild caught primates and promote a switch to captive bred animals reared in adequate welfare conditions at the earliest possible date. At the same time, good standards of husbandry and care should be set by the Community for captive breeding centres. A monitoring system should be established to verify that these standards are adhered to. It

should only be allowed to obtain animals from centres which conform to such standards, be they located within the Community or in third countries.

7. The necessity of using non-human primates in toxicity testing should be reviewed as a matter of urgency.

8. The use of chimpanzees in experimentation should be prohibited. Those remaining in laboratories should be properly retired or rehabilitated.

9. Statistics on the use of animals in genetic engineering should be gathered and published alongside other statistics on use of animals in experimentation. They should include the number of animals born with phenotypic defects or not surviving to birth, and the percentage of survivals from research projects.

10. Assessment of research projects involving genetic engineering of animals is governed by Community rules applying to animal experimentation in general. This assessment should include a full ethical review which takes animal welfare into account. Such a review should in any case be applied to all experiments involving animals.

Chapter 5

Animals in Sport, Entertainment and Exhibitions

WELFARE OF ANIMALS IN ZOOS

Reasons for concern

The European Commission estimates that there are over a thousand zoos in the European Community today. Some collections are publicly owned, some privately. The definition of a zoo used by the Commission incorporates any establishment, except circuses and pet shops, where live animals are kept for exhibition, and to which members of the public have access on seven or more days of the year. The definition therefore embraces zoological collections, animal parks, safari parks, bird gardens, dolphinaria, aquaria and specialist collections, including those for invertebrates. Some 250 of the zoos belonging to the IUDGZ – The World Zoo Organisation[21] are involved in more than 80 captive breeding programmes for endangered species. In 1996, 230 zoos are members of the European Association of Zoos and Aquaria (EAZA), whose membership overlaps with that of the IUDGZ, and in whose work it participates. It is therefore probable that no more than 25% of zoos in European Union countries belong to such professional organisations.

Modern zoos claim to fulfil four objectives: conservation, research, public education and public recreation. The emphasis on particular objectives varies from zoo to zoo. There is considerable concern that more than 50% of the establishments qualifying as zoos under the European Commission's definition do not fulfil these objectives acceptably in animal welfare terms. A survey carried out by Zoo Check in 1987, with the assistance of funding obtained from the European Community through Eurogroup, revealed that welfare problems such as the following were widespread:

- barren, cramped conditions in which the animal had neither the space nor the materials to fulfil its natural behavioural activities;

---

[21] Full title: International Union of Directors of Zoological Gardens – The World Zoo Organisation.

- enclosures where the animal had no opportunity to avoid the constant public gaze;
- enclosures constructed in such a way as to risk causing injury to the animals contained in them;
- lack of facilities to care for sick animals;
- inadequate or unsuitable diet;
- animals of normally social species kept singly.

There is, in addition, doubt as to whether zoos can ever provide suitable environments in which to keep animals such as the polar bear or cetacean species such as dolphins and orcas.

Economic and consumer factors

It is estimated that zoos throughout the world collectively attract approximately 350 million visitors each year, although it is suggested that attendances are declining in Europe. The experience of seeing a live animal at close quarters is a fascinating one which many people recall with pleasure. However, in recent years, the growth of wildlife documentary films and magazines has raised both the awareness of the public and their expectations, so that the unsuitable and downright poor conditions in which some animals are kept has come under increasing criticism in Europe. This criticism is voiced within the zoo industry itself, with the result that professional organisations such as EAZA have been strongly supportive of the introduction of EC legislation to ensure basic standards within the industry.

Animal collections are expensive to house and maintain properly. The specialised veterinary and environmental requirements of dolphins and orcas are particularly so, and this, coupled with the imposition of standards and conditions for keeping them in certain Member States, and EC import controls, is probably the reason behind the decline in the number of dolphinaria in northern Europe, although dolphin shows appear to retain their popularity as a source of entertainment in tourist areas in Spain. It is to be expected that the upgrading of facilities resulting from the imposition of general standards for zoos of all types would result in the closure of many. Specialisation in a few more easily kept species could be one survival possibility for smaller establishments.

Zoos seriously working in conservation and supportive research still need to finance these aspects of their work, at least in part, from the sale of tickets to the viewing public. They are therefore dependent on demand for zoo exhibitions as a form of recreation. The sponsorship they attract from local businesses, which is an increasing source of funding, is also dependent on the attractiveness to the public of the animal exhibits and the recreational amenities on offer.

Legislation

National legislation among the EU Member States ranges from comprehensive specific controls, such as the UK's Zoo Licensing Act of 1981, to authorisation and registration requirements for public health and planning reasons. National disease control regulations are applicable to animal imports in all Member States.

The trade and exchange of endangered or vulnerable species is governed by the Convention on International Trade in Endangered Species (CITES). Within the EU, this is implemented through Council Regulation 3626/82 (see p. 46). These instruments limit the import or export of the most strictly protected wild animal species to essentially non-commercial purposes, such as captive breeding for conservation. Animals which are permitted to be traded subject to quotas may be imported and exported for commercial purposes, such as public exhibition, subject to certain conditions. Zoos may import, export or exchange any animal in connection with conservation work related to the particular species.

Council Directive 91/628/EEC on the protection of animals during transport lays down conditions for the shipment of wild animals and animals of non-domesticated species.

In 1991 the European Commission put forward a proposal for a Council Directive laying down minimum standards for the keeping of animals in zoos. The proposal would have required zoos to apply to nationally appointed authorities for a licence, which would only be granted if an inspection team, consisting of a representative of the appointed licensing authority and two zoo management experts, was satisfied that they could fulfil the requirements of the legislation. Zoos which failed to meet the required standards within twelve months would lose their licences. The licences would have been subject to review every six years. The proposed Directive would have required zoos to ensure that animals were kept under conditions suited to their behavioural, social and biological needs. It would also have demanded provision of a high standard of veterinary and nutritional care by a sufficient number of properly trained staff. Zoos would have had to keep full records of births, deaths and acquisitions of animals. Zoo premises and records would have had to be open for inspection at any time by the licensing authority.

The proposed Directive was based on the recognised conservation concerns of the Community, and was destined to support Community legislation implementing CITES (see p. 46).

In June 1993, the proposal was approved by the European Parliament, subject to amendments which included annexing to the Directive a detailed code of practice for accommodation and care of animals in zoos.

However, there was a lack of political support from Member State governments, and the proposed Directive on zoos was later listed for withdrawal by the Commission following its review of Community legislation. The review was initiated at the end of 1992 and was undertaken as part of the institutional debate to define those areas in which the Community, rather than the individual Member States, should act, in accordance with the concept of subsidiarity expressed in the Treaty on European Union.[22] At the time of the European Council in Edinburgh in 1992, the Commission proposed instead the possible issue of a Recommendation on zoos to all Member State governments.[23]

The Draft Directive has now been republished by the Commission as a proposed Council Recommendation. An opinion from the European Parliament is expected early in 1997.

Possible EU initiatives

1. Member States which lack comprehensive welfare legislation covering the keeping of animals in zoos should introduce enforceable standards as soon as possible.

2. Further consideration should be given to the case for introducing a Community Directive rather than a Recommendation.

USE OF ANIMALS IN CIRCUSES

Reasons for concern

Circuses present a number of potential welfare problems. Training methods may not always be humane, and furthermore are used to make animals perform acts for which they would otherwise have no normal inclination. The animals must travel constantly during the performance season, during which they live in cramped mobile wagons. In such conditions it is all but impossible to provide larger species with an environment suitable to their natural behaviour. Primate species, which normally live in social groups, may be kept singly. Housing facilities in circus winter quarters can be inadequate, with the animals confined in buildings with no outdoor access for two to three months at a time.

---

[22] Treaty on European Union, Title II, Article G.5 inserting a new Article 3b to the Treaty establishing the European Community.

[23] *European Council in Edinburgh, 11/12 December 1992, Conclusions of the (UK) Presidency,* Annex 2 to Part A, p. 13.

Economic and consumer factors

Circus animals, particularly larger species, are expensive to maintain properly. In addition, many members of the public are aware of the welfare problems and boycott performances where animals are used. This increasing doubt as to the ethicality of using live animals, particularly of non-domesticated species, for public entertainment, is reflected in the UK by the prohibition of performances involving animals by a small number of local and municipal authorities, and in other countries by legislation banning the use of animals.

Legislation

Finland has, since 1986, prohibited the use in circuses of apes, elephants, carnivores, seals, rhinoceros, hippopotamus, ruminants, ungulates, marsupials, birds of prey, ostriches and crocodiles. All circuses must apply for a permit from the Ministry of Agriculture and Forests, which is empowered to set safety and welfare conditions for performances by visiting foreign circuses.

Within the EU, Denmark's national legislation bans the use of animals of non-domesticated species for circus performances. However, this has allowed the continuing use of a small number of Asian elephants, on the basis that these are used as working animals in their countries of origin. Exemptions can be granted, for example for the use of sea lions, provided that the veterinary authorities are satisfied that transport and accommodation facilities are acceptable from the welfare point of view. German federal law requires circuses to demonstrate that they can provide winter quarters for their animals before they can obtain a licence to perform. General animal welfare law is applied in other Member States.

There is no Community welfare legislation dealing with circuses as such. However, they must comply with the controls on the purchase, sale or movement of animals laid down in Council Regulation 3626/82 on the implementation in the Community of the Convention on International Trade in Endangered Species of Wild Fauna and Flora and the new Regulation on possession of and trade in wildlife which is shortly due to replace it (see p. 46). They must also comply with the provisions of Council Directive 91/628/EEC on the protection of animals during transport.

In 1992, representatives attending the eighth meeting of Parties to The Convention on International Trade in Endangered Species (CITES) adopted two Resolutions for controlling the use of CITES-listed species by circuses. The first called for standardisation of the certificates issued to travelling live animal exhibitions to denote captive-bred animals and animals acquired before the Convention came into force. Increased inspection and monitoring of the movements of travelling animal shows was also demanded. The second Resolution recommended the use of microchips to identify live animals of CITES Appendix I species traded for scientific research and other permitted exchanges and, ultimately, to identify CITES Appendix I and II animals used in travelling exhibitions and circuses.

Possible EU initiatives

1. Community legislation on the protection of animals during transport and on the implementation of CITES should be actively enforced where applicable to circuses, taking into account the content of the two Resolutions passed at the CITES Conference in 1992.

2. Consideration should be given to the introduction of legislation banning the use of non-domesticated species, including all CITES Appendix I species, by circuses. This could take the form of an amendment to Community legislation implementing CITES.

PERFORMING ANIMALS IN GENERAL ENTERTAINMENT

Reasons for concern

Animals are used in cabaret acts, on stage in plays, in television and cinema films made for entertainment, and in film and still photography for advertising. On an ethical level, some of the uses of animals in advertisements has been criticised because, if not actually cruel, it often ridicules the animals. Training methods, and the conditions in which the animals are constrained during and between performances are potential problem areas. Teeth and claws may be removed.

Chimpanzees – a highly protected species in decline in the wild – have been used for entertainment in bars and as props by street photographers in, for example, southern Spain, although this has reduced in recent years. Tiger and lion cubs have also been used for this purpose. The animals often suffer cruelly and are discarded when too large to be useful.

In film work, the desire for realism can lead to cruel treatment or accidental injury and even death for the animals involved. Horses are particularly at risk. Many feature films are made, either in part or totally, in countries where animal welfare legislation is either inadequate or not enforced.

Economic and consumer factors

As far as advertising is concerned, the presence of an animal helps to sell the product, either by creating amusement or by projecting a particular image with which the advertiser wants to associate the product, such as the physical power of the tiger or the speed of the horse.

The use of trained animals in filming can be costly, but this may be offset if filming takes less time.

Complaints from the viewing public are common if television films contain scenes which give the impression of involving, or actually do involve, cruelty to the animals shown.

Legislation

There is no specific Community legislation for the welfare of animals used in general entertainment or for the licensing of their handlers. However, animals of non-domesticated species could fall under certain provisions of Community legislation on the trade in and possession of specimens of species of wild fauna and flora which is in process of revision (see section on international wildlife trade, p. 46).

The transportation conditions of animals other than those classified as personal pets should conform to the requirements of Council Directive 91/628/EEC on the protection of animals during transport. Certain Community and/or national health legislation could also apply to the movement of performing animals between Member States and to and from the Community.

The European Convention for the Protection of Pet Animals addresses some aspects of the use of performing animals. Article 7 of the Convention states that no pet animal should be trained in such a way as to jeopardise its health or well being, either by forcing it to exceed its natural capabilities or by the use of artificial means which cause injuries or unnecessary pain, suffering or stress. Article 9 deals with the use of pet animals in advertising, entertainment, exhibitions, competitions and similar events. It states that no pet animal should be used for these purposes unless the organiser has created the necessary conditions to ensure that the animal is treated according to its ethological needs, that it is fed and watered, and that its health and well-being are not put at risk.

However, these provisions do not appear to apply to animals which are kept primarily for commercial purposes, rather than primarily for private enjoyment and companionship. Furthermore, the Convention can only be effective through implementation in the legislation of those Council of Europe Member States which have ratified it.

In practice, therefore, the welfare of performing animals and the licensing of their trainers is provided for to varying degrees by the national legislation of individual countries. One of the better examples is the Danish animal welfare law of 1991, which states that animals must not be trained or used for performance, circus exhibitions, film-making or other similar purposes if significant discomfort is caused to the animal.

Possible EU initiatives

1. The Multilateral Consultation of the Parties to the European Convention for the Protection of Pet Animals should look at the ways in which Articles 7 and 9 of the Convention are currently applied and should consider whether it is necessary to clarify the scope of the Convention, possibly through a Protocol of Amendment, to ensure the well-being of animals, normally kept as pets within the definition of the Convention, when these are used in advertising or in stage, film, television and other forms of entertainment.

2. European Union Member States should ensure the full application of licensing requirements for the possession of animals falling under the new European Parliament and Council Regulation on the trade in and possession of specimens of species of wild fauna and flora, which is to be introduced shortly.

3. Member States of the European Union and Council of Europe should ensure that their national legislation provides adequate protection for performing animals used in advertising and entertainment.

EQUINE COMPETITIONS

Reasons for concern

Horses are used competitively in show jumping, three-day events and racing. Such activities may make unreasonable demands on the animals, for example through excessively difficult obstacles or jumps. Safeguards to ensure that the horses are fit enough to take part may be inadequate. Excessive use of the rider's whip is also viewed with concern. Training methods for the animals used in professional and sponsored equine competitions have given rise to concern, not only to animal welfare organisations and the public, but also to the governing bodies of the sports.

Equine competitions take place at the amateur, as well as professional level. Many leisure riders, including children, take part with their animals in club and national competitions for the pleasure of doing so, but must still ensure that safety and other factors affecting the animals' well-being are adequately taken care of.

Economic and consumer factors

Equine competitions are often very popular with the general public. They are usually well publicised and the larger events are generally broadcast on television. Horses and riders can become household names. Commercial sponsorship of show-jumping and three-day events, and of the competitors and their horses, capitalises on this popularity, but can place great pressure on riders, both to achieve success and to take part regularly in a larger number of competitions.

Horse racing is a well-established industry in many countries. It is associated with, and partly funded by, betting.

Legislation

There is no Community legislation dealing with the welfare of horses used in competition and sporting events. However, various Community health and transport Directives would apply to animals (particularly for competition or breeding purposes registered equidae) moving between Member States or to and from non-Community countries.

Aspects of the welfare of horses used in competitions are covered in the European Convention for the Protection of Companion Animals. Article 7 of the Convention states that no pet animal should be trained in such a way as to jeopardise its health or well-being, either by forcing it to exceed its natural capabilities or by the use of artificial means which cause injuries or unnecessary pain, suffering or stress.

Article 9 of the Convention deals with the use of pet animals in exhibitions, competitions and similar events. It states that no pet animal should be used for these purposes unless the organiser has created the necessary conditions to ensure that the animal is treated according to its ethological needs, that it is fed and watered, and that its health and well-being are not put at risk. These provisions should certainly apply to horses in non-professional events.

Possible EU, Council of Europe or other initiatives

1. Member States which do not already do so should ensure that their animal welfare legislation gives adequate general protection to equines.

2. Equine sports are generally regulated by their own governing bodies, both at national and international level. Eurogroup for Animal Welfare and its member organisations have taken part in discussions with these bodies on various aspects of concern, and hope to continue to do so.

GREYHOUND RACING

Reasons for concern

The modern sport of greyhound racing developed as a spin-off from hare coursing (see p. 116) and is now the more widespread and popular activity of the two. In each country where it is practised, the sport is regulated by a national association which maintains stud books and collects registration fees from dog owners and tracks. The sport is associated with betting, which partly funds the industry.

From an animal welfare point of view, there is concern over the common risk of muscle, tendon and bone injuries resulting from racing and poor training. Although against the rules, it is reported that animals may none-theless be given drugs to enable them to run despite injuries.

Also of concern is the treatment of dogs which are retired or are among the high percentage rejected because they do not make the grade as racers. In the United Kingdom, the Retired Greyhound Trust takes in approx-imately 600 dogs a year, while various other charities also try to find homes for unwanted ex-racing greyhounds. However, there is some evidence to suggest that redundant greyhounds may be put down illegally using cruel methods by owners who do not wish to pay the modest veterinary fee for humane destruction. Unwanted greyhounds are frequently supplied to research institutions in Europe – in most cases illegally.

Racing greyhounds are traded between Community countries and exported elsewhere. Concern over transport conditions for the animals has led to research, partly funded by Aer Lingus, aimed at improving transport methods. The transportation of greyhounds by road from Ireland to Spain is of concern because of the length and conditions of the journey.

A final concern relates to the oversupply of greyhounds in relation to demand for them as racing or coursing animals or simply as pets. In 1991, Irish greyhound breeders were given the opportunity to benefit from a subsidy under an EC funding Regulation designed to facilitate diver-sification by traditional farmers in certain countries. While the funding may have helped to improve conditions in certain breeding units, it is likely that it has led to an increase in the number of dogs bred.

Economic and consumer factors

In the United Kingdom, official betting on greyhound races amounts to some £2 million a year. In 1991 the Parliamentary Select Committee on Home Affairs conducted an inquiry into the greyhound racing industry. Submissions made by interested parties, including animal welfare organisa-tions, included the suggestion that a reasonable sum of money from the industry should be made available to subsidise the care and adoption of retired racing dogs no longer wanted by their owners.

In the Republic of Ireland, approximately 25,000 greyhounds are registered annually, and an estimated 8,000 people earn a living or supple-ment their income from the greyhound breeding and racing industry. Some 10,000 Irish-bred greyhounds are sold to a number of countries each year, but around 80% go to the United Kingdom.

In April 1991, the Irish Department of Agriculture instituted a subsidy to greyhound breeders under its Alternative Farm Enterprise Allowance scheme. The scheme continues and is partly funded with EU structural funds. The purpose of the scheme is to finance diversification by traditional farmers in a limited number of countries.

Grant applicants in Less Favoured Areas were eligible to receive up to 50% of the cost of a project, while applicants in other rural areas could receive up to 40%. No individual project was allowed to cost more than £5,000 or less than £500. The money was available to subsidise the cost of improving or constructing fencing, kennelling and other facilities for the dogs. Applicants, who were mainly expected to be existing breeders when the scheme was set up, were subject to inspection by the Bord na gCon, on behalf of the Department of Agriculture.

In Spain, the sport of greyhound racing has been in economic decline for some years and some tracks have closed. In Denmark, on the other hand, the sport went through something of an upsurge in the 1970s, when the number of tracks increased from one to six.

In any country where the sport is practised, racing greyhounds are generally owned by private individuals, or groups of individuals, for whom the financial incentives come from betting, prizes and the breeding possibilities of a champion animal. These potential gains are offset by registration, training and maintenance costs.

Legislation

There is no Community legislation for the general welfare of greyhounds. However, Council Directive 91/628/EEC on the protection of animals during transport applies to the shipment of commercially traded dogs. In addition, greyhounds traded between registered commercial holdings, such as commercial breeders, within the Community might have to comply with the health certification requirements of the so-called 'Balai' Directive 92/65/EEC, agreed in June 1992, not least if they wish to avoid the quarantine requirements otherwise imposed for importation to the UK and Ireland. This measure deals with the health rules governing intracommunity trade in animals not specifically covered by other Community legislation.

Article 19.4 of Council Directive 86/609/EEC of 24 November 1986 on the approximation of laws, regulations and administrative provisions of the Member States regarding the protection of animals used for experimental and other scientific purposes requires that animals used for experimentation should be purpose bred and obtained from licensed suppliers and/or breeders, unless authorisation is given to do otherwise. It further states that stray animals of domestic species shall not be used in experiments. Allegations that racing greyhounds were being sold to laboratories in breach of this legislation are frequently made, particularly in Spain and Portugal.

In so far as greyhounds are pets of their owners, certain provisions of the European Convention for the protection of pet animals apply to their welfare. Article 7 of the Convention requires that animals should not be trained in a way that is detrimental to their health or welfare. Article 8 requires the registration of commercial dog breeders to ensure that they conform to good animal welfare practice. Article 9 states that pet animals shall not be used in competitive events if their welfare is put at risk. It further states that no substances or treatments shall be administered to alter the animal's natural level of performance, either during competitions or at any other time.

Professional sporting rules are laid down by the racing associations in each country. These typically cover the fitness of the dogs, including provisions for veterinary inspection, the number of races in which the animals are allowed to take part in a given period of time, and so on.

Possible EU, Council of Europe or other initiatives

1. Council Directive 86/609/EEC of 24 November 1986 on the approximation of laws, regulations and administrative provisions of the Member States regarding the protection of animals used for experimental and other scientific purposes requires that animals used for experimentation should be purpose bred and obtained from licensed suppliers and breeders, other than in exceptional circumstances. This provision should be properly enforced.

ANGLING

Reasons for concern

There is growing evidence, much of it from the Netherlands and the United Kingdom, to show that fish feel pain and fear. It is common angling practice to return cyprinids and other coarse fish alive to the water after capture. Being captured is presumably unpleasant, since fish afterwards usually avoid bait and hooks. However, although pain from injury has often been considered as the major source of unpleasantness, it seems that the restriction of freedom and accompanying fear are contributing factors. The playing of the fish before landing may also be stressful and exhausting. Concern includes the use of keep nets and of vertebrate live bait.

Certain types of angling competition have caused serious concern in Germany, where prosecutions have been taken, and fines imposed, against anglers for causing unnecessary and prolonged suffering to fish held in keep nets for many hours.

Lost or discarded tackle can prove hazardous to other wildlife. In the United Kingdom, the incidence of lead poisoning in swans has been reduced by a ban on the use of lead for the manufacture of most sizes of anglers' weights (see p. 48). In some areas, the mere presence of anglers may cause disturbance to waterfowl. There is concern also over the killing of birds to prevent predation in game fisheries.

Economic and consumer factors

Angling is a very popular hobby in many countries. As a consequence, there is considerable economic interest in the manufacture and sale of equipment, the sale and rent of fisheries, and tourism.

In the United Kingdom, angling associations have worked to make their members aware of the problems caused by discarded tackle and the need to avoid disturbance of birds and other riverside wildlife. Anglers also play a part in monitoring pollution of lakes and rivers.

Legislation

Some freshwater fish species are listed in Annexes IV and V of Council Directive 92/43/EEC on the conservation of natural habitats and of wild fauna and flora. With regard to the effect of angling on other animals and birds, both this Directive and the Directive on the conservation of wild birds require that the habitat of protected species should not be disturbed, and that killing of predators in the vicinity of game fisheries should be a last resort, used only if predation is a significant problem and there is no other way of dealing with it.

Possible EU and other initiatives

1. The use of lead to manufacture those sizes of anglers' weights capable of being swallowed by birds should be phased out by all Member States which have not yet done so. This would be in line with their obligations under Community legislation for the protection of wildlife and natural habitats.

2. Further research by Member States into the actual extent of bird and mammal predation on game fisheries would be useful.

3. Efforts should be made by national authorities and angling associations to make sure that anglers are aware of wildlife protection issues affected by their sport, and that they are also fully aware of any codes of practice for the correct handling of fish.

FIELD SPORTS

Reasons for concern

The recreational pursuit of animals takes place in various ways and involves a number of different species. Deer are shot during defined seasons in most

European countries, but are still hunted with hounds in the United Kingdom (with the exception of Scotland, where it is illegal) and France. In the United Kingdom, red deer stags are hunted in the autumn and the spring. Fallow deer buck are hunted in September and the winter months. Red deer hinds are hunted from November to the end of February. In Northern Ireland and the Republic of Ireland, carted deer hunts are still practised between the end of September and March. In this version of the sport, the animal is selected from an enclosure and brought to the meet. It is then chased by riders and hounds. When brought to bay, it is not killed, but recaptured and returned to the herd it came from.

Foxhunting with hounds is carried out in the United Kingdom and the Republic of Ireland. Mink are also hunted using hounds. The chase is a terrifying experience for animals hunted in this way, and the final kill may be cruel. This type of hunting is also a source of concern for the disturbance it causes to other wildlife. For example, mink hunts may disturb the breeding sites of protected species such as otter and waterside birds.

In many EU countries, hares, if hunted, are shot. In the United Kingdom and Ireland, however, they may also be hunted with hounds. The season for this activity continues into the period when the animals are beginning to produce young. Hares are also used in coursing events, the main purpose of which is to demonstrate the speed and ability of the dogs involved. The spectators bet on the results. On the British mainland, hare coursing takes two forms: static coursing, when hares are driven on to a particular field to be pursued by two dogs, usually greyhounds, and rough coursing in which the hares are flushed out by a line of coursers and supporters. In Northern Ireland and the Republic of Ireland, enclosed coursing is practised. Here the hare is caught and released from a holding pen into a series of linked enclosed areas. Should the dogs catch the hare, it may not always be possible for course attendants to remove and humanely kill it. A form of hare coursing is also understood to take place in Spain.

The commonest field sport in the EU as a whole is shooting, with deer, wildfowl, pheasant, partridge, grouse and pigeon among the typical quarry. Action to phase out the use of lead shot, particularly in wetlands, is referred to in the section on protection of wildlife and habitats in Europe (see p. 48). Concern over the competence of those who take up shooting, for example in handling guns correctly, knowledge of relevant laws, and ability to distinguish between species which are protected and those which are game, is leading to the introduction of testing of hunters prior to granting of licences in some countries. The number of wounded, unretrieved animals and birds has also led to legislation requiring that trained dogs accompany shoots in Denmark. However, in addition to these points, certain methods of artificially rearing game birds for shooting are of concern.

Pheasant, partridge and mallard are among species which are reared for shooting in various ways in most, if not all, countries where shooting takes place. One method involves incubating eggs removed from a small aviary stock of captive pheasants and placing them in fenced runs with chicken foster-mothers. Some other methods are more or less comparable with the intensive rearing of domestic poultry. In Denmark, for example, one million, or approximately half, the pheasant, partridge and mallard shot each year come from game rearing establishments, about one-third of which are commercially run. Concern over the conditions in which these birds are reared and released, particularly for the larger commercial shoots, has led to changes in the law to prevent the rearing of game birds for shooting in darkened indoor accommodation. Rearing pheasants and partridge in darkness is one way of preventing the feather-pecking and cannibalism which otherwise occurs if these species are reared in intensive conditions. Other preventive measures in current use, for other poultry and other countries also, include so-called spectacles or masks, which are attached through the nostrils and inhibit the birds' forward vision, and beak rings, which prevent full closure of the beak and inhibit normal feeding. The tips of the birds' beaks are usually trimmed before transportation to the release site. More severe trimming is known to take place. Danish research indicates that only 10–20% of released birds are actually shot, and most of the remainder die of disease or lack of food during the first autumn or winter. The terrain into which they are released is usually already inhabited by as many wild game birds as its resources will support, and the artificially reared birds do not compete well with their wild counterparts.

Swedish and French research on hares bred for shooting shows that artificially reared hares have only one-fifth the survival rate of wild hares, between shooting seasons.

Economic and consumer factors

Field sports generate economic activity, both directly and indirectly. An estimated 9,500 people are employed, full- or part-time, by hunt organisers in the United Kingdom. Employment and trade are also generated by the demand for hunting and shooting equipment. Substantial income may be derived from foreign tourists' participation in commercial shoots.

The rearing of game species for shooting is a niche production sector of agriculture with export possibilities. To take again Denmark as an example, pheasant rearing establishments produce around 240,000 young each year at a total value of DKr 10 million. Although most of the pheasants are sold to Danish buyers, partridge production is mainly export-oriented. 430,000 birds valued at DKr 13 million are sold annually, together with 850,000 eggs worth DKr 5.5 million.

Denmark exports some wild hares (caught in nets) to Italy as also does Poland and parts of the former Soviet Union.

Animal welfare organisations are opposed to hunting because of its cruelty. This view is also taken by a majority of the public in many countries, including the United Kingdom, where many county authorities into which England and Wales are divided have banned hunting with hounds across land which they own. Some farmers and other landowners also refuse permission for hunting. As an alternative, drag hunts take place in Germany and the Netherlands, and are also generating some interest in the United Kingdom. This reflects the real pleasure for many hunt participants of riding and being in the countryside, but without the pursuit of animal quarry. A combination of conservation and pest control reasons are often used as a justification for the continuation of hunting deer, foxes and mink with hounds. However, the usefulness of such hunting for these purposes is not supported by reliable modern research.

Shooting can be viewed as a nuisance in countries where there are large numbers of shooters and legislation allows access to otherwise private land in pursuit of game.

Legislation

There is no Community regulation of field sports other than the provisions of Council Directive 79/409/EEC on the conservation of wild birds and Council Directive 92/43/EEC on the conservation of natural habitats and or wild fauna and flora which are more fully described on p. 51. These measures are concerned with the protection of European wildlife, and therefore prohibit hunting or shooting of certain animals and birds. They also prohibit disturbance of their habitat, particularly during the breeding season. The killing of migratory birds is forbidden during the period when they are returning to their breeding grounds. Indiscriminate hunting methods are also prohibited. The mountain hare (*lepus timidus*) is listed on Annex V of Council Directive 92/43/EEC, which means it may be subject to management measures. The brown hare (*lepus capensis*) is not listed for any form of protection under this legislation.

A Commission proposal for amendment of Council Directive 79/409/EEC on the conservation of wild birds was presented to the Council of Ministers in March 1994. The Directive already allows Member States to fix their own hunting season dates, with the proviso that migratory birds shall not be shot during the return journey to their breeding grounds. However the Commission proposal would extend the possibilities for spring shooting of migratory birds beyond the present limits. The European Parliament have rejected this proposal and suggested a single cut-off date of 31 January each year. A common position is now awaited.

Within the Council of Europe, the Standing Committee of the European Convention for the protection of animals kept for farming purposes is currently finalizing a Recommendation on domestic fowl (*Gallus gallus*) to take into account the keeping of chickens for meat. It is also developing the Recommendation to include ducks, turkeys, guinea fowl, quail, partridges, pheasants and pigeons. It is not known if this will extend to commercial rearing of birds for shooting. However, birds artificially reared for shooting are treated under Danish, and probably other, national legislation as farmed poultry until they are released into the wild.

Possible EU and Council of Europe initiatives

1. Member States should ensure that the provisions of Community legislation on the conservation of wild birds and on the conservation of habitats and wild fauna are implemented in such a way that the exercise of field sports does not disturb wildlife designated for protection.

2. In connection with the above, Community Member States should link the issue of shooting licences to a certificate of competence, based on demonstration of knowledge. France, Denmark, Germany and the Netherlands have already introduced some form of skills test linked to licensing.

3. The extended Council of Europe Recommendation on domestic fowl should take into account the artificial rearing of game bird species for shooting.

4. EU Member States which still permit the hunting of live quarry with hounds and coursing could consider prohibiting such activities, since these are out of step with the general premises of the other legislation for the welfare and protection of animals which they have.

TRADITIONAL ENTERTAINMENTS AND FOLKLORIC EVENTS INVOLVING CRUELTY TO ANIMALS

Reasons for concern

Animals are still used in a variety of traditional entertainments or folkloric events in a number of Community Member States. There is generally some level of distress or outright cruel treatment for the animals involved. Mistreatment includes harassment, beating with sticks, and killing.

Festive Celebrations

Cockerels, geese, pigeons, snakes, cats, squirrels, pigs, goats and, most frequently, cattle, are used in a variety of festive celebrations in parts of the

Community. The festivities may be linked to the time of year or to super-stitions attached to religious festivals and the celebration of village patron saints. Sometimes the animal involved is viewed as the embodiment of the negative characteristics of human nature, and so is killed in a ritual rejection of sin and evil. For example, during festivals held in two villages of the Campania, Italy, during August, people wearing blindfolds beat cockerels to death. The animals are partly buried in the ground, heads protruding. Similar events take place in Spain. In Tordesillas, Valladolid, blindfolded girls strike out with long sticks at live cockerels suspended from a rope. Elsewhere in the Zamora and Guadalajara areas, partially buried cockerels are clubbed to death or decapitated in accordance with local custom. Live geese, suspended from a rope, are also decapitated by young men in Caspio de Tajo, Toledo. In the village of Manganeses de la Polverosa, Zamora, a live goat is thrown from the belfry of the church tower. Efforts to stop this particular festival have been made by the Spanish authorities in recent years, resulting in violent confrontation between police and local people in 1992. Villagers in Villanueva de la Vera, Cáceres, continue to maltreat a donkey as they drive it through the streets each February. Donkeys are the focus of mistreatment in village festivals in the Piemonte and Lazio regions of Italy also.

Bulls are a particular focus of festivities in Spain, but not only through organised bullfights, which are discussed separately below. In the town of Coria, a number of streets are cordoned off and a bull is released into them and made to run past the crowd, who shoot metal darts at the animal, and also throw objects such as bottles. The animal is killed at the end. The festivities take place over several days, using a new bull each day. In the Valencia region, several villages celebrate by driving a bull through the streets. These animals have balls of tar and other flammable material attached to their horns. The tar balls are ignited and the terrified animals run amid a shower of sparks.

Some of the Spanish folk festivals involving animals have been docu-mented on video and in photographs. Since the late 1980s, five of the seventeen Autonomous Communities into which Spain is divided have adopted their own regional animal welfare laws. These areas (Cataluña, Madrid, Murcia, Castilla-La Mancha and the Canary Islands) have pro-hibited the mistreatment of all animals in public entertainments and fiestas, with the exception of bulls. Organised bullfights and certain types of bull fiesta, as opposed to local festive customs involving other animals, are regu-lated nationally. Since animal welfare is mostly devolved to regional level in Spain, although a number of older national laws exist, it is hoped that those Autonomous Communities which have not yet adopted even limited general welfare laws will do so shortly. In 1989, a Report on possible legal action against events involving cruelty to animals was adopted by the European

Parliament's Environment Committee, but could not be adopted by the Parliament as a whole. The Resolution accompanying the Report asked countries which had not yet enacted comprehensive, modern animal welfare laws to do so as soon as possible. It also expressed concern over the brutalising effect which public events involving animal cruelty could have on young people.

Bullfighting

Within the Community, bullfighting takes place in Spain, Portugal and southern France. It is also practised in Mexico and a number of South American countries. Whatever its cultural significance, from the animal welfare point of view it is a source of considerable cruelty to the bulls and horses involved. The modern Spanish bullfight consists of three basic stages. When the bull is released into the arena, it is faced by the matador, who will use his cape to test the bull's reactions. Next, two mounted men (the picadors) carrying lances enter the ring. One of them will spear the bull's shoulder muscles, twisting the lance before removing it. The horses ridden by the picadors wear protective padding of a specified weight, but this does not fully protect them from the impact of collision, if the bull charges them. Horses fall and are gored from time to time, but no records are kept of horse injuries.

After this, two or three men on foot will attempt to place banderillas (colourfully decorated metre-long spears) in the bull's neck muscles. The blades are barbed so that they will remain embedded in the flesh. These opening stages are designed to confuse the bull and weaken it, so that it will lower its head to facilitate the kill. This takes place in the third and final stage of the contest. After some passes with the cape, the matador will attempt to kill the bull – ideally with one stroke – using a sword with a curved tip and horizontal stop bar a short distance up the blade. The sword must pierce the bull behind the head to sever the spinal chord or an artery. If the swordstroke fails to kill the bull, a knife is used to finish it. Under new rules introduced in 1992, if the matador is unable to deliver the deathstroke within ten minutes of the start of this final phase of the contest, the bull can be removed to a pen or slaughtered. If matador and audience consider that the animal showed exceptional bravery, the bull can be reprieved and returned to the ranch for breeding. All in all, the bull's ordeal in the ring lasts about twenty minutes. Up to six bullfights may feature in an afternoon's programme.

This standard type of bullfight, where the matador fights on foot, dates from the eighteenth century. The older form of contest, where the bullfighter is mounted on horseback, is still practised, principally at Ronda, which is the oldest bullring in Spain. Horses used in this contest are protected only by their agility and the rider's skill, and are more highly-bred animals than those used by the picadors in the modern bullfight. Rules for these and other categories of bullfight, together with the 'bull running' or *encierro* fiestas such as that held at Pamplona, are laid down under a national Regulation issued through the Spanish Ministry of the Interior. In addition to novice contests using younger bulls and inexperienced bullfighters, there are also mock-bullfights where small men in costume tease and chase calves in the arena. The calf is not supposed to be killed during these events, while bulls used in *encierros* are meant to be slaughtered afterwards away from public view. Altogether, some 30,000 bulls a year die as a result of bullfights and related activities in Spain.

It has been repeatedly alleged that trainee bullfighters are allowed into slaughterhouses in southern Spain to practise their killing technique. Should this prove to be so, it would be a breach of the Community's present and future legislation on the protection of animals at the time of slaughter or killing, which exempts only the killing of animals in cultural events (i.e., during the bullfight itself).

The standard Spanish style of bullfight is practised in Mexico and South America. Within the EU, it is also used in southern France. The Portuguese bullfight varies in that picadors are not used, and the law states that the bull must not be killed in the ring. All these types of bullfight fall into the category of event which would be prohibited under animal welfare laws in all other EU Member States.

A different kind of contest, the *courses libres* traditional in Provence, do not involve torture or killing of the bull. In these contests, a cockade or rosette is placed between the bull's horns. Young men attempt to pluck out the cockade whilst dodging the bull's horns. Bulls used in these contests are used more than once, and the best ones can become quite well known.

Bullfighting of all kinds has long been televised in Spain and France, but a new concern is the broadcasting of Mexican bullfights on Luxembourg-based satellite television. These programmes can be received in EU countries where bullfighting itself would be illegal.

In 1994/1995, EC funds available to Member States under regional extensification programmes associated with the Common Agricultural Policy were being paid to the breeders of fighting bulls. Breeders of fighting bulls in Spain are registered nationally. Details of their animals are listed in a national stud register. The so-called *lidia* bulls (the name comes from a word meaning 'to fight') are generally described as smaller and more agile than the beef-producing cattle of ordinary livestock farming. They range open pasture and their contact with human beings is minimised because of their future role in the ring. However, beef cattle and fighting bulls may be kept by the same farmer, and this may have made it difficult to discern which activity the funds are subsidising. Following a public outcry the

Commission amended the rules under which these grants are paid and it is hoped that this will prevent a repeat of this scandal.

Cockfighting

The sport of pitting of game cocks to fight was introduced from Asia to Europe around 500 BC. It was enthusiastically adopted by the Greeks and the Romans and spread north. Opposed by Christian clergy, it nonetheless became popular in Belgium, the Netherlands, France, Germany Italy, Spain and the United Kingdom. By the mid-nineteenth century it had begun to die out in some areas and was banned in the United Kingdom in 1849. It was also banned in Belgium in 1935, but continues illegally in both countries. It would not be permissible in many other countries today. French law bans the sport other than in the Nord-Pas de Calais, where there is an unbroken tradition. The sport is allowed to continue in the Canary Islands under local law.

Before a fight, spurs of metal or bone are slipped over the natural spurs of the birds. Between 4 and 6 cm long, these are designed to help the bird inflict damage on its opponent. The gamecocks are usually pitted in a fight to the death, although under modern rules there is an option to withdraw a badly injured bird. The birds are bred for aggression, and may be given alcohol before a fight to increase their excitement.

Dogfighting

Dog fighting is known to occur illegally in Germany, the Netherlands, Ireland, Italy and the United Kingdom, where it had previously died out in the nineteenth century. It may take place in other Member States. The dogs are bred for size and aggression. Fights are usually to the death, with losers in any case too badly injured to survive. Preparation for fights includes the use of drugs to enhance stamina and cropping of ears. Some dog fight enthusiasts travel abroad to follow their interest.

Economic and consumer factors

There is no particular economic significance attached to folk festivals involving animals, as these are local events and not generally tourist attractions, although there have been one or two attempts to make them so. Traditional customs involving animals have fallen into disuse in many places, or have been modified to omit the live animal.

The economics of bullfighting have long been a subject of debate, and few figures are available. However, it is estimated that overall ticket sales for bullfights in Spain are worth about 33,000 million pesetas annually. Of the 20 million bullfight tickets sold in Spain, it is believed that a substantial number are used by tourists in holiday areas. There is also a certain amount of municipal support in the form of funding for refurbishment of bullrings. Overall, although efforts are made to promote the activity in some parts of the country, in others fewer contests are being organised and arenas are half empty. A survey by the Spanish Ministry of Culture in the mid-1980s indicated that more than half the population disliked bullfighting. In France, on the other hand, there has been an upsurge of interest in recent years, but this may be a short-lived trend.

Bullfighting is a seasonal activity, employing relatively few people on a full-time basis. However, the most successful bullfighters can command quite a fan following and a high fee, possibly boosted through advertising sponsorship. Commercial sponsorship of bullfights does take place, although in the face of protests from members of the public and animal welfare organisations, at least one international company has instructed its concessionaires not to become involved in this way. To a breeder, the value of a fighting bull can be in the region of 2–3 million pesetas.

There is no economic significance to activities such as cockfighting and dogfighting, except to the human participants, who gamble quite heavily on the outcome of contests. In modern society, both activities are regarded with distaste by most people.

Legislation

There is no Community legislation dealing with the welfare of animals used in bullfighting, traditional festivals, or other activities involving combat between animals or between man and animals. It has generally been considered that the use of animals in essentially cultural activities was a matter for action by the Member States concerned.

Community legislation for the protection of animals at the time of slaughter or killing does not apply to activities of a cultural nature, and so would not cover the killing of bulls in the bullring or in festivities. However, it would be breached by the training of bullfighters using slaughter cattle in abattoirs.

The Council of Europe's Recommendation concerning cattle contains special provisions for calves. This states that calves kept for farming purposes shall not be used in the course of public spectacles or demonstrations if such use is likely to be detrimental to their health and welfare. The calf provisions were adopted by the Standing Committee of the European Convention on the protection of animals kept for farming purposes in June 1993. The Standing Committee is now finalizing a new Recommendation concerning domestic fowl. This states that poultry bred for farming purposes shall not be used to achieve any other goal, including public spectacles or demonstrations, if such use is likely to be detrimental to their health and welfare. The Council of Europe Recommendations concerning sheep and goats also stipulate that these animals shall not be used in public spectacles or demonstrations if it is damaging to their health and welfare. All the Recommendations depend for their effect on being expressed in national and/or Community legislation. Five Autonomous Communities in Spain have enacted laws banning the mistreatment of animals, with the exception of bulls, in local fiestas.

Within Spanish national law, a special Regulation covers all aspects of bullfighting, including the registration of bull breeders and all professional grades of bullfight participants. This law, which is issued by the Ministry of the Interior, was revised in 1992. It also regulates the establishment of bullfighting schools, where children can learn the trades of the bullring.

The only Spanish regional animal welfare legislation which deals with bullfighting is the Canary Islands law, which bans it (bullfighting is not, in any case, a local tradition), and the Catalan law which prohibits construction of new arenas, use of portable bullrings, and the establishment of bullfighting schools.

The Canary Islands law allows the continuation of cockfighting, provided it is conducted on closed premises with no children under 16 present. Cockfighting is banned under other Spanish regional laws and is illegal in most EU Member States. However, French legislation allows bullfighting and cockfighting in areas where these activities have a continuous tradition.

Dogfighting is illegal in those Spanish regions which have adopted animal welfare laws and in other EU Member States.

Possible EU initiatives

1. It is hoped that Member States will modernise or introduce legislation as necessary to prevent cruel treatment of animals in public events, and that responsible treatment of animals will be among the values encouraged through national education systems. Such action was called for in a European Parliament Motion for Resolution on residual ancestral customs in 1992.

Chapter 6

Animal Welfare and the European Union Treaty System

Animal protection law at Member State and European levels

Each of the present 15 Member States of the European Union has enacted legislation for the protection of animals, some as long as 150 years ago. These laws, as they stand, vary in their content and level of detail, in the way they are applied, and in the extent to which particular human activities are exempted from the protective provisions they generally apply to actions in relation to animals. Some have been periodically updated and assiduously invoked, while others have remained untouched for 50 years or so, lying more or less ignored on the statute book and rarely enforced. All, however, derive from and express the principle that to inflict cruelty upon an animal, whether by deliberate action or by neglect of care, is intrinsically wrong.

The Council of Europe, to which 40 countries, including all EU Member States, belong, has drawn up, and continues to develop, five Conventions on various aspects of animal welfare, while administering a sixth on nature protection. The Council's contribution to the development of international ethical standards for the use of animals by man is motivated by its concept of the dignity of man, which it views as in dissociable from the respect which man owes to his environment and to the animals which live therein.[24]

Over the last twenty years, legislation for the protection of animals has also been enacted by the European Community, or the European Economic Community as it formerly was. These laws are based on a combination of mostly trade-related provisions which are in turn founded upon the objectives of the Treaty of Rome, by which the European Economic Community was established in 1957. This basic Treaty has since been modified by the Single European Act, finalized in 1986, and the Treaty on European Union which entered into force in 1993. The objectives of the European Community, stated in Article 2 of the Treaty of Rome, make no specific mention of animal protection, although it has always been

---

[24] Speech by Deputy Secretary General of the Council of Europe to the Plenary Session of Eurogroup for Animal Welfare, Strasbourg, 23 November 1990.

recognised, within certain limits, as a reason for prohibiting or restricting trade between Member States under Article 36 of the Treaty.

However, in 1992, the formally stated objectives of the Community were amended by the Treaty on European Union to include promotion of 'sustainable ... growth *respecting the environment*' and 'the raising of the ... *quality of life*'.[25] The protection of animals can be viewed as an integral part of respect for the environment and improvement of the quality of life, and from that it may be argued that animal protection now features implicitly among Community objectives. It has certainly, during the last decade, already begun to feature among the practical tasks arising from the objectives of the Community's successive action programmes on the environment.

In addition, the Declaration on the protection of animals, which is appended to the Treaty on European Union, acknowledges the potential to affect animal welfare of certain areas of activity falling within the scope of Community legislation. It lists these as the common agricultural policy, transport, the internal market and research. It further recognises that both the Community institutions and the Member States have a role to play in ensuring that full consideration is given to animal welfare, whenever Community legislation in these areas is formulated and implemented.

From the animal welfare point of view, two questions arise from this situation. Will animal protection generally be interpreted as a component of environmental protection, and thus implicit within the revised objectives of the Treaty establishing the European Community? If so, will that be sufficient to ensure that adequate regard is paid to animal welfare when Community legislation, in the areas listed by the Declaration on the protection of animals, is being drafted? All Member States already have an obligation to implement Community legislation once adopted, be it for the protection of animals or anything else. However, whether they, and the law-making institutions of the Community, are obliged to consider the effects on animal welfare of proposed legislation in the four areas listed by the Declaration is less clear. If animal protection is truly a part of environmental policy, which is itself intended to be 'integrated into the definition and implementation of other Community policies',[26] then such consideration would be an obligation. If, on the other hand, animal protection is viewed, perhaps rather illogically, as separate from all other areas of environmental protection, then it would not. Certainly, the Declaration on the protection of animals is a welcome political statement, but one which, if it stands alone, could in practice be no more than a pious expression of good intent.

---

25 Treaty on European Union, Title II, Article G, modifying Article 2 of the Treaty establishing the European Economic Community, 7 February 1992.

26 Title XVI, Article 130r, Treaty on European Union, 7 February 1992.

The legal basis of Community legislation for animal protection

In the absence of any explicit Treaty reference to the desirability of enacting laws for animal protection, or for ensuring that other measures do not have destructive effects, on what basis has the present, quite substantial, body of Community legislation dealing with animal welfare come into existence?

Community legislation on the protection of animals used for experimental or other scientific purposes is based on Article 100 of the Treaty of Rome. Article 100, now supplemented by Article 100a, allows the Community to take action to harmonize the laws of Member States in order to ensure the proper functioning of the internal market.

A similar consideration lies behind the introduction of Community measures in the agricultural sector, where Community Directives for the protection of animals on the farm, in transportation, and at slaughter are based on Article 43 of the Treaty of Rome. This Article allows the Community to introduce measures for the common organization of the market in agricultural products. Live animals, fish, crustaceans, molluscs, birds' eggs and parts of animals are all defined by the Treaty as agricultural products[27] obtained through farming or fisheries. The animal protection legislation is therefore introduced in order to prevent distortion of competition within the single market, such as might otherwise arise from too wide a variation in national rules. It therefore helps to fulfil the objectives of the common agricultural policy, which are set out in Article 39 of the Treaty of Rome. Indeed, this is the basis of the argument for the necessity of Community farm animal welfare action, which was put forward by the Commission in 1993[28] when it carried out a review of Community legislation in relation to the subsidiarity principle expressed in the Treaty on European Union.[29] The Commission further noted that the Community is a party to the European Convention for the protection of animals kept for farming purposes, and takes part in the work arising from the European Conventions on animal transport and slaughter, to which all or most of its Member States are parties. This is held to imply, not only the need to ensure the even application of these Conventions within the Community, but also an international obligation to ensure that they are complied with. This international obligation would also, by that reasoning, extend to the implementation of the European Convention dealing with animal experimentation.

International obligations are also linked to the introduction of Community legislation for the implementation of the Convention on International Trade

---

[27] Treaty establishing the European Economic Community, Article 38 and Annex II.

[28] *Communication from the Commission to the Council and the European Parliament on the Protection of Animals*, COM (93) 384 final, 22 July 1993.

[29] Treaty on European Union, Title II, Article G,B.5, inserting a new Article 3b to the Treaty establishing the European Economic Community.

in Endangered Species (CITES). The new revised version of the Regulation implementing CITES, which deals with trade in and possession of specimens of species of wild fauna and flora, was based on Articles 100a and 113 of the Treaty establishing the European Community. Article 100a[30] allows the harmonization, or approximation, of Member States' national laws, in order to establish the internal market. Common environmental protection measures are embraced in this Article. Article 113 allows Community action to implement a common commercial policy between Member States in dealings with non-member countries. The underlying principle of the legislation is, therefore, the need for common trade rules, here in relation to environmental protection.

The CITES Regulation is now based on Article 130s. Article 130s allows the Community to legislate in pursuit of its environmental objectives, and was only incorporated into the Treaty of Rome through the Single European Act in 1986.

The Community's environmental policy, including the protection of nature and natural resources, and therefore of animals, began to evolve following the Community Summit in Paris in 1972, but it did not find expression in the Treaty of Rome until amendments were introduced by the Single European Act and the Treaty on European Union. In the meantime, environmental protection legislation, including that dealing with animals, was provided for, in a more or less piecemeal way, by action taken under either Article 100, as was the case with the Directive on animal experimentation, or Article 235 of the Treaty of Rome. Article 235 provides the possibility for the Community to fulfil its objectives in relation to areas where the Treaty does not otherwise provide the necessary powers. The Community's Regulation banning the commercial importation of whales and whale products, the original Regulation implementing CITES, the Directive on the conservation of wild birds, and the Directive banning the importation of products derived from hooded and harp seal pups were all introduced on this basis. Animal protection has therefore been dealt with only as an indirect concern of the Community, the passage of legislation coming primarily as a spin-off from the need to ensure the internal and external functioning of the common market, and secondarily from the development of Community environmental protection policy, which is itself derived from the need to apply common rules to ensure that the common market works.

As far as its Treaty status goes, animal protection is in a situation which is not dissimilar to that of general environmental protection before the Single European Act. The need for Community action on animal protection is broadly acknowledged, albeit reluctantly by some, but is not clearly

---

[30] Article 100a was inserted in the Treaty establishing the EEC by Article 18 of the Single European Act in 1986.

stated in the Treaty establishing the Community. Animal protection, like environmental protection, must, if it is to be effective, permeate the full range of Community activities which may potentially affect it. If animal protection is to be explicitly referred to in the Treaty, this must therefore be done in such a way as to make clear that it must be considered in the context of the categories of activity noted in the Declaration on the protection of animals.

Animal protection as a treaty obligation

Efforts to obtain clear references to the need for animal protection in the Treaty establishing the European Community are rooted in two concerns. The first is the wish to ensure that legislation for animal protection can be straightforwardly enacted at Community level whenever necessary, and that steps can be taken to avoid unnecessary negative impingements on animal welfare resulting from Community activity.

The second is the wish to ensure effective implementation and enforcement of Community legislation for the protection of animals. This second concern arises particularly from the history of poor enforcement, which has accompanied the development of legislation on the protection of animals during transport and slaughter. In March 1991, this concern motivated the presentation, to the President of the European Parliament, of a petition urging amendment of the Treaty of Rome to take better account of the needs of farm animals during transport. The petition was supported by more than 2 million signatures. There have been two other significant petitions. The first in 1982, against the killing of baby seals in Canada, attracted 3.5 million signatures and led to the Community ban on the import of baby seal products. The second in June 1991, opposing the use of animals for testing cosmetics, was signed by 2.5 million people.

In the United Kingdom, animal welfare organisations have raised, with their government, the possibility of invoking Article 36 of the Treaty, to prevent the despatch of live animals to other Member States which fail to apply Community animal protection measures properly. However, on the basis of past judgments by the Community's Court of Justice, Article 36 is difficult to invoke in areas where harmonised legislation exists, as is the case with farm animal welfare. It would, furthermore, be of little use from the animal welfare viewpoint, since any action would be specific to the case in connection with which it was invoked, and problems with the proper implementation of animal protection legislation touch more than one country and other areas besides those related to farm animals. It would, moreover, be no solution to these problems from the standpoint of the Community's paramount concern, which is to ensure the smooth functioning of internal dealings between its Member States.

If the protection of animals were explicitly acknowledged among the Community's objectives, either in its own right or as a specified part of the Community's overall environmental concerns, it would enhance the status of legislation concerning animals and might therefore lead both to optimum provision and better implementation.

Initiatives to place animal protection in the Community Treaty

Attempts over the years to place animal protection among the objectives of the Treaty have met with two problems: first, that of finding the right approach, and second, that of countering opposition to the concept. Some Member States have considered that action in this area, and on general environmental matters, is too great a departure from the economic activities on which the Community Treaty is largely based. However, the development of Community legislation shows that animal and environmental protection action are in fact closely linked to the economic functioning of the Community. Furthermore, the Community's objectives are now defined more broadly.

The first attempt to insert a Treaty reference to animal protection was made in 1983, in the opinion of the European Parliament's Committee on Institutional Affairs, which was drawn up in response to the draft Treaty later adopted as the Single European Act. This Report, adopted by the full Parliament in 1984, recommended the inclusion of the following text under the heading 'Environmental Policy': 'The Union shall take measures designed to provide for animal protection.' This reference was lost at a later stage of negotiation.

In March 1991, during the Intergovernmental Conferences on Economic and Political Union, the German Government proposed that the protection of farm and laboratory animals should be expressly included among the objectives of the Treaty of Rome. At the same time, a Motion for Resolution was tabled in the European Parliament. Broader in its scope, this suggested the inclusion of two references to animal protection in the Treaty. The first should list it as one of the objectives of Community environment policy under Article 130r, and the second, under Article 39.2, as one of the factors to be taken into account during implementation of the objectives of the common agricultural policy.

In response to these ideas, the Foreign and Commonwealth Office of the United Kingdom suggested that the Declaration on the protection of animals, with its comprehensive and explicit list of areas with potential to affect animal welfare, be adopted and appended to the Treaty on European Union. This was agreed by EC Heads of Government when the Treaty was finalised at the European Council in Maastricht in December 1991. The Declaration states:

The Conference calls upon the European Parliament, the Council and the Commission, as well as the Member States, when drafting and implementing Community legislation on the common agricultural policy, transport, the internal market and research, to pay full regard to the welfare requirements of animals.

From 1993, the European Parliament has three times expressed the opinion that a revised Treaty should include animal protection and provide animals with a new status of 'sentient animals' rather than goods or agricultural products.

- The 1993 report by Ms Christine Oddy MEP adopted by the Committee on legal affairs and citizens' rights. This report concluded *inter alia*, that 'there should be a new Article inserted into the Treaty of Rome similar to the existing Article 130 r-t for the environment ensuring that animal welfare is a component of all Community policies'.

- The 1994 report by Mr Gianfranco Amendola MEP on behalf of the Committee on the Environment, Public Health and Consumer Protection. In the motion for a resolution, the Parliament 'calls on the Community to make provision after Union for further amendment of the Treaties to enable animals to be treated as sentient beings'.

- The 1993 report by Mr Richard Simmonds MEP on behalf of the Committee on Agriculture, on the Communication from the Commission to the Council and the European Parliament on the protection of animals stated in its motion for a resolution 'calls for the Treaty of Rome to be amended on the occasion of the Intergovernmental Conference in 1996 to clarify Community competence in animal welfare'.

The Intergovernmental Conference process

The EU Treaty system is being reviewed under the auspices of the IGC, which started its proceedings in Turin on 29 March 1996.

On 17 May 1995, the European Parliament adopted the Martin and Bourlanges report, drawn up on behalf of the Institutional Affairs Committee, on the operation of the Treaty on European Union with a view to the 1996 Intergovernmental Conference. Paragraph 10 (vii) reads as follows:

The existing Treaty articles on environmental policy should be strengthened and simplified, so that environmental protection and concern for animal welfare and conservation become fundamental principles of the European Union and are effectively and fully integrated with other EU policies; environmental protection should be included in Article 3 of the Treaty as a Union objective.

The adopted resolution was then forwarded to the Council, the Commission, the members of the Reflection Group on the IGC and to the governments and parliaments of the Member States.

On 16–18 October 1995, a public hearing on the 1996 IGC organised by the Parliament's Institutional Committee took place at the initiative of Mrs Dury MEP and Mrs Maij-Weggen, MEP. The hearing was open to all organisations representing Europe's citizens. Numerous organisations gave their views on fields such as the environment and animals. Two major themes were developed by the speakers, namely the need to give animals a new status in the Treaty and the need to improve the transport of live animals. At this occasion, Eurogroup for Animal Welfare restated its belief that the welfare of animals must be established as one of the Union's basic principles.

Eurogroup for Animal Welfare, together with other animal welfare organisations, prepared a comprehensive document on the status of animals. This document suggests that the following Title and Article should be inserted in the Treaty of Rome:

TITLE XVI bis

ANIMAL WELFARE

Article 130t bis

1. Community policy on agriculture, transport, the internal market and research shall pay full regard to the welfare requirements of the animals used or produced in these sectors.

2. Live animals, although included in the terms 'goods' or 'products' in the Treaty shall be considered as sentient beings and be treated accordingly in Community legislation.

3. The Council, acting in accordance with the procedure referred to in Article 189c, shall take decision in order to achieve the objectives referred to in paragraph 2 of this Article.

4. The measures adopted pursuant to this Article shall not prevent any Member State from maintaining or introducing more stringent measures to protect the welfare of animals. Such measures must be compatible with this Treaty. They shall be notified to the Commission.

Future EU action

Member State Governments should take the opportunity of the IGC to include specific references to animal protection in the body of the Community Treaty, so making it clear beyond all further doubt that the Community's objectives include provision to legislate for the protection of animals. Thereby, proper consideration for the welfare requirements of animals would be a duty upon all Community institutions and Member States, whenever Community legislation on the common agricultural policy, transport, the internal market and research was proposed, as well as implemented.

Chapter 7

Animal Welfare and International Trade

In recent years it has become obvious that trade agreements could conflict with national and European legislation drafted to secure non-trade objectives, i.e. environment or more particularly animal protection.

Tensions between trade rules and animal protection policies might arise due, *inter alia*, to the fact that, while the international trade regime seeks the substantial reduction of tariffs and barriers to trade, the achievement of animal protection objectives often requires the control of trade in certain categories of products. Since 1991, the number of GATT challenges and threatened challenges to environmental, conservation and animal protection regulations have increased significantly.

GATT/WTO rules

GATT and since the conclusion of the Uruguay Round in 1994 in Marrakech, WTO (World Trade Organisation), is the heart of the multi-lateral trading system. Its aim is to promote trade and therefore to remove trade barriers and distortions in order to prevent a repeat of the mistakes of the protectionism of the 1930s which contributed to global depression.

The Basic Principles

To be GATT compatible, animal protection measures have to comply with certain basic trade requirements, mainly the principle of non-discrimination between exporting countries (Article I) and the principle of non-discrimination between domestic and imported countries (Article III).

Article III, §1 recognises the validity of 'internal taxes and other internal charges and laws, regulations and requirements affecting the internal sale, offering for sale, purchase, transportation, distribution or use of products' so long as the measure in question is not applied to imported or domestic products 'so as to afford protection to domestic production'.

Furthermore, Article XX permits trade restrictions that are necessary to 'protect public morals', 'to protect human animal or plant life or health' or 'to relate to the conservation of exhaustible natural resources'. Theoretically, these exceptions apply to all environmental and animal

135

protection objectives but in practice the commonly accepted interpretation is that 'trade rules allow countries to take any measures necessary for protecting the environment or animal protection within their own territory if they are *not discriminatory, arbitrary* and do not result in *disguised restriction* on international trade' (cf. European Commission Communication to the Council and to the Parliament on Trade and Environment, (COM(96) 54), final).

Processes and Production Methods

GATT/WTO rules make an important distinction between product-related and non-product-related Processes and Production Methods (PPMs). Product-related PPMs are trade measures based on the characteristics of the product itself, for example a ban on the importation of gasoline containing amounts of heavy metals and benzene. Non-product-related PPMs are relevant to trade measures based on the way products are produced or processed, but which are not detectable in the final product.

Methods of production are of central importance for animal protection. Many conservation and animal welfare laws as well as environmental measures incorporate non-product related PPMs. A PPM may lead to the loss of migratory species and shared living resources or to the suffering of animals. For instance, the EU Leghold Trap Regulation 3254/91, the US Law banning the importation of tuna caught in driftnets which exceed the UN rule of 2.5 km (High Seas Driftnet Enforcement Act), the US Marine Mammal Protection Act are based on non-product related PPMs.

According to recent jurisprudence, it is clear that quantitative import and export prohibitions or restrictions based on non-product related PPMs, imposed on products whose characteristics do not cause themselves any harm to animals or the environment, are considered inconsistent with GATT/WTO rules. The two GATT panels, Tuna-Dolphin I and Tuna-Dolphin II have found that non-product-related measures violate GATT. In both, the panel held that a US Law restricting the importation of canned yellowfin tuna caught by purse-seines were quantitative restrictions prohibited under Article XI of GATT. Moreover, the US Regulation was not an internal measure as contemplated under Article III, §1 of GATT because the US Law did not regulate tuna as a product, but rather regulated the method used to harvest tuna. Considering these two previous GATT Panel decisions, it is obvious that existing conservation and animal protection laws will be vulnerable to a GATT challenge.

Concerning product-related measures, GATT Article III allows each country to impose on imported products the same requirements in force for domestic 'like products' as long as this does not result in treatment less favourable for imports. The Agreement on Technical Barriers to Trade (TBT) and the Agreement on Sanitary and Phytosanitary measures (SPS) complement GATT/WTO rules. While the TBT regime aims to ensure transparency in the preparation, adoption and application of technical regulations and standards, it states that technical regulations must not create 'unnecessary obstacles to international trade' and that they 'shall not be more trade restrictive than necessary to fulfil a legitimate object'. Furthermore, one of the main objectives of the TBT is to promote international harmonisation of standards and technical regulations. The TBT contains provisions allowing countries not to apply international standards only if they would be ineffective or inappropriate to achieve a legitimate object. The main problem in this case is that it may be difficult to achieve the highest level of animal protection through harmonisation by conforming with international standards.

GATT/WTO rules and Multilateral Environmental Agreements

Many existing Multilateral Environmental Agreements (MEAs) contain trade provisions for the achievement of their environmental goal. The three main examples of MEAs are the Convention on International Trade in Endangered Species of Wild Fauna and Flora (CITES, 1973), the Montreal Protocol on Substances that Deplete the Ozone Layer (1987), and the Basel Convention on the Control of Transboundary Movements of Hazardous Wastes and their Disposal (1989). At the time of their adoption, there was no suggestion that they could conflict with GATT rules. Now, the relationship between the provisions of the multilateral trading system and trade measures taken pursuant to MEAs is one of the important issues of the trade and environment debate. It is also relevant in view of the status of future MEAs.

While there is still no formal acceptance that agreements such as CITES cannot be overruled by GATT, it is generally recognised that the trade related aspects of the MEAs will continue to be considered legitimate, at least with regard to the parties to the MEA. However, there is a doubt that regional conventions such as those adopted by the Council of Europe are likely to be accepted as legitimate when conflicting with GATT. The GATT panel in the Tuna Dolphin I case was the first to officially address this issue. It suggested that an 'international cooperative arrangement' to protect dolphins would be consistent with GATT but the basis for this observation is not clear from the panel's reasoning.

The WTO Committee on Trade and Environment

The Committee on Trade and Environment (CTE) was formally established with detailed terms of reference at the Marrakesh GATT Ministerial Conference in April 1994. Considering its mandate and work programme, the CTE is the main forum for addressing the relationship between trade and environment. It aims first to identify the relationship between trade measures and environmental measures, in order to promote sustainable development and secondly to make appropriate recommendations on whether any modifications to the provisions of the multilateral trading system are required.

The Marrakesh Decision adopted a seven-point work programme for the CTE:

1. The relationship between the provisions of the multilateral trading system and trade related environmental measures including MEAs;

2. The relationship between environmental policies relevant to trade and environmental measures with trade effects and the WTO rules;

3. The WTO's treatment of :

   (a) environmental charges and taxes;
   (b) environmental Production and Processing Methods, including standards and technical regulations, packaging, labelling and recycling;

4. The WTO's provisions relating to the transparency of measures intended to ensure environmental protection which have significant trade effects;

5. The compatibility of WTO and MEA dispute settlement mechanisms;

6. The effect of environmental measures on market access, especially in relation to developing countries, and environmental benefits of trade liberalisation;

7. The issue of exports of domestically prohibited goods.

In accordance to the terms of reference of the CTE agreed in Marrakech, the CTE should address three fundamental aspects, the need for rules to enhance positive interaction between trade and environmental measures for the promotion of sustainable development, the avoidance of protectionist trade measures and the surveillance of trade measures used for environmental purposes.

Within these terms of reference and in addition to a heavy agenda, the CTE is also required to follow the work under the Decision on Trade in Services and the Environment and the relevant provisions of the Agreement on Trade-Related Aspects of Intellectual Property Rights. Furthermore, it has been asked to draft rules relating to relations with inter-governmental and non-governmental organisations referred to in Article V of the WTO.

Trade and environment was on the agenda of the first biennial meeting of the Ministerial Conference which took place in Singapore in December 1996. On that occasion the report from the CTE was discussed and its initial work programme and terms of reference were reviewed but no changes were recommended even though the lack of progress was criticised by several countries.

Apart from CTE, various international fora participate in this trade and environment debate, mainly the Commission on Sustainable Development (CSD) a body in charge of monitoring the implementation of Agenda 21 of the Rio Conference on Environment and Development, the UNEP/UNCTAD and the Organisation for Economic Co-operation and Development (OECD). The OECD Joint Session of Trade and Environment Experts has been analysing and discussing trade and environment issues since April 1991.

The trade and environment debate and the European institutions

The European Parliament

Early in January 1993, the European Parliament adopted its first resolution on trade and the environment on the basis of an own initiative report submitted by the Committee on External Economic Relations (REX), with an opinion by the Committee on the Environment, Public Health and Consumer Protection. In this report, the Parliament asked for the establishment within the framework of the proposed Multilateral Trade Organisation (now WTO), of a committee dealing with trade and environment issues, to replace the ineffective EMIT Group that had existed under GATT since 1970.

Another resolution adopted by the European Parliament on 24 March 1994 embodied the recommendations of the EP to the Commission concerning the negotiations in the Trade Negotiation Committee of GATT on an agreement on a Trade and Environment Work Programme. As a consequence, the EP became the only political, directly elected body to present a formal position before the end of the negotiations in April 1994.

On 14 December 1994, the Parliament gave its assent to the conclusion of the results of the Uruguay Round of Multilateral Trade Negotiations and the following day it adopted resolution B4-0464/94 in which paragraph 24 is worded as follows:

[The EP] emphasizes the need for the WTO at last to link trade issues to environmental, social, consumer and animal protection issues with the aim of accommodating conflicting interests and insists that WTO decisions must on no account be permitted to threaten existing international or EU standards. [Paragraph 25] urges the Commission to secure a moratorium on GATT/WTO challenges to such legislation in order to facilitate constructive discussion within the Trade and Environment Committee (TEC) to press for maximum transparency in this committee and to report immediately and then annually thereafter on progress being made with these matters.

On 23 May 1996, the EP held a debate on trade and the environment in its Plenary session. On this occasion, the EP adopted a report from the REX

Committee with an opinion from the Environment Committee. In the resolution the Parliament regrets 'that some of the demands contained in its resolutions of January 1993 and March 1994 have not been taken into account, e.g. the call for a WTO Environment Council, a moratorium on all decisions by the GATT/WTO panel pending the amendment of GATT Article XX, a fully worked-out programme of measures to be taken by the GATT Ministerial Conference to follow-up the UNCED Conference...'. It also demands that substantial progress should be made for the Singapore meeting on:

- 'the acceptance of internationally agreed MEAs';

- 'increased transparency and openness in WTO procedures, including participation by NGOs and other relevant experts';

- 'non-mandatory and non-discriminatory ecolabelling schemes';

- 'dispute settlement procedures which take account of the provisions of both trade and environment instruments';

- 'improved co-operation and consultation between the WTO and international environmental agencies'.

Another report on the WTO by the REX Committee with an opinion by the Environment Committee is under consideration by the EP. It is a more general one and does not raise the animal protection interference with GATT rules.

The European Commission

On 26 February 1996, the Commission adopted a Communication to the Council and the Parliament on Trade and Environment (COM (96) 54). The document, presented by Trade Commissioner Sir Leon Brittan and Environment Commissioner Ritt Bjerregaard, proposes arguments to show how trade and the environment can be reconciled, and draws attention to the fact that trade itself need not be environmentally damaging.

The main conclusions reached by the Commission in its communication are the following:

- 'The most effective way of dealing with environmental problems is through international and multilateral agreements';

- 'It might be appropriate to further clarify the status of measures necessary to protect the environment under GATT Article XX';

- 'The multilateral trading system should accommodate, under clear and predictable rules, the use of trade measures taken in the framework of MEAs';

- 'Unilateral bans against a country may be allowable in exceptional circumstances if that country is violating some fundamental legal duties under international environmental law';

- 'A possible WTO regime should include some substantive provisions to avoid discrimination and trade distortions in the whole process of the operation of eco-labelling schemes';

- 'A proper dispute procedure should be developed including appropriate enforcement mechanisms for existing and future MEAs';

- 'Transparency within the CTE and increased NGO participation is needed.'

Possible EU initiatives

1. NGOs need access to relevant information about the work of the WTO to be able to submit views throughout the discussions and to have the opportunity to be represented to relevant meetings;

2. Interpretation of the WTO rules relating to process and production methods should be reviewed to enable distinctions to be made between 'like products' on the basis of their production method;

3. Clarification of the application of Article XX is required with regard to paragraphs (a), (b) and (g), in particular to establish that Article XX(a) exception applies to animal protection laws;

4. The legitimacy of existing and future MEAs must be recognised;

5. To ensure that governments can protect the integrity of their national laws and not suffer any unfair trade disadvantage as a result of third countries operating lower standards of animal or environmental protection than those existing within their own nation;

6. NGOs and other groups which have a legitimate interest in the outcome of certain WTO Disputes Settlements Procedures should establish their right to participate in these procedures, ie to present evidence to the panel, to submit briefs, to be included in the panel of advisers.

PART II

Summary of Legislation Relative to Animal Welfare at the Levels of the European Community and the Council of Europe

Introduction

BACKGROUND TO THE EUROPEAN UNION

The six founding countries – Belgium, Federal Republic of Germany, France, Italy, Luxembourg and the Netherlands – met on 25 March 1957 to sign the Treaty of Rome establishing the European Economic Community and the European Atomic Energy Community (Euratom). Since then the EEC has changed its name to become the European Community (EC) (see below) and expanded to include Denmark, Ireland and the United Kingdom (1973), Greece (1981), Spain and Portugal (1986) and Austria, Finland and Sweden (1995). The European Community now has 15 Member States representing 393 million citizens.

The objectives of the EC are defined within the articles of the Treaty of Rome. Those which have some bearing on animal welfare are listed in Appendix XI. On 17 February 1986, the Treaty was amended by the Single European Act which expands the Community's formal competence, pursues new objectives (e.g. improvement of the environment) and ensures a smoother functioning of the Community by enabling the Institutions to exercise their powers under conditions most in keeping with Community interests. It came into force on 1 July 1987.

In December 1991 the heads of government and of state of the Member States met as the European Council in Maastricht and agreed the Treaty on European Union. As well as bringing in further major changes to the Community structure the Treaty, known as the Maastricht Treaty, established the 'European Community' (EC) as the formal legal title of what had been the EEC. Whilst being largely a statement of political intent this Treaty contains relatively few legally specific commitments.

Confusion abounds over when to use the terms European Union and European Community; but it should be remembered that the two are not synonymous. The difference can be explained by looking at the two elements of the Treaty on European Union: the first element effects substantial amendments to the Treaty of Rome including the change of name to the EC; the second element establishes the European Union and gives it competence in two areas in which the Community has none. These areas of competence exclusive to the European Union and therefore dealt with outside the scope of EC law are the Common Foreign and Security Policy, the successor to the European Political Co-operation, and Justice and Home Affairs. The

European Union therefore is wider than the European Community, although founded on it.

The Maastricht Treaty also strengthened the provision within the Treaty of Rome on the environment and in December 1991 the European Council adopted a Declaration on the Protection of Animals calling upon the European Parliament, the Council and the Commission, as well as Member States, when drafting and implementing legislation on the common agricultural policy, transport, the internal market and research, to pay full regard to the welfare requirements of animals.

1. The Commission – initiator and executive

The Commission is composed of 20 Members (Commissioners) appointed for five years and acting in the interest of the Community. (In January 1995 this term was extended from four to five years to coincide with the elections to the European Parliament.) Commission decisions are taken on a collegiate basis, although specific competence are allocated to each Member.

The tasks of the Commission are:

- to ensure that the Community rules and principles of the Common Market are respected;

- to propose to the Council of Ministers measures likely to advance the development of Community policies;

- to implement Community policies, whether based on Council decisions or directly on the Treaty's provisions;

- to be the guardian of the Treaties.

The administrative staff, based mainly in Brussels, consists of approximately 15,000 officials, divided between 24 Directorates-General. The DGs most relevant to animal welfare are DGVI (Agriculture) and DGXI (Environment), with specific issues touching the competence of others.

The Secretariat General of the Commission is also responsible for the publication of official documents in the *Official Journals* (OJ). There are two series of OJs: The *C series* publishes Community information, for example Court Cases, minutes of European Parliament Plenary Sessions, Economic and Social Committee opinions or Commission proposals; the *L series* publishes legislative documents such as Regulations, Directives or Decisions.

2. The Economic and Social Committee – advisory representation

The Economic and Social Committee of (ECOSOC or ESC) is the official consultative and representative body of economic and social interest groups set up by the Treaty of Rome and the Single European Act.

It consists of 222 members appointed for four years and divided into three groups: Employers, Workers and Various Interests, i.e. farmers, cooperatives, consumers, industries, the professions, environmentalists, etc. It is a purely advisory committee, but is consulted by the Council and Commission for opinions on most draft Community measures. The ESC also issues opinions on its own initiative to draw attention to particular topics.

3. The European Parliament – public participation

The European Parliament has 626 Members elected every five years by universal suffrage. These Members form political rather than national groups and to date are divided as follows (abbreviations shown in brackets):

215 Socialists (PSE), 182 members of the European People's Party (PPE), 43 members of the Liberal Democratic and Reformist Group (ELDR), 27 Greens (V), 33 members of the European United Left (GUE), 20 members of the Group of the European Radical Alliance (ARE), 57 members of the Group Union for Europe (UPE) and 49 independents (NI or Ind).

In 1994 the number of MEPs was increased from 518 to 567 to reflect German unification. Greece, Spain, France, Italy, Netherlands, Portugal and the UK also gained slightly more seats. In January 1995 the number of MEPs increased again to reflect the addition of the three new Member States; Austria, Finland and Sweden.

The Single European Act enhanced the European Parliament's role in the legislative process by the introduction of the 'cooperation procedure'. This introduces a 'second reading' of legislation by Parliament whose rejection of a proposal at that stage alters voting requirements in Council from qualified majority to unanimity on certain issues under Article 100A. Although this still means that the Parliament cannot insert its own views nor prevent a unanimous Council overriding it, Parliament's influence has increased. This is especially so where Parliament is able to form an alliance with the Commission and at least one Member State making unanimity impossible and forcing the Council to accommodate Parliament's views. Lobbyists should bear this in mind when the cooperation procedure is being used.

The Maastricht Treaty on European Union further strengthened Parliament's power and influence by the introduction of a power of veto, albeit in limited areas of Community competence.

The European Parliament has the following advisory and supervisory powers conferred by the Treaty of Rome and the Single European Act:

● supervision of the Commission and the Council, partly through debating their programmes and reports, partly through oral and written questions;

- consultation on Commission proposals before the Council makes a decision on the text as revised by the Commission;

- budgetary powers which allow it to take part in major decisions on Community expenditure.

The Parliament has a staff of about 3,000 officials, based mainly in Luxembourg. It has 20 Committees established to discuss subjects in detail and holds plenary sessions in Strasbourg every month with representatives of the Commission and the Council of Ministers present.

There are generally two types of *Working Document* used:

1. *Motions for Resolution* (B series) which if they are adopted by the European Parliament become Resolutions published in the Official Journal; or

2. *Reports* (A series) drawn up either at the initiative of one of the Parliament's specialist Committees on the basis of Motions for Resolution or in response to Commission proposals.

Commission Proposals published in Official Journals as C series documents which are transmitted to the European Parliament and to the Economic and Social Committee (on proposals relating to economic and social matters) for an opinion.

4. The Council of Ministers – decision maker

The Council of Ministers is composed of Ministers from Member State Governments. Each government is president of the Council for six months in rotation. The Ministers responsible for particular fields meet several times a year to make decisions on issues pertaining to that field. The Council therefore makes the major policy decisions of the Union and to this end adopts legislation in the form of:

- *Regulations*, which have general application and are binding in their entirety, being directly applicable to all Member States;

- *Directives*, which are binding equally on all Member States as regards the results to be achieved but leave each Member State to decide how to implement them;

- *Decisions*, which are binding in their entirety upon those to whom they are addressed;

- *Recommendations*, which are not binding.

The Council of Ministers is assisted by the Committee of Permanent Representatives (COREPER), which is composed of senior civil servants from each Member State, usually Diplomats, and reporting to COREPER are the Council's working groups which consist of expert officials from the Member States and examine all new legislation in their particular field. COREPER coordinates the ground work for Council meetings.

5. The Court of Justice – servant of the Community law

The Community Court of Justice, sitting in Luxembourg, comprises 15 judges and is assisted by nine advocates-general. The Court's role is:

- to quash, at the request of a Community institution, government, or individual, any measures adopted by the Commission, Council or national governments which are incompatible with the Treaties;
- to pass judgment, at the request of a national court, on the interpretation or validity of points of Community law.

Through its judgments and interpretations the Court of Justice is helping to create a body of Community law which will apply to all.

6. The Court of First Instance

Set up by the Council of Ministers in October 1988 the Court of First Instance began to hear cases in November 1989. It sits in Luxembourg and hears cases in chambers of three or five judges and has 15 members altogether.

Its jurisdiction and therefore its usefulness to the ECJ is severely limited by the constraints of Article 168a of the Treaty which makes it impossible for the Court of First Instance to hear and determine actions brought by Member States, Community institutions or references made by national courts under Article 177. Such cases account for about two-thirds of the ECJ's workload. The Court of First Instance's jurisdiction mainly covers staff disputes between the servants of the Community and its institutions, although it can determine actions brought against a Community institution by natural or legal persons under Article 173 or 175 EEC relating to the implementation of competition rules applicable to undertakings. For those cases falling within the competence of the Court of First Instance there is a limited right of appeal to the European Court of Justice.

The Maastricht Treaty amended Article 168a to enable the Council, acting unanimously on a request from the ECJ and after consulting the Commission and European Parliament, to transfer any area of the ECJ's jurisdiction to the Court of First Instance, except for Article 177 rulings. Whilst this indicates a long term shift in the ECJ's role to one of appellate court, any change has yet to be seen. The Court of First Instance is therefore of little use in the alleviation of delays in the judicial system.

7. The Court of Auditors

The Court of Auditors was set up by Treaty in 1975 and given the status of the fifth Community institution by the Maastricht Treaty. Its 15 members are appointed by agreement of the Member States for a term of six years. Their role is to check that revenue is received and expenditure incurred 'in a lawful and regular manner' and that the Community's financial affairs are properly managed. Its findings are set out in annual reports drawn up at the end of each year.

THE COUNCIL OF EUROPE

Founded in 1949, the Council of Europe now has a membership of 40 parliamentary democracies and represents in excess of 765 million citizens across Europe.

The aims of the Council of Europe as laid down in its statute are:

- to work for greater European unity;

- to uphold the principle of parliamentary democracy and human rights;

- to improve living conditions and promote human values.

The main areas of activity in which European Conventions have been drawn up include Human Rights; Social Questions; Education, Culture, Sport; Youth; Public Health; Environment; Architectural Heritage; Local and Regional Authorities and Legal Affairs. The protection of animals falls into the last category.

The Council of Europe works through two main organs – the Committee of Ministers representing the governments of the 40 Member States; and the Parliamentary Assembly representing the 36 national parliaments. Their structure and roles are summarised in Figure 1.

1. The Committee of Ministers

The Committee of Ministers is the decision-making body of the Council of Europe and the channel through which governments directly determine its work. The Committee decides what action should be taken on the recommendations from the Parliamentary Assembly and on proposals from the various committees working within the Council's framework, for example the Committee of Experts for the Protection of Animals, later the ad hoc Committee (CAHPA), and now replaced by the Multilateral Consultation of representatives of the Member States. The Committee of Ministers also establishes the Council's work programme and provides a permanent forum for the Member States to discuss a wide range of political issues.

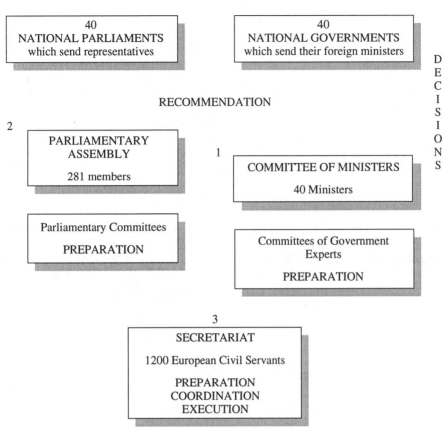

Figure 1

The members of the Committee of Ministers are the Foreign Ministers of each Member State, each of whom holds the presidency in turn for a six month period. Between the meetings of the Foreign Ministers, their Deputies, who act as permanent representatives of the governments, supervise the Council's regular work and thus have practically the same decision-making powers as the Ministers.

The decisions of the Committee of Ministers take the form either of *Recommendations* to governments – policy statements proposing a common course of action to be followed – or of European *Conventions* and *Agreements* which are binding on the States that ratify them. The preparatory work for the drawing up of Conventions and Recommendations is done by committees of government experts.

2. The Parliamentary Assembly

The Parliamentary Assembly of the Council of Europe plays a role in promoting democratic government and respect for human rights throughout the world. Although the Assembly is a consultative body and has no legislative powers its recommendations to the Committee of Ministers have been the starting point for action in many areas of the Council of Europe's work.

The Parliamentary Assembly has 281 members who are elected or appointed by the national parliaments from among their own members. The Assembly meets in Strasbourg three times a year and its debates, which are public, cover all aspects of European life.

3. The Secretariat

The Secretariat serves the Committee of Ministers, the Parliamentary Assembly and the inter-governmental committees. It is divided into directorates corresponding to the eight fields of activity of the Council's work programme and also controls the administration of the Council of Europe.

The various Institutions and their roles within the European Union can be summarised in Figure 2.

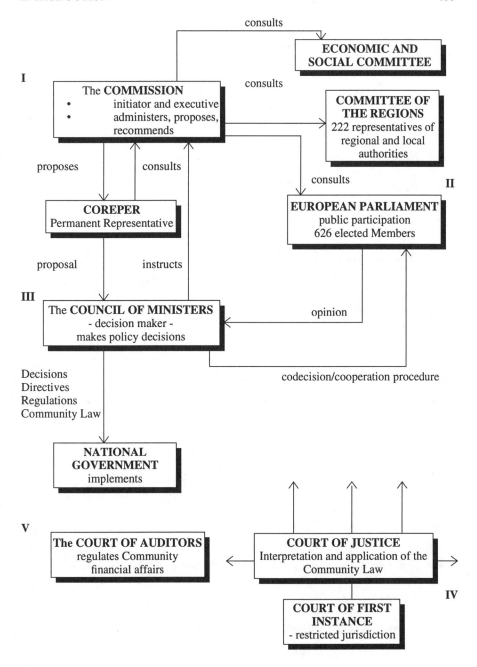

Figure 2

Index to Principal Legislation

EUROPEAN COMMUNITY

Wild Animals

Council Directive 79/409/EEC

of 2 April 1979 on the conservation of wild birds.
(OJ L.103 25/4/79)

Council Regulation (EEC) 348/81

of 20 January 1981 on common rules for the import of whale products.
(OJ L.39 12/12/81)

Council Decision 82/72/EEC

of 3 December 1981 concerning the conclusion of the Convention on the conservation of European wildlife and natural habitats.
(OJ L.38 10/2/82)

Council Decision 82/461/EEC

of 24 June 1982 concerning the conclusion of the Convention on the conservation of migratory species of wild animals.
(OJ L.210 9/7/82)

Council Regulation (EEC) 3626/82

of 3 December 1982 on the implementation in the Community of the Convention on international trade in endangered species of wild fauna and flora.
(OJ L.384 31/12/82)

Council Directive 83/129/EEC

of 28 March 1983 concerning the importation into Member States of skins of certain seal pups and products derived therefrom.
(OJ L.91 9/4/83)

Council Regulation 3094/86

concerning the use of drift-nets for tuna fishing.

Council Directive 89/370/EEC

of 8 June 1989 amending Directive 83/129/EEC concerning the importation of skins of certain seal pups and products derived therefrom.
(OJ L.105 14/6/89)

Commission Regulation (EEC) 2496/89

of 2 August 1989 on a prohibition on importing raw and worked ivory derived from the African elephant into the Community.
(OJ L.240 17/8/89)

Council Regulation (EEC) 3254/91

of 4 November 1991 prohibiting the use of leghold traps in the Community and the introduction into the Community of pelts and manufactured goods of certain wild animal species originating in countries which catch them by means of leghold traps or trapping methods which do not meet international humane trapping standards.

Council Directive 92/43/EEC

of 8 May 1992 on the conservation of natural habitats and of wild fauna and flora.
(OJ L.206 22/7/92)

Farm Animals

Council Directive 74/577/EEC

of 18 November 1974 on the stunning of animals before slaughter.
(OJ L.316 26/11/74)

Council Decision 78/923/EEC

of 19 July 1978 concerning the conclusion of the Convention on the protection of animals kept for farming purposes.
(OJ L.323 17/11/78)

Council Directive 88/146/EEC

of 7 March 1988 prohibiting the use in livestock farming of certain substances having hormonal action.
(OJ L.70 16/3/88 p. 16)

Council Directive 88/166/EEC

of 7 March 1988 laying down minimum standards for the protection of laying hens kept in battery cages.
(OJ L.74 19/3/88)

Council Decision 88/306/EEC

of 16 May 1988 on the conclusion of the European Convention for the Protection of Animals for Slaughter.
(OJ L.137 2/6/88)

Council Decision 90/424/EEC

of 26 June 1990 introduces EC financial support for the cost of implementing Community legislation on disease control and testing for residues of veterinary medicine and for the cost of the new veterinary inspection system needed after the abolition of internal frontiers.

Council Directive 90/425/EEC

of 26 June 1990 establishes the framework for veterinary inspection for live animals after the abolition of internal frontiers.

Council Directive 90/426/EEC

of 26 June 1990 concerns the movement of horses between Member States and third countries.

Council Directive 90/427/EEC

of 26 June 1990 concerns the free movement of breeding horses and their ova or sperm, criteria for the identification of such horses and the recognition of stud books.

Council Directive 90/428/EEC

of 26 June 1990 concerns the removal of all barriers to the free movement within the Community for horses taking part in competitions.

Council Directive 90/667/EEC

of 27 November 1990 controls the disposal of cadavers, slaughter offal, bodies of diseased animals and spoiled meat. It allows the use of low risk waste for feeding zoo animals, packs of hounds and on maggot farms.

Council Regulation (EEC) 1907/90

of 26 June 1990 on certain marketing standards for eggs.
   In force: 1 July 1991.
(OJ L.173 6/7/90 p. 5)

Council Regulation (EEC) 1906/90

of 26 June 1990 on certain marketing standards for poultry.
In force: 1 July 1991.
(OJ L.173 6/7/90 p. 1)

Council Directive 91/628/EEC

of 19 November 1991 on the protection of animals during transport.
(OJ L.340 11/12/91)

Council Directive 91/629/EEC

of 19 November 1991 laying down minimum standards for the protection of
calves.
(OJ L.340 11/12/91)

Council Directive 91/630/EEC

of 19 November 1991 laying down minimum standards for the protection of
pigs.
(OJ L.340 11/12/91)

Council Decision 92/583/EEC

of 14 December 1992 on the conclusion of the Protocol of amendment to
the European Convention for the Protection of Animals kept for Farming
Purposes.

Council Decision 93/119/EC

of 22 December 1993 on the protection of animals at the time of slaughter
or killing.

Council Decision 95/29/EC

of 29 June 1995 amending Directive 91/628/EEC concerning the protection
of animals during transport.

Council Decision 97/2/EC

of 17 December 1996 amending Directive 91/629/EEC laying down minimum standards for the protection of calves. (OJ L.25, 28.1.97, p. 24)

Experimental Animals

Directive 76/768/EEC

on harmonisation of the laws of Member States on Cosmetic Products.

Council Directive 86/609/EEC

of 24 November 1986 on the approximation of laws, regulations and administrative provisions of the Member States regarding the protection of animals used for experimental and other scientific purposes.
(OJ L.358 18/12/86)

Council Resolution

of 24 November 1986 on the signature by Member States of the European Convention on the protection of vertebrate animals used for experimental and other scientific purposes.

Council Directive 87/18/EEC

of 18 December 1986 on the harmonisation of laws, regulations and administrative provisions relating to the application of the principles of Good Laboratory Practice and the verification of their applications for tests on chemical substances.
(OJ L.15 17/1/87 p. 29)

Council Directive 88/320/EEC

of 9 June 1988 on the inspection and verification of Good Laboratory Practice (GLP).
(OJ L.145 11/6/88 pp. 35–7)

Council Decision 89/569/EEC

of 28 July 1989 on the acceptance by the European Community of an OECD decision/recommendation on compliance with the principles of Good Laboratory Practice.
(OJ L.315 28/10/89 p. 1)

Commision Directive 90/18/EEC

of 18 December 1989 adapting to technical progress the Annex to Council Directive 88/320/EEC on the inspection and verification of Good Laboratory Practice (GLP).
(OJ L.011 13/1/90 p. 37)

Commision Decision 90/67/EEC

of 9 February 1990 setting up an Advisory Committee on the Protection of Animals Used for Experimental and Other Scientific Purposes.
(OJ L.044 20/2/90 p. 30)

Council Directive 92/32/EEC

of 30 April 1992 amending for the seventh time Directive 67/548/EEC on the approximation of the laws, regulations and administrative provisions relating to the classification, packaging and labelling of dangerous substances.
(OJ L.154 5/6/92)

Genetic Engineering and Biotechnology

Council Directive 89/556/EEC

of 25 September 1989 regulates the trade in bovine embryos.

Council Directive 90/220/EEC

of 23 May 1990 on the deliberate release into the environment of genetically modified organisms.
(OJ L.117 8/5/90, p. 16)

Summary

The Directive controls the deliberate release of genetically modified organisms either directly or via products containing them. It does not apply to the carriage of such organisms.

Council Directive 90/219/EEC

of 23 May 1990 on the contained use of genetically modified microorganisms.
(OJ L.117 8/5/90, p. 1)

COUNCIL OF EUROPE

Wildlife

Convention No. 104

on the conservation of European wildlife and natural habitats (Bern 19/9/74).

Food Animals

Convention No. 65

for the protection of animals during international transport (Paris 13/7/68).

Additional Protocol No. 103

to the European Convention for the protection of animals during international transport (Strasbourg 10/5/79).

Convention No. 87

for the protection of animals kept for farming purposes (Strasbourg 10/3/76).

Additional Protocol No. 145

to the European Convention for the protection of animals kept for farming purposes (Strasbourg 6/2/92).

Convention No. 102

for the protection of animals for slaughter (Strasbourg 10/5/79).

Experimental Animals

Convention No. ETS 123

for the protection of vertebrate animals used for experimental and other scientific purposes (Strasbourg 31/5/85).

Companion Animals

Convention No. ETS 125

for the protection of pet animals (Strasbourg 1/10/87).

INTERNATIONAL

Washington Convention

on international trade in endangered species of wild fauna and flora (CITES) (Washington DC 6/3/73).

Bonn Convention

on the conservation of migratory species of wild animals (Bonn 23/6/79).

Judgments of the European Court of Justice

International Trade in Wild Fauna and Flora

29/11/90 *Case C-182/89*: Commission *v*. French Republic.
France failed to fulfil its obligations under Regulation 3626/82 by issuing import permits in February 1986 for more than 6,000 skins of endangered wild cats (*felis wiedii* and *felis geoffroyi*) from Bolivia. The French Republic was ordered to pay costs.

Birds

31/07/85 *Case 236/85*: Commission *v* Netherlands
Non-implementation of Council Directive 79/409/EEC.
(OJ C.240 21/9/85 p. 4)

08/07/85 *Case 247/85*: Commission *v* Belgium
Non-Implementation of Council Directive 79/409/EEC.
(OJ C.240 21/9/85 p. 4)
Ruling against Belgium and Italy.
(OJ C.204 31/7/87)

13/08/85 *Case 252/85*: Commission *v* France
Non-Implementation of Council Directive 79/409/EEC.
(OJ C.235 14/9/85 p. 5)
Ruling against France for failure to adopt within the prescribed period all legal measures necessary to comply with Directive 79/409/EEC (27/4/88).

20/08/85 *Case 262/85*: Commission *v* Italy
Non-Implementation of Council Directive 79/409/EEC.
(OJ C.235 14/9/85)

01/10/85 *Case 412/85*: Commission *v* Germany
Non-Implementation of Council Directive 79/409/EEC.
(OJ C.357 31/12/85)
Ruling against Germany for allowing derogations to the provisions of the Birds Directive which are not in accordance with its aims.
(OJ C.274 13/10/87 p. 4)

13/10/87   *Case 236/86.*
The Court of Justice brought a Ruling against the Netherlands for non-conformity of national legislation with certain aspects of Directive 79/409/EEC in relation to Articles 5, 8 and 9.

04/10/88   *Case 288/88*: Commission *v* Federal Republic of Germany
Action on grounds that a number of provisions of federal hunting laws and independent provisions of the Länder had not been brought into line with the provisions of Directive 79/409/EEC.
The Court of Justice ruled that the Federal Republic of Germany had not fulfilled its obligations under the Birds Directive by not bringing a number of provisions into its federal and regional hunting laws.

28/02/89   *Case 57/89*: Commission *v* Federal Republic of Germany
The Commission brought an action against the Federal Republic of Germany alleging that draining and dyking protected areas in the Leybrucht and Rysumer Nacken Bonn infringed Article 4 of Directive 79/409/EEC.
Case Dismissed.

02/05/89   *Case 157/89*: Commission *v* Italy
Court found against Italy regarding the hunting of certain birds during breeding and migration.

03/90   *Case 334/89*: Commission *v* Italy
Ruling on 17/1/91 against Italy for Non transposal of Directive 85/411/EC which amends the Birds Directive.

23/05/90   *C-169/89*
the Court of Justice ruled that a Dutch gourmet food shop was not in breach of the Birds Directive when it was read in conjunction with Article 36 of the Treaty.

09/90   *Case C-155/90*: Commission *v* Ireland
for not being more specific and providing inadequate controls under Article 9 of the Birds Directive.

30/11/90   *Case C-355/90*: Commission *v* Spain
Spain found guilty of failing to fulfil its obligations under the Birds Directive by not giving special protection area status for wild birds to the Santona marshes which were threatened by fish farms, garbage and road construction.
Spain was ordered to pay costs.

19/12/94   *Case C-435/92*
between 'Association pour la protection des animaux sauvages' and Prefects of Maine-et Loire and Loire-Atlantique on the interpretation of Art 7 §4 of Directive 79/409/EE and the setting of dates for the opening and closing of the hunting season.

8/2/96   *Case C-149/94*: Commission *v* Didier Vergy. The Court of Justice ruled that Directive 79/409/EEC is not applicable to specimens of birds born and reared in captivity.
(OJC.95 30/3/96 p. 2)

7/3/96   *Case C-118/94* between the Associazione Italiana per il World Wildlife Fund and others and the Regione Veneto on conditions for exercise of the Member States' power to derogate. The Court ruled that Article 9 of Directive 79/409/EEC authorises the Member States to derogate from the general prohibition on hunting protected species laid down by Articles 5 and 7 of the Directive only by measures which refer in sufficient detail to the factors mentioned in Article 9 (1) and (2).
(OJ C.180 22/6/96 p. 1)

11/7/96   *Case C-44/95*: Regina *v* Secretary of State for the Environment on Directive 79/409/EEC on the conservation of wild birds and Directive 92/43/EEC on the conservation of natural habitats of wild fauna and flora.
The Court ordered that a Member State may not, when designating a special Protection Area, take account of economic requirements as constituting a general interest superior to that represented by the ecological objective of Directive 79/409/EEC.

Farm Animal Welfare

23/12/88   *Case C-131/86*: United Kingdom *v* Council of European Communities
An application, pursuant to Articles 173 and 174 EEC Treaty, for the annulment of Council Directive 86/113/EEC of 25 March 1986 laying down minimum standards for the protection of laying hens kept in battery cages. The UK argued: that the legal basis of the Directive was insufficient as it was based only on Article 43 EEC when it should also have been based on Article 100 EEC; that the text of the Directive differs from that considered by the Council. The first argument failed but the second argument succeeded. The Directive was therefore declared void.

22/12/93   *Case C-348/92*: Commission *v* Ireland
failure to transpose directives on breeding animals of porcine species, sheep and goats.

5/10/94   *Case C-323* on artificial bovine insemination and geographical monopolies. ECJ insisted that Articles 90(1) and 86 of Treaty of Rome do not preclude a Member State from granting to approved bovine insemination centres certain exclusive rights within a defined area.
(OJ N°C331, 26.11.94, p. 2)

12/10/95   *Case C-257/94*: Commission *v* Italy for failure to transpose Directive 91/685/EEC introducing Community measures for the control of classical swine-fever and Council Directive 91/688/EEC on health and veterinary inspection problems upon importaion of bovine, ovine and caprine animals. The Court ordered the Italian republic to pay the costs.

Biotechnology

29/6/95   *Case C-170/94*: Commission *v* Hellenic Republic
failure to transpose directives 90/219/EEC and 90/220/EEC on genetically modified organisms.
Court ordered Hellenic Republic to pay costs.
(OJ N°C229, 2.9.95, p. 8)

Chapter 1

Wild Animals

INTERNATIONAL TRADE IN WILD FAUNA AND FLORA

Existing Legislation

Council Regulation (EEC) 3626/82 of 3 December 1982 on the implementation in the Community of the Convention on international trade in endangered species of wild fauna and flora.
In force: 1 January 1984.
(OJ L.384 31/12/82)

Summary

The Convention's fundamental aim is to establish worldwide controls over wildlife trade in order to protect certain species of wild fauna and flora against over-exploitation. It prohibits commercial international trade in the rarest wild animal and plant species and requires an export licence from the country of origin and an import licence from country of destination for trade in further listed species. Such permits are granted under strict conditions: e.g. that it is not detrimental to the survival of the species, that the specimen is transported with the minimum of risk of injury, damage to health or cruel treatment and that the recipient is suitably equipped to house and care for it. Each party is required to establish Management Authorities and Scientific Authorities to ensure that these conditions are met.

The EEC Regulation aims to ensure a uniform and effective implementation of CITES within the European Community and goes further in establishing a list of species given special treatment by the Community. (See Appendix III for list of signatories.)

Council Regulation (EEC) 3645/83 of 28 November 1983 amending Regulation 3626/82 on the implementation in the Community of CITES.
(OJ L.367 28/12/83 p. 1)

Alters Article 4 to allow amendments to the Convention Appendices to be incorporated into the EEC Regulation.

Commission Regulation (EEC) 3418/83 of 28 November 1983 laying down provisions for the uniform issue and use of the documents required for the implementation in the Community of CITES.
(OJ L.344 7/12/83 p. 1)

Also covers, *inter alia*, the field hitherto covered by Commission Regulation 3786/81 laying down provisions for the implementation of the common rules for imports of whale or other cetacean products.

Commission Regulation (EEC) 3646/83 of 12 December 1983 amending Regulation 3626/82 on the implementation in the Community of CITES.
(OJ L.367 28/12/83 p. 2)

Amendments to the Annexes following the CITES Meeting in Gabarone 19–20 April 1983.

Commission Regulation (EEC) 577/84 of 5 March 1984 amending for the third time Regulation 3626/82 on the implementation in the Community of CITES.
(OJ L.64 6/3/84 p. 9)

Transfers the Giant Panda from Appendix III to I of the Convention.

Commission Regulation (EEC) 1451/84 of 24 May 1984 amending Annex A to Regulation 3626/82 on the implementation in the Community of CITES.
(OJ L.140 26/5/84 p. 21)

Amends Appendix II of the Convention to include seven species of snake.

Commission Regulation (EEC) 1452/84 of 24 May 1984 amending Annex C to Regulation 3626/82 on the implementation in the Community of CITES.
(OJ L.140 26/5/84 p. 21)

To conform with the new taxonomic system for birds.

Council Regulation (EEC) 1831/85 of 27 June 1985 amending Regulation 3626/82 on the implementation in the Community of CITES.
(OJ L.173 3/7/85 p. 1)

Amendments to Annex A with respect to cyclamen plant species.

Commission Regulation (EEC) 2384/85 of 30 July 1985 amending Regulation 3626/82 on the implementation in the Community of CITES.
(OJ L.231 29/8/85 p. 1)

Amendments to the Annexes following the CITES Meeting in Buenos Aires 22 April–3 May 1985.

Council Regulation (EEC) 2295/86 of 21 July 1986 amending Regulation 3626/82 on the implementation in the Community of CITES.
(OJ L.201 24/7/86 p. 1)

Following the decisions taken at the Fourth Meeting of the Conference of Parties to CITES, amends Articles 2 and 6 (2) of Regulation 3626/82 in order to take account of the revised control system for plants listed in Appendix II and III and animals listed in Appendix III of the Convention.

Council Regulation (EEC) 1422/87 of 21 May 1987 amending Regulation 3626/82 on the implementation in the Community of CITES.
(OJ L.136 26/5/87 p. 1)

In view of the successful ranching operations involving birdwing butterflies, all species are transferred from part 1 of Annex C to part II except for *Ornithoptera alexandrae* which is still endangered.

Commission Regulation (EEC) 1540/87 of 22 May 1987 amending Regulation 3626/82 on the implementation in the Community of CITES.
(OJ L.147 26/5/87)

Following the Meeting of the Committee on the CITES Convention and the alterations to the Annexes.

Commission Regulation (EEC) 3143/87 of 19 October 1987 amending Regulation 3626/82 on the implementation in the Community of CITES.
(OJ L.299 22/10/87)

Commission Regulation (EEC) 869/88 of 30 March 1988 replacing Annex B to Council Regulation 3626/82 on the implementation in the Community of CITES.
(OJ L.87 31/3/88, p. 67)

Commission Regulation (EEC) 3188/88 of 17 October 1988 amending Council Regulation 3626/82 on the implementation in the Community of CITES.

Amendments to Appendix III of Annex A to Regulation 3626/82 in accordance with the opinion of the Committee on the Convention on International Trade in Endangered Species of Wild Fauna and Flora.
(OJ L.285 19/10/88 p. 1)

Commission Regulation (EEC) 610/89 of 9 March 1989 amending Council Regulation 3626/82 on the implementation in the Community of CITES.

Incorporates amendments to Appendices I and II relating to Madagascar and Malawi accepted by Member States parties to the Convention.

Commission Notice 89/C327/01 of 30 December 1989 lists the names and addresses of the Management and Scientific Authorities designated by the Member States in accordance with Article 7 of Regulation 3626/82.

Commission Notice 89/C327/02 of 30 December 1989 lists the ports of entry and exit designated by the Member States for trade with third countries in accordance with Article 16 of Regulation 3626/82.

Commission Regulation (EEC) 197/90 of 17 January 1990 amending Council Regulation 3626/82 on the implementation in the Community of CITES.
   Revises the Appendices of Regulation 3626/82 to take account of changes in CITES listing adopted at the Seventh CITES Conference at Lausanne (October 1989). (As a result of the change in the Appendix listing of the African elephant, Regulation 2496/89 prohibiting imports of ivory is redundant, see Elephants – Ivory.)
(OJ L.29 31/1/90)

Council Directive 91/628/EEC of 19 November 1991 on the protection of animals during transport and amending Directives 90/425/EEC and 91/496/EEC.
In force: 1 January 1993.
(OJ L.340 11/12/91)

Summary

The Directive applies to the transport of most animals including categories of wild animals (except, perhaps, *insectivora*). The Council shall lay down appropriate additional conditions for the transport of certain types of animal such as wild birds and marine mammals (Article 3).
   The Commission is required to submit a report drawn up on the basis of an opinion from the Scientific and Veterinary Committee on various welfare parameters associated with the transport of animals (Article 13).

Council Directive 95/28/EC of 29 June 1995 amending Directive 91/628/EEC concerning the protection of animals during transport.
(OJ N°.L 148, 30.6.95, p. 52)

Summary

This Directive introduces a distinction between standard vehicles and improved vehicles. However, it fails to introduce a European-wide maximum journey time of 8 hours for slaughter animals. In standard vehicles, animals cannot be transported for more than 8 hours before unloading for 24 hours. In improved ones, different rules apply according to the species transported.

In accordance with Article 13, the Commission shall submit proposals on vehicle standards and criteria to be met by staging points. These proposals are still pending. Before 31 December 1999, the Commission shall submit a report to the Council on the experience acquired by the Member States since the implementation of this Directive.

For further information see Transport of Animals in the Farm Animals section.

Regulation EC 1771/94 adopted by Commission. Lays down provisions for the introduction into the Community of pelts and manufactured goods of certain wild animal species. Prohibition on introduction into the Community of pelts of animals in Annex I of Regulation EEC 3254/91 and of the other goods listed in Annex II of that Regulation entered into force on 1/1/95. The Regulation is to enter into force in full on 1/1/96.

Regulation 558/95 amending Council Regulation 3626/82 on implementation of CITES within the Community. Amendments incorporate proposals put forward by Member States at the ninth session of the Conference of the Parties to the Convention (Fort Lauderdale 18/11/94) – Appendices I, II, III of Annex A and parts 1 and 2 of Annex C are amended.
(OJ N° L 79, 7.4.95, p. 12)

Commission Regulation (EC) No. 2727/95 of 27 November 1995 amending Council Regulation (EEC) No. 3636/82 on the implementation in the Community of CITES.

Work in Progress

Under the French Presidency the Council of Ministers have discussed a new text for the proposed new EC wildlife trade Regulation. The new draft regulation has been shortened and simplified making it easier to enforce. Unfortunately all references to animal protection have been taken out. In February 1996, the Council published its common position. The second reading of the Parliament took place in September 1996, where the Parliament adopted – with amendments – Mrs van Putten's report on the CITES Common Position. On 9 December, the Environment Council adopted the proposed Regulation on the protection of species of wild fauna and flora by regulating trade therein. This Regulation is applicable from 1 June 1997. It covers endangered animals and plants as well as any products made from such species.

By means of this Regulation the Community will be able to ensure better application and enforcement of the CITES Convention. The species covered are those listed in the Annexes to the Convention with the addition of a series of 'priority' species. The Regulation comprises four Annexes reflecting the level of protection increasing from Annex D (statistical monitoring only) to Annex A (total trading ban). The greater the threat of extinction facing the species in question, the more restrictive conditions have been fixed for introducing them into the Community. Finally, the Regulation also covers infringements which Member States will be required to penalize.

The ordinary meeting of the parties to CITES to be held in June 1997.

Action by the European Court of Justice

29/11/90   Judgment of the European Court of Justice in Case C-182/89: *Commission of the EC* v *French Republic*. France failed to fulfil its obligations under Regulation 3626/82 by issuing import permits in February 1986 for more than 6,000 skins of endangered wild cats (*felis wiedii* and *felis geoffroyi*) from Bolivia.

The French Republic was ordered to pay costs.

1991   File closed on the infringement proceedings against Spain regarding use of chimpanzees by beach photographers, first initiated in 1988.

Background

Washington Convention

06/03/73   The Convention on International Trade in Endangered Species of Wild Fauna and Flora (CITES) was formed in Washington. It came into effect on 1 July 1975 with the ratification of ten out of the 57 States which had signed it. (See Appendix III for Signatories).

02/11/76   First Ordinary Meeting of the Conference of the Parties to CITES, held in Bern, Switzerland. One of its prime achievements was to establish the Bern criteria for guidelines for listing or removing species from Appendix I or II. A Resolution was also adopted urging parties to the Convention to limit eventually the keeping of pet species in Appendix I to those which can be bred in captivity.

17/10/77   A Special Working Session was held in Geneva, Switzerland. There it adopted, among others, a Resolution (S.S.1.1.) recognising the necessity of international directives for the preparation and shipment of live specimens of the species listed in the Appendices. The general principles for this were also laid down.

19/03/79	Second Ordinary Meeting of the Conference of the Parties of CITES held in San José, Costa Rica. Adopted the Guidelines for Transport and Preparation for shipment of live wild animals and plants. Adopted Resolution 2.12 defining bred in captivity and establishing criteria for allowing captive breeding or artificial propagation operations, for example not endangering wild populations, establishing a parental breeding stock which avoids in-breeding, and managing them correctly in a controlled environment.
22/06/79	First Extraordinary Meeting of the Conference of Parties to CITES held in Bonn, Germany. Adopted an amendment to Article XI(3)(a) creating financial provisions to enable the secretariat to carry out its duties.
1980	Publication of 'CITES Guidelines for Transport and Preparation for shipment of live wild animals and plants' in UNIPUB Edition 1980.
13/03/81	Third Ordinary Meeting of the Conference of the Parties to CITES held in New Delhi, India. Adopted a Resolution on the criteria necessary for allowing ranching of Appendix I species. These include:

- possibility of the local populations to withstand the pressure of trade in ranched animals;

- that the operation is in accordance with conservation requirements;

- that ranching products are clearly identified;

- that the operation is carried out at all stages in a humane way.

Resolution 3.16 was adopted recommending parties to find suitable means for implementing the Transport Guidelines.

Resolution 3.17 recommends the development of an international reporting system for species that are stressed during transport.

19/04/83	Fourth Ordinary Meeting of the Conference of Parties to CITES held in Gabarone, Botswana. Three Resolutions were adopted of relevance to animal welfare:

Resolution 4.15 on the control of captive breeding and ranching operations. Includes establishing a Register of captive breeding operations;

Resolution 4.20 on drawing up CITES guidelines for transport of live wild animals by air, in accordance with IATA Guidelines;

Resolution 4.21 on an internal reporting system for species that are stressed during transport which can then be communicated to the Management Authority of the export country.

30/04/83   Second Extraordinary Meeting of the Conference of the Parties to CITES held immediately after the ordinary meeting in Gabarone; Article XXI of CITES was amended to allow the EEC to accede to the Convention.

03/05/85   Fifth Ordinary Meeting of the Conference of Parties to CITES held in Buenos Aires, Argentina. Adopts, amongst many others, a Resolution 5.12 on establishing quota systems for export of raw ivory from 1 December 1985; Resolution 5.16 asking the Technical Committee of CITES to review and develop recommendations on the establishment of reporting and monitoring procedures for ranching operations and captive breeding operations.

Resolution 5.18 asking the Technical Committee to establish a Working Group for recommendations on air transport. Also urges parties to consider adopting domestic legislation in this matter.

12/85   CITES Secretariat published a Manual on 'Ivory Trade – Control Procedures'.

07/87   Sixth Ordinary Meeting of the Conference of the Parties to CITES held in Ottawa, Canada.

09/10/89   Seventh Ordinary Meeting of the Conference of the Parties to CITES held in Lausanne, Switzerland. Adopted proposal to list the African elephant (*Loxodonta africana*) on Appendix I.

06/03/92   Eighth Ordinary Meeting of the Conference of the Parties to CITES held in Kyoto, Japan. Adopted Resolutions to implement Article IV of CITES in relation to trade in wild birds (weak version of submitted drafts); criticised enforcement of CITES in some EC countries, but urged acceptance of amendment to allow EC accession.

07/92   Standing Committee recommended to CITES Secretariat that trade with Italy be suspended due to failure to enforce the Convention's provisions.

7/11/94	The Ninth Meeting of the Parties to CITES was held in Fort Lauderdale in the USA. Extension of permission to trade in raw vicuna wool; approval of US proposal for CITES to look into shark-fin trade; approval for Appendix II listing given for box turtles, tarantulas, scorpions and hippopotamus; South African proposal of downlisting the White Rhino to allow trade in live animals and hunting trophies, approved until next conference.
9/94	South African and Sudanese governments request the downlisting of their African elephant populations from Appendix I to Appendix II of CITES. Motion agreed in Parliament under the topical and urgent debate procedure to refuse this.
11/94	South African authorities withdraw their proposal for downlisting of African elephant from Appendix I to Appendix II of CITES.

European Community

14/03/77	The Council authorised the Commission to enter into negotiations for the Community to accede to the Convention on International Trade in Endangered Species of Wild Fauna and Flora.
17/05/77	Council Resolution on the continuation and implementation of a European Community policy and action programme on the environment. This stressed that 'the protection of wild fauna and flora is a matter for the Community as a whole and that implementation of CITES is an important measure for protecting these species'. (OJ C.139 13/6/77 p. 1)
23/05/80	Motion for a Resolution 1-200/80 by Mr Lynge, Ms Gredal, Mrs Groes, Mr Fich, Mr Glinne, Mr Adams, Mr Albers, Mr Gautier, Mr Griffiths, Mr Jaquet, Mrs Fuillet, Mr Delors, Mr Hänsch, Mr Seeler, Mr van Minnen, Mr von der Vring, Mr Sieglerschmidt, Mr Walter and Mrs Viehoff on Community trade in products made from endangered animal species.
21/07/80	COM(80)413 Proposal for a Council Regulation (EEC) on the implementation of CITES. Submitted to the Council by the Commission. (OJ C.243 22/9/80 p. 16)
01/08/80	The Council asked the ECOSOC for an opinion.

26/02/81	The ECOSOC adopted by a large majority the proposal for a Council Regulation on the implementation of CITES. (OJ C.138 9/6/81 p. 5)
1981	The Commission published in its Environment and Quality of Life Series a Report on 'The Preliminary Status of the Marine Mammals of major relevance to Europe'. Ref: EUR 7317.
22/10/81	Report 2-579/81 on behalf of the Environment Committee on the proposal for a Council Regulation on the implementation of CITES.
20/11/81	European Parliament adopted the Resolution on the implementation of CITES. (OJ C.327 14/12/81 p. 105)
03/12/82	The Council adopted Council Regulation (EEC) 3626/82. (OJ L.384 31/12/82)
30/09/83	The Commission submitted a Communication to the Council for a proposal to amend Article 4 of Regulation 3626/82 in order to allow the adoption of amendments made at the Conference of the Parties to CITES into the Regulation Annexes. (OJ C.272 11/10/83 p. 7)
10/83	The Council asked the European Parliament and the ECOSOC for their opinion.
28/10/83	The Parliament approved the Commission proposal. (OJ C.322 28/11/83 p. 279)
28/11/83	Council Regulation (EEC) 3645/83 amending Regulation 3626/82. (OJ L.367 28/12/83 p. 1)
01/01/84	Council Regulation 3626/82 entered into force.
02/04/85	COM(85)128 final the Commission submitted a Communication to the Council for a proposal to amend Annex C to include the cyclamen species (except *Cyclamen persicum*) which are threatened by the high rate of Community imports of the bulbs of these species. (OJ C.112 7/5/85 p. 7)
05/85	The Council asked the European Parliament and the ECOSOC for their opinion.
30/05/85	The ECOSOC approved the proposal.

06/85	Report A2-60/85 on behalf of the Environment Committee on the Commission's proposal to amend Regulation 3626/82. Rapporteur: Beate Weber (S-D).
14/06/85	The European Parliament adopted a Resolution concluding the consultation procedure for the Commission proposal to amend Regulation 3626/82. (OJ C.175 15/7/85)
27/06/85	The Council adopted Council Regulation (EEC) 1831/85 amending Regulation 3626/82.
1986	The CITES-EC Annual Report for 1984 was published.
04/86	COM(86)167 final the Commission submitted a Communication to the Council for a proposal to amend Annex C of Council Regulation 3626/82. In view of the successful bird-wing butterfly ranching operations within the Community it was suggested that certain species be moved from Annex C Part 1 to Annex C Part 2. (OJ C.97 25/4/86 p. 7)
05/86	The Council asked the European Parliament and the ECOSOC for their opinions.
08/86	The ECOSOC approved the Commission's proposal. (OJ C.207 18/8/86 p. 27)
12/11/86	Report A2-153/86 on behalf of the Environment Committee on the Commission's proposal to amend Regulation 3626/82. Rapporteur: Hemmo Muntingh (S-NL).
01/12/86	The European Parliament adopted a Resolution concluding the consultation procedure for the Commission's proposal to amend Regulation 3626/82. (OJ C.175 12/1/87 p. 76)
22/01/87	Motion for a Resolution B2-1470/86 by Mr Martin, Mrs Crawley, Mr Hoon, Mr Elliott, Mr McMahon, Mr Newens and Ms Tongue on the importation of young chimpanzees into Spain.
21/05/87	Council Regulation (EEC) 1422/87 amending Council Regulation 3626/82. (OJ L.136 26/5/87 p. 1)
09/87	The CITES-EC Annual Report for 1985 was published. This consists of a cumulative report showing all trade in CITES specimens between the Community and the rest of the world.

19/10/87	Commission Regulation (EEC) 3143/87 amending Council Regulation 3626/82. Replaces Appendices I, II and III of Annex A and parts 1 and 2 of Annex C. (OJ L.299 22/10/87) Motion for a Resolution 2-299/87 by Mrs Bloch von Blottnitz on poaching of animals protected by CITES. COM(87)711 final/2: Communication from the Commission on the results of the Sixth Ordinary Meeting of the Parties to CITES, held in Ottawa in July 1987.
30/03/88	Commission Regulation (EEC) 869/88 replacing Annex B to Council Regulation 3626/82. Bases the Annex on the combined nomenclature drawn up to reflect implementation of the Harmonised Commodity Description and Coding System in the Community. (OJ L.87 31/3/88 p. 67)
27/04/88	Motion for a Resolution 2-213/88 by Mrs Bloch von Blottnitz on the implementation and reform of the regulations currently in force on the implementation in the Community of the Convention on international trade in endangered species of wild fauna and flora.
03/05/88	Motion for a Resolution 2-0221/88 by Mr Wedekind, Mrs Maij-Weggen, Mr Mertens, Mrs Lentz-Cornette and Mrs Schleicher on improving the scientific bases of nature protection and species conservation in the European Community.
09/06/88	Report A2-180/88 drawn up on behalf of the Environment Committee on the implementation of the CITES Regulation in the European Community (concerning the implementation in the Community of the Convention on International Trade in Endangered Species of Wild Fauna and Flora [the Washington Convention]). Rapporteur: Hemmo Muntingh (S-NL).
09/88	Publication of *Application of CITES in the European Economic Community* in two volumes, a report giving an overview of the application of European Community law related to CITES, prepared by the World Conservation Monitoring Centre and the IUCN Environmental Law Centre.
13/10/88	European Parliament adopted a Resolution on the implementation of the CITES Regulation in the European Community (Council Regulation (EEC) 3626/82). (OJ C.290 14/11/88 p. 142)

17/10/88	Commission Regulation (EEC) 3188/88 amending Council Regulation 3626/82. Further amendment of Appendix III, of Annex A. (OJ L.285 19/10/88)
1989	The CITES-EC Annual Report for 1987 was published.
09/03/89	Commission Regulation (EEC) 610/89 amending Council Regulation 3626/82 on the implementation of CITES in the Community. Incorporates amendments to Appendices I and II relating to Madagascar and Malawi being accepted as Parties to the Convention.
30/12/89	Commission Notice 89/C327/01 lists the names and addresses of the Management and Scientific Authorities designated by the Member States in accordance with Article 7 of Regulation 3626/82.
30/12/89	Commission Notice 89/C327/02 lists the ports of entry and exit designated by the Member States for trade with third countries in accordance with Article 16 of Regulation 3626/82.
1990	The CITES Annual Report for 1988 was published.
17/01/90	Commission Regulation (EEC) 197/90 amending Council Regulation 3626/82 on the implementation of CITES in the Community.
02/02/90	Opinion of the Environment Committee on Petition 471/87 by Miss McKeever which protests against the use of chimpanzees by Spanish beach photographers. The Committee supports the petitioner's view that this exploitation is objectionable. It contravenes Regulation 3626/82, which prohibits the import and exploitation of chimpanzees by beach photographers.
28/01/91	Motion for a Resolution B3-43/91 by Mrs Muscardini on the survival of lemurs in Madagascar.
04/91	Motion for a Resolution B3-1380/90 by Mrs Ewing and others calling for a ban on the import of wild caught birds. Rapporteur: Caroline Jackson (ED-UK).
07/91	Motion for a Resolution B3-701/91 by Mrs Muscardini calling for the EC to take measures to help end indiscriminate killing of the tapir for its hide. Referred to Environment Committee.

13/09/91   Report A3-212/91 Report by Mrs Jackson on Motion for a Resolution B3-1380/90 calling for a ban on the import of wild caught birds was debated and passed by Plenary.

11/91   Motion for a Resolution B3-1230/90 by Mr Stewart and 20 others calling for a ban on import, cross border transport and sale of wild caught birds.

1992   The CITES-EEC Annual Report for 1989 was published.

11/92   Rapporteur appointed for Motion for Resolution B3-1061/92 on live wild animal trade and transport. Rapporteur: Mr Killilea (RDE-IRL).

18/12/92   COM(91)448 final proposal for a Council Regulation laying down provisions with regard to possession of and trade in specimens of species of wild fauna and flora published by Commission.

01/93   COM(91)448 referred to Environment Committee. Rapporteur: Hemmo Muntingh (S-NL). First reading of the report in the Environment Committee scheduled for November 1992. A supplementary opinion is to be delivered by the Committee on Economic and Monetary Affairs and Industrial Policy.
            Rapporteur: Astrid Lulling (PPE-LUX).

Summary

            COM(91)448 is intended to supersede and update Regulation 3626/82. Its most significant addition is a new Appendix D which contains most animals and plants not already covered by Annex A, B and C of 3626/82, requiring an import declaration for the species it covers.

24/3/93   Environment Committee discussed new report [PE 204.175 + PE 204.175/ann] on Commission proposal [COM(91)0488 final] for Council Regulation laying down provisions with regard to possession of and trade in specimens of species of wild fauna and flora. Council working group to meet on 6/7 April to check annexes B C D for reduction. Rapporteur: Mr Muntingh.

6/5/93   [PE 204.175 + PE 204.175/Am.44-70] discussed in Environment Committee.

10/6/93   MEPs adopt Report [PE 204.175 rev] on Comm Proposal [COM(91)0488 final] for Council Reg laying down provisions for possession of and trade in specimens of species of wild fauna and flora.

24/6/93	Amended report on Commission proposal.

19/7/94   Regulation EC 1771/94 adopted by Commission. Lays down provisions for the introduction into the Community of pelts and manufactured goods of certain wild animal species. Prohibition on introduction into the Community of pelts of animals in Annex I of Regulation EEC 3254/91 and of the other goods listed in Annex II of that Regulation to enter into force on 1/1/95.

4/10/94   Council of Ministers discuss proposal for Regulation replacing REGULATION 3626/82/EEC on implementation of CITES with a text aimed at generally protecting wild flora and fauna from the harmful consequences which trade has for their conservation status and harmonising the effects of the national measures adopted in this area.

9/94   South-African and Sudanese governments request the downlisting of their African elephant populations from Appendix I to Appendix II of CITES. Motion agreed in Parliament under the topical and urgent debate procedure to refuse this.

11/94   South African authorities withdraw their proposal for downlisting of African elephant from Appendix I to Appendix II of CITES.

10/3/95   Regulation 558/95 amending Council Regulation 3626/82 on implementation of CITES within the Community. Amendments incorporate proposals put forward by Member States at the ninth session of the Conference of the Parties to the Convention (Fort Lauderdale 18/11/94) – Appendices I, II, III of Annex A and parts 1 and 2 of Annex C are amended.
(OJ N°L 79, 7.4.95, p. 12)

5/95   Under the French Presidency the Council of Ministers have discussed a new text for the proposed new EC wildlife trade Regulation. The new draft regulation has been shortened and simplified making it easier to enforce. Unfortunately all references to animal protection have been taken out. In February 1996, the Council published its common position. Under the second reading procedure Parliament will be able to give its opinion on this revised proposal.

21/11/95   The Environment Committee examined the legal basis of the CITES Convention and voted for a change in legal basis, from Articles 100A and 113, which put the emphasis on trade, to Article 130s, which calls for a cooperation procedure and puts the emphasis on the environment instead.

27/11/95 Commission Regulation (EC) No. 2727/95 amending Council Regulation (EEC) No. 3636/82 on the implementation in the Community of CITES.

26/2/96 Common Position (EC) No. 26/96 of 26 February 1996 adopted by the Council, with a view of adopting a Council Regulation on the protection of species of wild fauna and flora by regulating trade therein.
(OJ N° C 196, 6.7.96, p. 58)

11/6/96 Report A4-0000/96 Report of 11 June drawn up on behalf of the Committee on the Environment, Public Health and Consumer Protection, on the COMMON POSITION established by the Council with a view to the adoption of a Regulation on the protection of wild fauna and flora by regulating trade therein. Rapporteur: Maartje van Putten (PSE-NL).

18/9/96 Second reading of Report A4-0000/96 by Mrs van Putten on CITES. Adopted by Parliament with some amendments. The amendments adopted by Parliament which the Commission stated they will support include:

- inclusion of a reference to the Wild Birds Directive;

- Annex D (the monitoring Annex for non-CITES species) must have a representative number of species;

- improvement in enforcement of CITES in the EU;

- Member States to give a bi-annual report on the implementation and enforcement of the Regulation.

9/12/96 On 9 December, the Environment Council adopted the proposed Regulation on the protection of species of wild fauna and flora by regulating trade therein. Regulation 26/96/EC is applicable from 1 June 1997. It covers endangered animals and plants as well as any products made from such species.

By means of this Regulation the Community will be able to ensure better application and enforcement of the CITES Convention. The species covered are those listed in the Annexes to the Convention with the addition of a series of 'priority' species. The Regulation comprises four Annexes reflecting the level of protection increasing from Annex D (statistical monitoring only) to Annex A (total trading ban).

The greater the threat of extinction facing the species in question, the more restrictive conditions have been fixed for introducing them into the Community. Finally, the Regulation also covers infringements which Member States will be required to penalize.

CONSERVATION OF MIGRATORY SPECIES OF WILD ANIMALS

Existing Legislation

Council Decision 82/461/EEC of 24 June 1982 concerning the conclusion of the Convention on the conservation of migratory species of wild animals. (OJ L.210 9/7/82 p. 10)

Summary

Parties to the Convention acknowledge the importance of migratory species and their habitats and aim to take appropriate and necessary steps (either individually or in cooperation) to conserve such species and their habitat. In particular, action should be taken to promote research, provide immediate protection for endangered species listed in Appendix I and provide Agreements for the conservation and management of species listed in Appendix II.

For endangered species listed in Appendix I, Range States (i.e. those who have jurisdiction over part of the species' migratory range) must endeavour to conserve and restore habitats, remove obstacles affecting their migration and eliminate factors that may endanger the species further. Moreover, the taking, hunting, fishing, capturing, harassing or deliberate killing of such species is prohibited unless for extraordinary reasons.

Agreements between Range States regarding species listed in Appendix II should endeavour to restore their population levels to a favourable conservation status with the aid of research, and to promote the conservation and management of their habitats.

Work in Progress

None.

Background

Bonn Convention

23/06/79   Bonn Convention on the conservation of migratory species of wild animals.
             Drafted in the context of the United Nations Environment Programme (UNEP).

	Entered into force: 1 November 1983 after ratification by 15 Nations. (See Appendix I for signatories.)
26/10/85	First Meeting of the Conference of Parties to the Bonn Convention held in Bonn.
11/09/91	The agreement to protect European species of bats made under Article IV was concluded.
12/09/91	Negotiations on the text of an Agreement on the Conservation of Small Cetaceans of the Baltic and North Seas under Article IV were concluded.
04/12/91	Bats Agreement opened for signature and will come into force 90 days after five Range States have become Parties to it.
17/03/92	North and Baltic Seas Small Cetacean Agreement opened for signature and will come into force 90 days after six Range States have expressed their intent to be bound by it.

European Community

15/06/79	Council Decision for the Commission to take part in the negotiations for the conclusion of the Convention on the conservation of migratory species of wild animals.
18/04/80	Commission Communication to the Council on the results of the negotiations on the conclusion of the Convention on the conservation of migratory species of wild animals and a proposal for a Council Decision.
23/04/80	COM(80)187 final proposal from the Commission for a Council Decision. (OJ C.151 19/6/80 p. 4)
06/05/80	The Council asked the European Parliament and the ECOSOC for their opinions on the proposal.
24/09/80	Opinion of the ECOSOC: 'The Committee regrets that the Community has not yet become a full signatory of the Convention on the conservation of migratory species of wild animals'. (OJ C.300 18/11/80)
03/06/81	Report 1-243/81 drawn up on behalf of the Environment Committee on the proposal from the Commission to the Council for a decision on the conclusion of the Convention

on the conservation of migratory species of wild animals.
Rapporteur: Joannes Verroken (PPE-B).

13/11/81	Opinion of the European Parliament. (OJ C.327 14/12/81 p. 95)
24/06/82	Council Decision 82/461/EEC. (OJ L.210 9/7/82 p. 10)
05/06/85	Motion for a Resolution 2-403/85 by Mr Roelants du Vivier on the conclusion of regional Agreements with third countries concerning the protection of migratory species.
30/10/85	Commission Communication to the Council on the Report of the Community on the Bonn Convention on the conservation of migratory species of wild animals.
19/11/86	Public Hearing organised by the Environment Committee of the European Parliament on the extent of application within the European Community and its Member States of legislation on the protection of wildlife and its environment. Included discussion of the Birds Directive, Bonn Convention, Bern Convention and CITES.
26/09/88	Report A2-0179/88 drawn up on behalf of the Environment Committee on the implementation of the Bern Convention (on the conservation on European wildlife and natural habitats) and the Bonn Convention (on the conservation of migratory species of wild animals) in the European Community. Rapporteur: Hemmo Muntingh (S-NL).
12/10/88	European Parliament adopted a Resolution on the implementation of the Bern and Bonn Conventions in the Community. (OJ C.290 14/11/88 p. 54)
05/92	Draft Agreement on the Conservation of Small Cetaceans of the Mediterranean and Black Seas discussed by the Parties to the Barcelona Convention in the context of the Review of the Mediterranean Action Plan for small cetaceans.
21/6/93	Report A3-193/93 on trade in wild fauna and flora was debated in Parliament. One hundred and one amendments tabled by the environment committee were adopted.
28/6/93	Discussion in Environment Council meeting of forthcoming Council Regulation on possession of and trade in specimens of species of wild fauna and flora.

9/94   South-African and Sudanese governments request the down-listing of their African elephant populations from Appendix I to Appendix II of CITES. Motion agreed in Parliament under the topical and urgent debate procedure to refuse this.

25/7/95   Report by Mrs Van Putten was discussed for the first time in the Environment Committee of the Parliament. It was adopted by Plenary on 18 September 1996.

CONSERVATION OF EUROPEAN WILDLIFE AND NATURAL HABITATS

Existing Legislation

Council Decision 82/72/EEC of 3 December 1981 concerning the conclusion of the Convention on the conservation of European wildlife and natural habitats.
(OJ L.38 10/2/82)

Summary

The aims of the Convention are to conserve wild flora and fauna and their natural habitats, especially those species and habitats whose conservation requires the cooperation of several States, and to promote such cooperation. Particular emphasis is given to endangered and vulnerable species including migratory species.

Contracting Parties shall take requisite measures to maintain the population of wild fauna and flora at, or adapt it to, a level which corresponds in particular to ecological, scientific and cultural requirements, while taking account of economic and recreational requirements and the needs of sub-species, varieties or forms at risk locally.

Steps shall be taken to promote national policies for the conservation of wild fauna, flora and natural habitats, with particular attention to endangered and vulnerable species, especially endemic ones and endangered habitats in accordance with the provisions of the Convention. Moreover, where the capture or killing of listed endangered species is involved, non-discriminatory methods and in particular the use of nets, traps, snares and poisons shall be prohibited.

Contracting Parties undertake in their planning and development policies and their measures against pollution to have regard to the conservation of wild flora and fauna.

Each Party shall promote education and disseminate general information on the need to conserve species of wild flora and fauna and their habitats.

Council Directive 85/337/EEC on environmental impact assessments.
(OJ L.175 5/7/85 p. 40)

Council Directive 85/338/EEC of 27 June 1985 on the adoption of a Commission work programme concerning an experimental project for gathering, coordinating and ensuring the consistency of information on the state of the environment and natural resources in the European Community (the CORINE programme).
(OJ L.176 6/7/85 p. 14)

The CORINE Biotopes Project is one of the priorities for the Commission's work programme. Currently, a Register of Biotopes of major importance for nature conservation is being compiled on an on-line computer system. This includes information on the size, genetic diversity, and threatened species in each of the delineated Biotope areas and is intended to help the implementation of the Birds Directive and the Bern Convention.

Council Regulation (EEC) 2242/87 of 23 July 1987 on the continuation of action by the Community relating to the Environment (ACE 1987–1992).
(OJ L.207 29/7/87 p. 7)

Following on from the ACE Programme 1984–1987, this Regulation extends the scope of financial support to projects aimed at contributing towards the protection, maintenance or re-establishment of areas of particular Community-wide importance for the conservation of nature and especially of seriously threatened biotopes which are the habitat of endangered species. Hence, research priorities will concentrate on monk seals, brown bears, marine turtles and bats as well as birds.

Council Decision 90/150/EEC of 22 March 1990 on the proposal to extend the CORINE programme.
(OJ L.81 28/3/90 p. 38)

Council Directive 92/43/EEC of 21 May 1992 on the conservation of natural habitats and of wild fauna and flora.
(OJ L.206 22/7/92)

Came into force mid-1994.

Summary

The Directive will complement Directive 79/409/EEC on the conservation of wild birds and implement the non-bird parts of the Convention for the Conservation of European Wildlife and Natural Habitats to which the Community is a signatory.

The Directive will contribute towards ensuring bio-diversity through the conservation of natural habitats and of wild fauna and flora.

It has a number of Annexes which:

- identify specific types of habitat requiring protection;

- list species the habitat of which requires protection;

- provide the criteria for selecting sites requiring protection;

- list species requiring strict protection;

- list species the exploitation of which may be subject to management;

- identify prohibited methods of capture and killing and modes of transport.

Because of their failure to transpose this Directive into national law, about half of the Member States have received formal warning letters from the Commission.

Moreover, under the terms of Directive 92/43/EEC, the Member States were required to draw up a list of special conservation sites to the European Commission before June 1995, so that the 'Natura 2000' network of special protection areas in Europe could be set up. Many Member States have yet to submit their lists. As Natura 2000 network has to be created by June 1998, this delay could mean postponing the application of the Directive.

Council Regulation (EEC) 1973/92 of 21 May 1992 establishing a financial instrument for the environment (LIFE).
(OJ L.206 22/7/92)

Summary

The objective of LIFE is to contribute to the development and implementation of Community environmental policy and legislation by financing priority action within the Community; action with third countries around the Mediterranean and Baltic; in exceptional circumstances regional or global actions provided for in international agreements.

An Annex defines the fields of action eligible for Community financial assistance.

Council Regulation (EEC) 2078/92 of 30 June 1992. See Farm Animals General. Aid programme funds, *inter alia*, environmentally friendly farming or set aside of farmland for at least 20 years with a view to use for environmentally friendly purposes, in particular for establishment of biotope reserves or natural parks or protection of hydrological systems (additional monies for this Regulation are available under Structural Funds).

Regulation 609/95 adopted by Commission. Amends Regulation 1091/94 laying down certain detailed rules for the implementation of Council Regulation 3528/86 on the protection of the Community's forests against atmospheric pollution.
(OJ No. L 71, 31.3.95, p. 25)

Commission Opinion of 18 December 1995 on the intersection of the Peene Valley (Germany) by the planned A 20 motorway pursuant to Article 6 (4) of Council Directive 92/43/EEC on the conservation of natural habitas of wild fauna and flora.
(OJ No. L 6, 9.1.99, p. 14)

Work in Progress

Under Council Regulation (EEC) 1973/92 establishing a financial instrument for the environment, the Commission was to submit a report by 31/12/94 on the implementation of the Regulation and make proposals for any adjustment to be made with a view to continuing the action beyond the first stage.

The Council was due to decide on the implementation of the second phase as from 1 January 1996.

Background

Council of Europe

28/09/73   At its Fifteenth Sitting, the Consultative Assembly recommended that the Committee of Ministers:
'define a coherent policy for the protection of wildlife, with a view to establishing European regulations – if possible by means of a convention – and involving severe restrictions on hunting, shooting, capture of animals needing protection, fishing and egg-collecting and the prohibition of bird netting'.

24/03/76   The Second European Ministerial Conference on the Environment recommended the Committee of Ministers to set up within the Council of Europe an ad hoc Committee of experts, with instructions to draft a legal instrument on the conservation of wildlife, with particular reference to migratory species and natural habitats (Resolution No. 2).

06/76   Twenty-eighth Ordinary Session. The Consultative Assembly recommended that the Committee of Ministers set up a

Committee of experts and instruct it to submit a draft convention on the conservation of wildlife.

At the Twenty-ninth Meeting of the Committee of Ministers an ad hoc Committee for the Protection of Wildlife was created.

11/76   First Meeting of the ad hoc Committee under the chairmanship of Gunnar Seidenfaden (Denmark).

19/12/78   The text of the draft Convention was submitted to the Committee of Ministers.

18/06/79   The Committee of Ministers adopted the draft Convention.

19/09/79   At the Third European Ministerial Conference on the Environment in Bern the Convention on the Conservation of European Wildlife and Natural Habitats was opened for signature. (For signatories see Appendix II.)

A Standing Committee was set up to monitor its application.

13–15/09/82   First Meeting of the Standing Committee of the Convention on the Conservation of European Wildlife and Natural Habitats.

04/12/84   The Standing Committee met and decided to amend the annexes to the Convention on the Conservation of European Wildlife and Natural Habitats. As a result of the decision they decided to carry out a series of studies on invertebrates and freshwater fish within Europe.

The Committee also adopted Recommendation No. 3 (1984) relative to the establishment of national inventories for three types of natural habitat.

It also discussed the practice of spring hunting in Greece and Cyprus.

04/12/85   At its Fourth Meeting, the Standing Committee continued its discussion on amending Annexes II and III of the Bern Convention. It also decided to study the big endangered species one after another in Special Working Groups. The first Working Group would concentrate on the monk seal *Monachus monachus*.

The first biennial Reports on derogations made under Article 9 of the Convention were discussed.

04/12/86   At its Fifth Meeting, the Standing Committee continued its discussion on the amendments to the Annexes to the Bern Convention and proposals were submitted by the

Netherlands, Switzerland and Portugal respectively for the introduction of freshwater fish, invertebrates and other vertebrates in the Annexes.

The Standing Committee adopted Recommendation No. 5 (1986) on the means of pursuit of people who are capturing, killing and illegally trading in protected birds and Recommendation No. 6 (1986) on the protection of monk seals in the Mediterranean.

06/87   The First Meeting of the Working Group on turtles discussed a draft Recommendation on the protection of sea turtles and decided to submit it to the next meeting of the Standing Committee.

12/87   At its Sixth Meeting, the Standing Committee adopted amendments to Annexes II and III of the Bern Convention to include additional species. Also adopted were:

- Recommendation No. 7 (1987) concerning the protection of marine turtles and their habitat;

- Recommendation No. 8 (1987) concerning the protection of marine turtles in Dalyan and other important areas in Turkey;

- Recommendation No. 9 (1987) concerning the protection of the loggerhead turtle (*Caretta caretta*) in Laganas Bay, Zakynthos (Greece).

Further working groups were set up to deal with wolves (*Canis lupus*) and bears (*Ursus*).

29/04/88   Report on behalf of the Committee on the Environment, Regional Planning and Local Authorities on Environment Policy in Europe (1984–87). Rapporteur: Mr Fajardo. Contained a draft Recommendation.

06/05/88   Recommendation 1078 (1988) on environment policy in Europe (1984–7) adopted by the Parliamentary Assembly of the Council of Europe.

05/88   Workshop on the Situation and Protection of the Brown Bear (*Ursus arctos*) in Europe. Held at Covadonga (Asturias), Spain. Recommended, *inter alia*, strengthening the basis of legal protection of the brown bear.

12/88   Seventh Meeting of the Standing Committee. The Committee decided to hold a meeting of the Working Group on the wolf in June 1989, to include a study on the lynx in its 1989 work programme, and to hold a seminar on invertebrates. It adopted:

Recommendation No. 10 (1988) concerning the protection of the brown bear (*Ursus arctos*);

Recommendation No. 11 (1988) concerning the protection of the common seal (*Phoca vitulina*) and its habitat;

Recommendation No. 12 (1988) concerning measures for the protection of critical biotopes of endangered amphibians and reptiles.

06/06/89   Eighth Meeting of the Standing Committee. Provisions relating to the conservation of habitats were discussed.

21/06/89   First meeting of the Working Group on the wolf. Received Report 'Status and conservation needs of the wolf (*Canis lupus*) in the Council of Europe Member States and Finland'. Draft Recommendation on the protection of the grey wolf (*Canis lupus*) in Europe modified and endorsed to recommend:

- wolf to be fully protected in certain zones, whilst hunted according to existing regulations in Turkey, Spain, Greece and Finland;

- Italy to create protected areas;

- improved compensation to farmers;

- reinforcement of natural prey species;

- elimination of stray and feral dogs;

- organisation of educational campaigns;

- banning of drives for wolf control;

- enforcement of the ban on the use of poisons, poisoned baits and other indiscriminate means of killing;

- Greece and Turkey to remove wolf from list of pest species;

- Greece to enforce protection measures, draw up a national management plan, participate in a joint Balkan plan;

- Spain and Portugal to draw up a joint management plan.

12/89   Ninth Meeting of the Standing Committee on the Bern Convention adopted the following Recommendations:

- No. 17 (1989) on the protection of the wolf (*Canis lupus*);

● No. 18 (1989) on the protection of the indigenous cray-fish in Europe.

10/90   The Sixth Council of Europe Ministerial Conference, held in Brussels on 11–12 October, discussed extending the Bern Convention to cover Eastern Europe and Africa.

10/90   The Secretariat of the Bern Convention organised a seminar on the situation, conservation needs and re-introduction of the lynx in Europe, in Neuchâtel on 17–19 October.

Two recommendations were adopted at the end of the seminar.

01/91   Tenth Meeting of the Standing Committee of the Bern Convention.

The Committee adopted a new version of Appendix I to the Convention (protected plants) and the following Recommendations:

● No. 19 (1991) on the protection of the pardel lynx (*Lynx pardinus*) in the Iberian peninsular;

● No. 20 (1991) on the protection of the European lynx (*Lynx lynx*);

● No. 21 (1991) on the conservation of hymenoptera and their habitats;

● No. 23 (1991) on the protection of the habitat of the Orsini's viper (*Vipera ursinii rakosiensis*) in Hungary;

● No. 24 (1991) on the protection of some beaches in Turkey of particular importance to marine turtles.

12/91   Eleventh Meeting of the Standing Committee to the Bern Convention.

The Committee agreed to invite a number of European states to accede to the Convention in light of the dissolution of the USSR and discussed a report on the extension of the Convention to Africa. A procedure for African states to accede to the Convention was agreed.

The Committee also adopted the following Recommendations:

● No. 25 (1991) on the conservation of natural areas outside protected areas proper;

● No. 26 (1991) on the conservation of some threatened reptiles in Europe;

- No. 27 (1991) on the conservation of some threatened amphibians in Europe;

- No. 28 (1991) on the use of non-toxic shot in wetlands;

- No. 30 (1991) on conservation of species in Appendix I;

- No. 31 (1991) on the conservation of the European mink (*Mustela lutreola*);

- No. 33 (1991) on the conservation of the natterjack toad (*Bufo calamita*) in Ireland.

1993	Iceland, Malta and Romania acceded to the Convention on the Conservation of European Wildlife and Natural Habitats, which now has twenty-nine Contracting Parties.

1993   Iceland, Malta and Romania acceded to the Convention on the Conservation of European Wildlife and Natural Habitats, which now has twenty-nine Contracting Parties.

Twelfth Meeting of the Standing Committee to the Bern Convention.

The Committee has agreed to extend the geographic area of the Convention to the whole of the continent of Europe and to North Africa. Appendix I (strictly protected flora species) has been amended to include 591 species.

1993   Thirteenth meeting of the Standing Committee to the Bern Convention.

1995   Fourteenth meeting of the Standing Committee to the Bern Convention. The following Recommendations were adopted:

- No. 43 (1995) on the conservation of threatened mammals in Europe.

- No. 44 (1995) on the conservation of some threatened plants in Central Europe.

- No. 45 (1995) on controlling proliferation of *Caulerpa taxifolia* in the Mediterranean.

- No. 46 (1995) on the proposed Iruena dam site, Salamanca, Spain.

1996   Fifteenth meeting of the Standing Committee to the Bern Convention.

The Committee welcomed Tunisia's accession and Poland's presence as a Contracting Party.

The Committee also adopted the following Recommendations:

- No. 47 (1996) on the conservation of European semi-aquatic insectivora.

- No. 48 (1996) on the conservation of European globally-threatened birds.

- No. 49 (1996) on the protection of some wild plant species which are subject to exploitation and commerce.

The Committee also discussed the situation of marine turtles in Laganas Bay (Zakynthos). It found that Greece had achieved only limited progress with respect to the Decision of 24 March 1995. Therefore it decided to finance an expert to analyse the legal situation in Greece relevant to this matter.

The Committee further examined urgent cases concerning the implementation of Recommendations Nos. 26 and 27 on the conservation of some threatened reptiles and amphibians.

The Committee's next meeting was held on 2–6 September 1996.

European Community

Bern/Bonn Conventions

27/03/79	Recommendation from the Commission to the Council authorising the Commission to participate in the negotiations to conclude the Convention on the Conservation of European Wildlife and Natural Habitats. (COM(79)146 final).
20/07/79	COM(79)414 final the Commission submitted to the Council a proposal for a Council Decision. (OJ C.210 22/8/79 p. 12)
25/10/79	Opinion of the ECOSOC. (OJ C.53 3/3/80 p. 50)
09/05/80	Report 1-152/80 on behalf of the Committee on the Environment, Public Health and Consumer Protection on the proposal for a Council Decision on the conclusion of the Bern Convention. Rapporteur: Hemmo Muntingh (S-NL).
17/06/80	Opinion of the European Parliament. (OJ C.175 14/7/80 p. 17)
03/12/81	Council Decision 82/72/EEC concerning the conclusion of the Convention on the conservation of European wildlife and natural habitats.
03/09/82	EEC deposited its instrument of approval for the birds element only (see Appendix II).

12/09/84   Motion for a Resolution 536/84 by Mrs Bloch von Blottnitz on the infraction of the Bern Convention by Italy.

04/06/85   Motion for a Resolution 400/85 by Mr Roelants du Vivier on Commission Regulations implementing the 1979 Bern Convention on the conservation of wildlife and natural habitats.

27/09/85   Motion for a Resolution 939/85 by Mrs Bloch von Blottnitz on the violation of the Bern Convention by Greece.

19/11/86   Public Hearing organised by the Environment Committee on the implementation of legislation on the protection of wildlife and its environment. Included discussions on the Birds Directive, the Bonn and Bern Conventions and CITES.

26/09/88   Report A2-0179/88 drawn up on behalf of the Environment Committee on the implementation of the Bern Convention and the Bonn Convention in the European Community. Rapporteur: Hemmo Muntingh (S-NL).

12/10/88   European Parliament adopted a Resolution on the implementation of the Bern and Bonn Conventions in the European Community.
             (OJ C.290 14/11/88 p. 54)

12/07/90   Motion for a Resolution B3-1385/90 by Mrs Garcia Arias and others on the application of the Bern Convention by the Commission.

ACE

13/01/83   Commission submitted to the Council a proposal for a Council Regulation on action by the Community relating to the environment (ACE).
             (OJ C.30 4/2/83 p. 8)

06/04/83   Report 1-101/83 drawn up on behalf of the Committee on the Environment, Public Health and Consumer Protection on the Commission proposal for a Regulation on ACE.
             Rapporteur: Stanley Johnson (ED-UK).

15/04/83   The European Parliament adopted a Resolution concluding the consultation procedure on the Commission's proposal for ACE.
             (OJ C.128 16/5/83 p. 88)

28/04/83   The ECOSOC gave its opinion on the ACE proposal.
             (OJ C.176 4/7/83 p. 1)

28/06/84	Council Regulation (EEC) 1872/84 on action by the Community on the environment (ACE). (OJ L.176 4/7/84)

28/06/84   Council Regulation (EEC) 1872/84 on action by the Community relating to the Environment (ACE 1984–1987). (OJ L.176 4/7/84)

One of the first priorities of the ACE Programme was to accord Community financial support to projects providing an incentive and aimed at contributing towards the protection, maintenance or re-establishment of seriously threatened biotopes which are the habitat of endangered species, and bearing particular importance within the Community to the application of Directive 79/409/EEC on the conservation of wild birds.

16/12/86   Council Resolution on the strengthening of Community action in favour of the environment (ACE). (OJ C.3 7/1/87)

30/12/86   COM(86)485 proposal for a Council Regulation on action by the Community relating to the environment (ACE). (OJ C.18 24/1/87)

07/01/87   The Council asked the European Parliament and the ECOSOC for their opinions on ACE.

10/04/87   Report 22/87 on behalf of the Environment Committee on the proposal for a Council Regulation (ACE). Rapporteur: Simone Martin (LDR-F).

15/05/87   European Parliament adopted a Resolution on continuation of action by the Community relating to the Environment. (OJ C.156 15/6/87 p. 199)

02/07/87   Opinion of the ECOSOC on the proposal for a Council Resolution on ACE. (OJ C.232 31/8/87 p. 4)

23/07/87   Council Regulation (EEC) 2242/87 on the continuation of action by the Community relating to the Environment. (OJ L.207 29/7/87 p. 8)

30/07/88   Commission Communication (COM(88)409) pursuant to Article 10 of Council Regulation (EEC) 1872/84. (ACE) (OJ C.200 30/7/88 p. 3)

CORINE

16/10/83	COM(83)528 final a Proposal by the Commission for a Council decision on the adoption of a work programme for the first phase of the implementation of an information system on the state of the environment and natural resources in the Community (CORINE programme). (OJ C.291 27/10/83 p. 8)
09/03/84	COM(83)528 final ECOSOC delivered its opinion on the proposal for a Council decision on the CORINE programme. (OJ C.140 28/5/84 p. 24)
10/09/84	COM(83)528 final Environment Committee decided to draw up a report on the Commission's proposal for a decision on the CORINE Work Programme. Rapporteur: Beate Weber (S-D).
07/11/84	Report 2-951/85 by Beate Weber (S-D) on the Commission's proposal for a Council decision on the CORINE Work Programme.
06/11/84	The European Parliament adopted a Resolution concluding the procedure of consultation over the Commission's proposal for the adoption of a Work Programme (CORINE). (OJ C.337 17/12/84 p. 421)
27/06/85	Council Decision 85/338/EEC on a Work Programme for CORINE.
22/09/89	COM(89)542 a Proposal for a Council decision extending the lifetime of the CORINE environmental data bank project to cover the period until the European Environmental Agency is set up.
15/11/89	CES 1244/89 ECOSOC opinion on the Commission's proposal to extend the lifetime of the CORINE environmental data bank project (COM(89)542).
14/02/90	Report A3-35/90 drawn up on behalf of the Environment Committee on the Commission's proposal to extend the lifetime of the CORINE environmental data bank project (COM(89)542). Adopted by the European Parliament.
22/03/90	Council Decision 90/150/EC of 22 March 1990 on the proposal to extend the CORINE programme. (OJ L.81 28/3/90)

27/03/92   COM(92)23 final, Vols I and II a proposal for a Council Resolution on a Community programme of policy and action in relation to the environment and sustainable development (ACE).

01/07/92   CES 808/92 ECOSOC adopted its opinion on COM(92)23. Rapporteur: Mr Boisseree.

ENVIREG

01/03/90   CES 217/90 ECOSOC opinion on the Commission programme of regional actions designed to contribute to the protection of the environment and to promote socio-economic development (ENVIREG), (DOC. XVI/418/89).

16/03/90   Report A3-46/90 drawn up on behalf of the Regional Policy Committee on a regional action programme on the initiative of the Commission concerning the environment (ENVIREG).
Rapporteur: Panayotis Lambrias (PPE-GR). Adopted by the European Parliament.

18/12/95   Common Position No. 17/95 adopted by the Council with a view to adopting Council Regulation (EC) No. .../96 of amending Regulation (EEC) No. 1973/92 establishing a financial instrument for the environment (LIFE).
(OJ C 134, 6/5/96, p. 1)

17/1/96   COM (95) 720 final Amended proposal for a Council Directive amending Directive 85/337/EEC on the assessment of the effects of certain public and private projects on the environment.
(OJ No. C 81, 19.3.96, p. 14)

26/1/96   COM (96) 25 final Amended proposal for a Council Regulation amending Council Regulation (EEC) No. 1973/92 establishing a financial instrument for the Environment (LIFE).
(OJ C 92, 28/3/96, p. 7)

2/5/96   Judgment by European Court of Justice on Case C-133/94 *Commission* v *Belgium* for failure to transpose Directive 85/337/EEC on the assessment of the effects of certain public and private projects on the environment.
(JO C 197, 6/7/96, p. 4)

5/96   Commission Communication of Decisions to grant Commu-
                nity financial support for demonstration projects forwarded
                under the LIFE instrument concerning the environment.
                (OJ C154, 29/5/96, p. 5)

15/7/96   Council Regulation (EC) No. 1404/96 amending
                Regulation (EEC) No. 1973/92 establishing a financial
                instrument for the environment (LIFE).
                (OJ L 181, 20/7/96, p. 1)

ACNAT

21/06/90   COM(90)125 final a Proposal for a Council regulation on
                action by the Community relating to nature conservation
                (ACNAT) to be considered by the Environment Committee
                with an opinion from the Budgets Committee. Rapporteur:
                Carlos Pimenta (LDR-P).
                    Opinion from Budget Committee: Annemarie Goedmakers
                (S-NL).

18/10/90   CES 1211/90 ECOSOC adopted its opinion on the
                Commission's proposal for a regulation instituting the
                ACNAT programme (COM(90)125).

13/12/90   Report A3-322/90 by Mr Pimenta on behalf of the
                Environment Committee on a proposal for a regulation
                instituting EC funding for the ACNAT programme
                (COM(90)125) adopted by the European Parliament.

Parks and reserves

19/09/85   Motion for a Resolution 928/85 by Mr Nordmann and Mrs
                Lentz-Cornette on the establishment and conservation of
                Community nature reserves.

24/09/86   Motion for a Resolution 857/86 by Mrs Barbarella on the
                conservation of nature.

17/10/86   Motion for a Resolution 1014/86 by Mr Romera i Alcàzar on
                the measures needed to protect and conserve natural parks.

17/11/86   Motion for a Resolution 1184/86 by Mr Graziani on
                Community parks and nature reserves.

27/05/87   Report 65/87 drawn up on behalf of the Environment
                Committee on the establishment and conservation of

Community nature reserves. Rapporteur: Marcelle Lentz-Cornette (PPE-LUX).

10/07/87   The European Parliament adopted the Resolution on the establishment and conservation of Community nature reserves.
(OJ C.246 14/9/87 p. 121)

03/05/88   Motion for a Resolution 2-0221/88 by Mr Wedekind and others on improving the scientific bases of nature protection and species conservation in the European Community.

21/03/90   Motion for a Resolution B3-637/90 by Mr de la Camara Martinez on establishing a Community green flag to designate ecologically valuable natural areas.

27/06/90   Motion for a Resolution B3-1294/90 by Mrs Banotti on ensuring that environmental impact assessments are compulsory for all projects receiving structural fund money.

08/11/90   Motion for a Resolution B3-1908/90 by Mr Welsh on the impact of structural fund projects on wildlife habitats.

25/01/91   Motion for a Resolution 16/91 by Mr Kostopoulos on the protection of national parks.

Species

17/01/85   Motion for a Resolution 1476/84 by Mrs Squarcialupi and others on the protection of wild birds and mammals during times of cold weather.

03/05/85   Motion for a Resolution B2-253/85 by Mr Muntingh on swan deaths from lead poisoning.

05/06/85   Motion for a Resolution 402/85 by Mr Roelants du Vivier on the need for a Community information programme on the protection of wildlife and the natural environment.

13/03/86   Motion for a Resolution 14/86 by Mr Tridente on the survival of wildlife in Europe.

20/01/87   Motion for a Resolution 1393/86 by Mrs Bloch von Blottnitz on the protection of the Eurasian otter.

28/02/87   Motion for a Resolution 1545/86 by Mrs Garcia Arias and others on the protection of bears, wolves and other wild animals in danger of extinction.

06/01/89	Report A2-0339/88 drawn up on behalf of the Environment Committee on the protection of brown bears in the European Community. Rapporteur: Marcelle Lentz-Cornette (PPE-LUX).
31/01/89	Report A2-0377/88 drawn up on behalf of the Environment Committee on wolf conservation. Rapporteur: Carlo Graziani (COM-I).
17/02/89	European Parliament adopted a Resolution on the protection of brown bears in the European Community.
17/02/89	European Parliament adopted a Resolution on wolf conservation.
11/09/89	Motion for a Resolution B3-155/89 by the Green group on protection of the waters, marine fauna and forests in the Mediterranean area.
14/09/89	Motion for a Resolution B3-48/89 by Mr Lima and Mr Pisoni on the creation of a European fund for the conservation of flora and fauna.
20/12/89	Motion for a Resolution B3-751/89 by Mrs Diez De Rivera Icaza on preserving the biological diversity of the Community.
01/90	Motion for a Resolution B3-84/90 by the Green Group on the risk that the brown bear would become extinct in France.
07/02/90	Motion for a Resolution B3-237/90 by Mrs Muscardini and others on the protection of wolves and their habitats in the Apennines.
08/10/90	Motion for a Resolution B2-1385/90 by Mrs Garcia Arias and others on the implementation of the Bern Convention in the European Community. Referred to Environment Committee. Rapporteur: Ken Collins (S-UK) appointed 09/11/90.
27/05/92	Environment Committee adopted the draft report by Mr Collins.
12/06/92	Report A3-0214/92 by Mr Collins on the implementation of the Bern Convention in the European Community adopted by the European Parliament.
15/2/94	Report by Mr Jean-Pierre Raffin (V-F) on protection of brown bear voted on by Environment Committee.

14/3/94   Raffin Report on protection of brown bear adopted un-
                animously in Environment Committee.

Habitats Directive

19/10/87   Adoption of the Resolution of the Council of the European
                Community and the representatives of the Governments of
                the Member States, on the continuation and implementation
                of a European Community policy and action programme on
                the environment 1987–92.
                (The Fourth Environment Action Programme).
                (OJ C.70 18/3/87 p. 3)
                     Under Chapter 5.1 'Conservation of nature and natural
                resources', it identified a need for 'a Community instru-
                ment aimed at protecting not just birds but all species of
                fauna and flora; and not just habitats of birds, but the
                habitat of wildlife – animals and plants – more generally.
                Such a comprehensive framework should ensure that,
                throughout the Community, positive measures are taken to
                protect all forms of wildlife and their habitat'. It further
                stated that 'urgent action is also needed for the better
                implementation of the Birds Directive and the Bern
                Convention'.
                     In response, the Commission produced a proposal for a
                directive on the protection of natural and semi-natural
                habitats and of wild fauna and flora.

31/08/88   COM(88)381 final Commission proposal for a Council
                directive on the protection of natural and semi-natural habi-
                tats and of wild fauna and flora.

24/11/88   COM(88)381 final referred to Environment Committee.
                Rapporteur: Hemmo Muntingh (S-NL).

29/09/89   Report A3-39/89 by Mr Muntingh on the proposal for a
                habitats directive (COM(88)381 final).

12/10/89   Report A3-39/89 referred back to Environment Committee
                by Parliament.

30/03/90   COM(90)59 supplementary annexes to the Commission's
                proposal for a habitats directive (COM(88)381) published
                by Commission.

17/10/90   Second Report A3-0254/90 on COM(88)381 final by
                Mr Muntingh accepted by Environment Committee.

18/10/90	CES 1210/90 ECOSOC adopted its opinion on the proposal for a habitats directive (COM(88)381 and COM(90)59).
19/11/90	Report A3-254/90 by Mr Muntingh on behalf of the Environment Committee on the proposed habitats directive (COM(88)381) and (COM(90)59) adopted by the European Parliament.
21/05/92	Council Directive 92/43/EEC on the conservation of natural habitats and of wild fauna and flora (OJ L.206 22/7/92)
12/92	Council of Ministers endorse The Fifth Environmental Action Programme 'Towards Sustainability' as the Community's main vehicle for implementation of Agenda 21.
1/2/93	Council pass resolution on A Community Programme of Policy and Action in Relation to the Environment and Sustainable Development. 'Towards sustainability The 5th Environmental Action Programme.

Under Chapter 5.3: 'The case for preserving nature and biodiversity ... is a necessary element in the overall maintenance of the ecological balance; furthermore, nature provides an invaluable genetic bank which is essential to medical, biological, agricultural and other scientific progress. The Community strategy will be aimed at the maintenance of European biodiversity primarily through sustainable land management in and around habitats of Community and wider importance.'.... 'The creation and maintenance of (the network of habitats based on the Natura 2000 concept) will be very much dependent on how carefully transport, agricultural and tourist policies are shaped and pursued in the future.'

Mid-1994	Council Directive 92/43/EEC on the conservation of natural habitats and of wild fauna and flora. To be implemented.
30/11/94	COM(94) 453 First progress report on the implementation of the Fifth Action Programme adopted. It highlighted progress made in five priority areas: industry, energy, transport, agriculture and tourism.
04/95	Report from the European Community to the Commission on Sustainable Development: 'On Progress Towards Implementation of Agenda 21'.
12/95	Commission Opinion on the intersection of the Peene Valley (Germany) by the planned A 20 motorway pursuant

to Article 6 (4) of Council Directive 92/43/EEC on the conservation of natural habitas of wild fauna and flora.
(OJ No. L 6, 9.1.99, p. 14)

10/1/96   COM (95) 624 final Commission's Report 1995 on the
implementation of the European Community programme of
policy and action in relation to the environment and sustainable development 'Towards sustainability'.

29/2/96   COM (95) 647 final Proposal for a European Parliament
and Council Decision on the review of the European
Community programme of policy and action in relation to
the environment and sustainable development 'Towards
sustainability'.
(OJ No. C 140, 11.5.96, p. 5)

29/5/96   ECOSOC's opinion on the Proposal for a European
Parliament and Council Decision on the review of the
European Community Programme of policy and action in
relation to the environment and sustainable development
'Towards Sustainability'.
(OJ C.212 22/7/96 p. 1)

10/6/96   Report A4-0000/96 on the Commission's proposal COM
95(647) on the review of the European Community programme of policy and action in relation to the environment
and sustainable development 'Towards sustainability'.
Rapporteur: Mrs Lone Dybkjaer (ELDR-DK)

13/11/96   Adoption by Parliament in Plenary of Mrs Dybkjaer's report
PE 217.883.

Wildlife and farming

11/10/88   Motion for a Resolution 2-790/88 by Mrs Ferrer i Casals
and others on the cessation of farming and on hunting and
agritourism as possible alternative activities.

17/01/90   Motion for a Resolution B3-67/90 by Mr Happart and
others on fitting farm machinery with a safety device so as
to protect wild animals.

European Environment Agency

12/07/89   COM(89)303 final Proposal for a Council regulation on
the European Environment Agency and the European
Environment Monitoring and Information Network.

The object is to ensure adequate national monitoring, integrated and comparable on a Community-wide basis, in order to facilitate the achievement of the environmental goals defined in the Treaty of Rome and the Community's environmental action programmes. Biotopes and nature conservation will be a principal area of concern, and the Agency will be entrusted with further development of work carried out under the CORINE programme.

15/11/89   CES 1246/89 ECOSOC adopted its opinion on the Commission's proposal to set up a European Environment Agency (COM(89)303).

02–03/90   Report A3-27/90 drawn up on behalf of the Environment Committee on the Commission's proposal to set up a European Environment Agency (COM(89)303).
Rapporteur: Beate Weber (S-D).
Adopted by Plenary in two stages on 14 February and 14 March.

15/6/95   Commission submitted a proposal for a Council Regulation establishing a Community observer scheme applicable to Community fishing vessels operating in the Regulatory Area of the Northwest Atlantic Fisheries Organisation (NAFO).
(OJ No. C211, 15.8.95, p. 13)

15/6/95   Commission submitted a proposal for a Council Regulation amending, for the second time, Regulation 3366/94 laying down for 1995 certain conservation and management measures for fishery resources in the Regulatory Area as defined in the Convention on Future Multilateral Cooperation in the Northwest Atlantic Fisheries.
(OJ No. C211, 15.8.95, p. 19)

13/10/95   In the European Parliament's Environment Committee the chairman, Mr Ken Collins, recommended approval of a Council resolution on the development and implementation of the EEA [PE 191.513].

MARINE WILDLIFE – GENERAL

Existing Legislation

Council Regulation (EEC) 3626/82 of 3 December 1982 on the implementation within the Community of the Convention on International Trade in Endangered Species of Wild Fauna and Flora. The commercial trade in many marine animals and plants is prohibited or controlled.

Council Directive 92/43/EEC of 21 May 1992 on the conservation of natural habitats and of wild fauna and flora. Protects many species of marine wildlife and coastal habitats.

Council Regulation (EEC) 345/92 of 27 January 1992 amending for the eleventh time Regulation 3094/86 laying down certain technical measures for the conservation of fishery resources.

Council Regulation (EEC) 3034/92 of 19 October 1992 amending for the fourteenth time Council Regulation (EEC) 3094/86 laying down certain technical measures for the conservation of fishery resources.

Summary

Bans the use of purse seine nets by EC registered vessels when used to catch tuna or other species where encirclement puts marine mammals at risk of capture or killing.

Council Regulation (EC) 1173/95 of 22 May 1995 amending for the sixteenth time Regulation (EEC) 3094/86 laying down certain technical measures for the conservation of fishery resources.

Council Regulation (EC) 2251/95 of 18 September 1995 amending for the eighteenth time Regulation (EEC) 3094/86 laying down certain technical measures for the conservation of fishery resources.

Council Regulation (EC) 3071/95 of 22 December 1995 amending for the nineteenth time Regulation (EEC) 3094/86 laying down certain technical measures for the conservation of fishery resources.

Council Regulation (EC) 1075/96 of 10 June 1996 amending Regulation (EC) No. 1626/94 laying down certain technical measures for the conservation of fishery resources in the Mediterranean.

Council Regulation (EC) 1076/96 of 10 June 1996 amending Regulation No. 3090/95 laying down certain conservation and management measures for fishery resources in the Regulatory Area as defined in the Convention on Future Multilateral Cooperation in the North West Atlantic Fisheries.

Commission Decision 96/384/EC of 21 June 1996 on certain protective measures in respect of infectious anaemia in salmon in Norway.
(OJ L.151 26/6/96 p. 35)

Council Regulation (EC) 1167/96 of 25 June 1996 amending, for the second time, Regulation (EC) No. 3090/95 laying down for 1996 certain conservation and management measures for fishery resources in the Regulatory Area in the Convention on Future Multilateral Cooperation in the North West Atlantic Fisheries.
(OJ L.155 28/6/96 p. 1)

Council Regulation (EC) 1168/96 of 25 June 1996 laying down for 1996 certain conservation and management measures for fishery resources in the Convention Area as defined in the Convention on Future Multilateral Cooperation in the North West Atlantic Fisheries.
(OJ L.155 28/6/96 p. 3)

Commission Regulation (EC) 1265/96 of 1 July 1996 establishing urgent conservation measures to protect the stock of North Sea herring.
(OJ L.163, 2/7/96 p. 24)

Work in Progress

Proposal for a Regulation on Drift Net Fishing is being discussed by Parliament and Council.

Background

Council of Europe

25/05/92	Hearing on marine mammals by the Sub-Committee on Fisheries (of the Committee on Agriculture) held in Iceland. Report available from the Council of Europe.

European Community

25/05/87	Report A2-57/87 drawn up on behalf of the Environment Committee on the protection of the environment and wildlife in Antarctica. Rapporteur: Hemmo Muntingh (S-NL).
09/87	European Parliament adopted the resolution on Antarctica.
27/11/87	Motion for a Resolution 2-1363/87 by Mr Muntingh on measures to combat marine litter.
09/01/91	Commission submitted COM(90)498 a proposal for a Regulation to establish the NORSPA programme.

27/02/91	Mrs Ria Ooman-Ruijten (PPE-NL) appointed Rapporteur by Environment Committee on the proposal for a Regulation establishing the NORSPA programme (COM(90)498).
25/04/91	First reading of Mrs Ooman-Ruijten's report on COM(90)498 at Environment Committee.
31/05/91	Mrs Ooman-Ruijten's report on the proposal for a Regulation establishing NORSPA adopted by the Environment Committee as Doc. A3-164/91.
09/07/91	A3-164/91 adopted in Plenary.
11/91	CES 698/91 opinion by ECOSOC on COM(90)498 adopted.
09/01/91	Commission submitted COM(90)498 a proposal for a Regulation to establish the NORSPA programme.
27/02/91	Mrs Ria Ooman-Ruijten (PPE-NL) appointed Rapporteur by Environment Committee on the proposal for a Regulation establishing the NORSPA programme (COM(90)498).
25/04/91	First reading of Mrs Ooman-Ruijten's report on COM(90)498 at Environment Committee.
31/05/91	Mrs Ooman-Ruijten's report on the proposal for a Regulation establishing NORSPA adopted by the Environment Committee as Doc. A3-164/91.
09/07/91	A3-164/91 adopted in Plenary.
11/91	CES 698/91 opinion by ECOSOC on COM(90)498 adopted.
15/07/92	COM(92)311 proposal to amend, for the fourteenth time, Regulation 3094/86 which lays down certain technical measures for the conservation of fishery resources, by way of a regulation to ban the use of purse seine nets by EC registered vessels when used to catch tuna or other species where encirclement puts marine mammals at risk of capture or killing.
19/10/92	Council Regulation (EEC) 3034/92 amending for the fourteenth time Council Regulation (EEC) 3094/86 laying down certain technical measures for the conservation of fishery resources.
11/92	COM(92) 204 final Socialist Group Rapporteur nominated for Commission proposal for a Council Directive introducing Community measures for the control of certain fish diseases.

17/12/92   Joint motion for resolution on financial aid to mitigate disaster caused by oil-tanker 'Aegean Sea' on 3/12/92 at Corunna.

19/1/93   Report on COM(92)133 final for a Council Decision concerning pollution in the North Sea adopted by Parliament.

21/1/93   Joint motion for a resolution concerning endorsement of financial aid from Commission towards the Braer Tanker disaster in the Shetlands adopted by Parliament.

27/1/93   ECOSOC adopted additional opinion on Commission proposal [COM(92)387 final] for an EEC Council regulation establishing a Community system for fisheries and aquaculture.

1/93   COM(92)458 final Mr McCubbin appointed rapporteur for proposal concerning placing of aquaculture animals and products on the market.

3/93   Agriculture Committee to draw up a report on agricultural aspects of accession of Finland, Austria, Sweden and Norway. (Problems anticipated with Norway's continued defiance of IWC moratorium.)

3/93   Commission followed recommendation by Veterinary Standing Committee to extend the ban on imports of live and non-eviscerated Atlantic salmon from Norway until 30 September.

10/3/93   COM(92)533 final proposal for a Council regulation harmonising various technical measures in Mediterranean fisheries designed to safeguard species such as the monk seal, dolphins, whales and tortoises. In a written reply to oral question on protection of species in the Mediterranean the Council to discuss this proposal on 18/3/93 at a technical level. Council stated that conservation and protection of species were important elements of the Community's Common Fisheries Policy.

24/3/93   Environment Council meeting resulted in a common declaration marking the creation of an international marine sanctuary in the Mediterranean between Corsica, Provence, Liguria and Tuscany for the protection of all species of marine mammals and restricts the use of drift-nets and off-shore sporting events.

3/93   Motion for a resolution [B3-0022/93] by Mr Fernandez-Albor on Community Action for the protection of the environment in the coastal areas and waters of Galicia referred to the Environment Committee.

24/3/93   ECOSOC adopted opinion on [COM(92)458 final] for a council directive amending Directive 91/67/EEC concerning animal health conditions governing the placing on the market of aquaculture animals and products.

2/4/93   Motion for a resolution B3-0451/93 on the interaction between marine mammals and fisheries.

24/11/93   Judgment of European Court of Justice on Case C-405/92 between Etablissements Armand Mondiet SA and Armement Islais on validity of Article 1 of Council Regulation 345/92 on conservation of fisheries resources.

24/11/93   Joint motion for a Resolution B3-1791 and 1793/93 in favour of a total ban of drift-nets by Community fishing fleets.

1994   Council adopts decisions regarding Union's accession to the Convention for the Protection of the Marine Environment in the Baltic Sea (Helsinki Convention in 1974).

6/4/94   Regulation 761/94 adopted by Commission. Amends Council Regulation 1956/88 – application of Scheme of Joint International Inspection and Surveillance adopted by NATO.

12/4/94   1,745th Council Meeting on Fisheries discussed the proposal for a Regulation on the use of Drift-nets by the Community fleet.

3/5/94   European Parliament voted against addressing the issue of drift-netting under the emergency procedure.

6/5/94   Report A3-0186/94 adopted. Interactions between seals and fisheries.

10/6/94   Council discussed proposal for Regulation on use of drift-nets – no conclusion as they had to wait for Parliamentary Opinion which had been delayed due to the vote on 3/5/94.

27/9/94   Decision published by Commission amending Annex to Commission Regulation (EEC) 55/87 on the permitted use of beam trawls within Community coastal areas. (OJ No. L259, 7.10.94, p. 27)

29/9/94   Report on proposal for a Council Regulation amending Regulation 3094/86 laying down technical measures for the conservation of fishery resources including banning of all drift-nets in Community waters by the end of 1994 was discussed and adopted by the European Parliament.

15/11/94   At CITES EU voted against Norway's proposal to resume global trade in whale products.

7/12/94   Antarctic Whale Sanctuary officially became a protected zone.

22/3/95   COM (95) 70 final Proposal for a Council Regulation (EC) amending for the fifth time Regulation (EEC) No. 1866/86 laying down certain technical measures for the conservation of fishery resources in the waters of the Baltic Sea, the Belts and the Sound.
(OJ C 91 12/4/95 p. 5)

6/4/95   Council concluded that as nothing new had been brought to the discussion control measures must be put in hand to ensure that the rules in force are complied with in full.

18/5/95   Joint motion for a resolution (B4-0743) on the moratorium on whaling was adopted. This resolution restates the Parliament's opposition to commercial whaling of any species of whales that are considered as endangered species by the International Whaling Commission. It further calls on the Commission to present a report based on the latest scientific information on interaction between whales and other species in the marine environment and to express to the IWC the EU's support for the continuation of the moratorium on commercial whaling as long as it is based on sound scientific findings.
Eurogroup believes this Resolution does not go far enough in supporting a moratorium on commercial whaling for all species as has been Parliament's position previously.

22/5/95   Council Regulation (EC) 1173/95 amending for the sixteenth time Regulation (EEC) 3094/86 laying down certain technical measures for the conservation of fishery resources.
(OJ L 118 25/5/95 p. 15)

22/6/95   Council Directive 95/22/EC amending Directive 91/67/EEC concerning the animal health conditions governing the placing on the market of aquaculture animals and products.
(OJ L 243 11/10/95 p. 1)

18/9/95   Council Regulation (EC) 2250/95 amending for the fifth time Regulation (EEC) No. 1866/86 laying down certain

technical measures for the conservation of fishery resources in the waters of the Baltic Sea, the Belts and the Sound.
(OJ L 230 27/9/95 p. 1)

18/9/95   Council Regulation (EC) 2251/95 amending for the eighteenth time Regulation (EEC) 3094/86 laying down certain technical measures for the conservation of fishery resources.
(OJ L 230 27/9/95 p. 11)

7/12/95   COM (95) 635 final Proposal for a Council Regulation (EC) amending Regulation (EC) No. 1626/94 laying down certain technical measures for the conservation of fishery resources in the Mediterranean.
(OJ C 41 13/2/96, p. 17)

14/12/95   COM (95) 670 final Proposal for a Council Regulation (EC) amending for the sixth time Regulation (EEC) No. 1866/86 laying down certain technical measures for the conservation of fishery resources in the waters of the Baltic Sea, the Belts and the Sound.
(OJ C 44 16/2/96 p. 6)

14/12/95   SEC (95) 2259 final Commission's Report on the enforcement of Community Legislation concerning the use of driftnets in 1995 in the NE Atlantic and the Mediterranean.

22/12/95   Council Regulation (EC) 3071/95 amending for the nineteenth time Regulation (EEC) 3094/86 laying down certain technical measures for the conservation of fishery resources.
(OJ L 329 30/12/95 p. 14)

22/1/96   Council Decision concerning the approval of the amendment to Article VII of the Convention on fishing and conservation of the living resources in the Baltic Sea and the Belts.
(OJ L 21 27/1/96 p. 69)

2/96   Report A4-0006/96 on COM (95)0040 – communication from the Commission to the Council on an evaluation of the biological impact of fisheries. Rapporteur: Brigitte Langenhagen.

12/2/96   The ECOSOC gave its opinion on the conservation of fishery resources and fishery rights.
(OJ C 39, 12/2/96 p. 32)

3/96   Oral question H-0155/96 by Josu Imaz San Miguel (PPE-S) on driftnets. Mr Imaz San Miguel pointed out that the Parliament had requested the banning of all driftnets. Commissioner Bonino replied that the Parliament'opinion referred to the 1994 Commission's proposal, which was presently being discussed in the Council. However, the Member States have not yet been able to reach a compromise agreement that would allow a qualified majority decision. Mrs Bonino further stated that the Commission would apply in 1996 similar control measures as in 1995.

Oral question H-158/96 by Jaime Valdivielso de cué (PPE-S) on driftnets.

Oral question H-0159/96 by Daniel Varela Suanzes-Carpegna (PPE-S) on driftnets.

27/3/96	The ECOSOC gave its opinion on the EC proposal for a Council Regulation amending Regulation 1626/94 laying down certain technical measures for the conservation of fishery resources in the Mediterranean. (OJ C.174 17.6.96 p. 34)
28/3/96	COM (96) 117 final Proposal for a council regulation (EC) laying down certain conservation and control measures applicable to fishing activities in the Antarctic. (OJ C.156 31/5/96 p. 10)
4/96	Oral question H-0225/96 by Carmen Fraga Estévez (PPE-S) on the case between the United States and Italy regarding the use of driftnets longer than 2.5 km.
30/4/96	COM (96) 128 final Proposal for a Council Regulation (EC) introducing transitional measures into Regulation (EC) No. 1626/94 laying down certain technical measures for the conservation of fishery resources in the Mediterranean. (OJ C 176 19/6/96 p. 14)
28/5/96	The ECOSOC gave its opinion on the Commission's proposal on measures for the conservation of fishery resources. (OJ C 153 28/5/96 p. 50)
29/5/96	COM (96) 232 final Proposal for a Council Regulation (EC) amending Regulation (EEC) No. 2847/93 establishing a control system applicable to the Common Fisheries Policy. The text proposes that Member States establish a satellite-based system to monitor the position of Community fishing vessels. This monitoring system should apply to vessels using driftnets longer than 1 km by 1 January 1997 and by 1 January 1999 to all other Community vessels exceeding 15 metres in length overall. (OJ C.209 20/7/96 p. 7)

30/5/96	COM (95) 212 final for a Proposal for a Council Regulation (EC) amending for the eighteenth time Regulation (EEC) 3094/86 laying down certain technical measures for the conservation of fishery resources. (OJ C 180 14/7/96 p. 5)
6/96	Oral question H-0409/96 by Jesus Cabezon Alonso (PSE-S) on the use of drift gill nets.
10/6/96	Council Regulation (EC) No. 1075/96 amending Regulation (EC) No. 1626/94 laying down certain technical measures for the conservation of fishery resources in the Mediterranean. (OJ L 142 15.6.96 p. 1)
10/6/96	Council Regulation (EC) 1076/96 amending Regulation No. 3090/95 laying down certain conservation and management measures for fishery resources in the Regulatory Area as defined in the Convention on Future Multilateral Cooperation in the North West Atlantic Fisheries. (OJ L 142 15/6/96 p. 3)
19/6/96	The European Parliament adopted a Resolution on Commission's proposal on fishing activities in the Antarctic.
19/6/96	The European Parliament adopted a Resolution on Commission's proposal on fishery resources in the waters of the Baltic Sea, the Belts and the Sound.
21/6/96	Commission Decision No. 96/384/EC on certain protective measures in respect of infectious anaemia in salmon in Norway. (OJ L.151 26/6/96 p. 35)
20/6/96	COM (96) 279 final Commission's proposal for a Council Directive amending Directive 93/53/EEC introducing minimum Community measures for the control of certain fish diseases. (OJ C.242 21/8/96 p. 13)
25/6/96	Council Regulation (EC) No. 1167/96 amending, for the second time, Regulation (EC) No. 3090/95 laying down for 1996 certain conservation and management measures for fishery resources in the Regulatory Area in the Convention on Future Multilateral Cooperation in the North West Atlantic Fisheries. (OJ L.155 28/6/96 p. 1) Council Regulation (EC) No. 1168/96 laying down for 1996 certain conservation and management measures for

fishery resources in the Convention Area as defined in the Convention on Future Multilateral Cooperation in the North West Atlantic Fisheries.
(OJ L.155 28/6/96 p. 3)

Council Decision (EC) No. 96/428/EC on acceptance by the Community of the Agreement to promote compliance with international conservation and management measures by fishing vessels on the high seas.
(OJ L.177 16/7/96 p. 24)

1/7/96   Commission Regulation (EC) No. 1265/96 establishing urgent conservation measures to protect the stock of North Sea herring.
(OJ L.163, 2/7/96 p. 24)

18/7/96   Decision 96/490/EC adopted by Commission on certain protective measures with regard to *Gyrodactylus salaris* in salmonids.
(OJ L 202 10/8/96 p. 21)

SEALS – HOODED AND HARP

Existing Legislation

Council Directive 83/129/EEC of 28 March 1983 concerning the importation into Member States of skins of certain seal pups and products derived therefrom.
(OJ L.91 9/4/83 p. 30)

Summary

Member States shall take or maintain all necessary measures to ensure that the products listed in the table below are not commercially imported into their territories:

No.	
1	Raw furskins and furs, tanned or dressed, including assembled in plates, crosses and similar forms: – of whitecoat pups of hooded seals – of pups of hooded seals (blue-backs)
2	Articles of the fur skins referred to in 1.

Applied from 1 October 1983 to 1 October 1985 pending a report to the Council by the Commission before 1 September 1985.

Council Directive 85/444/EEC of 27 September 1985 amending Directive 83/129/EEC concerning the importation into Member States of skins of certain seal pups and products derived therefrom.
(OJ L.259 1/10/85)
Extended application of Directive 83/129/EEC until 1 October 1989.

Council Directive 89/370/EEC of 8 June 1989 amending Directive 83/129/EEC concerning the importation into Member States of skins of certain seal pups and products derived therefrom.
Extends application of the original Directive *sine die*.

Work in Progress

None.

Background

European Community

17/04/80	Motion for a Resolution 1-106/80 by Mr Johnson, Mr Simpson, Mrs Weber, Mr Price, Mr Prag, Mr Newton-Dunn, Miss Roberts, Miss Hooper, Miss Forster, Mr Spicer, Mr Marshall and Mr Collins, on Community trade in seal products and in particular of products deriving from the 'whitecoat' pups of harp and hooded seals.
19/05/80	Motion for Resolution 1-106/80 referred to the Environment Committee.
25/11/81	Report 1-738/81 drawn up on behalf of the Environment Committee on Community trade in seal products and in particular in products deriving from the whitecoat pups of harp and hooded seals. Rapporteur: Johanna Maij-Weggen (PPE-NL).
15/02/82	Second Report 1-984/81 drawn up on behalf of the Environment Committee on Community trade in seal products and in particular in products deriving from the whitecoat pups of harp and hooded seals. Rapporteur: Johanna Maij-Weggen (PPE-NL).
11/03/82	1-47/82. The European Parliament adopted a Motion for Resolution, based on its reports, calling on the Commission to introduce, by means of a regulation, a ban on Community imports of all skins and products derived from young hooded and harp seals and on these and other

products coming from seals whose stocks are depleted, threatened or endangered.
(OJ C.87 5/4/82 p. 87)
Voting: 160–10 with 20 abstentions

24/06/82   The Council of Environment Ministers undertook to support early action for the protection of seals.

09/09/82   Motion for a Resolution 1-582/82 by Mr Johnson, Mrs Maij-Weggen, Mr Collins, Mr Vandewiele, Mrs Spaak, Mrs Castle, Sir Henry Plumb, Mr Curry, Mr Wittgenstein, Mr Berkhouwer, Mrs Scrivener, Mr Muntingh, Mr Spinelli, Mrs Squarcialupi, Mrs Weber, Mr McCartin, Mr Nord, Mrs Krouwel-Vlam, Lord Douro, Mr Israel, Mr Marshall, Mr Beyer de Ryke, Mr Enright, Mr Prag, Mr Spicer, Lord O'Hagan, Mr Bombard, Mr Irmer, Mr von Wogau, Mr Del Duca, Mr van Aerssen, Mr Rogalla, Mr Ghergo, Mr Fergusson, Mrs Fuillet, Mr Sherlock, Mr Simpson, Mr Mertens, Mr Verroken and Mr Howell on behalf of the European Democratic group with respect to the topical and urgent debate on the Commission's failure to implement the Parliament's resolution of 11 March 1982.

16/09/82   European Parliament adopted the resolution deploring the Commission's failure to introduce proposals for banning seal skin imports into the Community.
(OJ C.267 11/10/82 p. 47)

06/10/82   Commission resolved to send a draft regulation to the Council providing for a ban on imported products derived from whitecoat pups of harp seals and from pups of hooded seals: such a ban would come into force on 1 March 1983.
(OJ C.285 30/10/82 p. 7)

19/11/82   Parliament urged the Council to adopt the regulation banning the import of baby seal skins.
(OJ C.344 30/12/82 p. 132)

25/11/82   The ECOSOC delivered a favourable opinion on the draft Council Regulation.
(OJ C.346 31/12/82 p. 1)

05/01/83   Council Resolution. The Commission was asked to examine further in collaboration with the authorities of the countries concerned the methods, circumstances and scientific aspects of the killing of pups of harp and hooded seals as well as the possibilities of identification by marking.

In addition, to pursue exploratory talks with the countries concerned (Norway and Canada).
(OJ C.14 18/11/83 p. 1)

11/02/83   COM(83)71 final communication from the Commission to the Council concerning the prohibition of importation into the Community of certain baby seal skins and derivative products.

28/02/83   Directive 83/129/EEC adopted by Council.
(OJ L.91 9/4/83 p. 30)

23/08/83   Commission submitted a Report to Council in compliance with Article 2 of Council Directive 83/129/EEC concerning the importation into Member States of skins of certain seal pups and products derived therefrom. (COM(82)403.)

1983   The Commission published in its Environment and Quality of Life series: *Recommendations and Status Report on Harp and Hooded Seals*, revised version, Ref: EUR 7317.

02/08/84   Motion for a Resolution 2-432/84 by Mrs Castle on Community trade in seal products and in particular products deriving from the whitecoat pups of harp and hooded seals.

24/09/84   Motion for a Resolution 2-591/84 by Lord Bethell, Mr Seligman, Mr Howell, Mr Simpson, Mr Muntingh, Mr Sherlock, Mr de Courcy Ling, Dame Shelagh Roberts, Mr Beazley, Mr Griffiths, Lord Douro, Mr Marshall, Mr Pearce, Ms Quin, Mr Louwes, Mrs Maij-Weggen and Mr Jackson on the continuation of the EEC Directive concerning the importation into Member States of skins of certain seal pups and products derived therefrom.

01/03/85   Report 2-1785/84 drawn up on behalf of the Environment Committee on Community trade in seal products and in particular products deriving from the whitecoat pups of harp and hooded seals.
Rapporteur: Hemmo Muntingh (S-NL).

15/03/85   European Parliament adopted the Resolution on Community trade in seal products.
(OJ C.94 15/4/85 p. 128)
    Voting: 55–0

11/06/85   COM(85)246 final Commission submitted a Communication to Council for a proposal for a Council

Directive amending Directive 83/129/EEC extending the period of its enforcement.

27/09/85   Council Directive 85/444/EEC extending application of Directive 83/129/EEC until 1 October 1989.
(OJ L.259 1/10/85)

30/12/87   Implementation by Canadian Government of Royal Commission (Malouf) recommendation to end large vessel offshore seal hunt in Canadian waters, whilst permitting harvest of older seals by Inuits to continue.

04/07/88   Written Declaration 10/88 by Mr Muntingh on the extension of the directive on importation into Member States of skins of certain seal pups and products derived therefrom (85/444/EEC).

24/03/88   Submission to the Council of Commission Communication COM(88)147 final, a report on the seal situation, prepared in compliance with Council Directive 85/444/EEC of 27 September 1985 amending Council Directive 83/129/EEC.

21/04/88   The Commission published the annexes to its Communication COM(88)147 final.

12/09/88   Written Declaration 10/88 opened for signature.
Signed by 325 Members, it was subsequently forwarded to the Commission of the European Communities.

14/02/89   Norwegian Government prohibited taking of seal pups by Norwegian sealers during the 1989 hunt and announced decision to appoint two commissions, one to review the seal hunt in recent years, whilst the other to evaluate existing seal harvest regulations and practices.

17/03/89   The Commission published its proposal COM(89)112 final for a Council Directive amending Directive 83/129/EEC concerning the importation into Member States of skins of certain seal pups and products derived therefrom.

08/06/89   Council Directive 89/370/EEC of 8 June 1989 amending Directive 83/129/EEC concerning the importation into Member States of skins of certain seal pups and products derived therefrom.

4/4/95   Oral reply to an oral question concerning Norway's recent decision to resume seal-hunting to 'maintain the seal population at a reasonable level' and 'to enable scientists to set up a programme to research seal nutrition'. Answer by Mr Neil Kinnock on behalf of the Commission was that harp and hooded seals are not endangered species and that there was no doubt about the sustainability of a hunt at the levels proposed by Norway. As Norway will continue to ban commercial seal hunting the Commission had no reason to interfere in this matter.

18/1/96   Motion for a Resolution 0053/96 by Mrs Maij-Weggen, Mrs Banotti and Mrs Oomen-Ruijten on the resumption of seal hunting by Norway.

5/96   Oral question H-0310/96 by MaLou Lindholm (V-SU) on seal hunting.

           Oral question H-0059/96 by Doeke Eisma (ELDR-NL) on import of Norwegian seals into the UK.

SEALS – MONK

Existing Legislation

Council Regulation (EEC) 3626/82 of 3 December 1982 on the implementation in the Community of the Convention on International Trade in Endangered Species of Wild Fauna and Flora (CITES) lists monk seal in Appendix I.

Council Directive 92/43/EEC of 21 May 1992 on the conservation of natural habitats and of wild fauna and flora lists monk seal in Annexes II and IV.

Work in Progress

Mediterranean Action Plan under the Barcelona Convention (see 'International' below).

Background

International

03/04/82   Mediterranean coastal states party to the Convention on the Protection of the Mediterranean Sea Against Pollutants (Barcelona Convention) adopted a Protocol concerning Mediterranean Specially Protected Areas. It entered into force on 23 March 1986 and has been ratified by the European Community.

A Mediterranean Action Plan was formulated by the Parties to the Barcelona Convention at the Joint Expert Consultation in 1988, identifying threats to the monk seal and steps to be taken.

09-13/09/85   Meeting of the Parties to the Convention agreed protection of the monk seal a priority target to be achieved by 1995.

Council of Europe

19/09/79   Convention on the Conservation of European Wildlife and Natural Habitats (Bern) opened for signature.

15/09/86   First Meeting of a Working Group on *Monachus monachus*, set up by the Standing Committee of the Bern Convention.

04/12/86   The Fifth Meeting of the Standing Committee adopted Recommendation No 6 (1986) on the protection of monk seals in the Mediterranean.

05/88   Second Meeting of the Working Group on the Mediterranean Monk Seal *(Monachus monachus)* requested the Standing Committee to organise a Seminar to coordinate international action relative to the species.

27/10/88   Final Report on The Biology, Status and Conservation of the Monk Seal *(Monachus monachus)*.

09/12/88   The Seventh Meeting of the Standing Committee agreed to hold a seminar during 1989 on the coordination of international action on conservation of the monk seal.

20–22/9/89   A seminar to coordinate international efforts on behalf of the monk seal was held in Madeira as part of the 1989 work programme of the Standing Committee of the Convention on the Conservation of European Wildlife and Natural Habitats.

01–04/05/91   First of a number of periodical seminars to discuss scientific and technical issues relevant to the conservation of the monk seal.

02–06/12/91   Eleventh Meeting of the Standing Committee received seminar report and endorsed the principle of acting through the Barcelona Convention on any future captive breeding proposals.

European Community

21/06/83	Motion for a Resolution 1-452/83 by Mrs Schleicher, Mr Johnson, Mr Muntingh, Mrs Pantazi, Mr Eisma, Mrs Squarcialupi and Mr Lynge on the protection of the monk seal.
07/07/83	Motion for a Resolution 1-582/83 by Mr Kyrkos on the drawing up of a programme for saving Mediterranean seals.
08/02/84	Report 1-1401/83 drawn up on behalf of the Environment Committee on the protection of monk seals. Rapporteur: Hemmo Muntingh (S-NL)
17/02/84	The European Parliament adopted the resolution on the protection of monk seals. (OJ C.77 19/3/84 p. 112)
1984	The Commission published in its Environment and Quality of Life Series: *Report on the Special Measures for the Conservation of Monk Seals in the European Community*, Ref: EUR 9228.
21/07/87	Council Regulation (EEC) 2242/87 on action by the Community relating to the Environment (ACE) 1987–1992. Its priorities for financial support included projects on the conservation and protection of monk seals. (OJ L.207 29/7/87 p. 8)
29/10/87	Motion for a Resolution 2-1098/87 by Mr Muntingh and Mr Avgerinos on the protection of the monk seal in Greece.
20/11/87	Motion for a Resolution 2-1251/87 by Mrs Schleicher, Mr Sherlock, Mr Garcia, Mr Roelants du Vivier and Mrs Squarcialupi on the monk seal.
11/07/88	Report A2-151/88 drawn up on behalf of the Environment Committee on the protection of the monk seal. Rapporteur: Hemmo Muntingh (S-NL).
16/09/88	European Parliament adopted the Resolution on the monk seal. (OJ C.262 10/10/88)
04/92	Motion for a Resolution B3-243/92 by Mr Bandrés Molet on the risk of extinction of the monk seal
03/90	Motion for a Resolution B3-224/90 by Mrs Santos and others on the oil spill affecting the monk seal reserve on

	Madeira Archipelago. Environment Committee decided not to draw up a report.
22/11/90	B3-2024/90 European Parliament adopted Urgent Resolution on the monk seal.

SEALS – GREY AND COMMON

Existing Legislation

Council Directive 92/43/EEC of 21 May 1992 on the conservation of natural habitats and of wild fauna and flora lists common seal (*Phoca vitulina*) in Annex II.

Background

General

1988	From April to September 1988 a viral illness spread rapidly among grey and common seal populations of the North Sea, the Waddenzee, the Shetlands, Orkneys and the Irish coast. More than 10,000 seals had succumbed by the end of the year. Rescue and rehabilitation centres were established at Pieterburen in the Netherlands, Docking in the United Kingdom, and Sylt in the Federal Republic of Germany.
06/88	International scientific seminar in Bonn organised by the Federal Minister for Environment, Nature Conservation and Nuclear Safety to consider and assess the causes, potential development and possible consequences of seal deaths and algal growth in the North Sea and the Baltic.

Council of Europe

29/04/88	Report on behalf of the Committee on Regional Planning and Local Authorities on the protection of the North Sea against pollution. Rapporteur: Mr Ahrens. The report contained a draft Recommendation.
06/05/88	Order No. 438 on the protection of the North Sea against pollution was adopted by the Parliamentary Assembly of the Council of Europe.
09/12/88	The Seventh Meeting of the Standing Committee of the Convention on the Conservation of European Wildlife and Natural Habitats adopted Recommendation No 11 concern-

ing the protection of the common seal *Phoca vitulina* and its habitat.

European Community

09/06/88	Motion for a Resolution 2-509/88 by Mrs Bloch von Blottnitz and Mr Staes on the environmental disaster in the North Sea and the Baltic.
15/09/88	European Parliament adopted the Joint Resolution by Mr Roelants du Vivier, Mr Sherlock, Mr Collins, Mr Staes, Mrs Schleicher, Mrs Maij-Weggen, Mr Iversen, Mrs Anglade and Mr Coderch Planas on the death of seals and pollution in the North Sea and the Baltic (replacing Documents B2-643, 654, 665, 684, 735, 740 and 759/88).
1988	Programme to combat the seal disease set up by the Dutch National Institute of Public Health and Environmental Protection and the Seal Rehabilitation and Research Centre in Pieterburen (NL) assisted by a grant of ECU 50 000 from the Commission of the European Communities. Research undertaken in cooperation with centres at Cambridge and Kiel.
1989	ECU 900 000 allocated for seal research from European Community Budget. Budget Item 6617 on environmental studies will finance further investigation of the links between seal deaths and marine pollution.
28/3/94	Report No. A3-0186/94 by Killailea on the interaction between seals and fisheries.

WHALES

Existing Legislation

Council Regulation (EEC) 348/81 of 20 January 1981 on common rules for imports of whales or other cetacean products.
(OJ L.39 12/12/81)

Summary

Introduces a system of import licences for all primary whale products. These may only be granted under the Regulation for non-commercial purposes, such as scientific research. The list of products annexed to the Regulation covers whalemeat, whalebone, non-edible whalemeat, whale oils and fats and products such as leather goods, skins and footwear treated with oil from whales or other cetaceans.

Council Regulation (EEC) 3626/82 of 3 December 1982 on the implementation within the Community of the Convention on International Trade in Endangered Species of Wild Fauna and Flora.

Summary

Goes further than CITES itself by way of Annex C1 and C2. All cetacean species not on Appendix I of the Convention are listed in C1 which confers CITES Appendix I status upon them. Thus the keeping for sale, offering for sale or transport for sale of any cetacean or its products is prohibited. Regulation 3626/82 largely supersedes Regulation 348/81 above but the latter remains on the statute books and, therefore, extant.

Commission Regulation (EEC) 3418/83 of 28 November 1983 laying down provisions for the uniform issue and use of the documents required for the implementation in the Community of the Convention on the International Trade in Endangered Species of Wild Fauna and Flora.
(OJ L.344 7/12/83 p. 1)

Supersedes the provisions of Commission Regulation 3786/81 in light of the Convention on International Trade in Endangered Species of Wild Fauna and Flora (CITES) being implemented in the Community by Regulation 3626/82.

Council Directive 92/43/EEC of 21 May 1992 on the conservation of natural habitats and of wild fauna and flora lists all cetaceans in Annex IV.

Work in Progress

18/5/95   Resolution B4-0743 adopted in Parliament on the issue of the prohibition commercial whaling in EU waters. The Parliament reiterated its opposition to the commercial killing of any species of whales seen as an endangered species by the IWC; called on the Commission to present a report on the basis of the latest scientific information on the interaction between whales and other species in the marine environment; reiterated its call for a conservation area for cetaceans in the Southern Ocean; called on the Commission to express to the IWC the EU's support for the continuation of the moratorium on commercial whaling as long as it is based on sound scientific findings; stressed the need to keep a strict balance of quotas through the revised management procedure.

Background

Council of Europe

27/09/89   The Parliamentary Assembly of the Council of Europe received and debated a report on whaling by Mr Kjarten Johanssen and Lord Kinnoull.

Resolution 929 (89) on the future of whaling resulted from this debate. It called on the members of the Council of Europe to adhere strictly to IWC decisions, to promote non-lethal methods of research, to press for IWC powers to extend to small cetaceans.

European Community

20/07/79   Motion for a Resolution 1-243/79 by Mr Johnson, Miss Hooper and Mr Newton-Dunn.

04/09/79   Commission put before the Council a recommendation for a Decision authorising the Commission to negotiate on behalf of the Community for the establishment of a new International Convention on Whaling.

29/04/80   COM(80)150 final Proposal from the Commission to the Council for a Council Regulation on common rules for imports of whale products.
(OJ C.121 20.5.80 p. 5)

30/05/80   The European Parliament's Environment Committee appointed Mr Hemmo Muntingh (S-NL) Rapporteur.

25/09/80   Opinion of the ECOSOC.
(OJ C.300 18/11/80 p. 13)

08/10/80   Report 1-451/80 drawn up on behalf of the Environment Committee. Rapporteur: Hemmo Muntingh (S-NL).

16/10/80   The European Parliament adopted a Resolution on the proposal from the Commission to the Council for a Regulation on common rules for imports of whale products.
(OJ C.291 10/11/80 p. 46)

20/01/81   Council Regulation (EEC) 348/81 of 20 January 1981 on common rules for imports of whales or other cetacean products.
(OJ L.39 22/12/81)

22/12/81   Commission Regulation (EEC) 3786/81 of 22 December 1981 laying down provisions for the implementation of

the common rules for imports of whale or other cetacean products.
(OJ. L.377 31/12/81 p. 42)

1982

The International Whaling Commission agreed to an amendment to the Schedule:

catch limits for the killing for commercial purposes of whales from all stocks for the 1986 coastal and 1985/86 pelagic seasons and thereafter shall be zero.

18/11/82

Motion for a Resolution 882/82 by Mr Sherlock, Mr Johnson, Mrs Scrivener, Mr Remilly, Mr Flanagan, Mrs Maij-Weggen, Mr Muntingh, Mrs Squarcialupi and Mr Collins on commercial whaling adopted by the European Parliament.
(OJ C.334 10/12/82 p. 87)

02/02/83

Motion for a Resolution 1198/82 by Mr Sherlock and Mr Johnson on the failure of some members of the Whaling Commission to abide by the decision of the IWC to end commercial whaling.

24/11/83

Commission Regulation (EEC) 3418/83 laying down provisions for the uniform use of the documents required for the implementation of CITES.

13/09/84

Motion for a Resolution 2-555/84 by Mrs Jackson, Mr Sherlock and Mrs Schleicher on the Community response to the failure of certain members of the IWC to abide by the decision to end commercial whaling.

24/09/84

Motion for a Resolution 592/84 by Mr Sherlock, Sir Jack Stewart-Clark, Mr Lalor, Mr Louwes, Ms Quin, Mr Griffiths on the Community response to the failure of certain members of the International Whaling Commission to abide by the decision of the IWC to end commercial whaling.

28/02/85

Report 2-1780/84 drawn up on behalf of the Environment Committee on the Community response to the failure of certain Members of the IWC to abide by the decision to end commercial whaling. Rapporteur: Hemmo Muntingh (S-NL).

10/05/85

Second Report 2-22/85 drawn up on behalf of the Environment Committee on the Community response to the failure of certain members of the IWC to abide by the decision to end commercial whaling. Rapporteur: Hemmo Muntingh (S-NL).

European Parliament adopted the Resolution.
(OJ C.141 10/6/85 p. 477)

Motion for a Resolution 2-995/87 by Mr Griffiths and others on slaughter of whales in the Azores. Referred to Environment Committee and included in Report A2-356/88 by Mr Schmid on possible legal action against events involving cruelty to animals. (*See Animals in Sport and Entertainment.*)

07/01/88 Motion for a Resolution 2-1522/87 by Mrs Banotti, Mrs Maij-Weggen, Mr Sherlock and Mrs Squarcialupi on a draft whale resolution for the EEC.

05/88 Fortieth Meeting of the International Whaling Commission in Auckland, New Zealand. Scientific research programmes involving killing of whales put forward by Norway, Iceland and Japan rejected. The IWC's Humane Killing Working Group continued discussions begun in 1986 on the Faeroese pilot whale hunt.

19/12/88 Report A2-330/88 drawn up on behalf of the Environment Committee on a draft resolution of the European Economic Community on whaling. Rapporteur: Hemmo Muntingh (S-NL).

17/02/89 European Parliament adopted the Resolution on whaling (A3-330/88).

06/89 Forty-first Meeting of the International Whaling Commission in San Diego, USA.

17/05/90 European Parliament adopted Resolution on whaling moratorium.

07/90 Forty-second Meeting of the International Whaling Commission in Noordwijk, Netherlands.

05/91 Forty-third Meeting of the International Whaling Commission in Reykjavik, Iceland.

06/91 Motion for a Resolution B3-978/91 by the ED Group on the moratorium on whaling and a fish products trade ban with countries which resume whaling outside the IWC. Not withheld.

06/92	Forty-fourth Meeting of the International Whaling Commission in Glasgow, Scotland.
09/07/92	Parliament debated the decision by Norway to recommence commercial whaling. A joint motion for resolution was adopted. It condemned Norway and urged EC participation in the International Whaling Commission.
15/07/92	COM(92)316 Communication from the Commission to the Council concerning the conservation of whales within the framework of the International Whaling Commission. Commission is authorised to seek negotiation on EC accession to International Convention for the Regulation of Whaling (1946).
21/4/93	Issue of commercial whaling recommencement by Norway has been withdrawn from the list of urgent topics for debate and letter to be written by President of the House to the Norwegian Government to convey the opposition of Parliament to this activity.
15/11/94	Norway's attempt to resume global trade in whale products was rejected by CITES. EU voted against Norway's proposal in spite of sensitivity due to the forthcoming Norwegian referendum on joining EU.
12/94	Motion for a resolution submitted to Parliament calling on the European Commission to prepare legislation prohibiting commercial whaling in EU waters and by all EU Member Nations.
18/5/95	Resolution B4-0743 adopted in Parliament on the issue of the prohibition of commercial whaling in EU waters. The Parliament reiterated its opposition to the commercial killing of any species of whales seen as an endangered species by the IWC; called on the Commission to present a report on the basis of the latest scientific information on the interaction between whales and other species in the marine environment; reiterated its call for a conservation area for cetaceans in the Southern Ocean; called on the Commission to express to the IWC the EU's support for the continuation of the moratorium on commercial whaling as long as it is based in sound scientific findings; stressed the need to keep a strict balance of quotas through the revised management procedure.

8/95   Forty-fifth Meeting of the International Whaling Commission held in the USA.

6/96   Forty-sixth Meeting of the International Whaling Commission held in Aberdeen, UK. The Commission extended the moratorium on commercial whaling for a further year. A vote was taken on the use of the electric lance, the IWC did not get a strong enough majority in favour of the ban (16 in favour, 8 against and 8 abstentions).

A Resolution was adopted calling on Norway to stop all whaling activity and to respect the moratorium imposed. The Commission also called upon Japan to reconsider its plans to kill 540 minke whales in the coming year. Proposals were made for aboriginal whaling in the US and in Russia.

DOLPHINS

Existing Legislation

Council Regulation (EEC) 3626/82 of 3 December 1982 on the implementation within the Community of the Convention on International Trade in Endangered Species of Wild Fauna and Flora.

Summary

Goes further than CITES itself by way of Annex C1 and C2. All cetacean species not on Appendix I of the Convention are listed in C1 which confers CITES Appendix I status upon them. Thus the keeping for sale, offering for sale or transport for sale of any cetacean or its products is prohibited.

Council Regulation (EEC) 345/92 of 27 January 1992 amending for the eleventh time Regulation 3094/86 laying down certain technical measures for the conservation of fishery resources.
(OJ L.42 18/2/92)

Summary

Deals with the conservation of fish stocks and bans the use of drift nets over 2.5 km long in Community waters or by Community vessels anywhere in the world. Vessels which have been using drift nets in the North East Atlantic albacore tuna fishery for more than two years may continue to use drift nets up to 5 km long until the end of December 1993, provided they are submerged 2 m below the surface.

Council Directive 92/43/EEC of 21 May 1992 on the conservation of natural habitats and of wild fauna and flora lists all cetaceans in Annex IV. Bottle-nosed dolphin (*Tursiops truncatus*) and harbour porpoise (*Phocoena phocoena*) are also listed in Annex II.

Council Regulation (EEC) 3034/92 of 19 October 1992 amending for the fourteenth time Council Regulation (EEC) 3094/86 laying down certain technical measures for the conservation of fishery resources.

Summary

Bans the use of purse seine nets by EC registered vessels when used to catch tuna or other species where encirclement puts marine mammals at risk of capture or killing.

Council Regulation (EC) 1173/95 of 22 May 1995 amending for the sixteenth time Regulation (EEC) 3094/86 laying down certain technical measures for the conservation of fishery resources.
(OJ L 118 25/5/95 p. 15)

Council Regulation (EC) 2251/95 of 18 September 1995 amending for the eighteenth time Regulation (EEC) 3094/86 laying down certain technical measures for the conservation of fishery resources.
(OJ L 230 27/9/95 p. 11)

Council Regulation (EC) 3071/95 of 22 December 1995 amending for the nineteenth time Regulation (EEC) 3094/86 laying down certain technical measures for the conservation of fishery resources.
(OJ L 329 30/12/95 p. 14)

Council Decision of 22 January 1996 concerning the approval of the amendment to Article VII of the Convention on fishing and conservation of the living resources in the Baltic Sea and the Belts.
(OJ L 21 27/1/96 p. 69)

Council Regulation (EC) No. 1075/96 of 10 June 1996 amending Regulation (EC) No. 1626/94 laying down certain technical measures for the conservation of fishery resources in the Mediterranean.
(OJ L 142 15.6.96 p. 1)

Council Regulation (EC) 1076/96 of 10 June 1996 amending Regulation No. 3090/95 laying down certain conservation and management measures for fishery resources in the Regulatory Area as defined in the Convention on Future Multilateral Cooperation in the North West Atlantic Fisheries.
(OJ L 142 15/6/96 p. 3)

Work in Progress

None

Background

International

09/91   The Agreement on the Conservation of Small Cetaceans in
               the Baltic and North Seas under Article IV of the
               Convention for the Conservation of Migratory Species of
               Wild Animals was concluded in Geneva.

12/91   Draft Agreement on the Conservation of Small Cetaceans
               in the Mediterranean and Black Seas presented to the eleventh
               Meeting of the Standing Committee of the Bern Convention.

03/92   The Agreement on the Conservation of Small Cetaceans in
               the Baltic and North Seas under Article IV of the
               Convention for the Conservation of Migratory Species of
               Wild Animals was opened for signature.

05/92   Draft Agreement on the Conservation of Small Cetaceans in
               the Mediterranean and Black Seas discussed by the Parties to
               the Barcelona Convention in the context of the Review of the
               Mediterranean Action Plan for small cetaceans.

European Community

28/04/88   Motion for a Resolution 2-226/88 by Mrs Weber and others
               on the killing of dolphins by tuna fishermen in the Eastern
               Tropical Pacific.

19/12/88   Report A2-330/88 drawn up on behalf of the Environment
               Committee on a draft resolution of the European Economic
               Community on whaling. Refers to lack of protection for
               small cetaceans and possible extension of IWC role in that
               domain. Rapporteur: Hemmo Muntingh (S-NL).

17/02/89   European Parliament adopted the Resolution on whaling
               (A2-330/88).

02/08/89   Motion for a Resolution B3-12/89 by Mr Seligman on the
               danger to marine mammals and other non-target species from
               purse seine and drift-netting. Referred to the Fisheries
               Subcommittee with an opinion requested from the Environ-
               ment Committee (the Environment Committee subsequently

decided not to deliver an opinion). Rapporteur: Vasco Garcia (LDR-P).

14/09/89 Motion for a Resolution B3-155/89 by the Green Group on stricter compliance with water quality standards and a ban on drift-netting in the Mediterranean.

29/09/89 ACP-EC Joint Assembly adopted a resolution for a world-wide ban on drift-netting.

11/89 0-106/89. Rule 58 oral question with debate by Mrs Winifred Ewing (ARC-UK) and others on EC funding of a project to pipe raw sewage into Moray Firth.

02/90 Motion for a Resolution B3-1671/90 by Mr Bandres Molet and Mr Amendola on mass death of dolphins off the Balearic Islands. No report.

02/90 Motion for a Resolution B3-1977-90 by Mr Papoutsis on mass death of dolphins off the Balearics. No report.

02/90 Motion for a Resolution B3-1912/90 by Mr Morris on dolphins killed in tuna purse-seine and drift-nets. No report.

02/02/90 Agriculture Committee decided to draw up a report on B3-12/89 on the danger to marine mammals and other non-target species from purse-seine and drift-netting.

03/90 Motion for a Resolution B3-753/89 by Mr Papayannakis. Pollution in the Gulf of Volos and the effects on marine wildlife.

03/90 Motion for a Resolution B3-8/90 by Mr Muntingh on rising concentration of PCBs in the bodies of marine mammals.

03/90 Motion for a Resolution B3-601/90 by the Green Group on the impact of purse-seine and drift-nets on marine wildlife and an EC ban. Not withheld for debate.

04/90 Motion for a Resolution B3-748/90 by the Green Group banning drift-nets. Not withheld for debate.

27/04/90 Motion for a Resolution B3-264/90 by Mrs Piermont on ban on drift-netting. To be included in the Report being prepared by Mr Vasco Garcia (LDR-P).

27/04/90 Motion for a Resolution B3-1912/90 by Mr Morris on the killing of dolphins by tuna fishermen using drift and purse-seine nets. To be incorporated in Garcia Report.

06/90	Motion for a Resolution B3-805/90 by Mr Amendola on ban on drift-nets in the Mediterranean because they contravene the Bern Convention.
29/09/90	Fisheries Committee appointed Mr David Morris (S-UK) Rapporteur on the purse-seining section of Motion for a Resolution B3-12/89 by Mr Seligman.
10/90	Motion for a Resolution 1535/90 by Mrs Pollack. By-catch of dolphins in the Mediterranean.
21/05/91	The Fisheries Subcommittee considered and rejected the draft report by Mr Vasco Garcia (LDR-P) on drift-netting (based on Motions for Resolution B3-12/89, B3-264/90 and B3-805/90). The report was relegated to the archives.
31/05/91	COM(90)610 proposal to amend for the eleventh time Regulation 3094/89 on fisheries conservation. Seeks, *inter alia*, to ban the use in EC waters of drift-nets over 2.5 km long. Referred by Fisheries Council to Parliament. Rapporteur: Vasco Garcia (LDR-P).
27/07/91	Draft report by Mr David Morris (S-UK) on purse seining was adopted by the Fisheries Subcommittee.
09/91	Motion for a Resolution B3-668/91 on the relationship between trade and environment with reference to GATT. Referred to Committee on External Economic Relations. Rapporteur: Tom Spencer (ED-UK).
24/09/91	Draft report by Vasco Garcia on COM(90)610, proposal to amend for the eleventh time Regulation 3094/89 on fisheries conservation, adopted by Fisheries Subcommittee.
25/09/91	Agriculture Committee adopts Morris report (A3-0249/91) on purse seining.
11/10/91	Report A3-244/91 by Mr Garcia on COM(90)610 adopted by European Parliament.
28/10/91	Fisheries Council reached agreement on COM(90)610, a proposal to amend Regulation 3094/86 on fisheries conservation, banning drift-nets over 2.5 km long.
22/11/91	Doc. A3-0249/91 by Mr David Morris on purse seine netting in the Eastern Tropical Pacific, debated and adopted in Plenary.

27/01/92	Council Regulation (EEC) 345/92 amending for the eleventh time Regulation 3094/86 laying down certain technical measures for the conservation of fishery resources, limiting drift-nets used by EC fleets and in EC waters to 2.5 km length.
15/07/92	COM(92)311 proposal to amend, for the Fourteenth time, Regulation 3094/86 which lays down certain technical measures for the conservation of fishery resources, by way of a regulation to ban the use of purse seine nets by EC registered vessels when used to catch tuna or other species where encirclement puts marine mammals at risk of capture or killing.
19/10/92	Council Regulation (EEC) 3034/92 amending for the fourteenth time Council Regulation (EEC) 3094/86 laying down certain technical measures for the conservation of fishery resources.
12/93	Fisheries Council requested report on drift-netting and a proposal for the Commission on the future of the derogation contained in Article 9a of Council Regulation (EEC) No. 3094/86 permitting certain French vessels to use drift-nets of up to 5km until 31/12/93 which could only extended 'in the light of scientific evidence showing the absence of any ecological risk linked thereto'.
8/04/94	COM(94)50 final Published – The use of Drift-nets under the Common Fisheries Policy report covers three main geographic areas of fishing: Baltic Sea, North East Atlantic and Mediterranean with reference to inshore salmon fishing in the UK and Ireland.
22/5/95	Council Regulation (EC) 1173/95 amending for the sixteenth time Regulation (EEC) 3094/86 laying down certain technical measures for the conservation of fishery resources. (OJ L 118 25/5/95 p. 15)
12/7/95	Resolution B4-0942 on the use of drift-nets adopted by the European Parliament.
18/9/95	Council Regulation (EC) 2250/95 amending for the fifth time Regulation (EEC) No. 1866/86 laying down certain technical measures for the conservation of fishery resources in the waters of the Baltic Sea, the Belts and the Sound. (OJ L 230 27/9/95 p. 1)

18/9/95   Council Regulation (EC) 2251/95 amending for the eigh-
               teenth time Regulation (EEC) 3094/86 laying down certain
               technical measures for the conservation of fishery
               resources.
               (OJ L 230 27/9/95 p. 11)

7/12/95   COM (95) 635 final Proposal for a Council Regulation
               (EC) amending Regulation (EC) No. 1626/94 laying down
               certain technical measures for the conservation of fishery
               resources in the Mediterranean.
               (OJ C 41 13/2/96, p. 17)

14/12/95   COM (95) 670 final Proposal for a Council Regulation
               (EC) amending for the sixth time Regulation (EEC) No.
               1866/86 laying down certain technical measures for the
               conservation of fishery resources in the waters of the Baltic
               Sea, the Belts and the Sound.
               (OJ C 44 16/2/96 p. 6)

14/12/95   SEC (95) 2259 final Commission's Report on the enforce-
               ment of Community Legislation concerning the use of drift-
               nets in 1995 in the NE Atlantic and the Mediterranean.

22/12/95   Council Regulation (EC) 3071/95 amending for the nine-
               teenth time Regulation (EEC) 3094/86 laying down certain
               technical measures for the conservation of fishery resources.
               (OJ L 329 30/12/95 p. 14)

22/1/96   Council Decision concerning the approval of the amendment
               to Article VII of the Convention on fishing and conservation
               of the living resources in the Baltic Sea and the Belts.
               (OJ L 21 27/1/96 p. 69)

2/96   Report A4-0006/96 on COM (95)0040 – communication
               from the Commission to the Council on an evaluation of
               the biological impact of fisheries. Rapporteur: Brigitte
               Langenhagen.

12/2/96   The ECOSOC gave its opinion on the conservation of
               fishery resources and fishery rights.
               (OJ C 39 12/2/96 p. 32)

3/96   Oral question H-0155/96 by Josu Imaz San Miguel (PPE-S)
               on driftnets. Mr Imaz San Miguel pointed out that the
               Parliaments had requested the banning of all driftnets.
               Commissioner Bonino replied that the Parliament's opinion

referred to the 1994 Commission's proposal, which was presently being discussed in the Council. However, the Member States have not yet been able to reach a compromise agreement that would allow a qualified majority decision. Mrs Bonino further stated that the Commission would apply in 1996 similar control measures as in 1995.

Oral question H-158/96 by Jaime Valdivielso de cué (PPE-S) on driftnets.

Oral question H-0159/96 by Daniel Varela Suanzes-Carpegna (PPE-S) on driftnets.

27/3/96   The ECOSOC gave its opinion on the EC proposal for a Council Regulation amending Regulation 1626/94 laying down certain technical measures for the conservation of fishery resources in the Mediterranean.
(OJ C.174 17.6.96 p. 34)

28/3/96   COM (96) 117 final Proposal for a council Regulation (EC) laying down certain conservation and control measures applicable to fishing activities in the Antarctic.
(OJ C. 156 31/5/96 p. 10)

4/96   Oral question H-0225/96 by Carmen Fraga Estévez (PPE-S) on the case between the United States and Italy regarding the use of driftnets longer than 2.5 km.

30/4/96   COM (96) 128 final Proposal for a Council Regulation (EC) introducing transitional measures into Regulation (EC) No. 1626/94 laying down certain technical measures for the conservation of fishery resources in the Mediterranean.
(OJ C 176 19/6/96 p. 14)

28/5/96   The ECOSOC gave its opinion on the Commission's proposal on measures for the conservation of fishery resources.
(OJ C 153 28/5/96 p. 50)

30/5/96   COM (95) 212 final for a Proposal for a Council Regulation (EC) amending for the eighteenth time Regulation (EEC) 3094/86 laying down certain technical measures for the conservation of fishery resources.
(OJ C 180 14/7/96 p. 5)

6/96   Oral question H-0409/96 by Jesus Cabezon Alonso (PSE-S) on the use of drift gill nets.

10/6/96	Council Regulation (EC) No. 1075/96 amending Regulation (EC) No. 1626/94 laying down certain technical measures for the conservation of fishery resources in the Mediterranean. (OJ L 142 15.6.96 p. 1)
10/6/96	Council Regulation (EC) 1076/96 amending Regulation No. 3090/95 laying down certain conservation and management measures for fishery resources in the Regulatory Area as defined in the Convention on Future Multilateral Cooperation in the North West Atlantic Fisheries. (OJ L 142 15/6/96 p. 3)
19/6/96	The European Parliament adopted a Resolution on Commission's proposal on fishing activities in the Antarctic.
19/6/96	The European Parliament adopted a Resolution on Commission's proposal on fishery resources in the waters of the Baltic Sea, the Belts and the Sound.

TURTLES

Existing Legislation

Council Regulation (EEC) 3626/82 of 3 December 1982 on the implementation in the Community of the Convention on International Trade in Endangered Species of Wild Fauna and Flora includes all marine turtles listed in Appendix I of Annex A.
(OJ L.384 31/12/82)

The parts and products of these species are listed in Annex B, i.e. the hides, skins and shells whether worked or simply prepared.

Under the Regulation the sale, keeping for sale, offering for sale or transporting for sale of turtles, whether dead or alive or derivatives thereof is prohibited, subject to exemptions.

Council Directive 92/43/EEC of 21 May 1992 on the Conservation of natural habitats and of wild fauna and flora lists loggerhead (*Caretta caretta*), green turtle (*Chelonia midas*), Kemp's Ridley (*Lepidochelys kempii*) and hawksbill (*Eretmochelys imbricata*) in Annex IV. The loggerhead is also listed in Annex II.

Work in Progress

Mediterranean Action Plan under the Barcelona Convention (see 'International' below).

Background

International

03/04/82   Mediterranean coastal states Party to the Convention on the Protection of the Mediterranean Sea Against Pollutants (Barcelona Convention) adopted a Protocol concerning Mediterranean Specially Protected Areas. It entered into force on 23 March 1986 and has been ratified by the European Community.

            A Mediterranean Action Plan was formulated by the Parties to the Barcelona Convention at the Joint Expert Consultation in 1988, identifying threats to turtles and steps to be taken.

09–13/09/85   Meeting of the Parties to the Barcelona Convention agreed protection of turtles as a priority target to be achieved by 1995.

Council of Europe

19/09/79   European Convention No. 104 on the Conservation of European Wildlife and Natural Habitats (Bern). In force: 1 June 1982.

06/87   A Working Group of Experts on *Caretta* species and *Chelonia midas* was set up and met for the first time to discuss a draft Recommendation on the protection of sea turtles.

11/11/87   The Sixth Meeting of the Standing Committee adopted Recommendation No. 7 (1987) on the protection of marine turtles and their habitat, Recommendation No. 8 (1987) on the protection of marine turtles in Dalyan and other important areas in Turkey and Recommendation No. 9 (1987) on the protection of loggerhead turtles (*Caretta caretta*) in Laganas Bay, Zakynthos.

09/12/88   The Seventh Meeting of the Standing Committee adopted Recommendation No. 12 (1988) on the protection of important turtle nesting beaches in Turkey.

1989   The group of experts on marine turtles met to examine population status of and protection measures for marine turtles in the Mediterranean and to advise the Greek authorities. An on-the-spot appraisal of the situation on Zakynthos was made by an independent expert accompanied by a member of the Convention Secretariat.

09/12/89	The Ninth Meeting of the Standing Committee prepared measures for the consideration of the Greek government concerning Laganas Bay.

08/01/91   The Tenth Meeting of the Standing Committee adopted Recommendation No. 24 (1991) on the protection of some beaches in Turkey of particular importance to marine turtles.

02–06/12/91   The Eleventh Meeting of the Standing Committee of the Bern Convention was informed that a study to be undertaken by the Greek Government on the situation at Laganas Bay on the Greek island of Zakynthos would be completed within seven and a half months.

Some members of the Committee suggested that marine turtles should be included in the Agreement to prevent or reduce the incidence of accidental catch in nets and on long lines.

European Community

29/07/86   Motion for a Resolution B2-657/86 by Mrs Bloch von Blottnitz on the destruction of the breeding grounds of the loggerhead turtles on the Greek Island of Zante.

08/09/86   B2-657/86 referred to Environment Committee. Opinions from Budgets Committee and Committee on Youth, Culture, Education, Information and Sport (these opinions were subsequently not drawn up).

18/12/86   Environment Committee decided to draw up a report on Motion for a Resolution B2-657/86 and appointed Mr Muntingh Rapporteur.

12/07/88   Report A2-0152/88 drawn up on behalf of the Committee on the Environment, Public Health and Consumer Protection on the protection of turtles in Community waters (based on Motion for Resolution B2-657/86). Rapporteur: Hemmo Muntingh (S-NL).

16/09/88   European Parliament adopted the Resolution on protection of turtles in Community waters. (A2-0152/88).
(OJ C.262 10/10/88 p. 202)

18/11/90   COM(91)448 final a proposal for a Council Regulation laying down provisions with regard to possession and trade in specimens of species of wild fauna and flora.

KANGAROOS

Existing Legislation

Council Regulation (EEC) 3626/82 of 3 December 1982 on the implementation within the Community of the Convention on International Trade in Endangered Species of Wild Fauna and Flora.

Some species of tree kangaroo are included in Appendix II.

Work in Progress

18/11/90	COM(91)448 final a proposal for a Council regulation laying down provisions with regard to possession of and trade in specimens of species of wild fauna and flora. Proposes an Annex D which contains most animals and plants not already covered by Annex A, B and C of 3626/82, it permits import of the species it covers by way of an import declaration. Kangaroos and their products are included.

Background

European Community

19/10/83	Motion for a Resolution 1-886/83 by Mr Eisma, Mrs Lentz-Cornette, Mrs Seibel-Emmerling, Mr Johnson and Mr Beyer de Ryke on imports of kangaroo products in connection with conservation of the species.
09/10/84	Motion for a Resolution 1-643/84 by Mr Cottrell, Sir Jack Stewart-Clark, Mr Beyer de Ryke and Mr Lalor on imports of products of kangaroos in connection with conservation of species.
28/11/84	Environment Committee decided to draw up a report and appointed Mr Muntingh Rapporteur.
05/06/87	Report 2-91/87 drawn up on behalf of the Environment Committee on the import of kangaroo products. Rapporteur: Hemmo Muntingh (S-NL).
18/09/87	European Parliament adopted the Resolution on the importation of kangaroo products. (OJ C.281 19/10/87 p. 203)
03/88	Scientific Working Group of CITES discussed expanding the Convention to include an Annex D for the monitoring of imports of species originating outside the European Community.

07/88   Discussions between the Commission and the Management
               Committee and Scientific Working Group of CITES on the
               possibility of adding an Annex D to Regulation 3626/82.
               This would include all species of kangaroo not previously
               covered by the Convention in order to facilitate the monitor-
               ing of imports.

ELEPHANTS – IVORY

Existing Legislation

Council Regulation (EEC) 3626/82 of 3 December 1982 on the imple-
mentation in the Community of the Convention on International Trade in
Endangered Species of Wild Fauna and Flora.
(OJ L.384 31/12/82)

Elephas maximus (Asian elephant) and *Loxodonta africana* (African
elephant) are both listed in Appendix I of Annex A of the Regulation.
African elephant was added in October 1989.

The parts and products of these species are listed in Annex B, i.e. the
'tusks and substantial parts of the *Elephantidae* species', and 'articles made
wholly or partly of the ivory from these species'.

Under the Regulation the sale, keeping for sale, offering for sale or transporting for sale of elephants, whether dead or alive or derivatives thereof is
prohibited, subject to exemptions.

Commission Regulation (EEC) 2496/89 of 2 August 1989 on a prohibition
on importing raw and worked ivory derived from the African elephant into
the Community.
(OJ L.240 17/8/89)

The Regulation prohibits the general issue of import permits for
raw and worked ivory from the African elephant. However, under Article 1.2,
Member States may derogate from the general ban and issue permits for:

(a) musical instruments containing parts made of ivory which is proven to
    have been re-exported from the Community;

(b) antiques;

(c) hunting trophies where the hunting permit has been issued with a view
    to enhancing the survival of the population in question (the Commission
    to decide to which countries of origin this should apply);

(d) household goods personal effects (tourist souvenirs are not exempt from
    the import prohibition).

Member States must notify the Commission of any permit issued in
accordance with Article 1.2.

The Regulation was issued to prevent stock piling of ivory prior to the expected agreement to list African elephant on Appendix I of CITES.

Work in Progress

7/95	Proposal for a new EC Regulation on the implementation of CITES is being discussed in the European Parliament and the Council of Ministers.

Background

International

1985	In view of the large amount of poaching and illegal trade of this species the Conference of Parties to CITES, meeting in Buenos Aires, decided to establish a quota system for trade in raw ivory.
02–13/03/92	Eighth CITES Conference where two proposals to downlist the African elephant from Appendix I to II were presented. Both were defeated.
1994	The Ninth Meeting of the Parties to CITES was held in the USA.

European Community

14/07/83	Motion for a Resolution 1-584/83 by Mr Collins on imports of ivory in the Community.
19/07/83	Motion for a Resolution 1-602/83 by Mr Johnson on ivory imports into the EEC.
26/07/83	Motion for a Resolution 1-619/83 by Mrs Pruvot on imports of African ivory.
20/09/83	Motion for a Resolution 1-725/83 by Mrs van Hemeldonck on the import of ivory into the European Community.
24/11/83	The Environment Committee decided to draw up a Report on the basis of Motions for Resolution 1-584/83, 1-602/83, 1-619/83 and 1-725/83 and appointed Mr Johnson Rapporteur.
27/02/84	Report 1-1486/83 drawn up on behalf of the Environment Committee on the import of ivory into the Community. Rapporteur: Stanley Johnson (ED-UK).
20/12/88	Communication COM(88)721 to the Council on the conservation of the African elephant adopted by the Commission.

03/03/89   Commission Communication COM(88)721 discussed and
               endorsed by the Council.

08/06/89   The Council invited the Commission to make proposals for
               the Community to support listing the African elephant on
               Appendix I of the Convention on International Trade in
               Endangered Species to be made at the Conference of the
               Parties in October 1989, and to bring forward proposals to
               impose an immediate ban under Council Regulation 3626/82
               on the import into the Community of all raw and worked
               ivory. Pending the adoption of Community measures,
               Member States were invited to introduce urgent measures on
               a national basis to ban the import of all raw and worked ivory
               into their territory.

               In response, France suspended authorisation of further
               ivory import permits with effect from 5 June 1989, the
               United Kingdom announced a ban on all imports of raw
               and worked ivory on 9 June 1989, and on 20 June 1989 the
               Netherlands announced the banning of all ivory imports
               direct from Africa.

14/06/89   The Commission informed Member States that under Article
               10.1.b of Council Regulation (EEC) 3626/82 they should no
               longer authorise imports of African elephant ivory.

25/07/89   Motion for a Resolution 3-0001/89 by Mr Jackson on the
               decline of the elephant population caused by the trade in
               ivory.

02/08/89   Commission Regulation (EEC) 2496/89 on a prohibition on
               importing raw and worked ivory derived from the African
               elephant into the Community.
               (OJ L.240 17/8/89 p. 5)

18/11/90   COM(91)448 final a proposal for a Council Regulation
               laying down provisions with regard to possession of and
               trade in specimens of species of wild fauna and flora. (See
               CITES section for further information.)

06/90   Motion for a Resolution B3-659/90 by Mr Henri Saby and
               others on a ban on the ivory trade. Environment Committee
               decided not to draw up a report.

06/90   Motion for a Resolution B3-797/90 by Mr Peter Crampton
               and others on the UK decision to allow Hong Kong to sell
               its ivory stocks. Environment Committee decided not to
               draw up a report.

9/94   South-African and Sudanese governments request the downlisting of their African elephant populations from Appendix I to Appendix II of CITES. Motion agreed in Parliament under the topical and urgent debate procedure to refuse this.

11/94   South African authorities withdraw their proposal for downlisting of African elephant from Appendix I to Appendix II of CITES.

FROGS' LEGS

Existing Legislation

None.

Work in Progress

None.

Background

28/08/84   Motion for a Resolution 2-459/84 by Mr Pearce on imports of frogs' legs.

26/03/85   Motion for a Resolution 2-27/85 by Mr Muntingh, Mrs Seibel-Emmerling, Mr Newens, Mr Lalor, Mr Baget Bozzo, Mr Bombard, Mrs Castle, Mrs Bloch von Blottnitz, Mrs Squarcialupi, Mr Raftery, Mr Beyer de Ryke, Mr Griffiths, Mr Collins, Mr Adam, Mr Pearce, Mrs Lemass, Mr Elliott, Mr Turner, Mr Seligman, Mrs Roberts, Mrs Thome-Patenôtre, on a ban on frogs' legs imports to protect the rice cultures and health in India and Bangladesh.

18/09/86   Motion for a Resolution 2-168/86 by Mr Cassidy and Mr von Habsburg on the protection of animals and the environment in relation to India.

05/03/87   The Indian Government introduced a ban on the commercial killing and export of frogs.

13/05/87   Motion for a Resolution 2-328/87 by Mr Cassidy on the subject of a ban on Community imports of frogs' legs from India.

WILD BIRDS

Existing Legislation

Council Directive 79/409/EEC of 2 April 1979 on the conservation of wild birds.

In force: 6 April 1981.

(OJ L.103 25/4/79)

Summary

The Directive recognises that the preservation, maintenance or restoration of a sufficient diversity and area of habitats is essential to the conservation of all species of bird. Certain species of bird will be the subject of special conservation measures which will include the creation of protected areas.

Commercial interests will be prevented from exerting harmful pressure on exploitation levels by the imposition of a general ban on marketing.

Because of their high population level, geographic distribution and reproductive rate within the Community as a whole, certain species may be hunted, which constitutes acceptable exploitation.

Various means, devices or methods of large-scale or non-selective capture or killing and hunting with certain forms of transport are to be banned because of the excessive pressure which they exert on the number of the species concerned. (Methods of capture and species concerned are tabulated in the Directive.)

Every three years the Commission must prepare and transmit to the Member States a composite report based on information submitted by the Member States on the application of national provisions introduced pursuant to this Directive.

Council Regulation (EEC) 3626/82 of 3 December 1982 on the implementation in the Community of the Convention on International Trade in Endangered Species of Wild Fauna and Flora. Many species of birds are listed on the Appendices of the Convention.

(OJ L.384 31/12/82)

Council Resolution of 2 April 1979 concerning Directive 79/409/EEC on the conservation of wild birds.

Council Directive 81/854/EEC of 19 October 1981 adopting, consequent upon accession of Greece, Directive 79/409/EEC on the conservation of wild birds.

(OJ L.319 7/11/81 p. 3)

Following the Act of Accession of Greece in particular Annex I Chapter XIII, point 1(f) (OJ L.291 19/11/79), Greece is required to implement Directive 79/409/EEC directly into its legislation on its date of Accession to the EEC. The Directive also lists the species in the Annex to the Directive in the new official language.

Commission Directive 85/411/EEC of 25 July 1985 amending Council Directive 79/409/EEC on the conservation of wild birds.
(OJ L.233 30/8/85)
Adopts the Annex I of Council Directive 79/409/EEC to take account of the latest information on the situation as regards avifauna.

Council Directive 86/112/EEC of 8 April 1986 adopting, consequent upon the accession of Spain and Portugal, Directive 79/409/EEC on the conservation of wild birds.
(OJ L.100 16/4/86 p. 22)
Following their date of accession, Spain and Portugal are required to implement Directive 79/409/EEC immediately into national legislation. Act of Accession refers to Annex I, Chapter X, article 239.
(OJ L.302 15/11/85 p. 9)

Council Directive 90/656/EEC of 4 December 1990 on the transitional measures applicable in Germany with regard to certain Community provisions relating to the protection of the environment lays down how the territory of the former German Democratic Republic is to conform to the Birds Directive. The protection measures in Articles 3 and 4 of Directive 79/409/EEC must be undertaken by 31 December 1992 at the latest. Areas of special protection must be classified within six months of unification.
(OJ L.353 17/12/90)

Commission Directive 91/244/EEC of 6 March 1991 amending Council Directive 79/409/EEC on the conservation of wild birds. Replaces Annexes I and III to the Directive.
(OJ L.115 8/5/91)

European Court of Justice

08/05/85   The Commission decided to open infraction procedures pursuant to Article 169 against Member States for non-compliance with Council Directive 79/409/EEC.

31/07/85   The Commission brought legal action against the Netherlands for not implementing Council Directive 79/409/EEC. Case 236/85.
(OJ C.240 21/9/85 p. 4)

08/07/85	The Commission brought legal action against Belgium for not implementing Council Directive 79/409/EEC. Case 247/85. (OJ C.240 21/9/85 p. 4)
13/08/85	The Commission brought legal action against France for not implementing Council Directive 79/409/EEC. Case 252/85. (OJ C.235 14/9/85 p. 5)
20/08/85	The Commission brought legal action against Italy for not implementing Council Directive 79/409/EEC. Case 262/85. (OJ C.235 14/9/85)
01/10/85	The Commission brought legal action against Germany for not implementing the Birds Directive correctly. Case 412/85. (OJ C.357 31/12/85)
08/07/87	The Court of Justice brought a Ruling against Belgium and Italy for not implementing the Directive in their own legislation. Case 247/85. (OJ C.204 31/7/87)
17/09/87	The Court of Justice brought a Ruling against Germany for allowing derogations to the provisions of the Birds Directive which are not in accordance with its aims. Case 412/85. (OJ C.274 13/10/87 p. 4)
13/10/87	The Court of Justice brought a Ruling against the Netherlands for non-conformity of national legislation with certain aspects of Directive 79/409/EEC in relation to Articles 5, 8 and 9. Case 236/86.
27/04/88	The Court of Justice brought a Ruling against France for failure to adopt within the prescribed period all legal measures necessary to comply with Directive 79/409/EEC. Case 252/85.
04/10/88	The Commission brought an action against the Federal Republic of Germany (Case 288/88) on grounds that a number of provisions of federal hunting laws and independent provisions of the Länder had not been brought into line with the provisions of Directive 79/409/EEC.
28/02/89	The Commission brought an action against the Federal Republic of Germany (Case 57/89) alleging that draining and dyking protected areas in the Leybrucht and Rysumer Nacken Bonn infringed Article 4 of Directive 79/409/EEC.

02/05/89   The Commission brought an action against Italy (Case 157/89) for various contraventions of the Birds Directive.

11/89   The Commission took infringement proceedings against France for breach of Article 4 of the Birds Directive with regard to bridge building work on the Seine estuary.

03/90   The Commission brought Case 334/89 against Italy for not transposing Directive 85/411/EC which amends the Birds Directive.

23/05/90   In Case C-169/89 the Court of Justice ruled that a Dutch gourmet food shop was not in breach of the Birds Directive when it was read in conjunction with Article 36 of the Treaty.

03/07/90   The Court of Justice ruled that the Federal Republic of Germany had not fulfilled its obligations under the Birds Directive by not bringing a number of provisions into its federal and regional hunting laws. Case C-288/88.

09/90   The Commission brought Case C-155/90 against Ireland for not being more specific and providing inadequate controls under Article 9 of the Birds Directive.

30/11/90   Case C-355/90 Spain was found guilty of failing to fulfil its obligations under the Birds Directive by not giving special protection area status for wild birds to the Santona marshes which were threatened by fish farms, garbage and road construction. Spain was ordered to pay costs.

05/12/90   The Court of Justice dismissed Case 57/89 against the Federal Republic of Germany.

17/01/91   The European Court of Justice found against Italy in Case C-157/89 regarding the hunting of certain birds during breeding and migration, and Case C-334/89 for failing to implement Directive 85/411/EC.

10/92   The Commission announced proceedings on Special Protected Areas designation against the United Kingdom.

19/12/94   CASE C-435/92 – between 'Association pour la protection des animaux sauvages' and Prefects of Maine-et Loire and Loire-Atlantique on the interpretation of Article 7 §4 of Directive 79/409/EE and the setting of dates for the opening and closing of the hunting season.

8/2/96   Judgment of the Court in Case C-149/94 against Didier Vergy. The Court of Justice ruled that Directive 79/409/EEC is not applicable to specimens of birds born and reared in captivity.
(OJ C.95 30/3/96 p. 2)

7/3/96   Judgment of the Court in Case C-118/94 between the Associazione Italiana per il World Wildlife Fund and others and the Regione Veneto on conditions for exercise of the Member States' power to derogate. The Court ruled that Article 9 of Directive 79/409/EEC authorises the Member States to derogate from the general prohibition on hunting protected species laid down by Articles 5 and 7 of the Directive only by measures which refer in sufficient detail to the factors mentioned in Article 9 (1) and (2).
(OJ C.180 22/6/96 p. 1)

                    The Commission is initiating procedures against Member States which have failed to meet their obligations under Directive 79/409/EEC on wild birds. The Commission has sent an official warning to France, citing its failure to designate the Loire Estuary a special protection zone, as required by Directive 79/409/EEC. The Netherlands is to appear before the Court of Justice for having defined its protection zones inadequately.

Work in Progress

Following the adoption of the van Putten Report on hunting seasons, the Council is to adopt a Common Position with a view to amending the wild birds Directive.

Background

European Community

22/11/73   The programme of action of the European Communities on the Environment called for specific action to protect birds.
(OJ C.112 20/12/73 p. 40)

20/12/74   Commission Recommendation of 20 December 1974 to Member States concerning the protection of birds and their natural habitats.
(OJ L.21 28/1/75 p. 24)

	Summarises the study on aspects of bird protection carried out on behalf of the Commission by the 'Zoologische Gesellschaft von 1858' of Frankfurt-am-Main under the supervision of Professor Dr Bernhard Grzimek and recommends adhesion of the Community to the Convention on Wetlands of International Importance especially to Waterfowl Habitat (Ramsar 1971).
20/12/76	Proposal from the Commission to the Council for a Council Directive on bird conservation. (OJ C.24/1/77)
11/01/77	The Council asked the European Parliament and the ECOSOC for their opinions on the proposal.
14/02/77	The EP Environment Committee appointed Mr H.E. Jahn Rapporteur.
25/05/77	Opinion of the ECOSOC. (OJ C.152 29/6/77 p. 3)
31/05/77	Report 113/77 drawn up on behalf of the Environment Committee. Rapporteur: H.E. Jahn.
11/07/77	Resolution of the European Parliament embodying its opinion on the proposal from the Commission to the Council for a Directive on bird conservation. (OJ C.163 11/7/77 p. 28)
03/08/77	Modifications of a proposal presented by the Commission to the Council. (OJ C.201 23/8/77 p. 2)
30/05/78	The French Minister for the Environment rejected the Commission's draft Directive.
02/04/79	Council Directive 79/409/EEC on the conservation of wild birds. (OJ L.103 25/4/75)
06/04/81	Council Directive 79/409/EEC entered into force.
1981	Commission submitted a proposal to the Council on the application of Council Directive 79/409/EEC to Greece.
05/05/81	The European Parliament approved the proposal. (OJ C.144 15/6/81 p. 37)

19/10/81	Council Directive 81/854/EEC adopting Directive 79/409/EEC consequent upon accession of Greece. (OJ L.319 7/11/81)
1984	The Commission produced the first Report on the implementation of the Birds Directive.
17/01/85	Motion for a Resolution 1476/84 by Mrs Squarcialupi on the protection of wild birds and mammals during times of cold weather.
03/04/85	Motion for a Resolution 90/85 by Mrs Schleicher, Mr Alber, Mr Mertens on the Directive 79/409/EEC on the conservation of wild birds.
19/07/85	Commission submitted a Communication to the Council for a Commission Directive amending Council Directive 79/409/EEC on the conservation of wild birds. Changes were made to Annex I in order to take account of the latest scientific information.
25/07/85	Commission Directive 85/411/EEC amending Council Directive 79/409/EEC.
24/10/85	Motion for a Resolution 1130/85 by Mrs Braun-Moser and Mr Ciancaglini on the official authorisation of shooting in Belgium.
01/01/86	Spain and Portugal acceded to the European Economic Community.
1986	The Commission produced a Report on the review of zones of great interest for the conservation of migratory bird species from the Community to Africa. Published in Environment and the Quality of Life. EUR 10878. Commission also produced a Report on the Information Sheets on the species listed in Annex I of the Directive 79/409/EEC. Published in Environment and the Quality of Life. EUR 10879.
26/06/86	Motion for a Resolution 484/86 by Mr Remacle, Sir James Scott-Hopkins, Mr Wijsenbeek, Mr Borgo and Mr Zarges on the shooting of birds in Belgium and the conservation of wild birds.
11/09/86	Motion for a Resolution 812/86 by Mrs Bloch von Blottnitz on the hunting of migratory birds in Italy.

12/11/86   Motion for a Resolution 1166/86 by Mrs Bloch von Blottnitz and Mr Roelants du Vivier on bird catching in Belgium.

19/11/86   Public Hearing organised by the Environment Committee of the European Parliament on the extent of application within the Community and its Member States of legislation on the protection of wildlife and its environment. Consisted of discussion on the Birds Directive, Bonn and Bern Convention and CITES. Rapporteur: Hemmo Muntingh (S-NL).

21/11/86   Motion for a Resolution 1198/86 by Mrs Bloch von Blottnitz on the keeping and breeding of wild birds threatened with extinction.

09/06/87   Motion for a Resolution 454/87 by Mr Kuijpers and Mr Vandemeulebroucke on the need to protect wetlands.

14/07/87   Motion for a Resolution 733/87 by Mr Zarges and others on the conservation and control of *corvidae* in the European Community and the amendment of Council Directive 79/409/EEC.

16/07/87   Motion for a Resolution 2-749/87 by Mr Filinis on measures to redress the damage to the aquatic habitat of Prespes, a site of international importance, caused by preparatory work within the framework of the Integrated Mediterranean Programmes and national projects.

1987   The Commission published in its Environment and Quality of Life Series:

- a Report on a draft Community list of threatened species of wild flora and vertebrate fauna Vols 1 and 2. Ref: EUR 10930;

- a Report on the conservation of species of wild flora and vertebrate fauna threatened in the Community Vols 1 and 2. Ref: EUR 10931.

21/01/88   Motion for a Resolution 2-1567/87 by Mr Roelants du Vivier on the destruction of starlings' roosting sites by pesticides.

26/09/88   Report A2-0181/88 drawn up on behalf of the Environment Committee on the implementation of the Directive on the conservation of wild birds in the European Community. Rapporteur: Hemmo Muntingh (S-NL)

13/10/88   European Parliament adopted Resolution (A2-181/88) on the implementation of the Directive on the conservation of wild birds in the European Community.
(OJ C.290 14/11/88 p. 137)

10/89   Motion for a Resolution B3-288/89 by the Green Group on plans to build a military firing range in the Alcochete bird habitat. Not withheld for debate.

06/90   Motion for a Resolution B3-507/90 by Mr Juan Bandres Molet on construction projects in Txingudi Bay, Basque country, a wetland protected under the Birds Directive.

04/12/90   Council Directive 90/656/EEC on the transitional measures applicable in Germany with regard to certain Community provisions relating to the protection of the environment lays down how the territory of the former German Democratic Republic is to conform to the Birds Directive. The protection measures in Articles 3 and 4 of Directive 79/409/EEC must be undertaken by 31 December 1992 at the latest. Areas of special protection must be classified within six months of unification.
(OJ L.353 17/12/90)

18/02/91   Motion for a Resolution B3-157/91 by Mr Kostopoulos on the protection of wetlands and the conservation of birds of prey.

07/03/91   COM(91)42 proposal for a Directive amending Annex II to Directive 79/409/EEC on the conservation of wild birds.

27/03/91   COM(91)42 referred by Council to European Parliament and ECOSOC for opinions.

05/04/91   COM(91)42 proposal for a Directive amending Annex II to Directive 79/409/EEC on the conservation of wild birds referred to Environment Committee. Rapporteur: Hemmo Muntingh (S-NL)

29/05/91   CES 701/91 Opinion of ECOSOC on COM(91)42 proposal to change the status of certain corvid species, adopted. It proposes reviewing the Annexes every five years in order to be able to respond to changes in bird populations.

1992	Ninth annual report to the European Parliament on monitoring of the application of Community law includes information on the application of Directive 79/409/EEC on the conservation of wild birds in 1991. (OJ C.250 28/9/92)
18/03/92	Report A3-107/92 by Mr Muntingh on COM(91)42 adopted by Environment Committee.
14/05/92	Report A3-107/92 by Mr Muntingh on COM(91)42 proposal for a Directive amending Annex II to Directive 79/409/EEC on the conservation of wild birds adopted by European Parliament.
12/93	Commission presented second report (COM(93) 572 final) on application of Wild Birds Directive 79/409/EEC.
21/12/93	Report (PE 205.805) adopted by Environment Committee on protection and conservation of wild bird species in Community.
19/12/94	Judgment by European Court of Justice CASE C-435/92 – between 'Association pour la protection des animaux sauvages' and Prefects of Maine-et Loire and Loire-Atlantique on the interpretation of Article 7 §4 of Directive 79/409/EE and the setting of dates for the opening and closing of the hunting season.
10/2/94	Raffin report on Protection and Conservation of Wild Birds discussed and adopted in Parliamentary Plenary Session.
21/2/94	Directive 79/409/EEC – Council of Ministers adopt common position on proposed amendment.
1/3/94	COM (94) 39 final Commission's proposal for a Council Directive amending Directive 79/409/EEC on the conservation of wild birds. (OJ C.100 9/4/94 p. 12)

Summary

This new proposal does not set any definite date for closure of the hunting season for migratory birds, starting from the principle that the Member States are best placed to define the rules for the application of hunting principles. The text proposes that the Member States ensure that species to which hunting laws apply are not hunted during the rearing season nor during the reproduction period.

14/3/94	Directive 79/409/EEC – Environment Committee adopted draft decision of Councils common position amending Annex II.
28/3/94	Opinion of the Economic and Social Committee on the proposal for a Council Directive amending Directive 79/409/EEC on the conservation of wild birds. (OJ C.393 31/12/94 p. 93)
4/5/94	Directive 79/409/EEC Parliament adopts Common Position rejecting all rapporteur's amendments.
8/6/94	Directive 94/24/EC adopted. Amends Annex II to Directive 79/409/EEC on conservation of wild birds. (OJ No L164, 30.6.94, p. 9)
3/95	Directive 79/409/EEC on Conservation of Wild Birds was discussed at the March Environment Council meeting. Ministers of Environment were informed of the latest developments concerning the proposal to modify this Directive in regard to the Member States' capacity to determine hunting seasons for migratory species in the context of sustainable development. Committee of Permanent Representatives is due to resume work on this issue following the European Parliament's opinion.
25/7/95	Report A4-0337/95 drawn up on behalf of the Committee of the Environment, Public Health and Consumer Protection on the Commission's proposal for a Council Directive amending Directive 79/409/EEC on the conservation of wild birds (COM (94) 0039). Rapporteur: Maartje van Putten (PSE-N). The report on hunting seasons for wild birds was discussed for the first time in the European Parliament's Environment Committee.
31/10/95	Draft Opinion PE 214.345 of the Committee on Agriculture and Rural Development for the Committee on the Environment on the Commission's proposal COM (94) 0039. Draftsman: David John Alfred Hallam (PSE-UK). This opinion proposes to close up the hunting season on 31 January but allows hunting to continue until 28 February for species which are subject to strict management plans agreed between the Commission and the Member States.
15/2/96	The European Parliament adopted Mrs van Putten's report on the Commission's Proposal for amending Directive 79/409/

EEC. It introduces a single closing date for the hunting season of 31 January for the whole of the European Union.

FUR – WILD-CAUGHT AND TRADE – GENERAL

Existing Legislation

Council Regulation (EEC) 3254/91 of 4 November 1991 prohibiting the use of leghold traps in the Community and the introduction into the Community of pelts and manufactured goods of certain wild animal species originating in countries which catch them by means of leghold traps or trapping methods which do not meet international humane trapping standards.
(OJ L.308 9/11/91)

Summary

The leghold trap is defined in Article 1 and was to be prohibited in the Community by 1 January 1995. Imports of fur and fur products from 13 listed species are subject to Articles 3, 4 and 5 and were to be banned from 1 January 1995.

Council Directive 92/43/EEC of 21 May 1992 on the conservation of natural habitats and wild fauna and flora prohibits certain non-selective methods (Annex VI) of capture for species listed in Annex V.
(OJ L.206 22/7/92)

Regulation EC 1771/94 of 19 July 1994 adopted by Commission. Lays down provisions for the introduction into the Community of pelts and manufactured goods of certain wild animal species. Prohibition on introduction into the Community of pelts of animals in Annex I of Regulation EEC 3254/91 and of the other goods listed in Annex II of that Regulation to enter into force on 1/1/96.

Work in Progress

In accordance with Article 3 of Council Regulation (EEC) 3254/91 the Commission had to determine before 1 July 1994, as the result of a review undertaken in cooperation with the competent authorities of the countries concerned, whether sufficient progress is being made in developing humane methods of trapping in their territory, or adequate measures are in force to ban the use of the leghold trap. This process resulted in an agreement to postpone the introduction of import restrictions until 1 January 1996 as allowed for in the Regulation. In December 1995, the Commission forwarded a new text (COM (95 (737)) which proposed to postpone the import ban for a further year. The Commission has received a negotiating mandate from the Council and it is to enter into negotiations with Canada, the United States, Russia and third countries, with a view to achieving a framework agreement which is to be consistent with Regulation 3254/91.

The International Standards Organisation has attempted to draft humane trapping standards for mammals. The Technical Committee (TC191) appointed for this task has failed to reach agreement on performance criteria and has concentrated instead on a trap testing procedure. The Committee has proceeded to draw up draft standards for methods of testing of Restraining and Killing Traps. The next meeting of the TC191 was scheduled for November 1996.

Discussions between the Commission, USA, Russia and Canada on further restrictions have resulted in a working group having been set up with experts from the three parties. The report of the working group to develop humane trapping standards was published in July 1996.

On 9 December, the Environment Council adopted a statement by a qualified majority, with the Italian delegation dissenting. The Council refers to the Commission's report on the state of negotiations towards the establishment of agreed humane trapping standards. It rejects the compromise text proposed and requests the Commission to reopen negotiations with third countries, with a view to achieving a more satisfactory agreement. Furthermore, it requests the Commission to take the necessary steps as of 1st January 1997 for the introduction of an import ban to come into effect no later than 31 March 1997.

On 18 December however, the Commission decided to ignore the appeal by the Council of Environment and to go ahead with negotiations on the base of the agreement achieved. The Commission decision has been forwarded to the CITES Committee, composed of representatives of the Member States and headed by the Commission.

Background

European Community

16/10/84   Motion for a Resolution 2-736/84 by Mr Collins on an immediate ban on fur coat sales in the EEC.

21/01/88   Motion for a Resolution B2-1563/87 by Mrs Castle, Mr Elliott, Mrs Bloch von Blottnitz, Mr Garcia, Mr von

Habsburg, Mr Bombard, Mrs Thome-Patenôtre and Mr Beyer de Ryke on the steel-jawed leghold trap referred to the Environment Committee.

28/04/88   Motion for a Resolution 2-222/88 by Mrs Bloch von Blottnitz on cruelty labels for fur coats referred to the Environment Committee with opinion from the Economic Affairs Committee (which subsequently decided not to draw up an opinion).

15/06/88   Written Declaration 9/88 on the steel-jawed leghold trap. Submitted by Mrs Barbara Castle and Mr Madron Seligman signed by 272 Members of the European Parliament and subsequently forwarded to the Commission.

26/06/88   The Environment Committee decided to draw up a joint report on Motions for Resolution B2-1563/87 and B2-222/88. Rapporteur: Caroline Jackson (ED-UK).

31/08/88   COM(88)381 final a Proposal for a Council Directive on the protection of natural and semi-natural habitats and of wild fauna and flora. The proposed annex which lists prohibited methods of killing or capture contains a ban on the use of the leghold trap in the European Community.

24/11/88   COM(88)381 final referred to Environment Committee. Rapporteur: Hemmo Muntingh (S-NL).

01/12/88   The Environment Committee adopted the draft report by Mrs Jackson on Motions for Resolution B2-1563/87 and B2-222/88.

09/12/88   Report A2-303/88 drawn up on behalf of the Environment Committee on the harmonisation of legislation within the European Community on the manufacture, sale and use of the leghold trap. Rapporteur: Caroline Jackson (ED-GB).

17/02/89   Report A2-303/88 adopted by Parliament.

20/04/89   Report A2-98/89 drawn up on behalf of the Committee on External Economic Relations on relations between the EEC and Canada. (Contains references to fur trade.) Rapporteur: Hans-Jürgen Zahorka (PPE-D).

26/04/89   COM(89)198 final a Proposal for a Council Regulation on the importation of certain furs.

18/05/89	COM(89)198 Council decides to consult ECOSOC.
24/05/89	COM(89)198 Council asks Parliament to deliver an opinion.
26/05/89	European Parliament adopts the Resolution on relations between the EEC and Canada. (Report A2-98/89).
27/07/89	COM(89)198 is referred to Environment Committee with an opinion from the Committee on External Affairs. Rapporteur: Hanja Maij-Weggen (PPE-NL).
29/09/89	Report A3-39/89 by Mr Muntingh on the proposal for a habitats directive (COM(88)381 final).
12/10/89	Report A3-39/89 referred back to Environment Committee by Parliament.
01/12/89	COM(89)198 Following Mrs Maij-Weggen taking a national post the Environment Committee appointed Mrs Mary Banotti (PPE-IRL) to take over as Rapporteur.
30/03/90	COM(90)59 supplementary annexes to the Commission's proposal for a habitats directive (COM(88)381).
03/04/90	ECOSOC Environment Section adopted its opinion on COM(89)198. Draftsman: Mrs Flather.
26/04/90	CES 513/90 ECOSOC adopted its opinion COM(89)198.
30/05/90	Environment Committee adopted its report on COM(89)198 with an opinion from the Economic Affairs Committee. Rapporteur: Mrs Banotti.
07/06/90	Report A3-138/90 drawn up by Mrs Banotti on behalf of the Environment Committee on the Proposal from the Commission to the Council for a regulation on the importation of certain furs (COM(89)198 – C3-82/89) with opinion from the Committee on External Economic Relations (Draftsman: Mrs Aglietta). Included Report on visit to Canada 18–26 February 1990 by Mrs Banotti, Mr Muntingh, Mrs Weber, Mrs Bjornvig and Mr Killilea.
13/09/90	Report A3-138/90 adopted by Parliament.
17/10/90	Report A3-254/90 second report on COM(88)381 final by Mr Hemmo Muntingh accepted by Environment Committee.
18/10/90	CES 1210/90 ECOSOC adopted its opinion on the proposal for a habitats directive (COM(88)381 and COM(90)59).

19/11/90	Report A3-254/90 by Mr Muntingh on behalf of the Environment Committee on the proposed habitats directive (COM(88)381 and COM(90)59) adopted in Plenary.
25/03/91	COM(91)86 final amendment to the proposal for a Council regulation (EEC) on the importation of certain furs presented by the Commission.
04/11/91	Council Regulation (EEC) 3254/91 prohibiting the use of leghold traps in the Community and the introduction into the Community of pelts and manufactured goods of certain wild animal species originating in countries which catch them by means of leghold traps or trapping methods which do not meet international humane trapping standards.
21/05/92	Council Directive 92/43/EEC on the conservation of natural habitats and of wild fauna and flora prohibits certain non-selective methods (Annex VI) of capture for species listed in Annex V.
19/7/94	Regulation EC 1771/94 adopted by Commission. Lays down provisions for the introduction into the Community of pelts and manufactured goods of certain wild animal species. Prohibition on introduction into the Community of pelts of animals in Annex I of Regulation EEC 3254/91 and of the other goods listed in Annex II of that Regulation to enter into force on 1/1/96.
7/9/95	The Commission was questioned by Parliament on its position on the difficulty of adopting 'humane' trapping standards and of a possible WTO challenge to the Fur Regulation. The Commission's position is that the Fur Regulation has to be applied without further delay. The working group set up between the Community, Canada and USA aims to find out whether humane trapping standards exist. The Commission would enforce the ban as long as internationally agreed trapping standards had not been adopted. Discussions are being held with Canada over the effects of the Regulation on indigenous people and how they can be helped.

11/12/95   Statement by the Environment Commissioner, Mrs Ritt Bjerregaard, on leghold traps in the European Parliament. Presentation of the new Commission's proposal.

12/95   COM (95) 737 final. Proposal for a Council Regulation (EC) amending Council Regulation (EEC) No. 3254/91 prohibiting the use of leghold traps in the Community and the introduction into the Community of pelts and manufactured goods of certain wild animal species originating in countries which catch them by means of leghold traps or trapping methods which do not meet international humane trapping standards.

Summary

The new proposal deletes Article 3 of Regulation (EEC) No. 3254/91, which states that the import ban shall be implemented on 1 January 1995, to replace it with language that negotiations will be started with exporting counties to agree trapping standards. No deadline is given to complete these negotiations or for the implementation of the ban. If no agreement is reached, the Commission will list the species and countries which have not met the conditions of Article 3 (1), but no deadline is given for this list to be published. A review of the progress of the negotiations is to take place by 31st December 1996. The ban is to be applied on a species by species level. This proposal does not make any acknowledgement of the welfare problems involved.

12/12/95   The Commission was questioned by Parliament on its decision to defer once more the date of entry into force of the import ban as laid down in Regulation 3254/91. The Commission stated that the implementation of the ban, which was due to enter into force on January 1, 1996, depended on the existence of international trapping standards, which had not been set up by experts yet. The deferral should, according to the Commission, enable experts to come to an agreement on such standards. The Commission further stated that its decision had been taken in accordance with the Commission's right of initiative, and on basis of Articles 113 and 130s of the Treaty. The Parliament would take part in the decision following the cooperation procedure.

29/5/96   Opinion of the Economic and Social Committee on COM
           (95) 737 final.
           (OJ C.212 22/7/96 p. 48)

18/6/96   Debate in Parliament on leghold traps. Mr Carlos Pimenta
           introduced his report on the Commissions proposal.

19/6/96   Report A4-0151/96 on behalf of the Committee on the
           Environment, Public Health and Consumer Protection was
           adopted by the European Parliament. Rapporteur: Mr Carlos
           Pimenta (ELDR-P).

Summary

Mr Pimenta's Report maintains the integrity of Regulation 3254/91 and
keeps Article 3(1). The report specifies that the import ban remains in
force until a trapping standard is agreed. Once agreement is reached, the
Commission can submit a proposal to suspend the import prohibition.
The text sets a timetable for implementing the ban not exceeding 12
months. It keeps the intent of the original Regulation by applying the ban
to all species at once. It rejects implementation on the basis of individual
species, which is unworkable due to the indiscriminate nature of leghold
traps.

19/6/96   Resolution A4-0151/96 adopted by the European Par-
           liament on the Commissions proposal for amending
           Regulation (EEC) No. 3254/91.

5/6/96   Draft Opinion PE 216.532 on behalf of the Committee of
           External Relations for the Committee on the Environment.
           Draftsman: Mr Kyösti Toivonen (PPE-FI).

9/12/96   On 9 December, the Environment Council adopted a state-
           ment by a qualified majority, with the Italian delegation
           dissenting. The Council refers to the Commission's report
           on the state of negotiations towards the establishment of
           agreed humane trapping standards. It rejects the com-
           promise text proposed and requests the Commission to
           reopen negotiations with third countries, with a view to
           achieving a more satisfactory agreement. Furthermore, it
           requests the Commission to take the necessary steps as of
           1st January 1997 for the introduction of an import ban to
           come into effect no later than 31 March 1997.

On 18 December however, the Commission decided to ignore the appeal by the Council of Environment and to go ahead with negotiations on the base of the agreement achieved. The Commission decision has been forwarded to the CITES Committee, composed of representatives of the Member States and headed by the Commission.

Chapter 2

Farm Animals

FARM ANIMAL WELFARE – GENERAL

Existing Legislation

Council Decision 78/923/EEC of 19 June 1978 concerning the conclusion of the European Convention for the Protection of Animals kept for Farming Purposes.
(OJ L.323 17/11/78)

Summary

The Convention applies to the keeping, care and housing of animals used for farming purposes and seeks to establish a framework for minimum welfare standards, particularly for animals in modern stock farming systems. The EEC is a contracting party to the Convention and participates in the meetings of the Standing Committee of the Convention.

Directive 89/608/EEC of 21 November 1989 lays down how the national authorities responsible for enforcing legislation on veterinary and zoo-technical matters, specifically including animal welfare, shall cooperate with their colleagues in other Member States.

Council Decision 90/84/EEC of 26 February 1990 concerning the Second Agricultural Research Programme includes alternative livestock production systems for possible financing

Council Regulation (EEC) 2078/92 of 30 June 1992 on agricultural production methods compatible with the requirements of the protection of the environment and maintenance of the countryside. Sets up a Community aid scheme to include, *inter alia*, the rearing of animals of local breeds in danger of extinction up to ECU 100 per unit of livestock.

Council Decision 92/583/EEC of 14 December 1992 on the conclusion of the Protocol of amendment to the European Convention for the Protection of Animals kept for farming purposes.
(OJ L.395 31/12/92)

Council Directive 96/24/EC of 29/4/96 amending Directive 79/373/EEC on the marketing of compound feedingstuffs.

Council Resolution of 25/6/96 on measures to be implemented under veterinary policy.

Work in Progress

COM(92)192 final a proposal for a Council Directive concerning the protection of animals kept for farming purposes. Council decision is still awaited after the Parliamentary report on 19/11/92.

Background

Council of Europe

20/01/71   Assembly debate on Recommendation 620 (1971) on the problems of animal welfare in industrial stockbreeding based on a Report by the Committee on Agriculture.

07/71   Consultative Assembly debate on the draft Convention on Animal Welfare in Intensive Rearing appended to Recommendation 641 (1971).

    The draft had been elaborated by the Committee on Agriculture on the basis of a text presented by the World Federation for the Protection of Animals.

    The Council of Ministers decided to submit the draft Convention proposed by the Assembly to the Committee of Experts for the Protection of Animals.

25/01/74   The Committee of Experts for the Protection of Animals submitted a draft Convention to the Committee of Ministers.

    The Committee of Ministers requested the opinion of the European Committee on Legal Co-operation (CCJ).

    The Committee of Ministers adopted the text of the European Convention on the Protection of Animals kept for Farming Purposes.

10/03/76   European Convention No. 87 for the Protection of Animals Kept for Farming Purposes opened for signature.

    In force: 10 September 1978. (See Appendix VI.)

22/02/79   First Meeting of the Standing Committee of the European Convention for the Protection of Animals kept for Farming Purposes.

    The Committee drew up its Rules of Procedure.

11/79   Second Meeting of the Standing Committee.

1981–5/82   During this period the Committee solely concerned itself with egg laying hens. (See Battery Hens).

27/05/82   At the Seventh Meeting of the Committee it was decided to elaborate a draft recommendation concerning the welfare of pigs kept for farming purposes while waiting for the EEC to adopt its draft Directive on egg laying hens in battery cages.

08/03/83   At its Eighth Meeting the Committee discussed the draft recommendation on pigs.

1984–1986   The Standing Committee continued its discussion of the draft recommendations for pigs and laying hens.

18/11/86   At its Fourteenth Meeting the Standing Committee adopted:

- A Recommendation concerning poultry of species *Gallus gallus* kept to produce eggs;

- a Recommendation concerning pigs.

(See Battery Hens and Pigs).
At this meeting the Standing Committee also started elaborating a draft recommendation for cattle.

21/11/87   The Recommendations concerning pigs and poultry entered into force.

21/10/88   Third Report of the Committee of Ministers adopted at the seventeenth Meeting of the Standing Committee. This noted the Committee's work concerning pigs, poultry, fur animals and biotechnology. The Standing Committee also adopted the Recommendation concerning cattle.

26/09/89   Nineteenth Meeting of the Standing Committee postponed the proposed Appendix C to the Recommendation concerning cattle (Special Provisions for Veal Calves).

21/10/89   The Recommendation of 21 October 1988 concerning cattle took effect.

11/89   Council of Europe Centre Naturopa published 'Farming and Wildlife'.

23/01/90   Bureau of the European Convention for the Protection of Animals kept for Farming Purposes met and discussed various matters including the postponed recommendation on calves; it was agreed to draft recommendations on sheep and goats.

24/04/90	Twentieth Meeting of the Standing Committee of the European Convention for the Protection of Animals kept for Farming Purposes discussed recommendations on, respectively, pigs, poultry and cattle. Discussion of draft recommendations: an amendment to the Convention to cover biotechnology; veal calves; goats and sheep were deferred to the next meeting.
22/05/90	Draft interim report to Council of Ministers noted the work of the Standing Committee in relation to cattle, fur animals, sheep, goats and biotechnology.
16/10/90	Twenty-first Meeting of the Standing Committee of the European Convention for the Protection of Animals kept for Farming Purposes discussed a number of matters including the draft Protocol of amendment to the Convention, and the draft recommendations on sheep and goats. Also, due to the progress made at EC level in the discussion on the draft directive on the keeping of calves, the Standing Committee reopened the discussion on Appendix C.
22/05/91	Twenty-second Meeting of the Standing Committee of the European Convention for the Protection of Animals kept for Farming Purposes met to discuss a number of matters including the Appendix to the Recommendation on cattle concerning calves which was shelved until the EEC veal calf legislation has been completed; the draft Protocol of amendment to the Convention (which was agreed); the draft recommendations on sheep and goats; the draft recommendation on broilers. Elaboration of a Recommendation on poultry for slaughter begun.
08/10/91	Twenty-third Meeting of the Standing Committee of the European Convention for the Protection of Animals kept for Farming Purposes. Again the draft Appendix on calves was deferred until the EEC Directive is in force. The draft recommendation on sheep was considered. The draft recommendations on goats and broilers were deferred.
15/11/91	Protocol of amendment to the European Convention for the Protection of Animals kept for Farming Purposes adopted by the Committee of Ministers. Open for signature on 6 February 1992.
02/06/92	Twenty-fourth Meeting of the Standing Committee of the European Convention for the Protection of Animals kept for Farming Purposes.

19/10/92	Protocol of Amendment to the European Convention for the protection of animals kept for farming purposes (Strasbourg 06/02/92) – Cyprus signed.
20/10/92	European Convention for the protection of animals kept for farming purposes (Strasbourg 10/03/76) – accession by Slovenia.
11/92	Twenty-fifth Meeting of the Standing Committee of the European Convention for the Protection of Animals kept for Farming Purposes adopted unanimously the Recommendations concerning sheep and goats.
22/12/92	European Convention for the Protection of animals kept for farming purposes (Strasbourg 10/05/79) – ratified by Austria.
20/01/93	Protocol of Amendment to the European Convention for the protection of animals kept for farming purposes (Strasbourg 06/02/92) – Denmark ratified.
08/03/93	Protocol of Amendment to the European Convention for the protection of animals kept for farming purposes (Strasbourg 06/02/92) – Portugal ratified.
02/06/93	Protocol of Amendment to the European Convention for the protection of animals kept for farming purposes (Strasbourg 06/02/92) – Cyprus ratified.
3–11/6/93	Twenty-sixth Meeting of the Standing Committee of the European Convention for the Protection of Animals kept for Farming Purposes adopted Recommendations concerning special provisions for calves.
8/6/93	Following the adoption of the EC Directive on 19 November 1991, the Standing Committee adopted the completed draft Appendix C to the Recommendation on Cattle – Special provisions for Calves (Appendix C enters into force on 8/12/93).
2–5/11/93	Twenty-seventh Meeting of the Standing Committee of the European Convention for the Protection of Animals kept for Farming Purposes elaborated Recommendations concerning domestic fowl (broilers) and other poultry species (duck, goose, turkey, guinea-fowl, quail, partridge, pigeon, pheasant) and Ratites (ostrich, emu, rhea).
26–29/4/94	Twenty-eighth Meeting of the Standing Committee of the European Convention for the Protection of Animals kept

for Farming Purposes further elaborated Recommendations concerning domestic fowl (broilers) and other poultry species (duck, goose, turkey, guinea-fowl, quail, partridge, pigeon, pheasant) and Ratites (ostrich, emu, rhea).

23/11/94 Protocol of Amendment to the European Convention for the protection of animals kept for farming purposes (Strasbourg 06/02/92) – Switzerland signed.

30/03/94 European Convention for the protection of animals kept for farming purposes (Strasbourg 10/03/76) – accession by former Yugoslavian Republic of Macedonia.

15/11/94 Protocol of Amendment to the European Convention for the protection of animals kept for farming purposes (Strasbourg 06/02/92) – Germany ratified.

21/12/94 Protocol of Amendment to the European Convention for the protection of animals kept for farming purposes (Strasbourg 06/02/92) – Switzerland ratified.

29/12/94 European Convention for the protection of animals kept for farming purposes (Strasbourg 10/03/76) – accession by Bosnia Herzegova.

14/09/94 European Convention for the protection of animals kept for farming purposes (Strasbourg 10/03/76) – Accession by Croatia.

25–28/4/95 Twenty-ninth Meeting of the Standing Committee of the European Convention for the Protection of Animals Kept for Farming Purposes further elaborated Recommendations concerning domestic fowl (broilers) and other poultry species (duck, goose, turkey, guinea-fowl, quail, partridge, pigeon, pheasant) and Ratites (ostrich, emu, rhea).

28/11–1/12/95 Thirtieth Meeting of the Standing Committee of the European Convention for the Protection of Animals Kept for Farming Purposes examined Recommendations on pigs, poultry, cattle, fur animals, sheep and goats. Adopted a Recommendation on domestic fowl (*Gallus gallus*) replacing the Recommendation on poultry adopted on 21 November 1986. The Committee further examined Recommendations concerning domestic duck, Muscovy duck and crossbreeds of Muscovy and Pekin duck, and ratites.

23–26/4/96 Thirty-first Meeting of the Standing Committee of the European Convention for the Protection of Animals Kept for Farming Purposes examined Recommendations on pigs, poultry, cattle, fur animals, sheep and goats. It proposed amendments for the draft Recommendation concerning domestic duck, Muscovy duck and crossbreeds of Muscovy and Pekin duck, ratites and fur animals.

8–11/10/96 Thirty-second Meeting of the Standing Committee of the European Convention for the Protection of Animals Kept for Farming Purposes is due to examine the draft Recommendations on fur animals, domestic duck, Muscovy duck and hybrids of Muscovy duck and domestic duck, domestic goose and fur animals.

European Community

24/04/76 Proposal from the Commission to the Council for a Council Decision concluding the European Convention for the protection of farm animals.
(OJ C.133 14/6/76 p. 6)

10/05/76 The President of the Council consulted the European Parliament and the ECOSOC on the proposal.

19/05/76 The EP Committee on Agriculture appointed Mrs Gwyneth Dunwoody Rapporteur.

30/06/76 Opinion of the ECOSOC.
(OJ C.204 30/8/76 p. 26)

28/02/77 Report 566/76 drawn up on behalf of the Committee on Agriculture. Rapporteur: Gwyneth Dunwoody.

11/03/77 Opinion of the European Parliament.
(OJ C.83 4/4/77 p. 43)

19/06/78 Council Decision 78/923/EEC. The Council approved the European Convention for the Protection of Animals kept for Farming Purposes.
(OJ L.323 17/11/78 p. 12)

10/79 The Commission called together an ad hoc expert group on farm animal welfare.

02/80 The Commission set up a Farm Animal Welfare Programme as part of the Second Programme for Coordinated Agricultural Research. It had two lines of action:

- coordinated activity aimed at bringing researchers together by means of seminars on a wide range of topics;

- common activity aimed at funding research projects which it considered to be of priority in the European Community.

These concentrated on poultry welfare.

03/06/83   Motion for a Resolution 1-381/83 by Mr Woltjer, Mrs Seibel-Emmerling, Mr Eisma, Mrs van Hemeldonck, Mr Gatto, Mr Johnson, Mrs Krouwel-Vlam, Mrs Maij-Weggen, Mrs Pantazi, Mrs Vgenopoulos and Mrs Weber on animal welfare policy.

1984   The Commission produced an evaluation Report (1979–1983) of the Farm Animal Welfare Programme (EUR 9180 Report).

24/09/84   The Committee on Agriculture, Fisheries and Food decided to draw up a Report on animal welfare policy and appointed Mr Richard Simmonds Rapporteur.

10/06/85   Interim Report A2-62/85 on behalf of the Committee on Agriculture, Fisheries and Food on animal welfare policy. Rapporteur: Richard Simmonds (ED-UK).

12/07/85   The European Parliament adopted the Resolution on animal welfare policy.
(OJ C.229 9/9/85 p. 126)

19–20/06/86   The EP Committee on Agriculture, Fisheries and Food organised a Public Hearing on Animal Welfare. It brought together experts composed of animal welfarists, producers, vets, scientists and consumer representatives in order to discuss the intensive rearing of veal calves and pigs, the keeping of laying hens and the transport of live animals.

19/12/86   Report A2-211/85 on behalf of the Committee on Agriculture, Fisheries and Food on animal welfare policy. Rapporteur: Richard Simmonds (ED-UK).

20/02/87   European Parliament adopted Resolution on animal welfare policy (A2-211/85).
(OJ C.76 23/3/87 p. 162)

Called on the Commission to draw up a proposal for a Directive to embody the European Convention on the protection of animals kept for farming purposes. Also called for action concerning the intensive rearing of battery hens, pigs, veal calves and the transport of live animals.
Voting: 150–0 with two abstentions.

17/03/87   Motion for a Resolution 76/87 by Mrs Lizin on the effect of high tension electricity lines on livestock.

30/05/88   Motion for a Resolution 2-296/88 by Mrs Bloch von Blottnitz on imports of stuffed ducklings from China.

27/07/89   Commission proposal to amend Regulations 797/85, 1096/85, 1360/78, 389/82 and 1696/71 with a view to speeding up the adjustment of agricultural production structures referred to Agriculture Committee.

28/08/89   Environment Committee appointed Mrs Adriana Ceci (GUE-I) Rapporteur on COM(89)9 a proposal for a regulation concerning the trade in poultry and hatching eggs.

16/10/89   Report A3-51/89 on Commission proposal to amend Regulations 797/85, 1096/85, 1360/78, 389/82 and 1696/71 with a view to speeding up the adjustment of agricultural production structures. Debated in European Parliament and voted on. All animal welfare amendments were adopted. The Commission said it would support these animal welfare amendments.

21/11/89   Directive 89/608/EEC adopted by Agriculture Council, lays down how the national authorities responsible for enforcing legislation on veterinary and zootechnical matters, specifically including animal welfare, shall cooperate with their colleagues in other Member States.

22/03/90   Draft Report A3-77/90 by Mrs Ceci (GUE-I) on COM(89)9 a proposal for a regulation concerning the trade in poultry and hatching eggs, adopted by Environment Committee.

05/90   Report A3-77/90 by Mrs Ceci (GUE-I) on COM(89)9 debated in Plenary. Commissioner MacSharry objected to the references to animal welfare because they went beyond the scope of the regulation. The report was referred back to Environment Committee.

28/06/90   A3-77/90 on COM(89)9. Environment Committee considered interim report by Mrs Ceci (GUE-I), on one of the main points of conflict with the Commission.

19/04/91   A3-77/90 on COM(89)9 proposal for a regulation concerning the trade in poultry and hatching eggs. Adopted by European Parliament. Rapporteur: Adriana Ceci (GUE-I).

18/05/92	COM(92)192 final a proposal for a Council Directive concerning the protection of animals kept for farming purposes.
12/06/92	COM(92)192 final a proposal for a Council Directive concerning the protection of animals kept for farming purposes referred to Agriculture Committee. Rapporteur: Richard Simmonds (ED-UK).
30/06/92	Council Regulation (EEC) 2078/92 on agricultural production methods compatible with the requirements of the protection of the environment and maintenance of the countryside. Sets up a Community aid scheme to include, *inter alia*, the rearing of animals of local breeds in danger of extinction up to ECU 100 per unit of livestock.
06/92	COM(92)243 proposal for a Council decision on the conclusion of the Protocol of amendment to the European Convention for the Protection of Animals kept for Farming Purposes, referred to Agriculture Committee for report.
10/07/92	COM(92)243 proposal for a Council decision on the conclusion of the Protocol of amendment to the European Convention for the Protection of Animals kept for Farming Purposes, referred to Agriculture Committee. Rapporteur: Richard Simmonds (ED-UK).
22/10/92	ECOSOC opinion on the proposal for a Council Decision on the conclusion of the Protocol of amendment to the European Convention for the Protection of Animals kept for Farming Purposes. Rapporteur: Mr Wick. (OJ C.332 16/12/92)
3/11/92	COM[92]408 Commission proposal for a Council Regulation amending Regulation EEC/805/68 on the common organisation of the market in beef and veal. Parliament nominated Mr Hory (S-F) rapporteur.
3/11/92	Draft Report [PE201.355] by Mr Garcia (LDR-P) on BSE adopted by Parliamentary Agriculture Committee.
19/11/92	Draft Report [PE201.034] by Mr Debatisse (PPE-F) on Commission proposal [COM(92)148 final] for a Council Regulation concerning the identification and registration of animals was adopted by parliamentary agriculture committee. Amendments 1–16 inc were adopted; 17–21 were rejected and concerned mostly the method of marking or identifying cattle.

19/11/92	Report A3-339/92 by Mr Simmonds on proposal for a Council Directive concerning the protection of farm animals kept for farming purposes and on the conclusion of the Protocol of amendment adopted by Parliament. (OJ C.322 15/12/92)
14/12/92	Council Decision 92/583/EEC on the conclusion of the Protocol of amendment to the European Convention for the Protection of Animals kept for farming purposes. (OJ L.395 31/12/92)
1/93	COM(92)460 final amended Commission proposal concerning a regulation on the protection of animals at the time of slaughter or killing has been referred to the Agriculture and Environment Committees.
1/93	COM(92)324 on animal feedstuffs. Mr Borgo (PPE-I) appointed rapporteur.
27/1/93	Commission proposal [COM(92)3224 final] for a Council Regulation EEC on feedingstuffs intended for particular nutritional purposes.
5/2/93	ECOSOC adopted its opinion on commission proposal [COM(92)462 final] for a Council Directive amending Council directive [88/407/EEC] of 14 June laying down the animal health requirements applicable to intra-community trade in and imports of deep-frozen semen of domestic animals of the bovine species and extending it to cover fresh bovine semen. Rapporteur: Mr Proumens.
12/2/93	COM(92)0462 for a Council Directive amending Dir 88/407/EEC adopted by Parliament. Directive lays down animal health requirements applicable to intra-community trade in and imports of deep frozen semen of domestic bovines extended to cover fresh semen.
2/3/93	Future action concerning the Labelling of products was discussed at Council of Ministers consumer protection and information meeting. Resolution adopted containing an annex detailing issues to be addressed by the Commission, such as the relevancy of labelling, that it should 'not be misleading and contain information enabling consumers to make purchasing decisions based on the information they find important regarding a particular product'. Resolution concludes that the Commission should address the issues listed and present appropriate proposals by June 1994. Council recognises that

existing national legislation is insufficient for all products and that there is disparity of existing legislation on labelling which creates barriers to trade within the Community.

12/3/93 [COM(92)0428] proposal for a Council Regulation amending (EEC)2771/75 on the common organisation of the market in eggs.

12/3/93 [COM(92)0578] proposal for a Council Directive on the statistical surveys to be carried out on sheep and goat production.

12/3/93 COM(92)0579 proposal on a Council directive on the surveys to be carried out on bovine animals production.

1/4/93 Environment Committee discussion of Draft Report on Commission proposal [COM(91)536 final] for a Council Directive amending Directive 79/112/EEC on the approximation of laws relating to labelling, presentation and advertising of foodstuffs.

23/4/93 COM(93)0055 – MEPs adopted Commission proposal for a Council Directive amending Directive 89/556/EEC on Animal Health conditions governing intra-Community trade in and importation from third countries of embryos of domestic animals of the bovine species.

22/10/93 Commission submitted proposal for a Council Directive fixing principles governing the organisation of inspections in the field of animal nutrition.
(OJ No. C313 p. 10)

17/12/93 Directive 93/117/EC – adopted by Commission on analysis methods for control of feedstuffs.
(OJ No. 329, 30/12/93 p. 54)

17/12/93 Decision 93/682/EC – third amendment of Decision 93/197/EEC adopted by Commission.
(OJ No. L317, 18.12.93 p. 82)

22/12/93 Judgment by European Court of Justice on CASE C-348/92 *Commission* v *Ireland* failure to transpose directives on breeding animals of porcine species, sheep and goats.
(OJ No. C43, 12/2/94, p. 2)

10/1/94 Commission proposal for Council Directive amending and updating Directive 64/432/EEC on health problems affecting intra-Community trade in bovine animals and swine.
(OJ No. C33, 2/2/94 p. 1)

26/1/94   Decision 94/43/EC published by Commission – amending Decision 93/13/EEC on veterinary checks at Community border inspection posts on products from third countries.
(OJ L.23, 28/1/94 p. 33)

28/1/94   Commission proposal submitted for Council Directive amending Directive 90/428/EEC on trade in competition equidae.
(OJ C.51 19/2/94 p. 6)

31/1/94   Decision 94/63/EEC published by Commission – provisional list of third countries authorised to import into EC semen, ova, embryos of ovine, caprine, equine species, ova and embryos of porcine species.
(OJ L.28, 2/2/94 p. 47)

11/3/94   (COM(93)0587) Report by Mr Borgo on proposal for Council Regulation on approval of certain establishments operating in animal feed sector.

30/8/94   Amended proposal for a Council Directive fixing the principles governing the organisation of inspections in the field of animal nutrition.
(OJ C.242, 30.8.94, p. 11)

7/11/94   Regulations 2701/94 and 2703/94 adopted by Commission. Amends Annexes I, II, III of Council Regulation 2377/90 on procedure for establishment of maximum residue limits of veterinary medicinal products in foodstuffs of animal origin.

5/10/94   Case C-323 on artificial bovine insemination and geographical monopolies. ECJ insisted that Articles 90(1) and 86 of Treaty of Rome do not preclude a Member State from granting to approved bovine insemination centres certain exclusive rights within a defined area.
(OJ C.331, 26.11.94, p. 2)

21/12/94   Decision 94/988/EC adopted by Commission. Amends Decision 94/24/EC drawing up a list of border inspection posts preselected for veterinary checks on products and animals from third countries.

7/4/95   Decision 95/140/EC adopted by Commission amending Decision 91/449/EEC laying down the specimen animal health certificates in respect of meat products imported from third countries.
(OJ L.91, 22.4.95, p. 56)

| 7/4/95 | Directive 95/9/EC adopted by Commission amending Directive 94/39/EC establishing a list of intended uses of animal feeding stuffs for particular nutritional purposes.
(OJ L.91, 22.4.95, p. 35) |

| 4/5/95 | Directive 95/11/EC adopted by Commission amending Council Directive 87/153/EEC fixing guidelines for the assessment of additives in animal nutrition.
(OJ L.106, 11/5/95, p. 23) |

| 29/6/95 | Council Decision 95/29/EC amending Directive 91/628/EEC concerning the protection of animals during transport.
(OJ L.148 30/6/95 p. 52) |

| 10/7/95 | Directive 95/33/EC adopted by Commission amending Council Directive 82/471/EEC concerning certain products used in animal nutrition.
(OJ L.167, 18/7/95, p. 17) |

| 18/7/95 | Decision 95/287/EC adopted by Commission amending Decision 94/474/EEC concerning certain protection measures relating to bovine spongiform encephalopathy and repealing Decisions 89/469/EEC and 90/200/EEC.
(OJ L.181 1/8/95 p. 40) |

| 25/7/95 | Decision 95/332/EC adopted by Commission amending Council Decision 79/542/EEC and Commission Decisions 92/260/EEC, 93/195/EEC, 93/196/EEC and 93/197/EEC with regard to the animal health conditions and veterinary certification for the temporary admission and re-entry of registered horses and imports into the Community of equidae for slaughter, registered equidae and equidae for breeding and production from Morroco.
(OJ L.190 11/8/95 p. 9) |

| 19/9/95 | Decision 95/388/EC adopted by Commission determining the specimen certificate for intra-Community trade in semen, ova and embryos of the ovine and caprine species.
(OJ L.234 3/10/95 p. 30) |

| 18/9/95 | Decision 95/380/EC adopted by Commission amending Commission Decisions 94/432/EC, 94/433/EC and 94/434/EC laying down detailed rules for the application of Council Directives 93/23/EEC on the statistical surveys to be carried out on pig production, 93/24/EEC on the statistical surveys to be carried out on bovine animal production and Council |

Directive 93/25/EEC on the statistical surveys to be carried out on sheep and goat stocks.
(OJ L.228 23/9/95 p. 25)

12/10/95   Judgment of the Court in Case C-257/94 between the Commission of the European Communities and Italy for failure to transpose Directive 91/685/EEC introducing Community measures for the control of classical swine-fever and Council Directive 91/688/EEC on health and veterinary inspection problems upon importation of bovine, ovine and caprine animals. The Court ordered the Italian republic to pay the costs.

24/10/95   COM (95) 491 final Proposal for a council Directive amending Directive 92/117/EEC concerning measures for protection against specified zoonoses and specified zoonotic agents in animals and products of animal origin in order to prevent outbreaks of food-borne infections and intoxications.
(OJ C.13 118/1/96 p. 23)

13/10/95   Decision 95/434/EC adopted by Commission on the list of programmes for the eradication and monitoring of animal diseases qualifying for a financial contribution from the community in 1996.
(OJ L.256 26/10/96 p. 57)

24/10/95   Decision 95/469/EC adopted by Commission on the list of programmes of checks aimed at the prevention of zoonoses qualifying for a financial contribution from the Community in 1996.
(OJ L.269 11/11/95 p. 26)

31/10/95   Directive 95/55/EC adopted by Commission amending Council Directive 70/524/EEC concerning additives in feedingstuffs.
(OJ L.263 4/11/95, p. 18)

31/10/95   Decision 95/476/EC adopted by Commission on financial assistance from the Community for storage in Italy of antigen for production of foot-and-mouth disease vaccine.
(OJ L.271 14/11/95 p. 19)

15/11/96   Decision 95/491/EC adopted by Commission on financial aid from the Community for the operation of the Community reference laboratory for swine vesicular disease, Pirbright, United Kingdom.
(OJ L.282 24/11/95 p. 23)

18/11/95   Decision 95/483/EC adopted by Commission determining the specimen certificate for intra-Community trade in ova and embryos of swine.
(OJ L.275 18/11/95 p. 30)

1/12/95   Decision 95/535/EC adopted by Commission on an additional financial contribution from the Community for the eradication of classical swine fever in Germany.
(OJ L.304 16/12/95 p. 47)

12/12/95   Decisions 96/49-50-51/EC adopted by Commission approving the programme for the eradication of Aujeszky's disease for 1996 presented by Portugal, the Netherlands and the UK and fixing the level of the Community's financial contribution.
(OJ L.16 22/1/96 pp. 9–11)

12/12/95   Decisions 96/52-53/EC adopted by Commission approving the programme for the eradication of contagious bovine pleuropneumonia for 1996 presented by Spain and Portugal and fixing the level of the Community's financial contribution.
(OJ L.16 22/1/96 pp. 12–13)

13/12/95   Decisions 96/54-55-56 EC adopted by Commission approving the programme for the eradication of infectious haematopoietic necrosis for 1996 presented by Spain and Portugal and Finland and fixing the level of the Community's financial contribution.
(OJ L.16 22/1/96 pp. 14–16)

13/12/95   Decisions 96/57-58/EC adopted by Commission approving the programme for the eradication of enzootic bovine leucosis for 1996 presented by Spain and Sweden and fixing the level of the Community's financial contribution.
(OJ L.16 22/1/96 pp. 17–18)

13/12/95   Decision 96/5/EC adopted by Commission repealing decision 94/514/EC concerning certain protection measures with regard to foot-and-mouth disease in Greece.
(OJ L.1 3/1/96 p. 12)

13/12/95   Decisions 96/62-63-64/EC adopted by Commission approving the programme for the eradication of bovine brucellosis for 1996 presented by France, Ireland, Spain and Portugal and fixing the level of the Community's financial contribution.
(OJ L.16 22/1/96 pp. 2–5)

13/12/95   Decision 96/59/EC adopted by Commission approving the programme for the eradication of bovine brucellosis for 1996

presented by France, Italy and Portugal and fixing the level of the Community's financial contribution.
(OJ L.16 22/1/96 pp. 19–21)

15/12/95   Decision 96/70/EC adopted by Commission approving the programme for the eradication of bovine tuberculosis for 1996 presented by Spain and fixing the level of the Community's financial contribution.
(OJ L.16 22/1/96 p. 30)

19/12/95   Decision 96/32/EC adopted by Commission amending Decision 93/13/EEC laying down the procedures for veterinary checks at Community border inspection posts on products from third countries.
(OJ L.9 12/1/96 p. 9)

20/12/95   Decision 96/35/EC adopted by Commission amending Decision 95/357/EC drawing up a list of border inspection posts agreed for veterinary checks on products and animals from third countries detailed rules concerning the checks to be carried out by the veterinary experts of the Commission and repealing Decision 94/24/EC.
(OJ L.10 13/1/96 p. 40)

10/1/96   Decision 96/78/EC adopted by Commission laying down the criteria for entry and registration of equidae in stud-books for breeding purposes.
(OJ L.19 25/1/96 p. 39)

12/1/96   Decision 96/107/EC adopted by Commission concerning the specific financial contribution by the Community towards the eradication of foot-and-mouth disease in Greece.
(OJ L.25 1/2/96 p. 57)

Decision 96/79/EC adopted by Commission laying down the zootechnical certificates of semen, ova and embryos from registered equidae.
(OJ L.19 25/1/96 p. 41)

Decision 96/81/EC adopted by Commission amending Decisions 92/260/EEC, 93/196/EEC and 93/197/EEC with regard to the categories of male equidae to which apply the requirements on equine viral arteritis.
(OJ L.19 25/1/96 p. 53)

Decision 96/82/EC adopted by Commission amending Council Decisions 93/196/EEC and 93/197/EEC with regard to the animal health certificates for imports of equidae for

slaughter, registered equidae and equidae for breeding and production, with regard to piroplasmosis.
(OJ L.19 25/1/96 p. 56)

12/1/96   Decision 96/97/EC adopted by Commission amending Decision 92/542/EEC establishing lists of embryo collection teams and embryo production teams approved in third countries for export of bovine embryos to the Community.
(OJ L.23 30/1/96 p. 20)

Decision 96/80/EC adopted by Commission laying down the specimen pedigree certificates for the ova of breeding animals of the bovine species and the particulars to be entered on those certificates.
(OJ L.19 25/1/96 p. 50)

24/1/96   Decision 96/130/EC amending Decision 93/693/EC concerning a list of semen collection centres approved for the export to the Community of semen of domestic animals of the bovine species.
(OJ L.30 8/2/96 p. 50)

1/2/96   Opinion of the Economic and Social Committee on COM (95) 491 Opinion on the Proposal for a Council Directive amending Directive 92/117/EEC.
(OJ C.97 1/4/96 p. 29)

13/2/96   Publication of the list of coordinating authorities responsible for collecting data concerning competitions for equidae in accordance with Commission Directive 92/216/EEC.
(OJ C.41 13/2/96 p. 3)

14/2/96   COM (96) 44 final Commission's proposal for 27 Council Regulations on the price for agricultural products and related measures (1996/1997 Price Package). It proposes to delete the second premium for bulls and to increase the first premium to be given when the bull is 10 months of age.
(OJ C.125 27/4/96 p. 29)

16/2/96   Directive 96/6/EC adopted by Commission amending Council Directive 74/63/EEC on undesirable substances and products in animal nutrition.
(OJ L.49, 28/2/96, p. 29)

21/2/96   Directive 96/7/EC adopted by Commission amending Council Directive 70/524/EEC concerning additives in feedingstuffs.
(OJ L.51, 1/3/96, p. 45)

26/2/96   Decision 96/279/EC adopted by Commission amending Council Decision 79/542/EEC and Commission Decisions 92/260/EEC, 93/196/EEC and 93/197/EEC.
(OJ L.107 30/4/96 p. 1)

16/4/96   The Parliament questioned the Commission on antibiotics in animal feed (Question H-0262/96 by Inger Schörling (V-SU)).
The Parliament questioned the Commission on BSE. (Question H-0353/96 by Lyndon Harrison (PSE-UK)).

11/4/96   Decision 96/283/EC adopted by Commission approving the programme for the eradication of Aujeszky's disease in Luxembourg.
(OJ L.107 30/4/96 p. 16)

22/4/96   Decision 96/312/EC adopted by Commission amending Decision 92/452/EEC establishing lists of embryo collection teams and embryo production teams approved in third countries for export of bovine embryos to the Community.
(OJ L.118 15/5/96 p. 26)

29/4/96   Council Directive 96/24/EC amending Directive 79/373/EEC on the marketing of compound feedingstuffs.
(OJ L.125, 23/5/96 p. 33)

29/4/96   Directive 96/25/EC adopted by Commission on the circulation of feed materials, amending Directives 70/524/EEC, 74/63/EEC, 82/471/EEC and 93/74/EEC and repealing Directive 77/101/EEC (OJ L.125, 23/5/96, p. 35)

15/5/96   Regulation (EC) No. 874/96 adopted by Commission on imports of pure-bred breeding animals of the ovine and caprine species from third countries.
(OJ L.118 15/5/96 p. 12)

23/5/96   Report PE. 216.607 on behalf of the Committee on Agriculture and Rural Development on COM (96) 44 final (JO C.125 27/4/96 p. 29), adopted by Parliament on 23 May. Rapporteur: Mr Giacomo Santini (UPE-I).

Summary

The amendments adopted state that the premium shall be granted once in the life of each male bovine animal at the age of 10 months and that the premium must not be used to support the breeding of bovines for bull rings or fiestas in the EU.

29/5/96   Decision 96/352/EC adopted by Commission on financial assistance from the Community for storage in France of antigen for production of foot-and-mouth disease vaccine.
(OJ L.136 7/6/96 p. 38)

11/6/96   Decision 96/362/EC adopted by Commission amending Decision 96/239/EC on emergency measures to protect against bovine spongiform encephalopathy.
(OJ L.139 12/6/96 p. 17)

18/6/96   Council Conclusions on transmissible spongiform encephalopathies.
(OJ C.194 5/7/96 p. 1)

20/6/96   Commission Decision 96/381/EC adopted by Commission approving the measures to be implemented as regards bovine spongiform encephalopathy in Portugal.
(OJ L.149 22/6/96 p. 25)

21/6/96   Decision 96/404/EC adopted by Commission repealing Decision 91/56/EEC concerning certain protection measures relating to contagious bovine pleuropneumonia in Italy.
(OJ L.165 4/7/96 p. 39)

24/6/96   Decision 96/385/EC adopted by Commission approving the plan for the control and eradication of bovine spongiform encephalopathy in the UK.
(OJ L.151 26/6/96 p. 39)

25/6/96   Council Resolution on measures to be implemented under veterinary policy.
(OJ C.203 13/7/96 p. 1)

7/96   COM (96) 366 final Proposal for a Council Regulation (EC) supplementing Regulation (EEC) No. 2092/91 on organic production of agricultural products and indications referring thereto on agricultural products and foodstuffs to include livestock production.

7/96   The European Parliament established a temporary Committee of Inquiry on BSE. Mr Reimer Böge (PPE-D) appointed Chairman.

4/7/96   Decision 96/414/EC adopted by Commission concerning protective measures with regard to imports of animals and animal products from the former Yugoslav Republic of Macedonia due to outbreaks of foot-and-mouth disease.
(OJ L.167 6/7/96 p. 58)

11/7/96   COM (96) 223 final Proposal for a Council Regulation (EC) establishing a European Agency for Veterinary and Phytosanitary Inspection.
(OJ C.239 17/8/96 p. 9)

17/7/96   Resolutions B4-0879, 088, 0889, 0893, 0911, 0916 and 0922/96 Joint resolution adopted by the Parliament on the Commission's information policy on BSE since 1988 and measures it has taken to ensure compliance with the export ban and eradicate the disease.

18/7/96   Decision 96/509/EC and 96/510/EC adopted by Commission laying down pedigree and zootechnical requirements for the importation of semen of certain animals.
(OJ L.210 20/8/96 pp. 47–53)

19/7/96   Decision 96/499/EC adopted by Commission amending Decision 95/357/EC drawing up a list of border inspection posts agreed for veterinary checks on products and animals from third countries detailed rules concerning the checks to be carried out by the veterinary experts of the Commission and repealing Decision 94/24/EC.
(OJ L.203 13/8/96 p. 11)

23/7/96   Decision 96/463/EC adopted by Commission designating the reference body responsible for collaborating in rendering uniform the testing methods and the assessment of the results for pure-bred breeding animals of the bovine species.
(OJ L.192 2/8/96 p. 19)

Regulation (EC) No. 1433/96 adopted by Commission. Amends Annexes II and III of Council Regulation 2377/90 on procedure for establishment of maximum residue limits of veterinary medicinal products in foodstuffs of animal origin.
(OJ L.184 24/7/96 p. 21)

30/7/96   Decision 96/533/EC adopted by Commission fixing the Community financial contribution to the implementation of a sixth programme for the exchange of officials competent for veterinary matters.
(OJ L.226 7/9/96 p. 25)

4/9/96   Decisions 96/ 534 and 96/535/EC adopted by Commission on financial assistance from the Community for storage respectively in Italy and in the United Kingdom of antigen for production of foot-and-mouth disease vaccine.
(OJ L.229 10/9/96 p. 16)

6/9/96 Regulation (EC) No. 1742/96 amending Annexes I, II and III of Council Regulation (EEC) No. 2377/90 laying down a Community procedure for the establishment of maximum residue limits of veterinary medicinal products in foodstuffs of animal origin.
(OJ L.226 7/9/96 p. 5)

11/9/96 Decisions 96/539 -540/EC adopted by Commission on animal helth requirements and veterinary certification for imports into the Community of, respectively, semen and ova and embryos of the equine species.
(OJ L.230 11/9/96 pp. 23–8)

30/10/96 The Agriculture Council adopted the Commission's proposals on the beef and veal sector. The Commission proposal in relation to the single premium for bulls is accepted.

YIELD AND GROWTH PROMOTERS

Existing Legislation

Council Directive 88/146/EEC of 7 March 1988 prohibiting the use in live-stock farming of certain substances having a hormonal action.
(OJ L.70 16/3/88 p. 16)

Council Directive 85/639/EEC of 20 December 1985, the original measure prohibiting the use in livestock farming of substances having a hormonal action with effect from 1 January 1988 (OJ L.382 31/12/85 p. 228), was declared void by the Court of Justice on procedural grounds in February 1988. It was subsequently readopted as Council Directive 88/146/EEC on 7 March 1988.

Council Directive 88/299/EEC on trade in animals treated with certain substances having a hormonal action and their meat, as referred to in Article 7 of Directive 88/146/EEC.
(OJ L.128 21/5/88 p. 36)

Commission Decision 89/358/EEC of 23 May 1989 stipulates the measures to be taken when results of veterinary controls for growth hormones carried out in a Member State indicate the need for further investigation in other Member States or a third country.

Commission Decision 89/353/EEC of 24 May 1989 amending Decision 89/15/EEC on the importation of live animals and fresh meat from certain third countries.
(OJ L.146 30/5/89 p. 39)

In view of a USA/EEC agreement to approve holdings which give an assurance that they will not administer certain substances for fattening purposes to animals the meat of which is destined for human consumption, this Decision allows authorisation of beef and veal imports under certain conditions.

Commission Decision 90/8/EEC of 19 November 1989 amends Decision 89/15/EEC by allowing the import of beef and veal for human consumption from the USA from listed suppliers who undertake to provide meat produced without the use of hormones.

Commission Decision 90/152/EEC of 5 March 1990 permits the import of meat from dairy cattle as the US authorities have provided guarantees that these cattle have been used for milk production only.

Council Decision 90/218/EEC of 25 April 1990 places a moratorium on the administration of BST to dairy cows until 31 December 1990.

Council Decision of 11 December 1991 amending Decision 90/218/EEC on the placing on the market and administration of BST, which would have the effect of extending the ban on BST for a further two years, i.e. until 31 December 1993.

Council Decision of 22 December 1993 voted to prolong the moratorium on BST until 31 December 1994. Commission proposal to link the duration of the moratorium of use of BST to the milk quotas regime remained 'on the table'.

Council Regulation (EC) No. 894/96 of 29/4/96 amending Regulation (EEC) No. 805/68 on the common organisation of the market in beef and veal, with regard to penalties.

Council Directive 96/22/EC of 29/4/96 concerning the prohibition on the use in stockfarming of certain substances having a hormonal or thyrostatic action, and repealing Directives 81/602/EEC, 88/146/EEC and 88/299/EEC.

Council Directive 96/23/EC of 29/4/96 on measures to monitor certain substances and residues thereof in live animals and animal products and repealing Directives 85/358/EEC and 86/469/EEC and Decisions 89/187/EEC and 91/664/EEC.
(OJ L.125 23/5/96 p. 10)

Work in Progress

Moratorium on licensing of BST products for administration to dairy cows to be subjected to a report from the Commission by 1/7/98.

Council Decision of 22 December 1993 voted to prolong the moratorium on BST until 31 December 1994. Commission proposal to link the duration of the moratorium of use of BST to the milk quotas regime remained 'on the table'.

Council Decision of 15/12/94 to extend moratorium on the use of BST until 31/12/1999, although this date is linked with the milk quotas regime.

Background

European Community

14/10/86   Motion for a Resolution 2-988/86 by Mr Glinne, Mr Eyraud, Mrs Fuillet, Mr Thareau, Mr Bombard, Mr Remacle, Mr Collins, Mrs van Hemeldonck, Mr Vernimmen and Mr Woltjer on the effects and risks of using the BST-type hormone in the dairy industry.

Motion for a Resolution 2-434/87 by Mr Eyraud and others on the USA's refusal to comply with Community legislation on slaughterhouses and hormones, and the consequences of this refusal.

23/07/87   Motion for a Resolution 2-767/87 by Mr Graefe zu Baringdorf on the risks associated with the use of genetically engineered growth hormones in stock farming and the effects with regard to:

- natural animal husbandry;

- the preservation of traditional, environment-related farming;

- increases in output (surpluses);

- providing consumers with high-quality, nutritious food;

- animal feed imports and subsidised food exports between the Community and Third World countries.

04/02/88   Motion for a Resolution 2-1701/87 by Mr Collins, Mr Eyraud, Mrs Weber, Mr Thareau, Mr Glinne, Mrs Dury and Mrs Gadioux on the ban on hormones.

25/03/88   Report A2-30/88 drawn up on behalf of the Committee on Agriculture, Fisheries and Food on the effects and risks of using the growth hormones and the BST hormone in the dairy and meat industries. Rapporteur: José Happart (S-B).

05/07/88   European Parliament adopted the Resolution on the effects and risks of using the growth hormones and the BST hormone in the dairy and meat industries (Happart Report A2-30/88).

16/09/88   Joint Resolution on the use of hormones in meat production. (OJ C.262 10/10/88 p. 167)

12/10/88   European Parliament established a Committee of Inquiry into hormone use under the Chairmanship of Mr Reinhold Bocklet (PPE-D). Mr Carlos Pimenta (LDR-P) was appointed Rapporteur. The Committee met in November and December 1988.

20/01/89   Joint Resolution on the negotiations with the United States concerning the hormones conflict.
(OJ C.47 27/2/89 p. 161)

15/03/89   Report A2-11/89 drawn up on behalf of the Committee of Inquiry into the Problem of Quality in the Meat Sector on the findings of the Inquiry Committee. Rapporteur: Carlos Pimenta (LDR-P).

22/03/89   Report A2-16/89 drawn up on behalf of the Environment Committee on the USA's refusal to comply with Community legislation on slaughterhouses and hormones, and the consequences of this refusal. Rapporteur: Ken Collins (S-UK).

14/04/89   European Parliament adopted a Resolution on the USA's refusal to comply with Community legislation on slaughterhouses and hormones, and the consequences of this refusal (Collins Report A2-16/89).

21–23/06/89 During Agriculture Council meeting all states except UK opposed licensing of BST.

21/06/89   ECOSOC Opinion CES 749/89 on COM(88)779 final/2 – (SYN 189 and 190), the Commission's proposals for:

• a Council regulation laying down a Community procedure for the establishment of tolerances for residues of veterinary medical products;

• a Council directive amending Directive 81/851/EEC on the approximation of laws of the Member States relating to veterinary medicinal products;

• a Council directive extending the scope of Directive 81/851/EEC laying down additional provisions for immunological veterinary medicinal products.

14/07/89   Draft Report on behalf of the Environment Committee on COM(88)779 final/2. Growth and yield promoting substances are at present licensed under veterinary medicinal product legislation. The Commission has submitted a package of three legislative proposals (COM(88)779 final/2 – SYN 189 and

190) intended to contribute to the removal of barriers to the free movement of veterinary medicinal products and to the harmonisation of conditions for authorising the manufacture and marketing of new products. It intends to follow this package with proposals for a definitive procedure for Community level authorisation of veterinary medicinal products. Rapporteur: Ken Collins (S-GB).

13/09/89   The Commission formally requested that Member States should not license BST during the period leading up to the end of 1990 pending the results of further studies into safety aspects and the socio-economic impact.

19/09/89   Environment Committee held initial discussion on report by Ken Collins (S-UK) laying down EC standards for residues of veterinary drugs in animal products and authorisation of new drugs. Opinion from Agriculture Committee by Mrs Mechthild Rothe (S-D).

10/89   COM(89)379 proposal for a Council decision concerning the administration of bovine somatotrophin (BST) to cows as a productive aid to milk production. The Commission will report on developments by 1 October 1990 and Council shall decide whether or not to authorise BST before 31 December 1990. Referred to the Agriculture Committee. Rapporteur: José Happart (S-B).

15/10/89   CES 1247/89 ECOSOC opinion on COM(89)379.

16/11/89   Council Directive 87/519/EEC which amends Directive 74/63/EEC on undesirable substances and products in animal nutrition, ruled void by European Court in Case 11/88.

12/12/89   Agriculture Committee discussed a communication from the French Presidency on beta-agonists. Council was unanimously in favour of EC harmonisation of the use of growth and yield promoters and invited the Commission to present proposals.

01/02/90   Report A3-23/90 by Mr Happart on the proposal to institute a moratorium on the licensing of BST (COM(89)379), adopted by the Agriculture Committee.

19/02/90   Opinion by Mrs Ceci (GUE-I) was adopted as an Annex of A3-23/90.

19/02/90   Report A3-51/90 by Mr Collins on COM(88)779 (section dealing with residues of veterinary medicines in animal products) adopted by Environment Committee.

22/02/90	Report A3-50/90 by Mr Collins on COM(88)779 (establishment of EC system of mutual recognition between Member States for licensing veterinary drugs) adopted by Environment Committee.
14/03/90	Report A3-50/90 by Mr Collins adopted by European Parliament.
15/03/90	Report A3-51/90 by Mr Collins adopted by European Parliament.
25/04/90	Council Decision 90/218/EEC places a moratorium on the administration of BST to dairy cows until 31 December 1990.
26/06/90	Council Regulation (EEC) 2377/90 on residues of veterinary medicines in animal products.
	COM(90)135 concerning the licensing of veterinary medicines referred to European Parliament.
08/11/90	Report A3-295/90 on COM(88)135 laying down rules for the authorisation of new drugs. Rapporteur: Ken Collins (S-UK) on behalf of the Environment Committee.
11/12/90	COM(90)531 Commission proposal for a decision to extend the moratorium on administering BST to cows as dealt with in Decision 90/218/EEC for another two years, to 31 December 1993. Referred to Agriculture Committee with opinion from Environment Committee. Rapporteur for Agriculture Committee: José Happart (S-B).
11/01/91	Report A3-7/91 by Mr Happart on COM(90)531 adopted by the Agriculture Committee.
25/01/91	Report A3-7/91 by Mr Happart on COM(90)531 adopted by Plenary on the request from Council to adopt the urgency procedure. It was adopted without opinion from the Environment Committee.
30/01/91	CES 137/91 ECOSOC adopted report by Mr Silva on supporting proposal COM(90)531.
01/12/91	COM(91)522 Proposal for a decision amending Decision 90/218/EEC on the placing on the market and administration of BST, which would have the effect of extending the ban on BST for a further two years i.e. to 31 December 1993. (OJ C.24 31/1/92)

11/12/91	Council Decision amending Decision 90/218/EEC on the placing on the market and administration of BST, which would have the effect of extending the ban on BST for a further two years, i.e. until 31 December 1993 (COM(91)522).
11/02/92	COM(91)522 adopted by Agriculture Committee.
17/02/92	COM(91)522 approved by Parliament.
11/2/93	Commission statement on the use of hormones in stockbreeding. Environment and Agriculture Committees table a motion for a resolution entitled 'the use of hormones and illegal growth-promoting substances in beef production'; MEPs adopted the resolution.
17/12/93	Report A3-0426/93 adopted by Euro Parliament – Commission proposal for a Council Decision amending Decision 90/218/EEC concerning placing on the market and admin of Bovine Somatotrophin (BST).
2/9/94	ECOSOC's Agriculture and Fisheries Section adopted a report on the issue of the continual banning BST in the EU. In plenary session ECOSOC recommends maintaining the ban on the marketing of BST and its administration to dairy cows in the Community.
25/10/94	Commission's update version of its Communication to Council concerning Bovine Somatotrophin (BST) published.
15/12/94	Council of Ministers voted in favour of a prolongation of ban on administration and marketing of BST until 31/12/1999, but to be linked with the milk quotas regime. Commission will present report to ministers by 1/7/98 on tests and research Member States are entitled to carry out in order to obtain necessary scientific data to assess the effects of BST.
16/3/95	Resolution adopted by the European Parliament condemning the assassination of Belgian Inspector Karel Van Noppen on 20/2/95 and calling for the adoption by the Council and the Commission of urgent measures to tighten controls on the importing and use of certain hormonal substances by farmers as well as the trade in veterinary drugs
22/9/95	Joint Resolution adopted in Parliament on the conference on the growth activators in stockfarming. This resolution refers to

the Commission's announcement to convene a conference on the banning of hormones in late November 1995.

The Parliament calls on the Commission:

- to invite independent experts to this conference to assess risks and effects of the use of hormones on the health of consumers;

- to make it clear that this ban on hormones and the ban on use of BST also apply to imported products and foodstuffs;

- to strengthen procedures for monitoring use of hormones;

- to promote a system guaranteeing quality control of animal products by introducing a EU quality control label;

- to submit an annual report on the application of this legislation and the results achieved in combating fraud involving the use of hormones in meat production and stockfarming.

29/11–1/12/95	EU Conference on the use of hormones for growth promotion, at the initiative of the European Commission. Aims at assessing the development of substances used for growth promotion and their risks for human/animal health.
16/1/96	A joint debate was held in the European Parliament on the use of hormones in meat production.
18/1/96	Resolution adopted by the European Parliament on the impact of the conclusions of the Commission's scientific conference of growth promoters in meat production (29/11–1/12/95).

The Parliament:

- calls on the Commission and Council to oppose the import of hormone-treated meat in the EU, and wishes the total ban on the use of growth promoters in stockfarming to be maintained;

- calls on the Council to adopt a Council Regulation banning the use of stockfarming of certain substances having a hormonal or thyrostatic action and of beta-agonists;

- regrets that too little attention was given to the environmental impact of the use of growth-promoters, to expectations of consumers and to animal welfare;

       ● calls on the Commission to hold a follow-up conference without delay in cooperation with the European Parliament.

29/4/96   Council Regulation (EC) No. 894/96 amending Regulation (EEC) No. 805/68 on the common organisation of the market in beef and veal, with regard to penalties.
(OJ L.125 23/5/96 p. 1)

29/4/96   Council Directive 96/22/EC concerning the prohibition on the use in stockfarming of certain substances having a hormonal or thyrostatic action, and repealing Directives 81/602/EEC, 88/146/EEC and 88/299/EEC. (OJ L.125 23/5/96 p. 3)

29/4/96   Council Directive 96/23/EC on measures to monitor certain substances and residues thereof in live animals and animal products and repealing Directives 85/358/EEC and 86/469/EEC and Decisions 89/187/EEC and 91/664/EEC.
(OJ L.125 23/5/96 p. 10)

TRANSPORT OF ANIMALS

Existing Legislation

Council Decision 90/424/EEC of 26 June 1990 introduces EC financial support for the cost of implementing Community legislation on disease control and testing for residues of veterinary medicine and for the cost of the new veterinary inspection system needed after the abolition of internal frontiers.

Council Directive 90/425/EEC of 26 June 1990 establishes the framework for veterinary inspection for live animals after the abolition of internal frontiers.

Council Directive 90/426/EEC of 26 June 1990 concerns the movement of horses between Member States and third countries.

Council Directive 90/427/EEC of 26 June 1990 concerns the free movement of breeding horses and their ova or sperm, criteria for the identification of such horses and the recognition of stud books.

Council Directive 90/428/EEC of 26 June 1990 concerns the removal of all barriers to the free movement within the Community for horses taking part in competitions.

Commission Decision 90/552/EEC implements Directive 90/426/EEC. It designates areas in Spain and Portugal which are considered to be infected with African horse sickness.

Commission Decision 90/553/EEC stipulates that vaccinated animals from the areas identified in 90/552/EEC must be identified with a clear, indelible mark.

Council Decision 90/638/EEC of 27 November 1990 lays down criteria for funding under Council Decision 90/424/EEC.

Council Directive 91/628/EEC of 19 November 1991 on the protection of animals during transport and amending Directives 90/425/EEC and 91/496/EEC.
    In force: 1 January 1993.
(OJ L.340/17 11/12/91)

Summary

The Directive applies to the transport of:

(a) domestic solipeds and domestic animals;

(b) domestic birds and domestic rabbits;

(c) domestic mammals and birds;

(d) other mammals and birds;

(e) cold-blooded animals.

The Council shall lay down appropriate additional conditions for the transport of certain types of animal such as solipeds, wild birds and marine mammals (Article 3).

Decision 94/453/EC adopted by Commission. Amends or repeals some detailed rules on animal health and public health conditions required for imports of certain live animals and animal products from Austria, Finland, Norway and Sweden in application of the European Economic Area Agreement.
(OJ No. L187, 22.7.94, p. 11)

Council Decision 95/29/EC of 29 June 1995 amending Directive 91/628/EEC concerning the protection of animals during transport.

Work in Progress

According to Directive 95/29/EC, the Commission had to submit by 31 December 1995 proposals to the Council for the fixing of standards with which means of transport must comply. On December 17, the Commission tabled a new set of proposals on staging points as well as a route plan for animal transport. The proposals lay down conditions for hygiene arrangements, facilities and staff to be provided at each official halt. They also set out procedures for loading and unloading animals in transit. (JO N° L19, 22.1.97, P3U)

Before 31 December 1999 the Commission will report to Council on the implementation of Council Directive 95/29/EC by Member States.

Background

Council of Europe

1956	Karl Czerntz, the late President, and other Members of the Parliamentary Assembly tabled a motion for a recommendation on the prohibition of horses for slaughter.
1957	The Committee on Agriculture considered that the export of live horses and cattle for slaughter should not be prohibited.
28/10/57	Mr Wiley presented a Report to the Assembly on the regulation of live horses and livestock for slaughter (Resolution 134). The Resolution was adopted.
13/09/60	A motion for a recommendation on the regulation of the transport of live animals was tabled.
1961	The Assembly instructed the Committee of Ministers to draft a Convention for the regulation of the international transit of animals. Recommendation 287 (1961).
14/09/61	The Committee on Agriculture adopted a report on the international transit of animals and the accompanying draft Recommendation (Doc 1340).
22/09/61	The Assembly adopted Recommendation 287.
25/10/63	The Committee of Ministers adopted a Resolution allowing a Committee of Experts to be appointed to draft a Convention for the regulation of the international transit of animals.
1965	The Committee of Experts on the International Transport of Animals was established.
13/12/68	European Convention No. 65 for the protection of Animals During International Transport. The Committee of Ministers examined and adopted (with certain amendments) the draft Convention elaborated by the Committee of Experts. It also adopted Resolution (68) 23 concerning the same matter. (See Appendix IV for signatories.)
13/12/68	The Convention was opened for signature by the Member States.

20/02/71   The Convention entered into force.

10/05/79   Additional Protocol No. 103 to the European Convention for the Protection of Animals During International Transport allows for the accession of the EEC to the European Convention. (See Appendix V for signatories.)

01/10/80   Motion for a Recommendation on the protection of animals by Mr Dejardin and others urging that the Committee of Ministers report regularly to the Assembly on the application of the Convention by the signatory States (Doc 4626).

15/05/81   The ad hoc Committee of Experts (CAHTA) decided to submit to the Committee of Ministers a proposal concerning the international transport of animals destined for food purposes.

04/08/81   Parliamentary Assembly Report on the ill-treatment of horses during international transport. Rapporteur: Gerd Müller.
           A draft Recommendation was presented by the Committee on Agriculture.

30/09/81   Assembly Report on the ill-treatment of horses during international transport (amendments).
Presented by: Mr Cavaliere.

01/10/81   The Assembly adopted Recommendation 923 (1981) at its Thirty-third Ordinary Session on the ill-treatment of horses during international transport.

03/11/81   Report by the ad hoc Committee of Experts on the Transport of Animals (CAHTA) on the behaviour patterns of horses during transport.

11/12/81   Report of the ad hoc Committee of Experts on the Transport of Animals (CAHTA).

12/12/81   At its meeting CAHTA noted that the Member States of the European Community considered it necessary to pursue scientific studies on the transport of animals intended for slaughter before final conclusions could be drawn.

04/12/84   At its Fifteenth Meeting, the ad hoc Committee of Experts for the Protection of Animals (CAHPA) agreed to propose to the Committee of Ministers that its specific terms of reference be extended to cover problems raised by the transport of animals.

21/02/85   The Ministers' Deputies agreed to modify the terms of reference of the CAHPA and thus entrusted it with the tasks originally given to the CAHTA.

21/03/85   The Working Party of CAHPA produced a report in which it made proposals for starting work on the definition of the conditions under which the welfare of different animal species during transport would be ensured. Priority was given to the elaboration of a draft recommendation on the international transport of horses intended for slaughter.

06/85–05/87 CAHPA discussed the general conditions under which the welfare of horses during international transport would be best ensured, as well as the particular conditions for the transport of horses by rail, road, sea and air, which are the subject of separate appendices to the general conditions.

05/05/87   At the Nineteenth Meeting, CAHPA adopted the draft Recommendation on the international transport of horses and submitted it to the Committee of Ministers for decision.

17/09/87   Committee of Ministers adopted the Recommendation on the international transport of horses.

01/01/88   CAHPA was formally discontinued as the Council of Europe decided that it had concluded its work in the field of animal welfare. However, in order to monitor the implementation of those Conventions without a standing committee it was agreed to hold a multilateral consultation once a year, one of the first tasks being to work on the Convention on Transport and make proposals for amendments to the Committee of Ministers.

The Working Party of the Multilateral Consultation of Parties to the European Convention for the Protection of Animals during International Transport held its first meeting in The Hague, and prepared a draft Recommendation on the transport of pigs.

06/88   Recommendation on the transport of pigs was adopted by the Multilateral Consultation of the Parties to the European Convention for the Protection of Animals during International Transport.

22/09/88   Recommendation No. R (88) 15 on the Transport of Pigs adopted by the Committee of Ministers.

01/89	Working Party of the Multilateral Consultation discussed draft recommendations on the transport of cattle, sheep, goats, and poultry.
06/89	Second Meeting of the Working Party finalised the draft recommendation on the transport of cattle, together with parts of the draft recommendation on the transport of sheep and goats, and further considered the preliminary draft of the recommendation on the transport of poultry.
10/89	The Second Multilateral Consultation of Parties to the European Convention for the Protection of Animals during International Transport approved Recommendations for the transport of cattle, sheep, goats, and poultry.
07/11/89	The Additional Protocol No. 103 to the European Convention for the Protection of Animals during International Transport entered into force.
15/01/90	Recommendation No. R (90) 1 on the Transport of Cattle adopted by the Committee of Ministers.
21/02/90	Recommendation No. R (90) 5 on the Transport of Sheep and Goats adopted by the Committee of Ministers.
21/02/90	Recommendation No. R (90) 6 on the Transport of Poultry adopted by the Committee of Ministers.
18/9/95	Draft Report AS/Agr (1995) 31 rev. drawn up by the Council of Europe Committee on Agriculture and Rural Development, on animal welfare and livestock in Europe. Rapporteur: Mr Michels (D-PPE).
26/1/96	Recommendation 1289 (1996) on animal welfare and livestock transport in Europe adopted by the Parliamentary Assembly of the Council of Europe.
19–22/3/96	First Meeting of the Working Party for the Preparation of the Multilateral Consultation of Parties to the European Convention for the Protection of Animals during International Transport held in Strasbourg (ETS 65). The Working Party examined the implementation of the European Convention and identified major problems connected with the signature, ratification and/or implementation of the Convention.
	The next meeting of the Working Party for the Preparation of the Multilateral Consultation of Parties to the European Convention for the Protection of Animals during International Transport is scheduled for March 1997.

European Community

29/05/75	Proposal from the Commission to the Council for a Decision:

    1. Authorising the Commission to open negotiations with the Council of Europe on the accession of the Community to the European Convention for the protection of animals during international transport.

    2. Concluding the European Convention for the protection of animals during international transport and introducing the provisions necessary for its application to intra-Community trade.

(OJ C.133 14/6/75 p. 5)

09/06/75	The Council requested opinions from the European Parliament and the ECOSOC.
13/09/75	Report 304/75 on behalf of the Committee on Agriculture on the proposal from the Commission.
24/09/75	Opinion of the ECOSOC. (OJ C.286 15/12/75 p. 22)
17/10/75	European Parliament adopted Resolution expressing a favourable opinion on the Commission's proposal. (OJ C.257 10/11/75 p. 38)
18/07/77	Council Directive 77/489/EEC on the protection of animals during international transport. (OJ L.200 8/7/77 p. 10)
12/02/79	Proposal from the Commission for a Council Directive establishing measures for the implementation of Directive 77/489/EEC on the protection of animals during international transport. (OJ C.41 14/2/79)
04/04/79	Approval of the ECOSOC for the Commission's proposals. (OJ C.171 9/7/79 p. 20)
04/05/79	Report 129/79 drawn up on behalf of the Committee on Agriculture on the proposal from the Commission.
11/05/79	The European Parliament passed a resolution requesting the Commission to reconsider its proposal and if possible to propose alternative solutions. (OJ C.140 5/6/79 p. 131)

1981   The Council asked the Commission to assign to the Standing Committee on Agricultural Research the task of examining whether there are good physiological, ethological and economic reasons for limiting the final journey to the abattoir of animals intended for immediate slaughter and, if so, of recommending a maximum duration for such journeys.

08/04/81   Motion for a Resolution 1-111/81 by Mr von Habsburg and others on the transport of horses intended for slaughter.

12/05/81   Council Directive 81/389/EEC establishing measures necessary for the implementation of Directive 77/489/EEC on the protection of animals during international transport.
                (OJ L.150 6/6/81 p. 1)

02/10/81   The EP Committee on Agriculture decided to draw up a Report based on Motion for a Resolution 1-111/81.

24/11/81   The EP Committee on Agriculture appointed Mrs Luise Herklotz Rapporteur.

08/10/82   The EP Environment Committee was asked to deliver an opinion on the Draft Report of the Committee on Agriculture and appointed Mr Doeke Eisma draughtsman of the opinion.

20/04/83   The Committee on Agriculture considered and adopted the draft report of the Environment Committee.

29/04/83   Report 1-299/83 drawn up on behalf of the Committee on Agriculture, with an opinion from the Committee on the Environment appended. Rapporteur: Luise Herklotz (S-D).

09/06/83   The European Parliament adopted the Resolution on the transport of horses intended for slaughter.
                (OJ C.184 11/7/83 p. 133)

11/83   The Commission produced a Report on the international transport of farm animals intended for slaughter (EUR 9556).

16/02/84   Motion for a Resolution 1457/83 by Mr Eisma and Mr Woltjer on the international transport of farm animals.

05/03/85   Communication from the Commission to the Council concerning the protection of animals during international transport (COM(85)70).

03/85   RSPCA filed an official complaint to the Commission in a 150 page document on the non-implementation of Directive 77/489/EEC and 81/389/EEC by the United Kingdom and France.

15/04/85	Motion for a Resolution 2-74/85 by Mr Cryer, Mr Stevenson and Mr Stewart on the treatment of calves exported from the United Kingdom.
09/09/85	Motion for a Resolution B2-0735/85 by Mr Collins on the transport of live animals.
01/10/86	RSPCA filed a second complaint against France and the UK on the non-implementation of the Directives 77/489/EEC and 81/389/EEC.
12/86	France and UK agreed to bring their legislation on the international transport of animals into line with Directives 77/489/EEC and 81/389/EEC.
19/12/86	Report A-211/85 on behalf of the Committee on Agriculture, Fisheries and Food on animal welfare policy. Rapporteur: Richard Simmonds (ED-UK). (See Section on Farm Animal Welfare – General.)
20/02/87	European Parliament adopted the Resolution for an animal welfare policy (A-211/85). (OJ C.229 9/9/85 p. 126) The Resolution called on the Commission to limit the maximum journey time of transport to 24 hours, to investigate the problems of non-implementation and to propose guidelines for species-specific conditions for transportation.
1988	The Commission published the Code of Conduct for the International Transport of Horses, a series of guidelines for the transport of horses adapted from Council of Europe Recommendation No. R(87)17 adopted by the Committee of Ministers in September 1987. Text available in English and French.
06/89	Field Study into the International Transport of Animals and Field Study concerning the Stunning of Slaughter Animals published in one volume by the Commission (Ref. No. ISBN 92-825-9551-X).
29/06/89	COM(89)322 final proposal for a Council Regulation on the protection of animals during transport.
10/89	COM(89)322 proposal for a Council Regulation on the protection of animals during transport referred to Agriculture Committee. Rapporteur: David Morris (S-UK). Opinions from

Environment Committee, Budget Committee and Transport Committee.

20/12/89   COM(89)493 proposal for a Regulation to implement COM(88)383 the framework directive on veterinary inspection after 1992, referred to Agriculture Committee which charged the PPE with drawing up the report.

05/04/90   Report A3-45/90 by Mr David Morris (S-UK) on COM(89)322 with opinions from Environment and Transport Committees debated and adopted in plenary.

18/05/90   Report A3-86/90 on COM(89)493 debated and voted in Plenary.

06/90   Motion for a Resolution B3-856/90 by Mr Martin on extending the UK's Minimum Values Orders to all Member States.

05/06/90   COM(90)238 Commission amendments to COM(89)322 a proposal for a regulation on the transport of animals.

26/06/90   Council Directive 90/425/EEC the framework for veterinary inspection for live animals after the abolition of internal frontiers.

05/07/90   Case C-304/88 Court of Justice ruled against Belgium in that subjecting imports of live animals from other Member States to prior authorisation it was in breach of Article 30 of the Treaty of Rome.

09/90   Motion for a Resolution on the difficulties of moving cattle and sheep through France: B3-1580/90 Rainbow Group; B3-1587/90 DR Group; B3-1593/90 LDR Group; B3-1613/90 CG Group; B3-1586/90 ED Group; B3-1596/90 RDE Group; B3-1597/90 PPE Group; B3-1599/90 Socialist Group; B3-1646/90 GUE Group.

14/06/91   Report A3-169/91 on the proposal for a regulation on veterinary inspection of live animals entering the Community. Rapporteur: Mark Killilea (RDE-IRL).

22/10/91   COM(89)322 and COM(90)238 Agriculture Council reached political agreement on the bulk of the proposal.

19/11/91   Council Directive 91/628/EEC on the protection of animals during transport and amending Directives 90/425/EEC and 91/496/EEC. The Directive repeals and replaces Directives 77/489/EEC and 81/389/EEC.

05/92	COM(92)147 proposal for a Directive amending Directive 90/425/EEC concerning veterinary and zootechnical checks applicable in intra-Community trade in certain live animals and products with a view to the completion of the internal market. Referred to Agriculture Committee.
18/05/92	The Scientific and Veterinary Committee, Animal Welfare Section, reported to the Commission on the transport of farm animals in relation to Directive 91/628/EEC. On the basis of the report the Commission is now preparing a proposal for detailed rules on feeding, watering, loading, unloading, etc of animals in transit.
10/07/92	COM(92)211 final proposal for a Council Directive amending Directive 89/662/EEC concerning veterinary checks in intra-Community trade with a view to the completion of the internal market.
14/12/92	Motion for a resolution (B3-1755/92) tabled by Mr Tauran on the scandal of the transport of animals; rejected, but motion may be referred to a Committee.
16/3/93	Protection of animals during transport was discussed at the 1,648th Council meeting for Agriculture. Council asked the Commission to submit the additional proposals necessary for the implementation of the Directive. Commissioner Steichen replied that appropriate proposals would be submitted to the Council.
25/5/93	Parliamentary debate [B3-0149/93] on transport of farm animals.
9/93	David Morris appointed rapporteur on Proposal for a Council Directive [COM(93)330 final] concerning protection of animals during transport.
2/12/93	Draft report by Mr David Morris voted and adopted by Agriculture Committee. Max 8 Hour journey time retained.
15/12/93	Report A3-0404/93 adopted by Parliament.
3/2/94	Commission Decision based on Article 16 of Council Directive 91/628/EEC – rules on welfare of animals during transport in Greece.
22/7/94	DECISION 94/453/EC adopted by Commission. Amends or repeals some detailed rules on animal health and public health conditions required for imports of certain live animals and

animal products from Austria, Finland, Norway and Sweden in application of the European Economic Area Agreement. (OJ No. L187, 22.7.94, p. 11)

16/11/94   German Minister states in oral answer that Transport to be discussed before the end of the German Presidency.

15/2/95   Joint Motion for a Resolution on transport of live animals was adopted by European Parliament.

2/3/95   Complaint filed with the Commission by Eurogroup for Animal Welfare regarding Italy's violation of Council Directive 91/628/EEC on transport of animals by not enforcing border checks for horses arriving from Eastern European countries.

27–28/3/95 At the Council of Ministers meeting French Agriculture Minister Mr Jean Puech expressed regret that a decision had still not yet been reached. Commission had put forward some suggestions for technical improvements to the Presidency compromise which the Council is examining. President appealed to all delegations to make an effort so that the Council may reach a decision at a future meeting.

Commission's suggestions were for a draft proposal for a European Parliament and Council Directive relating to motor vehicles and their trailers transporting certain animals and amending Directive 70/156/EEC. This Directive was called for in Article 13 of the Transport Directive (91/628) It provides for suitability of vehicles and strength where transport of animals is concerned; vehicles must be roofed, equipped with adequate loading/unloading facilities, ventilation, partitions, lighting and be designed and constructed so that there is appropriate access for the purpose of inspecting and tending the animals during transport.

29/6/95   Council Directive 95/29/EC adopted. This Directive amends Directive 91/628/EEC concerning the protection of animals during transport. It lays down additional rules for the transport of farm animals. These include: space allowances on vehicles for the different farm animal species; watering and feeding intervals; journey time and rest periods. Journey times vary depending on whether or not a livestock vehicle possesses certain additional requirements laid down in the Directive. The new rules also include stricter requirements for transporters, journey plans, official inspections and enforcement procedures.

19/9/95   In an oral answer to an oral question in Parliament the
           Commission reiterated that if a Directive such as the
           Transport Directive is properly enforced by a Member State
           there is no legal basis for citizens to achieve their aims of
           defending animal welfare by resort to the European Court of
           Justice.

17/12/96   The Commission tabled a new set of proposals on staging
           points as well as a route plan for animal transport. (OJ No. L19,
           22.1.97, p. 34)

HUMANE SLAUGHTER

Existing Legislation

Council Directive 74/577/EEC of 18 November 1974 on stunning of
animals before slaughter.
In force: July 1975.
(OJ L.316 26/11/74 p. 10)

Summary

Member States must ensure that suitable measures are taken to induce death
as rapidly as possible after stunning, in accordance with appropriate
measures.

Stunning means a process effected by a mechanically operated instrument, electricity, or gas anaesthesia without adverse effects on the condition
of the meat, which when applied to an animal puts it into a state of in-
sensibility which lasts until it is slaughtered thus sparing it in any event all
needless suffering.

The stunning process must be approved by the competent authority and
carried out by a person who has the necessary qualifications and knowledge.

Any cruel treatment or unnecessary suffering on the part of the animals is
to be avoided in respect of emergency slaughtering.

The Directive does not affect provisions related to special methods of
slaughter which are required for particular religious rites.

Council Decision 88/306/EEC of 16 May 1988 on the conclusion of the
European Convention for the Protection of Animals for Slaughter.
(OJ L.137 of 2/6/88 p. 25)

Council Directive 90/667/EEC of 27 November 1990 controls the disposal
of cadavers, slaughter offal, bodies of diseased animals and spoiled meat. It
allows the use of low risk waste for feeding zoo animals, packs of hounds
and on maggot farms.

Council Directive 93/119/EC of 22 December 1993 on the protection of animals at the time of slaughter or killing.
(OJ No. 340 31/12/93 p. 21)

Decision 95/29/EC adopted by Commission. Amends Decision 94/382/EC on the approval of alternative heat treatment systems for processing animal waste of ruminant origin with a view to inactivate spongiform encephalopathy agents.
(OJ L.38, 18.2.95, p. 17)

Work in Progress

None.

Background

Council of Europe

04/07/73	The Consultative Assembly adopted Recommendation 709 (1973) on slaughter methods for meat animals, proposing that the Committee of Ministers invite the governments of Member States to conclude a European Convention on the humanisation and harmonisation of slaughter methods.
	The Committee of Ministers decided to ask the Committee of Experts for the Protection of Animals for an opinion on the Recommendation.
	The Committee of Experts advised the Committee of Ministers and assisted it in drafting a European Convention on slaughter methods for meat animals.
01/77	The Committee of Experts was transformed into the ad hoc Committee of Experts for the Protection of Animals (CAHPA).
10/05/79	European Convention No. 102 for the Protection of Animals for slaughter opened for signature.
11/06/82	Convention entered into force. (See Appendix VIII for signatories.)
01/01/88	CAHPA was dissolved but the multilateral consultations organised by the Council of Europe in order to monitor the implementation of their Conventions on animal welfare are, at some future point, to consider proposals for updating the Convention for the protection of animals for slaughter and monitoring its implementation.
05/06/90	First meeting of Working Party on Slaughter to discuss draft code of conduct on slaughter.

26/11/90   Second meeting of Working Party on Slaughter finalised a working draft of a code of conduct on slaughter.

19/03/91   Multilateral Consultation of parties to the European Convention for the Protection of Animals for Slaughter agreed the text of a draft Recommendation on the Slaughter of Animals.

17/06/91   Recommendation R(91)17 on the Slaughter of Animals adopted by Committee of Ministers. To be reviewed within 5 years of entry into force, i.e. 1996.

20/10/92   European Convention for the protection of animals for slaughter (Strasbourg 10/05/79) – Slovenia signed convention and acceded.

03/11/93   European Convention for the protection of animals for slaughter (Strasbourg 10/05/79) – Switzerland ratified.

30/03/94   European Convention for the protection of animals for slaughter (Strasbourg 10/05/79) – Former Yugoslav Republic of Macedonia acceded.

14/09/94   European Convention for the protection of animals for slaughter (Strasbourg 10/05/79) – Croatia signed and acceded.

29/12/94   European Convention for the protection of animals for slaughter (Strasbourg 10/05/79) – Bosnia Herzegovenia acceded. Date of entry into force is 30/06/95.

European Community

18/03/74   Proposal for a Council Directive on the stunning of animals before slaughter.
(OJ C.44 19/4/74 p. 27)

07/04/74   The President of the Council requested the European Parliament to deliver an opinion.
The President of the European Parliament referred this proposal to the Committee on Agriculture and asked it to consider whether the simplified consultation procedure could be adopted.

18/04/74   The Committee on Agriculture decided to adopt the simplified consultation procedure and instructed its Chairman to present the report to Parliament.

13/05/74   Report 82/74 drawn up on behalf of the Committee on Agriculture on the proposal from the Commission for a Council Directive on the stunning of animals before slaughter.

14/06/74   Opinion of the European Parliament.
             (OJ C.76 3/7/74 p. 52)

03/77   The Commission produced a Report as part of information on
             agriculture entitled: *'Review of Pre-slaughter Stunning in the
             European Community'*. (Ref. No. 30).

07/03/83   Motion for a Resolution 1-1343/82 by Mr Kyrkos on
             Community concern for Greek slaughterhouses.

23/10/87   Commission submitted COM(87)488, a proposal for a
             Council Decision on the conclusion of the European
             Convention for the Protection of Animals for Slaughter.

16/12/87   Opinion of the ECOSOC on COM(87)488.

22/01/88   Opinion of the European Parliament on COM(87)488.

16/05/88   Council Decision 88/306/EEC on the conclusion of the
             European Convention for the Protection of Animals for
             Slaughter.

06/89   *Field Study concerning the Stunning of Slaughter Animals*
             published by the Commission in one volume with Field
             Study into the International Transport of Animals (Ref. ISBN
             92-825-9551-X).

15/11/91   COM(91)136 proposal for a Council Regulation (EEC) on the
             protection of animals at the time of slaughter or killing.
             Referred to European Parliament and ECOSOC.
             (OJ C.314 5/12/91)

13/12/91   COM(91)136 referred to the Agriculture Committee.
             Rapporteur: David Morris (S-UK). With opinion from
             Environment Committee.

31/01/92   COM(91)136 Environment Committee appointed Sir James
             Scott-Hopkins draftsman.

04/92   ECOSOC adopted its opinion CES 360/92 on COM(91)136.
             Rapporteur: Mr Wick.

21/04/92   Environment Committee accepted Sir James Scott-Hopkins'
             draft opinion on COM(91)136.

08/07/92   Report A3-243/92 by Mr Morris incorporating Environment
             Committee opinion and other amendments on the protection
             of animals during slaughter, adopted by Parliament.

17/11/92   COM(92)460 final. Amended proposal for a Council Regulation
             (EEC) on the protection of animals at the time of slaughter or

killing, submitted by the Commission pursuant to Article 149(3) of the EEC Treaty.
(OJ C.328 12/12/92)

14/6/93   Agriculture Council discuss Commission proposal concerning protection of animals at time of slaughter or killing.

13/2/95   Decision 95/29/EC adopted by Commission. Amends Decision 94/382/EC on the approval of alternative heat treatment systems for processing animal waste of ruminant origin with a view to inactivate spongiform encephalopathy agents.
(OJ L.38, 18.2.95, p. 17)

18/7/96   Decision 96/449/EC adopted by Commission on the approval of alternative heat treatment systems for processing animal waste of ruminant origin with a view to inactivate spongiform encephalopathy agents.
(OJ L.184 24/7/96 p. 43)

LAYING HENS

Existing Legislation

Commission Regulation (EEC) 1943/85 of 12 July 1985 amending Regulation (EEC) No. 95/69 as regards certain marketing standards for eggs.
    Provides for descriptions of eggs from hens not kept in batteries so as to enable consumers to identify eggs from the principal non-battery production systems.

Council Directive 88/166/EEC of 7 March 1988 complying with the judgment of the Court of Justice in Case 131/86 (annulment of Council Directive 86/113/EEC of 25 March 1986) laying down minimum standards for the protection of laying hens kept in battery cages.
In force: 1 July 1987.
(OJ L.74 19/3/88 p. 83)

Summary

Council Directive 86/113/EEC of 25 March 1986 formed the original Community measure on battery hens but was annulled on procedural grounds as a result of an action brought by the United Kingdom. The Court of Justice ruled that unauthorised changes (which had been the object of neither the consultations nor the majority vote of the Council) had been made by the General Secretariat to the justification contained in the preamble. The stipulations of the Directive were not challenged, and after revision of the preamble to comply with the Court of Justice Ruling, the measure was re-adopted as Council Directive 88/166/EEC.

The Directive requires cages being constructed or used for the first time after 1 January 1988 to meet with certain minimum requirements: each hen must have at least 450 cm^2 available floor area and a feeding trough of 10 cm in length, the cage must be at least 40 cm high over 65% of its area and never lower than 35 cm. The floor must support at least three claws on each foot and not slope more than 14%.

All existing battery cages must conform with these minimum requirements by 1 January 1995.

Member States must also ensure that conditions for laying hens in battery cages are in accordance with the general requirements laid down in the Annex.

The Commission undertakes to carry out regular inspections of battery cages in order to ensure compliance with the Directive and to report by 1 January 1993 on scientific developments in the field of alternative rearing systems for laying hens.

Council Regulation (EEC) 1907/90 of 26 June 1990 on certain marketing standards for eggs.
In force: 1 July 1991.
(OJ L.173 6/7/90 p. 5)

Summary

Lays down compulsory requirements for labelling and allows additional information to be added such as type of farming.

Regulation 786/95 adopted by Commission amending Regulation 1274/91 introducing detailed rules for implementing Council Regulation 1907/90 on certain marketing standards for eggs.
(OJ L.79, 7.4.95, p. 12)

Regulation 3501/93 adopted by Commission – common organisation of market in eggs.
(OJ L.319, 21/12/93 p. 25)

Decision 95/141/EC – approval of establishment for the purposes of intra-community trade in poultry and hatching eggs submitted by Sweden.
(OJ L.92, 25.4.95, p. 25)

Council Regulation (EC) No. 818/96 of 29/4/96 amending Regulation (EEC) No. 1907/90 on certain marketing standards for eggs.
(OJ L.111, 4/5/96 p. 1)

Decision 95/141/EC of 10/4/95 – adopted by Commission. This Decision approves the plan for the approval of establishment for the purposes

of intra-community trade in poultry and hatching eggs submitted by Sweden.
(OJ L.92, 25.4.95, p. 25)

Regulation (EC) No. 2401/95 of 10/10/95 amending Regulation (EEC) No. 1274/91 introducing detailed rules for implementing Council Regulation 1907/90 on certain marketing standards for eggs.
(OJ L.246 13/10/95 p. 6)

Work in Progress

In November 1996 the European Commission published the Report of the Scientific Veterinary Committee on the welfare of laying hens. The report deals with various issues, such as housing systems for laying hens, assessment of welfare, behaviour disorders, productivity, egg quality and environment. It also analyses the different production systems (cages, enriched ages, non-cage systems). The Commission is due to forward a proposal amending Directive 88/166/EEC.

Background

Council of Europe

11/79	The Standing Committee on Farm Animal Protection, set up under Chapter II of the Convention for the protection of animals kept for farming purposes, held its second meeting and decided to adopt Recommendations for egg-laying hens, while maintaining close contact with the EEC on this matter.
05/80	At its Third Meeting the Standing Committee started to examine and evaluate the material presented by contracting parties, observers and experts.
12/81	During the Sixth Meeting, the Standing Committee unanimously adopted a draft proposal for a Recommendation concerning egg-laying hens.
04/82	The Standing Committee's Bureau met to consider the reactions of the different contracting parties to the proposal. Further slight amendments were made to the draft Recommendation.
27/05/82	The Standing Committee adopted its Recommendation at its Seventh Meeting but decided to wait until the EEC had adopted its draft Directive before proceeding further.

06/04/83   The Standing Committee transmitted the text of the draft Recommendation in its first triennial report to the Committee of Ministers.

18/11/86   At its 14th Meeting, the Standing Committee adopted the Recommendation concerning poultry of species *Gallus gallus* kept to produce eggs.
            (See Section on Farm Animal Welfare – General.)

21/11/87   Recommendation of 18 November 1986 concerning poultry of species *Gallus gallus* kept to produce eggs came into effect.

European Community

29/10/75   EEC Regulation 2771/75 on the common organisation of the market in eggs.
            (OJ L.282 1/11/75 p. 49)

            EEC Regulation 2772/75 on marketing standards for eggs.
            (OJ L.282 1/11/75 p. 56)

            The above two regulations are concerned with the quality and standards of eggs for the benefit of the consumer.

19/06/78   Council Decision 78/923/EEC the EEC approved the European Convention for the protection of animals kept for farming purposes.
            (OJ L.323 17/11/78 p. 12)

1979   Germany requested that the Council invite the Commission to consider the problem of the protection of egg-laying hens.

1980   The Commission started the Farm Animal Welfare Programme as part of the second Programme for Coordinated Agricultural Research. It supported six research contracts in poultry welfare.

14/07/80   Communication from the Commission to the Council on the intensive keeping of egg-laying hens, and draft resolution on the protection of egg-laying hens in cages.

22/07/80   Council Resolution on the protection of egg-laying hens in cages. The Council invited the Commission to submit a report. The study was undertaken by the Standing Committee for Agricultural Research.
            (OJ C.196 1/8/80)

31/07/81 COM(81)420 Proposal for a Council Directive laying down minimum standards for the protection of laying hens kept in battery cages, the scientific report of SCAR and a summary of the economic and marketing consequences.
(OJ C.208 18/8/81 p. 5)

20/08/81 The President of the Council requested opinions from the European Parliament and the ECOSOC.

25/08/81 The President of the European Parliament referred the proposal COM(81)420 to the Committee on Agriculture and to the Environment Committee for an opinion.

21/09/81 The Committee on Agriculture appointed Mr Teun Tolman Rapporteur.

20/10/81 The Environment Committee appointed Mrs Lieselotte Seibel-Emmerling draftsman.

26/11/81 The Environment Committee adopted its draft opinion.

02/12/81 The ECOSOC adopted its opinion on the proposal for a Council Directive.
(OJ C.343 31/12/81 p. 48)

08/12/81 Report 1-831/81 drawn up on behalf of the Committee on Agriculture. Rapporteur: Teun Tolman (PPE-NL).

18/12/81 The Report was referred back to the Committee on Agriculture at the request of the Rapporteur.

19/04/82 Second Report 1-95/82 drawn up on behalf of the Committee on Agriculture on the proposal from the Commission for a Directive on battery hens. Rapporteur: Teun Tolman (PPE-NL).

23/04/82 Opinion of the European Parliament.
(OJ C.125 17/5/82 p. 186)

06/82 COM(82)319 the Commission decided to modify its proposal and submitted its amendment to the Council.

11/09/84 Motion for a Resolution 2-476/84 by Mr Graefe zu Baringdorf on banning the keeping of hens in cages.

18/07/85 Commission Regulation (EEC) 1943/85 of 12 July 1985 amending Regulation (EEC) 95/69 as regards certain marketing standards for eggs.

Provides for descriptions of eggs from hens not kept in batteries so as to enable consumers to identify eggs from the principal non-battery production systems.

25/03/86   Council Directive 86/113/EEC laying down minimum standards for the protection of laying hens kept in battery cages. (OJ L.95 10/4/86 p. 45)

19/12/86   Report A2-211/85 on behalf of the Committee on Agriculture, Fisheries and Food on animal welfare policy. Rapporteur: Richard Simmonds (ED-UK). (See Section on Farm Animal Welfare – General.)

19/02/87   European Parliament adopted the Resolution on animal welfare policy in which it takes the view that research coordinated by the Commission is necessary in order to establish standards for alternative systems of keeping poultry, taking into account the economic conditions of this industry. (OJ C.76 23/3/87 p. 162)

23/02/88   Case 131/86 – United Kingdom *v* Council of European Communities

An application in the European Court of Justice, pursuant to Articles 173 and 174 EEC Treaty, for the annulment of Council Directive 86/113/EEC of 25 March 1986 laying down minimum standards for the protection of laying hens kept in battery cages. The UK argued: that the legal basis of the Directive was insufficient as it was based only on Article 43 EEC when it should also have been based on Article 100 EEC; that the text of the Directive differs from that considered by the Council. The first argument failed but the second argument succeeded. The Directive was therefore declared void.

07/03/88   Council Directive 88/166/EEC complying with the judgment of the Court of Justice in Case 131/86 (annulment of Council Directive 86/113/EEC of 25 March 1986 laying down minimum standards for the protection of laying hens kept in battery cages). (OJ L.74 19/3/88 p. 83)

26/06/90   Council Regulation (EEC) 1907/90 on certain marketing standards for eggs.

03/92   Report of Scientific Veterinary Committee, Animal Welfare Section, on the welfare of laying hens kept in different production systems. Forms the basis for the report to the Council of Ministers which the Commission is required to present together with appropriate proposals to revise Directive 88/166/EEC before 1 January 1993.

12/3/93   COM(92)0428 proposal for a Council Regulation amending Regulation (EEC)2771/75 on the common organisation of the market in eggs, (EEC)827/68 on the common organisation of the market in certain products listed in Annex II to the Treaty and (EEC)2658/87 on the tariff and statistical nomenclature and on the Common Customs Tariff (see also Poultry Kept for Meat).

20/12/93   Regulation 3501/93 adopted by Commission – common organisation of market in eggs.
               (OJ L.319, 21/12/93 p. 25)

6/4/95   Regulation 786/95 adopted by Commission amending Regulation 1274/91 introducing detailed rules for implementing Council Regulation 1907/90 on certain marketing standards for eggs.
               (OJ L.79, 7.4.95, p. 12)

10/4/95   Decision 95/141/EC – adopted by Commission. This Decision approves the plan for the approval of establishment for the purposes of intra-community trade in poultry and hatching eggs submitted by Sweden.
               (OJ L.92, 25.4.95, p. 25)

12/10/95   Regulation (EC) No. 2401/95 amending Regulation (EEC) No. 1274/91 introducing detailed rules for implementing Council Regulation 1907/90 on certain marketing standards for eggs.
               (OJ L.246 13/10/95 p. 6)

10/11/95   COM (95) 535 final Proposal for a Council Directive amending Directive 90/539/EEC on animal health conditions governing intra-Community trade in and imports from third countries of poultry and hatching eggs.
               (OJ C.15 20.1.96 p. 13)

29/2/96   Opinion of the ECOSOC on COM (95) 535 regarding animal health conditions governing intra-Community trade in and imports from third countries of poultry and hatching eggs.
               (OJ C.153 28/5/96 p. 46)

29/4/96   Council Regulation (EC) No. 818/96 amending Regulation (EEC) No. 1907/90 on certain marketing standards for eggs.
               (OJ L.111, 4/5/96 p. 1)

POULTRY KEPT FOR MEAT

Existing Legislation

Council Desicion 78/923/EEC of 19 June 1978 approves the European Convention on the protection of animals kept for farming purposes.
(OJ L.323 17/11/78 p. 12)

Council Regulation (EEC) 1906/90 of 26 June 1990 on certain marketing standards for poultry.
In force: 1 July 1991.
(OJ L.173 6/7/90 p. 1)

Summary

Lays down compulsory requirements for labelling, but these only concern durability, price and slaughterhouse of origin. Indication of the type of farming used is optional.

COM(92)0428 proposal for a Council regulation amending Regulations (EEC)2777/75 on the common organisation of the market in poultry meat, (EEC)827:68 on the common organisation of the market in certain products listed in Annex II to the Treaty and (EEC)2658/87 on the tariff and statistical nomenclature and on the Common Customs Tariff.

Commission adopted Regulation EEC/2891/93 amending Regulation 1538/91 introducing detailed rules for implementing Regulation 1906/90 on certain marketing standards for poultry meat.
(OJ L.263, 22/10/93, p. 12)

Council adopted Directive 93/120/EC amending Directive 90/539/EEC on animal health conditions governing intra-Community trade in and imports from third countries of poultry and hatching eggs.
(OJ L.340, 31/12/93 p. 35)

Council adopted Directive 93/121/EC amending Directive 91/494/EEC on animal health condition governing intra-Community trade in and imports from third countries of fresh poultry meat.
(OJ L.340 31/12/93 p. 39)

Decision 95/58/EC adopted by Commission amending Decision 94/85/EC drawing up a list of third countries from which the Member States authorise imports of fresh poultry meat.
(OJ L.55, 11.3.95, p. 41)

Decision 96/24/EC of 19/12/95 adopted by Commission approving the 1996 programme presented by Denmark for the monitoring and control of salmo-

nella in breeding poultry and setting the level of the Community's financial contribution.
(OJ L.8 11/1/96 p. 26)

Decision 96/93/EC of 12/1/96 adopted by Commission authorising Sweden to maintain its national measures as regards turkey thinotracheitis in application of Article 14 (4) of Council Directive 90/539/EEC.
(OJ L.21 27/1/96 p. 72)

Decision 96/247/EC of 25/3/96 adopted by Commission on financial contributions from the Community for the eradication of Newcastle disease in the Netherlands.
(OJ L.83 2/4/96 p. 17)

Decision 96/264/EC of 28/3/96 adopted by Commission on financial contributions from the Community for the eradication of Newcastle disease in Germany.
(OJ L.89 10/4/96 p. 45)

Regulation (EC) No. 1000/96 of 4/6/96 adopted by Commission amending Regulation (EEC) No. 1538/91 introducing detailed rules for implementing Council Regulation (EEC) No. 1906/90 on certain marketing standards for poultry.
(OJ L.134 5.6.96 p. 9)

Decision 96/482/EC of 12/7/96 adopted by Commission laying down animal health conditions and veterinary certificates for the importation of poultry and hatching eggs other than ratites and eggs thereof from third countries including animal heatlth measures to be applied after such importation.
(OJ L.196 7/8/96 p. 13)

Work in Progress

1994/95   Standing Committee of the European Convention for the Protection of Animals Kept For Farming Purposes preparing draft Recommendation on the Keeping of Poultry, Ducks, Ratites, Geese, Pheasants, etc. for meat.

Background

Council of Europe

19/11/73   A study was undertaken by the Committee of Experts for the Protection of Animals on the effects of goose cramming.

1974   The Report of the Committee of Experts for the Protection of Animals found no evidence of cruelty.

European Community

19/06/78   Council Decision 78/923/EEC approval of the European Convention on the protection of animals kept for farming purposes.
(OJ L.323 17/11/78 p. 12)

1980   The Commission started the Farm Animal Welfare Programme as part of the second Programme for Coordinated Agricultural Research. It supported six research contracts in poultry welfare.

15/10/80   Motion for a Resolution 1-486/80 by Mr Caborn on goose cramming to produce foie gras.

19/03/81   The Environment Committee (EP) decided to draw up a report based on Motion for a Resolution 1-486/80 and appointed Mr Francis Combe (L-F) Rapporteur.

27/04/82   Following the death of Mr Combe, Mrs Pruvot was appointed Rapporteur.

30/09/82   The Environment Committee adopted its Motion for a Resolution which 'considered that there is no reason to restrict or prohibit the cramming of geese to produce foie gras'.

05/10/82   Report 1-686/82 drawn up by the Environment Committee on goose cramming to produce foie gras. Rapporteur: Marie-Jane Pruvot (L-F).

07/02/83   Parliament adopted the resolution by Mrs Pruvot (1-686/82). Voting 76-62.
(OJ C.68 14/3/83 p. 10)
An amendment by Mr Tom Spencer (ED-GB), Mr Simmonds, Sir Fred Catherwood, Mr Moorhouse and Mr Moreland calling on the Commission to curtail the practice of goose cramming on animal welfare grounds was rejected. Voting 57-54.

17/03/86   Motion for a Resolution 2-21/86 by Mr Newens and others on the production of foie gras by goose cramming.

05/08/86   Motion for a Resolution 2-694/86 by Mr Marshall on the cruelty to geese involved in the manufacture of pâté de foie gras.

19/12/86	Report A2-211/85 on behalf of the Committee on Agriculture, Fisheries and Food on animal welfare policy. Rapporteur: Richard Simmonds (ED-UK). (See Section on Farm Animal Welfare – General).
19/02/87	European Parliament adopted the Resolution on animal welfare policy in which it takes the view that research co-ordinated by the Commission is necessary in order to establish standards for alternative systems of keeping poultry, taking into account the economic conditions of this industry. (OJ C.76 23/3/87 p. 162)
27/02/87	Motion for a Resolution 2-1646/86 by Mrs Banotti on the cruel practice of cramming ducks and geese for the production of foie gras.
08/05/87	Motion for a Resolution 309/87 by Mr Marshall on the future of pâté de foie gras production.
02/06/87	Motion for a Resolution 436/87 by Mr Hughes on the cruel practice of cramming ducks and geese for the production of foie gras.
02/06/87	Motion for a Resolution 437/87 by Mrs Boserup on the cruel practice of cramming ducks and geese for the production of foie gras. Referred to Environment Committee and included in Report A2-356/88 by Mr Schmid on possible legal action against events involving cruelty to animals. (See Animals in Sport and Entertainment.)
17/08/88	Motion for a Resolution 2-619/88 by Mr Ford, Mrs Seibel-Emmerling, Mrs van Hemeldonck, Mr Pearce, Ms Tongue, Mrs Lemass, Mrs Llorca Vilaplana, Mrs Ewing, Mr Seal, Mr Elliott, Mr Marshall, and Mrs Castle on the methods used to produce foie gras.
19/04/90	Report A3-309/90 by Mrs Ceci on COM(89)668 adopted by European Parliament. Includes recommendations on the stunning and slaughter of birds for foie gras production.
26/06/90	Council Regulation (EEC) 1906/90 on marketing standards for poultry lays down compulsory requirements for labelling, but these only concern durability, price and slaughterhouse of origin, indication of the type of farming used is optional.
28/09/90	COM(89)668 proposal for a regulation to lay down standards for the trade in fresh meat from poultry, pigeons and farmed

game birds. Referred to Environment Committee with opinions from Budgets Committee and Agriculture Committee. Rapporteur: Adriana Ceci (GUE-I).

12/06/92   COM(92)192 final a proposal for a Council directive concerning the protection of animals kept for farming purposes referred to Agriculture Committee. Rapporteur: Richard Simmonds (ED-UK).

19/11/92   Report A3-339/92 by Mr Simmonds on the protection of animals kept for farming purposes adopted by European Parliament.

12/3/93   COM(92)0428 proposal for a Council regulation amending Regulations (EEC)2777/75 on the common organisation of the market in poultry meat, (EEC)827:68 on the common organisation of the market in certain products listed in Annex II to the Treaty and (EEC)2658/87 on the tariff and statistical nomenclature and on the Common Customs Tariff.

21/10/93   Commission adopted Regulation EEC/2891/93 amending Regulation 1538/91 introducing detailed rules for implementing Regulation 1906/90 on certain marketing standards for poultry meat.
(OJ L.263, 22/10/93, p. 12)

22/12/93   Council adopted Directive 93/120/EC amending Directive 90/539/EEC on animal health conditions governing intra-Community trade in and imports from third countries of poultry and hatching eggs.
(OJ L.340, 31/12/93 p. 35)

22/12/93   Council adopted Directive 93/121/EC amending Directive 91/494/EEC on animal health condition governing intra-Community trade in and imports from third countries of fresh poultry meat.
(OJ L.340 31/12/93 p. 39)

22/12/94   Motion for a resolution tabled in Parliament on the alleviation of cruelty in the production of foie gras.

2/3/95   Decision 95/58/EC adopted by Commission amending Decision 94/85/EC drawing up a list of third countries from which the Member States authorise imports of fresh poultry meat.
(OJ L.55, 11.3.95, p. 41)

10/11/95   COM (95) 535 final Proposal for a Council Directive amending Directive 91/494/EEC on animal health conditions governing intra-Community trade in and imports from third countries
of fresh poultry meat.
(OJ C.15 20.1.96 p. 15)

19/12/95   Decision 96/24/EC adopted by Commission approving the
1996 programme presented by Denmark for the monitoring
and control of salmonella in breeding poultry and setting the
level of the Community's financial contribution.
(OJ L.8 11/1/96 p. 26)

12/1/96   Decision 96/93/EC adopted by Commission authorising
Sweden to maintain its national measures as regards turkey
thinotracheitis in application of Article 14 (4) of Council
Directive 90/539/EEC.
(OJ L.21 27/1/96 p. 72)

2/96   Opinion of the ECOSOC on COM (95) 535 regarding animal
health conditions governing intra-Community trade in and
imports from third countries of fresh poultry meat.
(OJ C.153 28/5/96 p. 46)

25/3/96   Decision 96/247/EC adopted by Commission on financial
contributions from the Community for the eradication of
Newcastle disease in the Netherlands.
(OJ L.83 2/4/96 p. 17)

28/3/96   Decision 96/264/EC adopted by Commission on financial
contributions from the Community for the eradication of
Newcastle disease in Germany.
(OJ L.89 10/4/96 p. 45)

4/6/96   Regulation (EC) No. 1000/96 adopted by Commission amending Regulation (EEC) No. 1538/91 introducing detailed rules
for implementing Council Regulation (EEC) No. 1906/90 on
certain marketing standards for poultry.
(OJ L.134 5.6.96 p. 9)

12/7/96   Decision 96/482/EC adopted by Commission laying down
animal health conditions and veterinary certificates for the
importation of poultry and hatching eggs other than ratites and
eggs thereof from third countries including animal heatlth
measures to be applied after such importation.
(OJ L.196 7/8/96 p. 13)

VEAL CALVES

Existing Legislation

Council Directive 91/629/EEC of 19 November 1991 laying down minimum standards for the protection of calves.
    In force: 1 January 1994.
(OJ L.340 11/12/91 p. 28)

Summary

The Directive specifies the amount of space and ventilation to be provided for calves confined for rearing and fattening in holdings of more than five animals.

All new installations shall be covered by the Directive from 1 January 1994 but existing installations will have until no later than 31 December 2003 to comply.

Article 6 requires the Commission to report by 1 October 1997 on farming systems which comply with the well-being of calves and to put forward appropriate proposals.

Council Directive 97/2/EC of 20 January 1997 amending Directive 91/629/EEC laying down minimum standards for the protection of calves.

Summary

Keeping calves in individual pens after the age of eight weeks shall be prohibited from 1/1/98 for all newly built or rebuilt holdings, and from 31/12/2006 for all holdings?

Work in Progress

European Community

In November 1995, the Scientific Veterinary Committee published its report on the Welfare of Calves. It reviews the scientific literature with reference especially to housing systems and management procedures which relate to housing, feeding and the maintenance of good welfare including good health. In its conclusions, the Committee makes a number of recommendations to improve the welfare of calves.

Following this report, the Commission published a proposal for a Council Directive amending Directive 91/629/EEC proposing to phase-out all veal crates by 2008. The Parliament gave an opinion on this proposal. The vote in Parliament took place in September 1996. The Council adopted the Commission proposal in January 1997.

The Commission also submitted a proposal for a Commission Decision amending the Annex to Directive 91/629/EEC. The proposal has been submitted to the Standing Veterinary Committee.

Background

Council of Europe

10/87   The Fifteenth Meeting of the Standing Committee of the European Convention for the Protection of Animals kept for Farming Purposes started the elaboration of a draft Recommendation on cattle.

03/88   The Sixteenth Meeting of the Standing Committee considered a revised version of the draft Recommendation on cattle, including Appendix C: Special Provisions for Calves.

10/88   The Seventeenth Meeting of the Standing Committee suspended adoption of the Recommendation on cattle to allow time for confirmation or otherwise of a reservation by the Belgian representative. The Committee interrupted its work on Appendix C: Special Provisions for Calves pending the drafting of EEC legislation.

21/10/88   The Recommendation concerning cattle was deemed adopted on this date. The provisions for calves were not included.

04/89   The Eighteenth Meeting of the Standing Committee heard that a draft EEC regulation on calves had been prepared by the Commission. It was decided that Appendix C (Special Provisions for Calves) to the Recommendation concerning cattle should not be taken up at this stage.

09/89   The Nineteenth Meeting of the Standing Committee further discussed the proposed provisions on calves.

24/04/90   The Twentieth Meeting of the Standing Committee deferred discussion of special provisions for veal calves pending the adoption of EEC legislation.

8/6/93   Standing Committee adopted 'Special Provisions for Calves'.

European Community

11/02/84   Motion for a Resolution 2-1536/84 by Mrs Castle on the rearing of veal calves.

05/12/84   Motion for a Resolution 2-1141/84 by Mr Mertens and others on the intensive rearing of calves and pigs.

19/12/86   Report A2-211/86 on behalf of the Committee on Agriculture, Fisheries and Food on animal welfare policy. Rapporteur: Richard Simmonds (ED-UK).
              (See Section on Farm Animal Welfare – General.)

20/02/87   The European Parliament adopted a Resolution on animal welfare policy.
              (OJ C.76 23/3/87 p. 162)

26/02/87   Motion for a Resolution 2-1637/86 by Mr Eyraud, Mrs Gadioux and Mr Thareau on the introduction of Community aid for the rearing of calves at foot.

19/06/89   COM(89)114 final the Commission published a proposal for a Council Regulation (EEC) concerning minimum standards for the protection of calves kept in intensive farming systems.
              (OJ C.214 21/8/89 p. 4)

24/10/89   Mr Richard Simmonds appointed Rapporteur for the Agriculture Committee on COM(89)114. Mrs Anita Pollack to draft an opinion for the Environment Committee.

06/11/89   Initial debate in Agriculture Committee on COM(89)114.

20/12/89   CES 1373/89 opinion of ECOSOC on COM(89)114 adopted. It advises against systematic and hasty implementation.

24/01/90   Opinion by Anita Pollack (S-UK) on COM(89)114 adopted by Environment Committee.

20/02/90   Draft report by Richard Simmonds (ED-UK) on COM(89)114 adopted by Agriculture Committee.

05/04/90   Report A3-53/90 by Mr Simmonds on COM(89)114 adopted by Parliament.

05/06/90   COM(90)237 Commission amendments to the proposal for a Regulation on the protection of calves.

25/06/90   Agriculture Council discussed calf proposals and asked COREPER to report back to a later meeting.

22/10/91   Agriculture Council agreed to adopt the proposal concerning minimum standards for the protection of calves kept in intensive farming systems as a Directive.

19/11/91   Council Directive 91/629/EEC laying down minimum standards for the protection of calves.

1/93   Agriculture Committee decided not to draw up a report on motion for a resolution [B3-897/92] on the health of cattle herds in the EC, especially in Piedmont.

19/9/95   In a written reply to a written question by Parliament, the Commissioner said that the Commission has requested the scientific veterinary committee to make a final report on the housing and feeding of calves before the end of 1995. An expert working group established by that committee will also look at the welfare of calves kept in different farming systems.

9/11/95   Report VI/5891/95 by the Commission's Scientific and Veterinary Committee on the welfare of calves. The report examines the need of calves, gives an outline of the different systems with regard to housing, management and diet and analyses the economic consequences of improving calf welfare.

26/1/96   COM (96) 21 final Proposal for a Council Directive amending Directive 91/629/EEC laying down minimum standards for the protection of calves.
              (OJ C. 85 22/3/96 p. 19)

Summary

The Commission proposes to ban individual pens for all calves after the age of 8 weeks:

- from 1 January 1998 for new/rebuilt buildings;

- from 1 January 2008 for all holdings.

It proposes to amend Article 6, which requires the Commission to report by 1 October 1997 on farming systems which comply with the well-being of calves and to put forward appropriate proposals, and to replace the date of 1 October 1997 by 1 January 2006.

Commission proposal for a Commission Decision amending the Annex to Directive 91/629/EEC laying down minimum standards for the protection of calves.

This proposal focuses on diet and housing conditions.

23/7/96   Opinion PE 217.888 for the Committee on Agriculture drawn up on behalf of the Committee on the Environment, on COM (96) 21. Draftsman: Mr Karl-Erik Olsson (ELDR-SU)

2/9/96   Report PE 217.832 on COM (96) 21, drawn up on behalf of the Committee on Agriculture and Rural Development, adopted by Parliament in September 1996. Amendments adopted by Parliament include:

- the date by which all holdings must comply with the amended Directive should be 2005;

- calves to have bedding, a dry lying area;

- the age of the calves after which group-housing is obligatory to be 6 weeks;

- enlargement of the exceptions to the group-housing rule.

The Commission only supported amendments on bedding, visual and tactile contact between calves if in crates and the Maastricht Declaration in the preamble. Rapporteur: Raul Miguel Rosado Fernandes (UPE-P).

PIGS

Existing Legislation

Council Directive 91/630/EEC of 19 November 1991 laying down minimum standards for the protection of pigs.
In force: 1 January 1994.
(OJ L.340 11/12/91 p. 33)

Summary

Member States must provide minimum standards of space depending on average weight for new installations by 31 December 2005 and for existing installations by 1 January 1998. Tethering of sows and gilts will be prohibited by 31 December 1995.

Article 6 requires that by 1 October 1997, and after consultation with the Scientific Veterinary Committee, the Commission will report on the welfare requirements of pigs in intensive systems and make proposals.

Background

Council of Europe

10/03/76   The Convention for the protection of animals kept for farming purposes was opened for signature.

22/02/79   The First Meeting of the Standing Committee set up under the Convention for the protection of animals kept for farming purposes. The Committee drew up its Rules of Procedure.

27/05/82   At its Seventh Meeting, the Standing Committee decided to elaborate a draft recommendation concerning the welfare of pigs kept for farming purposes.

11/03/83   At its Eighth Meeting, the Standing Committee considered the provisions of a 'Draft recommendation on Pigs'.

15/09/83   On the basis of information provided by the delegations, the Bureau revised the text of the 'Draft Recommendation on Pigs'. The Bureau also undertook the elaboration of the Draft Appendices for the different biological groups of pigs.

12/83–11/86 The Standing Committee continued to discuss the draft recommendation on pigs.

21/11/86   At its Fourteenth Meeting, the Standing Committee adopted the Recommendation concerning pigs.

21/11/87   The Recommendation of 21 November 1986 concerning pigs came into effect.

Subsequent meetings of the Standing Committee of the European Convention for the Protection of Animals kept for Farming Purposes received information from representatives and observers on the implementation of the Recommendation concerning pigs.

28/11–1/12/95 Thirtieth Meeting of the Standing Committee of the European Convention for the Protection of Animals Kept for Farming Purposes examined a Recommendation on pigs.

23-26/4/96   Thirty-first Meeting of the Standing Committee of the European Convention for the Protection of Animals Kept for Farming Purposes examined Recommendations on pigs.

European Community

05/12/84   Motion for a Resolution 2-1141/84 by Mr Mertens, Dr Sherlock, Mrs Lentz-Cornette, Mr Alber, Mrs Schleicher, Mrs Peus and Mr Lambrias on the intensive rearing of calves and pigs.

19/12/86	Report A2-211/86 on behalf of the Committee on Agriculture, Fisheries and Food on animal welfare policy. Rapporteur: Richard Simmonds (ED-UK).
19/06/89	COM(89)115 final Commission proposal for a Council Regulation (EEC) concerning minimum standards for the protection of pigs kept in intensive systems. (OJ C.214 21/8/89 p. 5)
19/09/89	Agriculture Committee appointed Mr Simmonds Rapporteur on COM(89)115.
24/10/89	Environment Committee will prepare an opinion on COM(89)115 to be drafted by Mrs Anita Pollack.
06/11/89	Agriculture Committee held initial debate on COM(89)115.
11/89	Motion for a Resolution B3-548/89 by the Green Group on the need for EC regulation of the pig farming sector, including measures to protect extensive farming from competition from intensive farming, to ban tethering and other practices and to reduce transport.
24/01/90	Environment Committee adopted the opinion by Mrs Anita Pollack (S-UK) on COM(89)115.
20/12/89	CES 1374/89 ECOSOC adopted its opinion on COM(89)115. It does not totally condemn stalls and tethers.
21/02/90	The draft report by Mr Richard Simmonds (ED-UK) on COM(89)115 was adopted by the Agriculture Committee.
05/03/90	Directives 90/118/EEC and 90/119/EEC to remove all barriers to the movement within the Community of boars, sows or embryos for breeding purposes, approved by Agriculture Council.
05/04/90	Report A3-53/90 by Mr Richard Simmonds (ED-UK) on COM(89)115 adopted by European Parliament.
05/06/90	COM(90)239 Commission amendments to COM(89)115, laying down minimum standards for the welfare of pigs.
28/10/91	Agriculture Council agreed to adopt proposal laying down minimum standards for the protection of pigs as a Directive.
19/11/91	Council Directive 91/630/EEC laying down minimum standards for the protection of pigs.
12/3/93	[COM(92)0577] proposal for a Council Directive on the statistical surveys to be carried out on pig production.

22/6/95	Directive 95/25/EC amending Directive 64/432/EEC on health problems affecting intra-Community trade in bovine animals and swine. (OJ L.243 11/10/95 p. 16)
12/10/95	Judgment of the Court in Case C-257/94 between the Commission of the European Communities and Italy for failure to transpose Directive 91/685/EEC introducing Community measures for the control of classical swine-fever and Council Directive 91/688/EEC on health and veterinary inspection problems upon importation of bovine, ovine and caprine animals. The Court ordered the Italian republic to pay the costs.
15/11/95	Decision 95/491/EC adopted by Commission on financial aid from the Community for the operation of the Community reference laboratory for swine vesicular disease, Pirbright, United Kingdom. (OJ L. 282 24/11/95 p. 23)
15/11/95	Decision 95/493/EC adopted by Commission repealing Decision 94/887/EC derogating from prohibitions relating to African swine fever for certain areas in Spain and repealing Council Decision 89/21/EEC. (OJ L. 282 24/11/95 p. 28)
15/11/95	Decision 96/30/EC adopted by the Commission approving the programme for the eradication of *Brucella Melitensis* for the year 1996 presented by Greece and fixing the level of the Community's financial contibution. (OJ L. 8 11/1/96 p. 33)
18/11/95	Decision 95/483/EC adopted by Commission determining the specimen certificate for intra-Community trade in ova and embryos of swine. (OJ L.275 18/11/95 p. 30)
1/12/95	Decision 95/535/EC adopted by Commission on an additional financial contribution from the Community for the eradication of classical swine fever in Germany. (OJ L. 304 16/12/95 p. 47)
15/12/95	Decision 96/69/EC adopted by Commission approving the programme for the eradication and surveillance of swine vesicular disease for 1996 presented by Italy and fixing the level of the Community's financial contribution. (OJ L.16 22/1/96 p. 29)

19/12/95   Decisions 96/25 to 96/28EC adopted by Commission approving the programme for the eradication and surveillance of African swine fever for the year 1996 presented by, respectively, Italy, Spain, Portugal and Germany and fixing the level of the Community's financial contribution.
(OJ L. 8 11/1/96 pp. 28–31)

20/12/95   Decision 96/23/EC adopted by Commission laying down the rules for technical and scientific measures concerning the control of classical swine fever and the financial contribution fom the Community.
(OJ L. 7 10/1/96 p. 10)

31/1/96   Decision 96/141/EC adopted by Commission amending Decision 95/296/EC concerning certain protection measures relating to classical swine fever in Germany and repealing Decision 94/462/EC.
(OJ L. 32 10/2/96 p. 36)

22/2/96   Decision 96/190/EC adopted by Commission amending Decision 93/244/EEC and concerning additional guarantees relating to Aujeszky's disease for pigs destined to regions free of the disease in Germany.
(OJ L. 60 9/3/96 p. 29)

25/3/96   Decision 96/238/EC adopted by Commission amending for the second time Decision 95/296/EC concerning certain protection measures relating to classical swine fever in Germany.
(OJ L. 78 28/3/96 p. 46)

5/6/96   Decision 96/141/EC adopted by Commission amending Decision 95/296/EC concerning certain protection measures relating to classical swine fever in Germany and repealing Decision 94/462/EC.
(OJ L.138 11/6/96 p. 23)

GAME MANAGEMENT AND GAME MEAT PRODUCTION

Existing Legislation

None.

Work in Progress

European Community

17/10/89   COM(89)496 final proposal for a Council Regulation concerning game meat and rabbit meat.

24/10/89	COM(89)496 referred to Environment Committee with opinion from Agriculture Committee and Legal Affairs Committee. Rapporteur: Caroline Jackson (PPE-UK).
13/09/90	Report A3-168/90 by Mrs Jackson on COM(89)496 adopted by European Parliament.
28/09/90	CES 371/90 opinion drafted by Mr Murphy on COM(89)496 adopted by ECOSOC.

COM(89)668 proposal for a regulation to lay down standards for the trade in fresh meat from poultry, pigeons and farmed game birds. Referred to Environment Committee with opinions from Budgets Committee and Agriculture Committee. Rapporteur: Adriana Ceci (GUE-I).

17/10/90	Draft report A3-309/90 by Mrs Ceci on COM(89)668 adopted by Environment Committee.
19/04/90	Report A3-309/90 by Mrs Ceci on COM(89)668 adopted by European Parliament. Includes recommendations on the stunning and slaughter of birds for foie gras production.

COM(89)496 proposal for a Council Regulation concerning game meat and rabbit meat being considered by Council expert working group.

14/04/91	Report A3-303/90 on proposal for a Regulation on the trade in poultry meat and meat from farmed game birds to prevent the spread of disease. Rapporteur: Jim Fitzsimmons (RDE-IRL).
17/6/96	Decision 96/389/EC adopted by Commission approving the plan for the monitoring and control of salmonella in fowl presented by Ireland. (OJ L.155 28/6/96 p. 60)
18/6/96	Decision 96/389/EC adopted by Commission approving the plan for the monitoring and control of salmonella in fowl presented by Finland. (OJ L.155 28/6/96 p. 61)
25/7/96	Decision 96/502/EC adopted by Commission approving the plan for the monitoring and control of salmonella in fowl presented by Sweden. (OJ L.204 14/8/96 p. 18)

Council of Europe

25–28/4/95	Twenty-ninth Meeting of the Standing Committee of the European Convention for the Protection of Animals Kept

for Farming Purposes further elaborated Recommendations concerning domestic fowl (broilers) and other poultry species (duck, goose, turkey, guinea-fowl, quail, partridge, pigeon, pheasant).

28/11–1/12/95 Thirtieth Meeting of the Standing Committee of the European Convention for the Protection of Animals Kept for Farming Purposes adopted a Recommendation on domestic fowl (*Gallus gallus*) replacing the Recommendation on poultry adopted on 21 November 1986.

FUR FARMING

Existing Legislation

Council Decision 92/583/EEC of 14 December 1992 on the conclusion of the Protocol of amendment to the European Convention for the Protection of Animals kept for Farming Purposes.
(OJ L.395 31/12/92)

Work in Progress

Council of Europe

The Recommendation concerning fur bearing animals is to be reviewed after five years of its entering into force, i.e. by the end of 1996.

European Community

COM(91)136 proposal for a Council Regulation (EEC) on the protection of animals at the time of slaughter or killing. Covers the killing of farm reared fur bearing animals in Article 10 and Annex F.

Background

Council of Europe

21/10/87 Meeting of the Bureau of the Standing Committee of the European Convention for the Protection of Animals kept for Farming Purposes agreed to recommend to the Standing Committee that the next Recommendation to be drafted should concern fur animals, on grounds that the welfare of these animals is not always ensured in the present intensive breeding systems, and an efficient legislation on this type of breeding is not enforced in all States party to the Convention.

03/88	Sixteenth Meeting of the Standing Committee of the European Convention for the Protection of Animals kept for Farming Purposes selected fur animals as the subject of its next Recommendation.
10/88	Seventeenth Meeting of the Standing Committee of the European Convention for the Protection of Animals kept for Farming Purposes considered the draft recommendation on fur animals elaborated by the Bureau in July 1988.
12/88	Meeting of the Bureau revised the draft recommendation on fur animals in accordance with the comments of the Standing Committee.
04/89	Eighteenth Meeting of the Standing Committee agreed to hold a meeting in Denmark in September 1989 in order to hear reports of the Danish experience in this field. The Meeting also agreed that the European Convention for the Protection of Animals kept for Farming Purposes should be amended by a Protocol of Amendment to make clear that the Convention also covered the killing and transport of fur animals.
06/89	Meeting of the Bureau of the Standing Committee further revised the draft recommendation concerning fur animals to include appendices on various species. It also amended the draft Protocol of Amendment to remove transport, since this did not form part of the draft recommendation.
26/09/89	Nineteenth Meeting of the Standing Committee in Copenhagen heard further submissions on the keeping of fur bearing animals and drafted recommendations on the keeping and killing of animals farmed for their fur.
02/90	Meeting of the Bureau of the Standing Committee further revised the draft recommendation concerning fur animals.
24/04/90	Twentieth Meeting of the Standing Committee further revised the draft recommendation on the keeping of fur animals.
16/10/90	Twenty-first Meeting of the Standing Committee on the Convention for the Protection of Animals kept for Farming Purposes finalised recommendations for the keeping of animals farmed for their fur.
19/10/91	The Recommendation concerning fur animals entered into force.

15/11/91   Protocol of Amendment to the European Convention for the
                Protection of Animals kept for Farming Purposes adopted
                by the Committee of Ministers. Open for signature on
                6 February 1992.

28/11–1/12/95   Thirtieth Meeting of the Standing Committee of the
                European Convention for the Protection of Animals Kept
                for Farming Purposes revised a Recommendation on fur
                animals. It covers stockmanship and inspection of fur
                animals, enclosures/housing, management, changes of phe-
                notype/genotype, and research. It gives special provisions
                for mink, polecats, foxes, coypu, chinchilla and methods of
                killing fur animals.

23-26/4/96   Thirty-first Meeting of the Standing Committee of the
                European Convention for the Protection of Animals Kept
                for Farming Purposes proposed amendments for the draft
                Recommendation concerning fur animals.

8–11/10/96   Thirty-second Meeting of the Standing Committee of the
                European Convention for the Protection of Animals
                Kept for Farming Purposes is due to examine the draft
                Recommendation on fur animals.

European Community

12/11/88   The Directorate-General for Agriculture (DGVI) of the
                Commission of the European Communities published a call
                for expressions of interest concerning a study of fur farming.

07/90   Commission published a study into the legal, technical and
                animal welfare aspects of fur farming (ISBN-826-0504-3).

10/07/92   COM(92)243 proposal for a Council Decision on the
                conclusion of the Protocol of Amendment to the European
                Convention for the Protection of Animals kept for Farming
                Purposes, referred to Agriculture Committee. Rapporteur:
                Richard Simmonds (ED-UK).
                (See Farm Animals General.)

Chapter 3

Experimental Animals

ANIMAL EXPERIMENTATION

Existing Legislation

Council Directive 86/609/EEC of 24 November 1986 on the approximation of laws, regulations and administrative provisions of the Member States regarding the protection of animals used for experimental and other scientific purposes.

In force: 24 November 1989.

(OJ L.358 18/12/86)

Summary

The aim of the Directive is to ensure that where animals are used for experimental and other scientific purposes the provisions laid down by law, regulation and administration in the Member States for their protection are approximated. Such harmonisation should ensure that the number of animals used is reduced to a minimum, that such animals are adequately cared for, that no pain, suffering, distress or lasting harm are unnecessarily inflicted but, where unavoidable, that these are kept to a minimum.

The Directive applies to the use of animals in experiments undertaken for:

1. development, manufacture, quality, effectiveness and safety testing of drugs, foodstuffs and other substances or products;

2. the protection of the environment in the interests of the health or welfare of man or animal.

The content of the Directive follows very closely that of the European Convention and aims to ensure that as far as the 12 Member States are concerned these will be observed. It does however go further in introducing elements specific to the European Community. These include prior notification of the experiment or the person to carry it out, prohibition of experiments on endangered species listed in Appendix I of CITES, elimination of unnecessary duplication of experiments and encouragement of research into alternatives to animals.

Council Resolution of 24 November 1986 on the signature by Member States of the European Convention for the protection of vertebrate animals used for experimental and other scientific purposes.
(OJ C.331 23/12/86)

Resolution of the Representatives of the Governments of the Member States of the European Community meeting within the Council of 24 November 1986 regarding the protection of animals used for experimental and other scientific purposes.
(OJ C.331 23/12/86)
Urges Member States to apply national provisions which are no less severe than those of the Directive where the purpose of the experiments on animals is listed in Article 2 of the European Convention but not covered by the Directive.

Council Directive 87/18/EEC of 18 December 1986 on the harmonisation of laws, regulations and administrative provisions relating to the application of the principles of Good Laboratory Practice and the verification of their applications for tests on chemical substances.
(OJ L.15 17/1/87 p. 29)

Council Directive 88/320/EEC of 9 June 1988 on the inspection and verification of Good Laboratory Practice (GLP).
(OJ L.145 11/6/88 pp. 35–7)

Council Decision 89/569/EEC of 28 July 1989 on the acceptance by the European Community of an OECD decision/recommendation on compliance with the principles of Good Laboratory Practice.
(OJ L.315 28/10/89 p. 1)

Commission Directive 90/18/EEC of 18 December 1989 adapting to technical progress the Annex to Council Directive 88/320/EEC on the inspection and verification of Good Laboratory Practice (GLP).
(OJ L.011 13/1/90 p. 37)

Commission Decision 90/67/EEC of 9 February 1990 setting up an Advisory Committee on the Protection of Animals Used for Experimental and Other Scientific Purposes.
(OJ L.044 20/2/90 p. 30)

Council Directive 92/32/EEC of 30 April 1992 amending for the seventh time Directive 67/548/EEC on the approximation of the laws, regulations and administrative provisions relating to the classification, packaging and labelling of dangerous substances.
(OJ L.154 5/6/92)

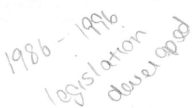
1986 – 1996. legislation developed

Summary

Article 15 is intended to avoid duplicate testing on animals by doing away with the need to renotify the same substance.

Work in Progress

European Community

Directive 86/609/EEC. Formal proposals resulting from the deliberations on the type of experimentation statistics to be collected by Member States under the Directive will be produced in due course.

The EC is discussing training for animal handlers and a system to gather statistics.

COM(92)23 final proposal for a Fifth Environmental Action Plan. Among targets this sets a 50% reduction in experiments on animals by the year 2000.

COM (95) 624 final Commission's Report 1995 adopted 10/1/96 on the implementation of the European Community programme of policy and action in relation to the environment and sustainable development 'Towards Sustainability'.

Protection of animals used for experimental purposes is mentioned under 'risk management'; 50% reduction by the year 2000 still mentioned as an aim and recent developments are highlighted, i.e. development of alternative methods and the role of ECVAM.

COM (95) 647 final Proposal for a European Parliament and Council Decision on the review of the European Community programme of policy and action in relation to the environment and sustainable development 'Towards sustainability'. Adopted 29/2/96. Under 'risk management', no mention is made of the 50% reduction target.
(OJ No. C 140, 11.5.96, p. 5)

PE 217.883: Report by Mrs Dybkjaer (ELDR.DK) on Commission proposal COM(95)647. Amendment adopted on 50% reduction of animal experimentation.

Council of Europe

Work is being undertaken to develop a system to gather statistics, and also in relation to training of laboratory workers who handle animals.

Background

Council of Europe

15/12/70   Report on the opinion of the Committee on Science and Technology (Doc 2874) concerning the problems arising out of the use of live animals for experimental or industrial purposes adopted by the Committee on Agriculture. Rapporteur: Mr Rinderspacher.

29/12/70   Opinion of the Consultative Assembly (Doc 2875).

20/01/71   The Assembly adopted Recommendation 621 (1971) on the problems arising out of the use of live animals for experimental or industrial purposes.

The Assembly recommended the Committee of Ministers to give a Committee terms of reference 'to draft international legislation setting out the conditions under which, and the scientific grounds on which, experiments on live animals may be authorised'.

1973   The Committee of Ministers proposed that a convention on the use of live animals for experimental purposes be drawn up and instructed the Committee of Experts for the Protection of Animals to do so.

01/78   Following the finalisation of the Convention for the Protection of Animals for Slaughter also drawn up by the Committee of Experts, now the ad hoc Committee of Experts (CAHPA), work began on the Convention on the use of live animals for experimental purposes. Proposals were submitted by the World Federation for the Protection of Animals (WFPA), the International Society for the Protection of Animals (ISPA) and the International Committee for Laboratory Animals (ICLA).

10/78   Second Meeting of CAHPA. The first Draft Convention was discussed and considered to be unsuitable. The Secretariat was given the task of preparing the second draft.

19/10/79   CAHPA submitted suggested revisions to the Draft Convention.

06/07/80   Basic principles for the European Convention for the Protection of Animals used for Experimentation Purposes were adopted by Eurogroup for Animal Welfare.

29/01/81	Petition presented to the Parliamentary Assembly on behalf of the World Coalition for the Abolition of Experiments on Animals.
26/11/82	At its Eleventh Meeting, CAHPA approved the following:

1. Draft European Convention for the Protection of Vertebrate Animals used for Experimental and other Scientific Purposes;

2. Draft Explanatory Report to the Convention.

08–09/12/82	European Public Parliamentary Hearing on the Use of Live Animals for Experimental and Industrial Purposes held at Palais de l'Europe, Strasbourg. (Eurogroup submitted a document entitled *Animal Experimentation – Areas of Concern: The Scope and Role of Legislation* by Judith Hampson BSc, PhD, and Sheila Silcock BSc, DipNutr.)
25/02/82	Preliminary Report of the Committee on Science and Technology on Animal Experimentation. Rapporteur: Mrs Aner. Proposals for modifying the Draft Convention in the light of the public hearing.
03/83	Submission of suggested amendments to the Draft Convention by Judith Hampson BSc, PhD, Sheila Silcock BSc, DipNutr, and Ian Milligan MA, LLB, for Eurogroup.
26/04/83	Doc 5049 was released containing:

1. Report on the Draft European Convention for the protection of animals in experimental purposes. Rapporteur: Mr Bassinet.

2. Draft Recommendation presented by the Committee on Science and Technology (adopted 26/4/83).

27/04/83	Draft Opinion for the Committee of Ministers on the proposed amendments in the report of the Committee on Science and Technology.
26–29/04/83	At the Twelfth Meeting of CAHPA the Committee finalised and adopted Appendices A and B of the Draft Convention for the Protection of Vertebrate Animals Used for Experimental and Other Scientific Purposes. This meeting marked the attendance for the first time by a scientific adviser to Eurogroup (Judith Hampson BSc, PhD).

CAHPA decided to submit to the Committee of Ministers for opening to signature by the Member Countries of the Council of Europe, the Draft Convention and the Draft Explanatory Report.

07/03/85   As decided by the Committee of Ministers, a meeting of technical experts chaired by Mr Stian Erichsen (Norway) took place to prepare the final examination of the Draft Convention by the Committee of Ministers.

31/05/85   The Committee of Ministers adopted the text of the Convention.

18/03/86   European Convention No. Ets 123 for the Protection of Vertebrate Animals used for Experimental and other Scientific Purposes was opened for signature. (See Appendix IX for signatories.)
Once the Convention has been ratified by four Member Countries, a five year period is given to the Member Countries to enable them to implement its provisions.

01/01/91   The European Convention (ETS 123) entered into force.

19/03/91   Multilateral Consultation agreed to devote its Fourth Consultation to be held in April 1992 to the European Convention for the Protection of Vertebrate Animals Used for Experimental and Other Scientific Purposes.

13/04/92   Second Meeting of the Working Party for the Preparation of the Multilateral Consultation of Parties to the European Convention for the Protection of Vertebrate Animals used for Experimental Purposes (ETS 123) discussed various possible amendments to the Convention, particularly concerning the breeding of animals carrying harmful genetic modifications for which a draft text was prepared.

24–27/11/92   First Multilateral Consultation of Parties to the European Convention for the Protection of Vertebrate Animals used for Experimental Purposes (ETS 123) – adopted resolution on the interpretation of certain provisions and terms of the convention.

03/11/93   European Convention No. Ets 123 for the Protection of Vertebrate Animals used for Experimental and other Scientific Purposes (Strasbourg 18/03/86) – Switzerland ratified.

30/11–3/12/93   Second Multilateral Consultation of Parties to the European Convention for the Protectin of Vertebrate Animals used for Experimental Purposes (ETS 123) – adopted resolution on education and training for persons working with laboratory animals.

09/12/93   European Convention No. Ets 123 for the Protection of Vertebrate Animals used for Experimental and other Scientific Purposes (Strasbourg 18/03/86) – Cyprus signed and ratified.

6–9/9/94   Fourth Multilateral Consultation of Parties to the European Convention for the Protection of Vertebrate Animals used for Experimental Purposes (ETS 123).

19/9/95   In the European Parliament Report A4 – 196/95 by David Bowe MEP. Under the Convention each party is required to provide yearly information about the numbers of animals used in experiments but because some Member States are not able to make annual data returns Mr Bowe will be accepting the submission of statistics every two years during a transition period of six years. He will also be calling for a 50% reduction in the number of animals used in tests by the year 2000 [PE 191.498] which is also the goal of the Fifth Environmental Action Programme.

For the Commission, Edith Cresson welcomed support for the amendment as a means of making the 1986 Convention and subsequent EU Directives more effective. She was optimistic about the European Centre for Alternative Testing at ISPRA developing new methods which would result in less animal testing and felt able to accept most of the other amendments tabled by Parliament subject to slight change of wording [PE 191.505.fin]

25–29/9/95   Fifth Meeting of the Working Party for the preparation of the Multilateral Consultation of the Parties to the European Convention for the protection of vertebrate animals used for experimental purposes (ETS 123). Issues raised included statistics, transport, sources of animals, housing, transgenic animals and euthanasia.

2/4/96   Hearing on the transport of laboratory animals – European Convention for the protection of vertebrate animals used for experimental purposes (ETS 123). Discussions mainly focused on the transport of primates and on air transport. A draft declaration of intent concerning the transport of laboratory animals was circulated (CONS 123 (96) 5 revised).

8–11/4/97   Next meeting of the Multilateral Consultation of the Parties to the European Convention for the protection of vertebrate animals used for experimental purposes (ETS 123). Transport of laboratory animals stands on the agenda.

European Community

24/11/83   Motion for a Resolution 1-1096/83 by Mrs Dury and Mr Glinne on regulations governing the Lethal Dose 50% Test.

09/01/84   Motion for a Resolution 1-1254/83 by Mrs Herklotz and Mrs Seibel-Emmerling on the limitation of animal experiments and the protection of experimental animals.

15/05/84   Report 1-213/84 drawn up on behalf of the Committee on Environment, Public Health and Consumer Protection on limiting animal experiments and the protection of experimental animals (based on Motions for Resolution 1-1096/83 and 1-1254/83). Rapporteur: Ursula Schleicher (PPE-D).

24/05/84   Resolution adopted by the European Parliament on the limitation of animal experiments and the protection of experimental animals (1-213/84).
(OJ C.172 2/7/84)

22/02/85   Commission Recommendation to Council (COM(85)54) for a Council Decision authorising the Commission to negotiate Community participation in the European Convention.

04/03/85   Letter from President Delors to Mrs Seibel-Emmerling and Sir Jack Stewart-Clark announcing the preparation by the Commission of a draft Directive on animal experimentation.

19/06/85   Motion for a Resolution 544/85 by Mr Martin and Mr Newens, on the continued Community approval of the use of LD50.

Motion for a Resolution 545/85 by Mr Newens and Mr Martin, on legislation for the protection of vertebrate animals used for experimental purposes.

10/10/85   Motion for a Resolution 2-0979/85 by Mrs Seibel-Emmerling, Sir Jack Stewart-Clark, Mrs Castle, Mr Seligman, Mrs Maij-Weggen, Mrs Thome-Patenôtre, Mrs

Squarcialupi, Mr Toksvig, Sir Henry Plumb, Mr Martin, Mr Muntingh, Mr Marshall, Dr Sherlock, Mr Seal, Mr Prout, Mrs Quin, Mr Griffiths, Mr Paisley, Mr Pearce, Mrs Jackson, Mrs Daly, Mr Newens, Mr Raftery, Mr Newton-Dunn, Mrs Braun-Moser, Mr Woltjer, Mr Adam, Mr Rogalla, Mrs Lemass, Mr Habsburg, Mr Cottrell, Mr Prag, Ms Tongue, Mrs Faith, Mrs Ewing, Mr Turner, Mr Hutton, Mr Falconer, Mr Elliott, Mr Gauthier, Mr de Courcy Ling, on the Commission's failure to act upon the Resolutions concerning the Directive on animal experiments.

18/12/85   COM(85)637 final proposal from the Commission for:

- a Council Directive on the protection of animals used for experimental and other scientific purposes; and

- the signature by the Community and Member States of the European Convention for the Protection of Vertebrate Animals used for Experimental and other Scientific Purposes.

(OJ C.351 31/12/85)

23/01/86   The Council requested opinions from the European Parliament and the ECOSOC on the proposal.

26/02/86   EP Environment Committee appointed Mrs Caroline Jackson Rapporteur.

07/03/86   Report 2-233/86 drawn up on behalf of the Environment Committee on the proposal for a Directive on the harmonisation of laws relating to the application of the principles of Good Laboratory Practice and verification of their application for tests on chemical substances. Rapporteur: Ursula Schleicher (PPE-D).

21/05/86   Opinion of the ECOSOC on the proposal for a Directive on the protection of experimental animals (COM(85)637 final).
(OJ C.207 18/8/86)

18/07/86   Report A-94/86 drawn up on behalf of the Environment Committee on the proposal for a Directive on the protection of experimental animals (COM(85)637 final). Rapporteur: Caroline Jackson (ED-UK).

12/09/86   Opinion of the European Parliament on COM(85)637 final.
(OJ C.255 13/10/86)
Vote: 150-0 with 2 abstentions.

04/11/86   Motion for a Resolution 1135/86 by Mrs Bloch von Blottnitz on the planned construction of an institute for breeding laboratory animals in Schinveld (Netherlands).

10/11/86   Commission amendments to the proposal for a Directive on the protection of animals used for experimental and other scientific purposes.
(OJ C.323 16/12/86)

24/11/86   Council Directive 86/609/EEC on the approximation of laws, regulations and administrative provisions of the Member States regarding the protection of animals used for experimental and other scientific purposes.
(OJ L.358 18/12/86)

15/12/86   COM(86)698 final The Commission submitted a proposal for a Council Directive on the inspection and verification of the organisational processes and conditions under which laboratory studies are planned, performed, recorded and reported for the non-clinical testing of chemicals (Good Laboratory Practice).

18/12/86   Council Directive 87/18/EEC on the harmonisation of laws, regulations and administrative provisions relating to the application of the principles of good laboratory practice and the verification of their application for tests on chemical substances.
(OJ L.15 17/1/87 p. 29)

10/02/87   The Commission signed the European Convention on behalf of the EEC.

08/03/87   Motion for a Resolution 2-73/87 by Mrs Bloch von Blottnitz on the banning of the use of LD50 tests in animal experiments.

23/03/87   Motion for a Resolution 2-129/87 by Mrs Bloch von Blottnitz on the setting up of a European Assessment and Coordination Centre for alternative and supplementary methods for use in animal experiments.

08/07/87   Report A2-118/87 drawn up on behalf of the Committee on Energy, Research and Technology on the proposal from the Commission to the Council (COM(86)549 final 2 – Doc. C2-152/86/III) for a regulation relating to a research and development coordination programme of the European Economic Community in the field of medical and health research (1987–9). Rapporteur: Dieter Schinzel (S-D).

28/07/89 Council Decision 89/569/EEC on the acceptance by the European Community of an OECD decision/recommendation on compliance with the principles of Good Laboratory Practice.

18/09/87 The European Parliament adopted a Resolution (A2-118/87) on the proposal COM(86)549 final 2 for a regulation relating to a research and development coordination programme of the European Community in the field of medical and health research (1987–9).
(OJ C.281 19/10/87 p. 169)

18/12/87 The Council adopted a Common Position with a view to the adoption of a Council Directive on the inspection and verification of the organisational processes and conditions under which laboratory studies are planned, performed, recorded and reported for the non-clinical testing of chemicals (Good Laboratory Practice) (doc. C2-190/86). Transmitted to the Parliament on 15 January 1988.

25/03/88 Report A2-28/88 drawn up on behalf of the Environment Committee concerning the Common Position of the Council (Good Laboratory Practice) (Doc. C2-273/87). Rapporteur: Beate Weber (S-D).

04/88 European Parliament Opinion (A2-28/88) on the Common Position of the Council (Doc. C2-273/87) (Good Laboratory Practice).

09/06/88 Council Directive 88/320/EEC on the inspection and verification of Good Laboratory Practice (GLP).

29/04/88 COM(88)243 final Commission Report on the possibility of modifying tests and guidelines laid down in existing Community legislation in compliance with Article 23 of Council Directive 86/609/EEC. This was adopted by the Commission on 27 April 1988 and transmitted to Parliament on 27 May 1988.

17/08/88 Motion for a Resolution 2-0618/88 by Sir Jack Stewart-Clark, Mr Seligman, Ms Tongue, Mrs Llorca Vilaplana, Mr Marshall, Mrs Squarcialupi, Mrs van Hemeldonck, Mr Bombard, Mr Coimbra Martins, Mrs Ewing, Mrs Castle, Mrs Jackson, Mrs Bjornvig, Mr Poulsen, Mr Elliott,

	Mrs Lemass, Mrs Lentz-Cornette and Mr Tomlinson on the use of chimpanzees for biomedical research.
21/11/88	COM(88)632 final – SYN 168 Commission proposal for a Council Decision adopting two specific research and technological development programmes in the field of the environment:

- STEP: Science and Technology for Environmental Protection;

- EPOCH: European Programme on Climatology and Natural Hazards.

Both 1989–92.
STEP includes research into alternatives to the use of animals in chemicals testing.

24/11/88	The Commission proposal on the STEP and EPOCH programmes (COM(88)632 final – SYN 168) was submitted to the Council. (OJ C.327 20/12/88)
09/01/89	Report A2-0352/88 drawn up on behalf of the Environment Committee on a reduction in the use of animals for experimental purpose (based on Motions for Resolution B2-73/87 and B2-129/87). Rapporteur: Carole Tongue (S-UK).
	(Drawn up in response to the Commission's Report COM(88)243 final of 29 April 1988 on the possibility of modifying tests and guidelines.)
23/01/89	Council authorised the Commission to participate in OECD negotiations on good laboratory practice.
17/02/89	European Parliament adopted Resolution on a reduction in the use of animals for experimental purposes (Tongue Report A2-0352/88).
20/03/89	Report A2-4/89 drawn up on behalf of the Committee on Energy and Research on COM(88)632 final – SYN 168, the Commission proposal for a Council Decision adopting the STEP and EPOCH research programmes. Rapporteur: Günther Rinsche (PPE-D).
31/03/89	CES 427/89 ECOSOC opinion on STEP and EPOCH programmes adopted.
03/04/89	Annex to Report A2-4/89.

| 12/04/89 | European Parliament adopted a Resolution on COM(88) 632 final – SYN 168 – STEP and EPOCH programmes (A2-4/89). |

12/04/89   European Parliament adopted a Resolution on COM(88) 632 final – SYN 168 – STEP and EPOCH programmes (A2-4/89).

18/05/89   COM(89)134 – SYN 168. The Commission's revised proposals for the STEP and EPOCH programmes.

20/06/89   Doc. C3-0011/89 – SYN 168 Common Position adopted by Council with a view to the adoption of a decision on two specific research and technological development programmes in the field of the environment STEP and EPOCH (1989–92).

10/07/89   COM(89)302 final – SYN 198 Commission proposal for a Council Decision on the conclusion, on behalf of the Community, of the European Convention for the protection of vertebrate animals used for experimental and other scientific purposes .

25/07/89   Doc. C3-0011/89 – SYN 168 Common Position on STEP and EPOCH referred to the European Parliament for an opinion.

09/89   Following a seminar on LD50 testing and classification schemes organised by DGXI (Environment), the Commission made a commitment to hold a further seminar to evaluate the feasibility of rationalising classification schemes and to introduce fixed dose procedure for classification, packaging and labelling as an acceptable test.

11/10/89   Parliament approved COM(89)302.

18/12/89   Commission Directive 90/18/EEC adapting to technical progress the Annex to Council Directive 88/320/EEC on the inspection and verification of Good Laboratory Practice (GLP).

01/90   CES 1122/89 ECOSOC in its opinion completely supports the proposal (COM(89)302).

09/02/90   Commission Decision 90/67/EEC setting up an Advisory Committee on the Protection of Animals Used for Experimental and Other Scientific Purposes.

11/90   Motion for a Resolution B3-1338/90 by Mrs Muscardini and others to end the use of animals to test cosmetics and medicines.

04/11/91   Communication from the Commission to the Council and Parliament concerning the establishment of a European Centre for the Validation of Alternative Methods (SEC(91)1794).

19/02/91   Report A3-302/90 on a proposal for a directive on the authorisation of pesticides and herbicides. As this is dependent on their toxicity and ecotoxicity testing must be carried out. Adopted by European Parliament. Rapporteur: José Luis Valverde Lopez (PPE-E).

06/91   Motion for a Resolution B3-234/91 by Mr Seligman and others pointing out that insufficient attention has been given to alternatives to the use of animals in biomedical research techniques resulting in an excessive use of wild-caught chimpanzees. It also calls for a register of all captive chimps.

09/10/91   Report A3-214/91 on COM(90)227 a proposal for a Council regulation (EEC) on the evaluation and the control of the environmental risks of existing substances. This includes LD50 and LC50 tests. Adopted by European Parliament. Rapporteur: Ursula Schleicher (PPE-D) on behalf of Environment Committee.

                  CES 275/91 ECOSOC opinion on COM(90)227. Draftsman: Mr Vidal.

04/11/91   Communication from the Commission to the Council and Parliament concerning the establishment of a European Centre for the Validation of Alternative Methods (SEC(91)1794).

12/12/91   Council adopted a common position on COM(90)227.

19/12/91   Report A3-7/92 by Mrs Roth-Behrendt on COM(90)488 adopted by Environment Committee.

12/02/92   Report A3-7/92 by Mrs Roth-Behrendt on COM(90)488 adopted by Plenary. The Commission did not accept all Parliament's amendments and Plenary voted to refer the report back to Committee.

30/04/92   Council Directive 92/32/EEC amending for the seventh time Directive 67/548/EEC on the approximation of the laws, regulations and administrative provisions relating to the classification, packaging and labelling of dangerous substances.

21/05/92	Report A3-7/92 by Mrs Roth-Behrendt on COM(90)488 discussed by Environment Committee and three compromise amendments were adopted.
10/06/92	Report A3-7/92 by Mrs Roth-Behrendt on COM(90)488 and its three compromise amendments was adopted by Plenary.
25/3/93	Commissioner for Consumer Affairs presented the Environment Committee with the Commission's objectives for 1993–5. As Council had been unanimous in approving the Common Position she doubted that the Ministers would accept the Parliament's amendment re Article 100a, showing Council's unwillingness to formally consult Parliament re postponing the date for a ban on the testing of cosmetics on animals.
20/4/93	Council's Common Position re Cosmetic Products undergoes a second reading and vote.
11/3/94	Motion for a Resolution in Seligman Report adopted pursuant to Rule 52 Alternative testing methods.
9/95	Council Proposal for a Directive for Adoption of the Council of Europe's European Convention ETS 123 for the Protection of Vertebrate Animals used for Experimental and other Scientific Purposes (Strasbourg 18/3/86).
19/9/95	In the European Parliament Report A4 – 196/95 by David Bowe MEP was adopted on the amended proposal for a Council Decision on the conclusion, on behalf of the Community, of the Council of Europe's European Convention ETS 123 for the Protection of Vertebrate Animals used for Experimental and other Scientific Purposes (Strasbourg 18/3/86) – (Com (94)0366 – C4-0000/94 – 94/ 0000(COD)). Under the Convention each party is required to provide yearly information about the numbers of animals used in experiments but because some Member States are not able to make annual data returns Mr Bowe will be accepting the submission of statistics every two years during a transition period of six years. He will also be calling for a 50% reduction in the number of animals used in tests by the year 2000 [PE 191.498] which is also the goal of the Fifth Environmental Action Programme. For the Commission, Edith Cresson welcomed support for the amendment as a means of making the 1986

Convention and subsequent EU Directives more effective. She was optimistic about the European Centre for Alternative Testing at ISPRA developing new methods which would result in less animal testing and felt able to accept most of the other amendments tabled by Parliament subject to slight change of wording [PE 191.505.fin]

10/1/96 COM (95) 624 final Commission's Report 1995 adopted on the implementation of the European Community programme of policy and action in relation to the environment and sustainable development 'Towards Sustainability'.

Protection of animals used for experimental purposes is mentioned under 'risk management'; 50% reduction by the year 2000 still mentioned as an aim and recent developments are highlighted, i.e. development of alternative methods and the role of ECVAM.

29/2/96 COM (95) 647 final Proposal for a European Parliament and Council Decision on the review of the European Community programme of policy and action in relation to the environment and sustainable development 'Towards sustainability'. Under 'risk management', no mention is made of the 50% reduction target.
(OJ C.140, 11.5.96, p. 5)

12/3/96 Oral question H-0199/96 from the European Parliament to the Commission on statistics on animal experimentation.

25/4/96 Judgment of the Court in Case C-274/93 between The Commission and Luxembourg for failure to implement Council Directive 86/609/EEC. Luxembourg to pay the costs.
(OJ C.180 22/6/96 p. 12)

16/7/96 COM (96) 243 final Commission amended proposal for a Council Decision on the conclusion, on behalf of the Community, of the European Convention for the protection of vertebrate animals used for experimental and other scientific purposes.
(OJ C. 266 13/9/96 p. 15)

COSMETICS

Existing Legislation

Directive 76/768/EEC – on harmonisation of the laws of Member States on Cosmetic Products.

Work in Progress

	COM(94) 606 final – 1994 Annual Report on the development, validation and legal acceptance of alternative methods to animal experiments.
14/7/95	Report by Mrs Roth-Behrendt on the 1994 Annual Report adopted by Parliament.
24/7/96	Report from the Commission – 1995 on development, validation and legal acceptance of alternative methods to animal experiments in the field of cosmetic products. The report outlines the different methods under development and validation, gives information on statistics on animal experiments and perspectives relating to the development of alternative methods for the various toxicity tests used in the evaluation of the safety of cosmetic ingredients and cosmetic products. It also highlights the major players involved in encouraging research in alternative methods. One of the report's conclusions was that validation had turned out to be more difficult and time-consuming than expected. A successful outcome can be expected for the validation of some tests, such as in vitro phototoxicity testing and skin corrosivity. (COM (96) 365 final)
1/97	Publication of Mrs Roth-Behrendt's report on the Commission 1995 Report.

Background

European Community

11/90	Motion for a Resolution B3-1338/90 by Mrs Muscardini and others to end the use of animals to test cosmetics and medicines.
05/02/91	COM(90)488 proposal for a directive to amend for the sixth time Directive 76/768/EEC on the approximation of the laws of the Member States relating to cosmetic products. It will remove intra-Community barriers to trade.
11/03/91	COM(90)488 proposal for a directive to amend for the sixth time Directive 76/768/EEC on the approximation of the laws of the Member States relating to cosmetic products, referred to Environment Committee. Rapporteur: Dagmar Roth-Behrendt (S-D).

04/07/91	CES 863/91 ECOSOC opinion on COM(90)488 on the marketing of cosmetics. Draftsman: Mr Proumens.

03/11/92 COM(90)488 proposal to amend Directive 76/768/EEC on the approximation of laws of the Member States relating to cosmetics products. Council of Consumer Affairs Ministers agreed Common Position which incorporates some of Parliament's amendments and will ban the sale in the EC of products containing ingredients tested on animals for use as cosmetics after 1 January 1998. The ban may be postponed for two or more years where validated alternative non-animal tests are not available. The Commission must report annually to the Parliament on the development of alternative tests.

17/12/92 Amendment of Directive 76/768/EEC Council of Ministers adopted the common position on the sixth amendment of the Directive on approximation of the Member States' laws relating to cosmetic products.

14/6/93 EC Ministers for Consumer Affairs met in Luxembourg to discuss Cosmetics issue. Agreed to make proposed ban on testing non-comprehensive and dependent on approval of technical committee. This contradicts Parliament's amendments and makes the ban subject to agreement by such countries as USA and Japan; it must therefore be worked out by the OECD.

COM(94) 606 final – 1994 Annual Report on the development, validation and legal acceptance of alternative methods to animal experiments.

19/6/95 Directive 95/17/EC adopted by the Commission relating to methods of analysis necessary for checking the composition of cosmetic products.
(OJ L.178, 28.7.95, p. 20)

14/7/95 Report by Mrs Roth-Behrendt on the 1994 Annual Report adopted by Parliament [A4 – 165/95]. A resolution from the environment committee expressing regret that the Commission has not yet been able to produce a detailed analysis on animal testing for cosmetics was approved. As well as demanding a report, Parliament has again insisted that experiments on animals should be banned by the beginning of 1998.

24/7/96 Report from the Commission – 1995 on development, validation and legal acceptance of alternative methods to animal experiments in the field of cosmetic products. The report outlines the different methods under development and validation, gives information on statistics on animal experiments and perspectives relating to the development of alternative methods for the various toxicity tests used in the evaluation of the safety of cosmetic ingredients and cosmetic products. It also highlights the major players involved in encouraging research in alternative methods. One of the report's conclusions was that validation had turned out to be more difficult and time-consuming than expected. A successful outcome can be expected for the validation of some tests, such as in vitro phototoxicity testing and skin corrosivity.
(COM (96) 365 final)

Chapter 4

Genetic Engineering and Biotechnology

BIOTECHNOLOGY ACTION PROGRAMMES

Existing Legislation

Council Decision 89/160/EEC on a first multiannual programme (1988–93) for biotechnology-based agro-industrial research and technological development (ECLAIR).
(OJ L.60 3/3/89 p. 48)

Council Decision 89/621/EEC adopting the BRIDGE (Biotechnology Research for Innovation, Development and Growth in Europe) programme.

Directive 94/15/EC adopted by Commission. Adapts to technical progress Council Directive 90/220/EEC on deliberate release into environment of genetically modified organisms.
(OJ L.103, 22/4/94 p. 20)

Work in Progress

1/3/95	European Parliament voted on Patenting Directive proposal and rejected by a great majority the compromise text agreed on between Parliament and Council delegations. Legal Affairs Committee has called upon the Commission to table a new proposal as soon as possible for a Directive designed to protect biotechnological inventions taking into account the ethical issues raised in debate on March 22/23.
12/95	The Commission made a new proposal on patenting, COM (95) 661, which permits the patenting of processes for modifying animal genetics on condition that the usefulness of the invention exceeds the suffering inflicted on the animal. This proposal will probably be voted by Parliament in the first part of 1997.
1/97	Publication of Mr Rothley's report (PSE-D) (PE.218.021).

Background

European Community

1985	European Community Biotechnology Action Programme (BAP) (1985–9). (OJ L.83 25/3/85 p. 1)
12/87	COM(87)667 final Commission proposal for a Council Decision to adopt a first multiannual programme (1988–93) for biotechnology-based agro-industrial research and technological development (ECLAIR). (OJ C.63 5/3/88 p. 7)
23/03/88	Opinion of the ECOSOC on the proposal for a Council Decision to adopt a first multiannual programme (1988–93) for biotechnology-based agro-industrial research and technological development (ECLAIR). (OJ C.134 24/5/88 p. 15)
08/08/88	Report A2-0170/88 drawn up on behalf of the Committee on Energy, Research and Technology on the proposal from the Commission of the European Communities to the Council (COM(87)667 final) for a decision to adopt a first multiannual programme (1988–93) for biotechnology-based agro-industrial research and technological development (ECLAIR). Rapporteur: Mauro Chiabrando (PPE-I).
14/09/88	European Parliament Opinion on ECLAIR (A2-0170/88).
28/10/88	COM(88)602 final – SYN 113 amended proposal for a Council Decision to adopt a first multiannual programme (1988–93) for biotechnology-based agro-industrial research and technological development – ECLAIR (European Collaborative Linkage of Agriculture and Industry through Research). (OJ C.294 18/11/88 p. 7)
17/11/88	Council adopted a Common Position with a view to the adoption of a decision on a First Multiannual Programme (1988–93) for biotechnology-based agro-industrial research and technological development – 'ECLAIR' (C2-237/88 – SYN 113).
03/01/89	COM(88)806 final – SYN 182 Commission proposal for a Council Decision adopting a specific research and technological development programme in the field of biotechnology (1990–4) (BRIDGE).

04/01/89   Report A2-344/88. Recommendation of the Committee on Energy, Research and Technology concerning the Common Position of the Council with a view to the adoption of a decision on a First Multiannual Programme (1988–93) for biotechnology-based agro-industrial research and technological development – 'ECLAIR' (C2-237/88 – SYN 113).

18/01/89   European Parliament Opinion concerning the Common Position of the Council with a view to the adoption of ECLAIR (A2-344/88).
(OJ C.47 27/2/89 p. 76)

09/02/89   COM(89)51 final – SYN 113 Commission submitted to the Council its re-examined proposal for Council Decision to adopt a first multiannual programme (1988–93) for biotechnology-based agro-industrial research and technological development (ECLAIR).
(OJ C.76 28/3/89 p. 13)

023/02/89   Council Decision 89/160/EEC on a first multiannual programme (1988–93) for biotechnology-based agro-industrial research and technological development (ECLAIR).
(OJ L.60 3/3/89 p. 48)

26/04/89   CES 555/89 opinion of the ECOSOC on the proposal for a Council Decision adopting a specific research and technological development programme in the field of biotechnology (1990–4) (BRIDGE) Biotechnology Research for Innovation, Development and Growth in Europe (COM(88)806 final – SYN 182).

28/04/89   Report A2-139/89 drawn up on behalf of the Committee on Energy, Research and Technology on the proposal from the Commission to the Council (COM(88)806 final – Doc. C2-340/88) for a decision adopting a specific research and technological development programme in the field of biotechnology (1990–4) – BRIDGE. Rapporteur: Roger Gauthier (RDE-F).

24/05/89   European Parliament Opinion on the BRIDGE programme (A2-139/89).

29/06/89   Council Decision 88/420/EEC revising the European Community Biotechnology Action Programme (BAP).

11/10/89   Report A3-38/89 drawn up on behalf of the Energy and Research Committee on the Council's Common Position on the BRIDGE biotechnology programme. Voted by Parliament. Rapporteur: Alain Pompidou (RDE-F).

27/10/89   Council Decision 89/621/EEC adopting the BRIDGE (Biotechnology Research for Innovation, Development and Growth in Europe) programme.

1990–1994   BRIDGE (Biotechnology Research for Innovation, Development and Growth in Europe) includes provision for the development of *in vitro* methods of toxicity evaluation.

18/04/91   SEC(91)629 Commission communication *Promoting the Competitive Environment for the Industrial Activities Based on Biotechnology Within the Community* (see also Genetic Engineering – Work in Progress).

09/10/91   Report A3-227/91 drawn up on behalf of the Energy and Research Committee on the proposal for a Council Decision to establish a new Community programme to support biotechnological research and development. Adopted by the European Parliament. Rapporteur: Enrico Falqui (V-I).

28/10/91   Research Council discussed and reached agreement on a Common Position on COM(90)160 a proposal for EC funding of biotechnological research. Includes work on transgenic animals.

11/91   Motion for a Resolution B3-1271/91 by Mr Porrazzini on Community biotechnology research and legislation on bio-technology ethics. Referred with SEC(91)629 to Energy and Research Committee. Rapporteur: Hiltrud Breyer (V-D).

16/12/92   COM(92)589 final amended proposal for Council Directive on legal protection of biotechnologies published.

2/93   COM(92)589 final referred to parliamentary committees: Legal Affairs, Agriculture, Economic, Energy, Environment, Development.

16/12/93   Council reached a political agreement on its common position regarding the legal protection of biotechnological inventions; Member States to implement Directive into national law by end 1996.

1/94   Council adopts common position regarding legal protection of Biotechnological inventions.

4/5/94	Rothley report on legal protection of biotechnological inventions was debated and voted on during May Plenary. Co-Decision procedure used; lack of absolute majority; Council been asked to refer report back to July session.
15/4/94	Directive 94/15/EC adopted by Commission. Adapts to technical progress Council Directive 90/220/EEC on deliberate release into environment of genetically modified organisms. (OJ L.103, 22/4/94 p. 20)
4/11/94	Commission adopted Decision 94/730/EC establishing simplified procedures concerning the deliberate release into the environment of genetically modified plants pursuant to Article 6 (5) of Council Directive 90/220/EEC. (OJ L.292, 12.11.94, p. 31)
23/1/95	Agreement reached by the Conciliation Committee at their second meeting on Legal protection of biotechnological inventions. Parliament will be asked to vote on the compromise.
1/3/95	European Parliament voted on Patenting Directive proposal and rejected by a great majority the compromise text agreed on between Parliament and Council delegations. Legal Affairs Committee has called upon the Commission to table a new proposal as soon as possible for a Directive designed to protect biotechnological inventions taking into account the ethical issues raised in debate on March 22/23.
29/6/95	Judgment by the European Court of Justice against the Hellenic Republic for failure to transpose Directives 90/219/EEC and 90/220/EEC on genetically modified organisms (Case C-170/94). (OJ C.229, 2.9.95, p. 8)
7/9/95	Regulation No. 2131/95/EC adopted by Commission. Amends Regulation EEC No 2349/84 on the application of Article 85(3) of the Treaty to certain categories of patent licensing. (OJ L.214, 8.9.95, p. 6)
13/12/95	COM (95) 661 final Commission's proposal for a European Parliament and Council Directive on the legal protection of biotechnological inventions.

The main points of the proposal include:

- inventions and discoveries;
- a clear exclusion from patentability of germ line gene therapy on humans;
- farmer's privilege as regards breeding stock.

The proposal permits the patenting of processes for modifying animal genetics on condition that the usefulness of the invention exceeds the suffering inflicted on the animal.

1/96	Oral question H-0004/96 from the Parliament to the Commission on the Commission's bioethics group.
11/1/96	Conference on biotechnology held by the European Commission.
14/5/96	Working document PE 216.340 on COM (95) 661 concerning the legal protection of biotechnological inventions. Rapporteur: Mr Willi Rothley (PSE-D).
10–11/6/96	Public hearing on biotechnology held at the European Parliament by the Legal Affairs Committee. Mr Willi Rothley presents his report on COM (95) 661.
1/97	Publication of Mr Rothley's report (PE 218.021).

GENETIC ENGINEERING

Existing Legislation

Council Directive 89/556/EEC of 25 september 1989 regulates the trade in bovine embryos.

Council Directive 90/220/EEC of 23 May 1990 on the deliberate release into the environment of genetically modified organisms.
(OJ L.117 8/5/90, p. 16)

Summary

The Directive controls the deliberate release of genetically modified organisms either directly or via products containing them. It does not apply to the carriage of such organisms.

Council Directive 90/219/EEC of 23 May 1990 on the contained use of genetically modified micro-organisms.
(OJ L.117 8/5/90, p. 1)

Summary

The Directive lays down common measures for the contained use of genetically modified micro-organisms. Proscribed and permitted techniques are identified in Annexes.

Council Decision 92/583/EEC of 14 December 1992 on the conclusion of the Protocol of amendment to the European Convention for the Protection of Animals kept for Farming Purposes.
(OJ L.395 31/12/92)

Summary

Extends the Convention to include biotechnology.

Work in Progress

The Commission has proposed a modification to Directive 90/219/EEC (COM (95) 0640).
     The Parliament has appointed Mr Antonio Trakatellis as rapporteur.

Background

Council of Europe

03/88	The Sixteenth Meeting of the Standing Committee of the European Convention for the Protection of Animals kept for Farming Purposes (T-AP) acknowledged the growing importance of biotechnology and discussed the application of the Convention to certain results of gene technology which were directly relevant to the protection of farm animals.
04/89	The Eighteenth Meeting of the Standing Committee agreed that the European Convention for the Protection of Animals kept for Farming Purposes should be amended by a Protocol of Amendment to make clear that the Convention also covered aspects of biotechnology related to the welfare of farm animals. The Standing Committee also agreed to draw the attention of the Committee of Ministers to developments in biotechnology and to invite Ministers' consider-

ation of possible Council of Europe action, preferably the elaboration of a new Convention.

06/89   The Meeting of the Bureau of the Standing Committee prepared a draft interim report to the Committee of Ministers on biotechnology in relation to farm animal welfare.

09/89   The Nineteenth Meeting of the Standing Committee in Copenhagen decided to formulate a proposal for amending the Convention to allow the Standing Committee to deal with all aspects of biotechnology.

05/12/89 First Council of Europe Symposium on Bioethics. The Standing Committee was invited to send an observer.

24/04/90 Twentieth Meeting of the Standing Committee of the Convention for the Protection of Animals kept for Farming Purposes further considered the draft Protocol and was careful not to interfere with any experimental breeding in laboratories.

16/10/90 Twenty-first Meeting of the Standing Committee further considered the draft Protocol.

22/05/91 Twenty-second Meeting of the Standing Committee approved the draft Protocol.

15/11/91 The Committee of Ministers adopted the Protocol of Amendment to the European Convention for the Protection of Animals kept for Farming Purposes.

06/02/92 Protocol of Amendment opened for signature (see Appendix VII).

23–27/11/92 Multilateral Consultation of Parties to the Convention on the Protection of Animals used for Experimental or other Scientific Purposes agreed the extent to which procedures, including breeding, concerning transgenic animals were covered by the Convention.

13/04/92 Second Meeting of the Working Party for the preparation of the Multilateral Consultation of the Parties to the European Convention for the Protection of Vertebrate Animals used for Experimental and other Scientific Purposes. The Convention covers genetically modified animals where these are harmful and do, or may, cause suffering if the modification is carried out for experimental and scientific purposes.

European Community

05/88
COM(88)160 proposal for a Council directive on the contained use of genetically modified micro-organisms and for a Council directive on the deliberate release to the environment of genetically modified organisms.

24/11/88
Opinion of the ECOSOC on the proposal for a Council directive on the contained use of genetically modified micro-organisms and for a Council directive on the deliberate release to the environment of genetically modified organisms.
(OJ C.23 30/1/89 p. 45)

28/04/89
Report A2-141/89 drawn up on behalf of the Environment Committee on the proposal from the Commission to the Council (COM(88)160 – C2-73/88) for a directive on the contained use of genetically modified micro-organisms and on the deliberate release to the environment of genetically modified organisms. Rapporteur: Gerhard Schmid (S-D).

Appended to the above document was a Report drawn up on behalf of the Committee on Energy, Research and Technology by Mr José Vicente Carvalho Cardoso (PPE-P).

22/05/89
Report A2-141/89 by Mr Schmid on COM(88)160-SYN131. European Parliament adopted an Opinion and Legislative Resolution.

08/06/89
The Environment Council considered Commission's amended proposals to COM(88)160: COM(89)409 which deals with contained use and COM(89)408 which deals with deliberate release of genetically engineered organisms. The Council decided that the directive on contained use should be based on Article 130S of the Treaty, which requires unanimity.

31/08/89
The Council sent a Common Position on COM(89)409 to Parliament (C3-130/89). It was referred to the Environment Committee. Rapporteur: Gerhard Schmid (S-D) appointed 26/09/89.

19/09/89
The Environment Council reached agreement by qualified majority on COM(89)408 (deliberate release).

30/11/89	The Social Affairs Council adopted a Common Position (SEC(89)2091) on COM(89)408 (deliberate release). It was referred to the European Parliament's Environment Committee. Rapporteur: Gerhard Schmid (S-D). Opinion from Energy and Research Committee.
24/01/90	Report A3-14/90 by Mr Schmid on COM(89)409 and C3-130/89 (contained use) adopted by Environment Committee with opinion from Legal Affairs Committee (Draftsman: Carlo Casini (PPE-I)).
14/03/90	Report A3-14/90 by Mr Schmid on the proposal for a directive on the contained use of genetically modified micro-organisms (COM(89)409) adopted by European Parliament.
14/03/90	Report A3-49/90 by Mr Schmid on the Common Position of the Council for a directive on the deliberate release to the environment of genetically modified organisms adopted by the European Parliament.
23/05/90	Council Directive 90/220/EEC on the deliberate release into the environment of genetically modified organisms.
23/05/90	Council Directive 90/219/EEC on the contained use of genetically modified micro-organisms.
18/10/90	CES 1213/90 ECOSOC opinion on COM(88)160 proposal for a Council Directive on the contained use of genetically modified micro-organisms and for a Council directive on the deliberate release to the environment of genetically modified organisms drafted by Mr de Tavernier.
19/04/91	SEC(91)629 Commission Communication to the Parliament and Council promoting a competitive environment for industrial activities based on biotechnology within the Community. This proposed the establishment of a group on ethics and biotechnology, with the aim of advising the Commission on promoting better public understanding. The Commission considered it could be desirable to include a member with expertise on the ethics of applying such techniques to animal husbandry. The group was appointed in early 1992 and its first task was to look at the ethics of using biotechnology to boost livestock performance.
29/6/95	Judgment of the Court in Case C-170/94 *Commission* v. *Hellenic Republic* for non-transposition of Directives

90/219/EEC and 90/220/EEC on genetically modified organisms. The Hellenic Republic to pay the costs.
(OJ C. 229 2/9/95 p. 8)

7/9/95   Regulation No. 2131/95 (EC) amending Regulation (EEC) No 2349/84 on the application of Article 85(3) of the Treaty to certain categories of patent licensing.
(OJ L.214, 8.9.95, p. 6)

16/1/96   Commission Decision amending Decision 91/448/EEC concerning guidelines for classification referred to in Article 4 of Council Directive 90/219/EEC on the contained use of genetically modified micro-organisms.
(OJ L.31 9/2/96 p. 25)

1/97   Publication of Mr Trakatellis' report on COM(95)06 40.

PATENTING OF LIVING ORGANISMS

Existing Legislation

None.

Work in Progress

The Commission has published its new proposal for a European Parliament and Council Directive on the legal protection of biotechnological inventions (COM (95) 661 final. The Parliament will have to give an opinion and the proposal will then be considered by the Council of Ministers.

Publication of Mr Rothley's report, rapporteur for the Legal Affairs Committee, on the Commission proposal PE218.021.

Background

European Community

17/10/88   COM(88)496 final – SYN 159 proposal for a Council Directive on the legal protection of biotechnological inventions. Referred to European Parliament and ECOSOC.

03/11/88   Commission proposal for a Council Directive on the legal protection of biotechnological inventions (COM(88)496) considered by the Council.

26/04/89   CES 550/89 Opinion of the ECOSOC on the proposal for a Council Directive on the legal protection of biotechnological inventions (COM(88)496 final – SYN 159).

10/89	COM(88)496 proposal to introduce the possibility of patenting biotechnological inventions including living organisms referred to the Legal Affairs Committee. Rapporteur: Willi Rothley (S-D).
22/05/90	COM(88)496 Legal Affairs Committee held a hearing of experts on the implications of this proposal. Agriculture Committee held a similar hearing on the same proposal.
10/90	Motion for a resolution B3-1538/90 by Mr Graefe zu Baringdorf and others on the ethical and animal welfare problems associated with the patenting of transgenic animals and the need for a moratorium on patents for animals until these problems have been examined.
28/07/91	Draft report by Mr Rothley on COM(88)496 adopted by Legal Affairs Committee.
17/12/91	Draft opinion by Mr Linkohr on COM(88)496 adopted by the Energy and Research Committee.
10/02/92	Report A3-126/92 by Mr Rothley on COM(88)496 referred by Plenary back to Legal Affairs Committee at the request of the Agriculture Committee.
21/05/92	Report A3-126/92 by Mr Rothley on COM(88)496 re-adopted by Legal Affairs Committee.
10/06/92	Report A3-126/92 debated by Parliament and referred back to Legal Affairs Committee for opinion on compatibility of the draft patenting Directive with UNCED Biodiversity Convention.
23/06/92	Report A3-126/92 by Mr Rothley on COM(88)496. The Legal Affairs Committee decided not to draw up a new report, it will prepare an opinion on the compatibility between the Rothley report and the Biodiversity Convention signed at Rio. Written opinion asked from the Commission Legal Service and from the Legal Service of the Parliament. The Environment Committee to provide an opinion by letter.
22/09/92	Report A3-126/92 by Mr Rothley on COM(88)496 re-adopted by Legal Affairs Committee.
29/10/92	Report A3-126/92 by Mr Rothley on COM(88)496 adopted by European Parliament.

29/10/92	Third Report [A3-286/92] by Mr Rothley on the legal protection of biotechnological inventions was adopted by the Parliament but Mr Elliott's amendment against the patenting of live animals was rejected.
9/2/93	Joint motion tabled on the first European patent on animals.
13/12/95	COM (95) 661 final Commission's proposal for a European Parliament and Council Directive on the legal protection of biotechnological inventions.

The main points of the proposal include:

- inventions and discoveries;

- a clear exclusion from patentability of germ line gene therapy on humans;

- farmer's privilege as regards breeding stock;

The proposal permits the patenting of processes for modifying animal genetics on condition that the usefulness of the invention exceeds the suffering inflicted on the animal.

1/96	Oral question H-0004/96 from the Parliament to the Commission on the Commission's bioethics group.
11/1/96	Conference on biotechnology held by the European Commission.
14/5/96	Working document PE 216.340 on COM (95) 661 concerning the legal protection of biotechnological inventions. Rapporteur: Mr Willi Rothley (PSE-D).
10–11/6/96	Public hearing on biotechnology held at the European Parliament by the Legal Affairs Committee. Mr Willi Rothley presents his report on COM (95) 661.
24/7/96	Working document PE 218.217 on COM (95) 0661 661 concerning the legal protection of biotechnological inventions. Rapporteur: Mrs Ulla Sandbaek (EDN-DK)
17/12/96	Adoption by Parliament's Environment Committee of Mrs Sandbaek's opinion on COM (95) 0661. (PE 219.413)
18/12/96	Adoption by Agriculture Committee of Mr Friedrich-Wilhelm Graefe zu Baringdorf (V-D)'s opinion on COM (95) 0661.
1/97	Publication of Mr Rothley's report on COM (95) 0661 for Legal Affairs Committee.

Chapter 5

Companion Animals

COMPANION ANIMALS – GENERAL

Existing Legislation

None.

Work in Progress

None.

Background

Council of Europe

20/04/79   Report on behalf of the Committee on Agriculture on the dangers of over-population of domestic animals for the health and hygiene of man and humane methods of limiting such dangers. Rapporteur: Mr Bizet.
            Included a draft Recommendation.

08/05/79   Assembly debate on Recommendation 860. Recommended that the Committee of Ministers instruct the appropriate inter-governmental expert committee to draw up a European Convention which should aim to:

1. control the trade in animals;

2. control animal populations.

22/01/80   Opinion on Recommendation 860 of the Ad Hoc Committee of Experts for the Protection of Animals (CAHPA).

06/80   The Committee of Ministers at its 320th Meeting at Deputy level instructed CAHPA 'to consider the appropriateness of elaborating one or more international instruments (convention or recommendation) at the European level, dealing with issues set out in sub-paragraphs (i) and (ii) of paragraph 5 of Assembly Recommendation 860 on the dangers of over-population of domestic animals for the health and hygiene of man, and on humane methods of limiting such dangers'.

01/81	The Committee of Ministers, at Deputy level, instructed CAHPA to examine the legal aspects of animal protection with a view to preparing appropriate instruments.
11/83	Work began on the draft Convention for the protection of pet animals.
05/84–06/85	The CAHPA continued to elaborate on the Convention for the protection of pet animals having decided that legal protection should be based on the safeguarding of the health and welfare of the pet animal itself as has been the case for the other Conventions of the Council of Europe. In the elaboration of the provisions, however, the Committee also took into consideration the conservation of threatened wild animal species, the inconveniences caused by stray animals, the danger that certain animals may present to the health or safety of man and the control of diseases.
06/06/86	At its Eighteenth Meeting, CAHPA finalised and adopted the final text of the Convention on the protection of pet animals. It decided to submit this to the Committee of Ministers, and invited them to decide on the question of whether the Draft Convention should provide for the possibility of signature by the European Economic Community.
	It was subsequently decided that the Convention should not contain the possibility of EEC participation.
13/11/87	European Convention No. ETS 125 for the Protection of Pet Animals was opened for signature.
	The EEC is not a contracting party. (See Appendix X for signatures and ratifications.)
01/05/92	European Convention for the Protection of Pet Animals entered into force following ratification by four Member States.
20/10/92	European Convention for the Protection of Pet Animals – Territorial Declaration and Reservation by Denmark on ratification.

28/06/93	European Convention for the Protection of Pet Animals – Reservation by Portugal on ratification.
03/11/93	European Convention for the Protection of Pet Animals – Switzerland ratified.
09/12/93	European Convention for the Protection of Pet Animals – Cyprus signed and ratified.
7–10/3/95	European Convention for the Protection of Pet Animals – Multilateral Consultation of Parties adopted a Resolution on surgical operations in pet animals and a Resolution on the breeding of pet animals.

European Community

20/01/83	Motion for a Resolution 1-1172/82 by Mrs de March on Community measures to prevent the theft and illegal traffic in pedigree and hunting dogs.
16/01/85	Motion for a Resolution 2-1429/84 by Mrs Thome-Patenôtre on the tattooing of cats and dogs in Europe. The President of the European Parliament referred this to the Committee on Legal Affairs and Citizens' Rights which subsequently decided not to draw up a report.
14/01/88	Motion for a Resolution 2-1553/87 by Mr Pearce on the Council of Europe Convention on Pets. No report.
23/10/89	Motion for a Resolution B3-390/89 by Mrs Ewing and others on the need for a system for permanent identification and compulsory registration of dogs. This is intended to reduce the nuisance created by stray dogs. Referred to the Environment Committee with opinion from Agriculture Committee. Rapporteur: Anita Pollack (S-UK).
29/05/90	Report A3-156/90 by Mrs Pollack adopted by Environment Committee.
23/11/90	Report A3-156/90 by Mrs Pollack on a European system of dog registration adopted by European Parliament.
04/92	Petition no. 267/91 on banning the breeding of certain types of dogs in the UK, referred to Environment Committee. Rapporteur: Tom Spencer (PPE-UK).

HEALTH CHECKS AND FREE MOVEMENT OF COMPANION ANIMALS

Existing Legislation

Council Decision 89/455/EEC of 24 July 1989 introducing Community measures to set up pilot schemes for the control of rabies with a view to its eradication or prevention.

Commission Decisions 90/328/EEC to 90/334/EEC of 23 May 1990 approve the measures taken by France, Italy, Luxembourg, Belgium, the Federal Republic of Germany and the Netherlands under Council Decision 89/455/EEC to set up pilot projects for the control and eradication of rabies.

Council Directive 92/65/EEC ('Balai' or 'Sweeping Up' Directive) of 13 July 1992 laying down animal health requirements governing trade in and imports into the Community of animals, semen, ova and embryos not subject to animal health requirements laid down in specific Community rules referred to in Annex A (I) to Directive 90/425/EEC. It includes cats and dogs traded for commercial purposes between commercial holdings.

Work in Progress

Under the 'Balai' Directive a proposal on the movement of privately owned pets between rabies-free areas of mainland EC territory has been agreed and was in place by 1st January 1993.

A second proposal on health checks for imported birds (other than poultry) is presently being prepared by the Commission.

Background

European Community

08/03/88 COM(88)836 final Commission proposal for a Council Regulation instituting a certificate for dogs and cats on visits of less than one year in the Member States and introducing Community measures to set up pilot projects for the control and eradication of rabies.

28/04/89 Report A2-145/89 Report drawn up on behalf of the Committee on Agriculture, Fisheries and Food on the proposal for a Council Regulation instituting a certificate for dogs and cats on visits of less than one year in the Member States and introducing Community measures to set up pilot projects for the control and eradication of rabies (COM(88)836 final). Rapporteur: Juan Luis Colino Salamanca (S-E).

26/05/89   European Parliament Opinion on COM(88)836 final (A2-145/89).

24/07/89   Council Decision 89/455/EEC introducing Community measures to set up pilot schemes for the control of rabies with a view to its eradication or prevention.

9/95   In response to a written question in Parliament on the quarantine requirements for guide dogs, Commissioner Flynn replied that Directive 92/65/EEC permits the UK and Ireland to impose strict quarantine restrictions to guide dogs as well. But Article 10 of this Directive, which provides for rabies control, is due to be reviewed before the end of 1997.

12/12/95   Decisions 96/42 to 96/48/EC approving the programme for the eradication of rabies for 1996 presented by France, Luxembourg, Belgium, Germany, Italy, Austria, and Finland, and fixing the level of the Community's financial contribution.
(OJ L.16 22/1/96 pp. 1–8)

Chapter 6

Animals – General

ANIMAL WELFARE – GENERAL

Existing Legislation

Council Declaration of December 1991 on the protection of animals calling upon the European Parliament, the Council and the Commission, as well as Member States, 'when drafting and implementing Community legislation on the common agricultural policy, transport, the internal market and research, to pay full regard to the welfare requirements of animals'.

Work in Progress

Opening of the Intergovernmental Conference on 29 March 1996, in Turin.

On 14 March 1996, the Parliament adopted Report A4-0068/96 on Parliament's opinion on the convening of the IGC and evaluation of the work of the Reflection Group with a view to the Intergovernmental Conference. Rapporteurs: Mrs Raymonde-Dury (PSE-B) and Mrs J. Maij-Weggen (PPE-N)
(PE 216.237)

Point 11.7 reads:

> Given the enormous interest shown by European citizens, the question of animal welfare should be given greater prominence and included as a new title VI B/Article 130 t in the Treaty of the European Union.

Background

18/02/83   Resolution of the Council of the European Community and the government representatives of the Member States, on the continuation and implementation of a European Community policy and action programme on the environment (1982–7). (OJ C.46 17/2/83)

Under the environment chapter of the Commission's programme for 1985, the Commission stated:

> An improvement in the quality of life also entails respect for animals in the Member States and in the Member

States' dealings with the rest of the world. The regular debates concerning the hunting of seal pups should not conceal the many questions raised by the exploitation of animals in Europe: the use of animals for experiments, factory farming, trade in animals and the processing of animals for consumption purposes. The Commission will examine all possible steps which can be taken in this connection.

19/12/83   Report 1-1200/83 drawn up on behalf of the Committee on Institutional Affairs on the preliminary draft Treaty establishing the European Union. Coordinating Rapporteur: Altiero Spinelli (COM-I).
Article 59 reads:

Environmental Policy
The Union shall take measures designed to provide for animal protection.

14/02/84   The European Parliament adopted the draft Treaty establishing the European Union, with 237 votes in favour, 31 against and 43 abstentions.
The reference to animal protection was later removed.

15/10/86   Draft Resolution of the Council of the European Community on the continuation and implementation of a European Community policy and action programme on the environment (1987–92).
(OJ C.70 18/3/87 p. 3)
Under Section 5.1.9 it states:

It will be important in the context of the Fourth Environment Programme to put some flesh on the above statement. Priorities will include the better enforcement of existing Community Directives relating to animal protection and the proposal of new Community measures where this is appropriate, e.g. for the protection of laboratory animals and the welfare of farm animals.

07/87   *Animal Welfare within the European Community.* Report prepared for the Commission of the European Communities.

22/07/87   Motion for a Resolution 2-766/87 by Mr Pasty, Mrs Thome-Patenôtre and Mrs Lemass on the creation of a European animal welfare prize.

10/05/88   COM(88)202 final Commission proposal for a Council Decision on preventing environmental damage by the implementation of education and training measures.

17/08/88   Motion for a Resolution 2-0620/88 by Mrs Bloch von Blottnitz on the creation of Community provisions governing the status of animals.

28/11/88   COM(88)484 final Commission proposal for a Council Directive on the freedom of access to information on the environment.

03/03/89   Report A2-417/88 drawn up on behalf of the Committee on Youth, Culture, Education, Information and Sport on the proposal from the Commission to the Council (COM(88)202 – C2-68/88) for a decision on preventing environmental damage by the implementation of education and training measures. Rapporteur: Ursula Schleicher (PPE-D).

07/03/89   Report A2-424/88 drawn up on behalf of the Environment Committee on the proposal from the Commission to the Council (COM(88)484 final) for a Council directive on the freedom of access to information on the environment. Rapporteur: Bram van der Lek (ARC-NL)

03/89   European Parliament adopted a Resolution (A2-417/88) on the Commission proposal for a decision on preventing environmental damage by the implementation of education and training measures (COM(88)202).

31/03/89   CES 438/89 ECOSOC opinion on COM(88)484 final – freedom of access to information on the environment.

13/04/89   European Parliament adopted a Resolution (A2-424/88) on the freedom of access to information on the environment (COM(88)484).

12/07/89   COM(89)303 final Commission proposal for a Council Regulation (EEC) on the establishment of the European Environment Agency and the European Environment Monitoring and Information Network. The European Centre for the Development of Alternatives to Animal Testing would come under the Agency. (See Conservation of European Wildlife and Natural Habitats.)

30/12/89   COM(89)411 the sixth annual report by the Commission on the implementation of EC legislation.

01/02/90	COM(89)658 a proposal for a regulation laying down EC rules for intra-Community trade in animals that are not already covered by specific regulations. These animals are cage birds, fur bearers, monkeys, deer and bees.

23/03/90   The Agriculture Committee decided to apply the simplified procedure for consideration of COM(89)658 and appointed the President, Mr Juan Luis Salamanca (S-E), Rapporteur.

18/05/90   Report A3-111/90 by Mr Salamanca on COM(89)658, a proposal for a regulation laying down animal health requirements for the placing on the market in the Community of animals and products of animal origin not covered in this respect by specific Community laws, was adopted by Plenary.

22/02/91   Motion for a Resolution B3-2162/90 by Mrs Muscardini referred to Environment Committee. It calls on the Community and its Member States to comply with the 1978 Declaration on the Rights of Animals drawn up by the Coalition Mondiale pour les Droits de l'Animal and for observance of this Declaration to be ensured through consultation with animal welfare societies. It also incorporates a call for a category on sentient animals to be included in the Treaty of Rome.

26/04/91   Environment Committee decided to draw up a report on B3-2162/90. Rapporteur: Gianfranco Amendola (V-I).

16/05/91   Motion for a Resolution B3-253/91 by Mr Seligman and others on insertion of animal protection in the Treaty of Rome referred to the Committee on Institutional Affairs with an opinion from the Environment Committee.

07/91   Motion for a Resolution B3-668/91 by Mr Pimenta and Mr Muntingh deplores that the relationship between animal welfare/environment is not on the agenda of GATT. Referred to the External Relations Committee. Rapporteur: Tom Spencer (PPE-UK).

30/10/91   Report A3-321/91 by Mr Amendola based on, but going further than, B3-2162/90 adopted by Environment Committee.

12/91   The European Council, meeting in Maastricht, agreed the following text of a Declaration on the protection of animals in response to an initiative by the UK Government following on from the German delegation's request to the Intergovernmental Conferences on Political and Economic Union to include references to farm and laboratory animal welfare in the draft Treaty on European Union:

The Conference calls upon the European Parliament, the Council and the Commission, as well as Member States, when drafting and implementing Community legislation on the common agriculture policy, transport, the internal market and research, to pay full regard to the welfare requirements of animals.

Done at Maastricht, 7 February 1992.
(OJ C.191, 29/7/92, p. 103)

02/92 — Report A3-321/91 by Mr Amendola on the status of animals debated by European Parliament and referred back to the Environment Committee following a request from the Agriculture Committee.

17/03/92 — The Agriculture Committee forwarded its opinion on the status of animals (A3-321/91) to the Environment Committee.

7/03/92 — Draft report by Mr Spencer on B3-668/91 was the subject of a preliminary exchange of views in the Environment Committee (A3-329/92).

22/04/92 — Environment Committee rejected the amended report by Mr Amendola on the rights of animals. The text therefore falls and will not return to Plenary.

11/92 — Motion for a Resolution B3-1096/92 by Mr Ken Collins pursuant to rule 63 on status of animals in the European Community.

19/1/93 — Report [A3-0380/92] by Mr White on a resolution B3-0908/92 concerning the application of the principle of subsidiarity to environment and consumer protection policy was adopted by Parliament.

6/5/93 — Report [PE 203.833] on condition and status of animals in Community discussed at Environment Committee.

18/10/93 — Commission submitted proposal for Council Directive relating to the zootechnical and genealogical conditions applicable to imports from third countries of animals, semen, ovules and embryos.
(OJ C.306, 12.11.93, p. 11)

29/10/93	Report [A3-0309/93] on Commission proposal for a Council Directive on financing of veterinary checks and inspections on live animals and certain animal products and amending Directive 91/496/EEC was voted on and adopted.
4/11/93	Report [PE 203.833] voted on by Agriculture Committee. Only two amendments were not adopted including that the status of animals be modified in the Treaty of Rome at the 1996 IGC and that animals be referred to as 'sentient beings'.
4/11/93	Report [PE 205.396] on status of animals in the Community. Amendments adopted except the removal of animals from the list of agricultural products contained in Annex II of the Treaty of Rome.
16/11/93	Parliament approves: Commission proposal [COM(93)110] for a Council Directive amending Directive 70/524/EEC concerning additives in animal feedingstuffs; proposal [COM(93)119] for Council Decision concerning the use of and marketing of enzymes, micro-organisms and their preparations in animal nutrition.
1/12/93	Commission proposal submitted to EP and Council for Regulation on novel foods and novel food ingredients. (OJ C.16, 19/1/94 p. 10)
14/12/93	Commission proposal for a European Parliament and Council Directive amending for second time Directive 83/344/EEC on extraction solvents used in production of foodstuffs and food ingredients. (OJ C.15, 18/1/94 p. 17)
14/12/93	Commission adopted Regulation 3425/93 amending Annexes I and II to Council Regulation 2377/90 laying down Community procedure for establishment of maximum residue limits of veterinary medicinal products in foodstuffs of animal origin. (OJ L.312, 15/12/93 p. 12)
15/12/93	Agriculture Committee adopted report on the protection of animals. Rapporteur Richard Simmonds welcomed Commission's communication stating that protection of animals is part of the CAP meaning that subsidiarity does not apply and existing directives on laying hens, pigs and calves will remain in force and proposals to amend the Transport Directive are under discussion.

20/12/93	Report (PE 203.833) adopted by Environment Committee. All Agriculture Committee amendments rejected.
22/12/93	Council adopt Resolution on strengthening of veterinary epidemiological surveillance measures. (OJ C.16, 19/1/94 p. 1)
7/1/94	Decision 94/24/EEC adopted on border inspection posts preselected for veterinary checks on products and animals from third countries. Repeals Decisions 92/430/EEC and 92/431/EEC.
21/1/94	PE 203.833 adopted in Plenary Session.
11/3/94	Report by Mr Borgo on proposal for Council decision amending Decision 90/424/EEC on expenditure in veterinary field adopted by Parliament.
19/3/94	Commission Communication 94/C 82/04 published. Re: Council Regulation EEC No. 2309/93 of 22/7/93 and Council Directives 93/39/EEC, 93/40/EEC, 93/41/EEC. (OJ C.82, 19/3/94 p. 4)
30/3/94	Decision 94/187/EC adopted by Commission. Import of animal casings from third countries. (OJ L.89 6/4/94 p. 18)
25/5/94	Decision 94/339/EC adopted by Commission laying down detailed rules for the application of Article 9 (1) of Council Directive 90/425/EEC concerning veterinary and zoo-technical checks applicable in intra-Community trade in certain live animals and products with a view to the completion of the internal market. (OJ L.151, 17.6.94, p. 38)
22/7/94	Directive 94/40/EC amending Council Directive 87/153/EEC fixing guidelines for the assessment of additives in animal nutrition. (OJ L.208, 11.8.94, p. 15)
8/9/94	Decision adopted by Commission fixing Community financial contribution to the implementation of a fourth programme for the exchange of officials competent for veterinary matters. (OJ L.248, 23.9.94, p. 28)
30/9/94	Decision adopted by Commission amending for fourth time Decision 92/571/EEC relating to new transitional measures

which are necessary to facilitate the move to the system of veterinary checks provided for in Council Directive 90/675/EEC.
(OJ L.256, 4.10.94, p. 30)

10/11/94 Commission adopts Decision 94/755/EC on Community financial assistance for improvement of the facilities for veterinary checks on Austria's external borders.
(OJ L.302, 25.11.94, p. 38)

21/11/94 Commission adopts Decision 94/756/EC on the list of programmes of checks aimed at the prevention of zoonoses qualifying for financial contribution from Community in 1995.
(OJ L.302, 25.11.94, p. 42)

25/11/94 Commission adopts Decision 94/769/EC on list of programmes for the eradication and monitoring of animal diseases qualifying for a financial contribution from Community in 1995.
(OJ L.305, 30.11.94, p. 38)

20/4/95 Draft opinion for the Committee on Institutional Affairs on the operation of the Treaty on European Union with a view to the 1996 Intergovernmental Conference was adopted by the Environment Committee. All amendments retained and to be discussed within the Institutional Affairs Committee before being discussed by the Parliament in Plenary (May 1995).

2/3/95 Decision adopted by Commission amending Decisions 94/187/EC, 94/309/EC and 94/446/EC laying down health requirements and certification for the import of certain products covered by Council Directive 92/118/EC.
(OJ L.69, 29.3.95, p. 45)

17/3/95 Decision 95/82/EC adopted by Commission amending Decisions 94/957/EC and 94/958/EC relating to transitional measures to be applied by Finland as regards veterinary checks.
(OJ L.66, 24.3.95, p. 26)

21/3/95 Decision 95/85/EC adopted by Commission determining for Sweden the number of Animo units which may benefit from the Community's financial contribution. (Animo is a computerised network linking veterinary authorities in the EU.)
(OJ L.68, 28.3.95, p. 29)

4/5/95   Directive 95/11/EC adopted by Commission amending Council Directive 87/153/EEC fixing guidelines for the assessment of additives in animal nutrition.
(OJ L. 106, 11/5/95, p. 23)

9/6/95   COM (95) 254 final Proposal for a Council Directive amending Council Directive 90/675/EEC laying down the principles governing the organisation of veterinary checks on products entering the Community from third countries.
(OJ C.185 19/7/95 p. 16)

22/6/95   Directive 95/25/EC amending Directive 64/432/EEC on health problems affecting intra-Community trade in bovine animals and swine.
(OJ L.243 11/10/95 p. 16)

10/7/95   Directive 95/33/EC adopted by Commission amending Council Directive 82/471/EEC concerning certain products used in animal nutrition.
(OJ L.167, 18/7/95, p. 17)

6/9/95   Decision 95/357/EC adopted by Commission drawing up a list of border inspection posts agreed for veterinary checks on products and animals from third countries, detailed rules concerning the checks to be carried out by the veterinary experts of the Commission and repealing Decision 94/24/EC.
(OJ L.211 6/9/95 p. 43)

13/9/95   Opinion of the Economic and Social Committee on COM (95) 254 laying down the principles governing the organisation of veterinary checks on products entering the Community from third countries.
(OJ C.301 13/11/95 p. 23)

13/10/95   Decision 95/434/EC adopted by Commission on the list of programmes for the eradication and monitoring of animal diseases qualifying for a financial contribution from the Community in 1996.
(OJ L.256 26/10/96 p. 57)

16–18/10/95   Public hearing held by the Parliament at the initiative of the Institutional Committee. Members of animal welfare organisations restated the need to give animals a new status in the Treaty and to improve transport of live animals.

24/10/95   Decision 95/469/EC adopted by Commission on the list of programmes of checks aimed at the prevention of zoonoses

qualifying for a financial contribution from the Community in 1996.
(OJ L.269 11/11/95 p. 26)

25/10/95   Directive 95/53/EC adopted by Commission fixing the principles governing the organisation of official inspections in the field of animal nutrition.
(OJ L.265 8/11/95 p. 17)

31/10/95   Directive 95/55/EC adopted by Commission amending Council Directive 70/524/EEC concerning additives in feedingstuffs.
(OJ L.263, 4/11/95, p. 18)

14/12/95   Judgment of the Court in Case C-132/94 between the European Commission and Ireland for failure to transpose Directive 90/675/EEC on veterinary checks on products entering the Community form third countries. Ireland to pay the costs.
(OJ C.64 2/3/96 p. 3)

Judgment of the Court in Case C-138/94 between the European Commission and Ireland for failure to transpose Directive 91/496/EEC regarding veterinary checks on animals entering the Community from third countries. Ireland to pay the costs.
(OJ C.64 2/3/96 p. 3)

Judgment of the Court in Case C-162/94 between the European Commission and Ireland for failure to transpose Directive 89/662/EEC concerning veterinary checks in intra-Community trade with a view to the completion of the internal market. Ireland to pay the costs.
(OJ C.77 16/3/96 p. 2)

14/12/95   Decisions 96/67-68/EC adopted by Commission approving the 1996 programme presened by Portugal and Greece for the control of echinococcosis/hydatidosis and setting the level of the Community' s financial contribution.
(OJ L.16 22/1/96 pp. 27–8)

19/12/95   Decision 96/32/EC adopted by Commission amending Decision 93/13/EEC laying down the procedures for veterinary checks at Community border inspection posts on products from third countries.
(OJ L.9 12/1/96 p. 9)

20/12/95   Decision 96/35/EC adopted by Commission amending Decision 95/357/EC drawing up a list of border inspection posts agreed for veterinary checks on products and animals from third countries detailed rules concerning the checks to be carried out by the veterinary experts of the Commission and repealing Decision 94/24/EC.
(OJ L.10 13/1/96 p. 40)

22/12/95   Council Directive 95/69/EC laying down the conditions and arrangements for approving and registering certain establishments and intermediaries operating in the animal feed sector and amending Directives 70/524/EEC, 74/63/EEC, 79/373/EEC and 82/471/EEC.
(OJ L.332 30/12/95 p. 15)

29/1/96   Decision 96/105/EC adopted by Commission relating to new transitional measures which are necessary to facilitate the move to the system of veterinary checks provided for in Council Directive 90/675/EEC.
(OJ L.24 31/1/96 p. 32)

1/2/96   Opinion of the Economic and Social Committee on COM (95) 491 Opinion on the Proposal for a Council Directive amending Directive 92/117/EEC.
(OJ C.97 1/4/96 p. 29)

16/2/96   Directive 96/6/EC adopted by Commission amending Council Directive 74/63/EEC on undesirable substances and products in animal nutrition.
(OJ L.49, 28/2/96, p. 29)

19/2/96   Decision 96/187/EC adopted by Commission amending Decision 95/357/EC drawing up a list of border inspection posts agreed for veterinary checks on products and animals from third countries detailed rules concerning the checks to be carried out by the veterinary experts of the Commission and repealing Decision 95/24/EC.
(OJ L.59 8/3/96 p. 59)

21/2/96   Directive 96/7/EC adopted by Commission amending Council Directive 70/524/EEC concerning additives in feedingstuffs.
(OJ L.51, 1/3/96, p. 45)

13/3/96   Report A4-0068/96 on Parliament's opinion on the convening of the IGC and evaluation of the work of the Reflection Group with a view to the Intergovernmental Conference

was adopted by Parliament. Rapporteurs: Mrs Raymonde-Dury (PSE-B) and Mrs J. Maij-Weggen (PPE-N)
(PE 216.237)
Point 11.7 reads:

> Given the enormous interest shown by European citizens, the question of animal welfare should be given greater prominence and included as a new title VI B/Article 130 t in the Treaty of the European Union.

11/4/96   Decision 96/283/EC adopted by Commission approving the programme for the eradication of Aujeszky's disease in Luxembourg.
(OJ L.107 30/4/96 p. 16)

29/4/96   Directive 96/25/EC adopted by Commission on the circulation of feed materials, amending Directives 70/524/EEC, 74/63/EEC, 82/471/EEC and 93/74/EEC and repealing Directive 77/101/EEC.
(OJ L.125, 23/5/96, p. 35)

19/3/96   Directive 96/17/EC adopted by Council amending the Annex to Directive 85/73/EEC on the financing of veterinary inspections and controls of animal products covered by Annex A to Directive 89/662/EEC and by Directive 90/675/EEC.
(OJ L.78 28/3/96 p. 30)

1/4/96   Decision 96/267/EC adopted by Commission amending Decision 95/357/EC drawing up a list of border inspection posts agreed for veterinary checks on products and animals from third countries detailed rules concerning the checks to be carried out by the veterinary experts of the Commission and repealing Decision 95/24/EC.
(OJ L.91 12/4/96 p. 76)

29/4/96   Council Directive 96/24/EC amending Directive 79/373/EEC on the marketing of compound feedingstuffs.
(OJ L.125, 23/5/96 p. 33)

17/5/95   Report by Martin/Bourlanges drawn on behalf of the Institutional Affairs Committee on the operation of the Treaty on European Union with a view to the 1996 Intergovernmental Conference adopted. Article 10 (vii) reads:

> The existing Treaty articles on environmental policy should be strengthened and simplified, so that

environmental protection and concern for animal welfare and conservation become fundamental principles of the European Union and are effectively and fully integrated with other EU policies; environmental protection should be included in Article 3 of the Treaty as a Union objective.

Adopted resolution has been forwarded to the Council, Commission, the members of the Reflection Group on the Intergovernmental Conference and the governmental parliaments of the Member States.

22/5/96	Decision 96/345/EC adopted by Commission laying down certain detailed rules oncerning on-the-spot checks carried out in the veterinary field by Commission experts in the Member States. (OJ L.133 4/6/96 p. 29)
30/5/96	Decision 96/357/EC adopted by Commission amending Decision 95/357/EC drawing up a list of border inspection posts agreed for veterinary checks on products and animals from third countries detailed rules concerning the checks to be carried out by the veterinary experts of the Commission and repealing Decision 95/24/EC. (OJ L.138 11/6/96 p. 18)
25/6/96	Council Resolution on measures to be implemented under veterinary policy. (OJ C.203 13/7/96 p. 1)
26/6/96	Council Directive 96/43/EC amending and consolidating Directive 85/73/EEC in order to ensure financing of veterinary inspections and controls on live animals and certain animal products and amending Directives 90/675/EEC and 91/496/EEC. (OJ L.162 1/7/96 p. 1)
23/7/96	Council Directive 96/51/EC amending Directive 70/524/EEC concerning additives in feedingstuffs. (OJ L. 235 17/9/96 p. 39)
11/9/96	Commission's list of enzymes, micro-organisms and their preparation in animal nutrition permitted for use in individual Member States. (OJ C. 263 11/9/96 p. 3)

ANIMALS IN SPORT AND ENTERTAINMENT

Existing Legislation

None.

Work in Progress

None.

Background

22/11/84	Motion for a Resolution 2-1060/84 by Mr Roelants du Vivier on the banning of certain forms of hunting, particularly riding to hounds.
03/05/85	Motion for a Resolution B2-253/85 by Mr Muntingh on swan deaths from lead poisoning.
13/05/85	Motion for a Resolution B2-531/85 by Mr Cottrell, Mr Bombard, Mrs Maij-Weggen, Mr Paisley, Mrs Ewing, Mr Anastassopoulos, Mr Pearce, Mr Huckfield, Mr Stewart, on bullfighting.
28/02/86	Motion for a Resolution B2-1674/85 by Mr Cottrell and others on the introduction of a ban on bullfighting in Spain, Portugal and Southern France.
10/04/86	Motion for a Resolution B2-89/86 by Mr Roelants du Vivier on the need to deal in a single report with bullfighting and all other popular practices involving the mutilation or killing of animals.
13/05/86	Motion for a Resolution B2-278/86 by Mr Cottrell on a 'Sport Aid' bullfight staged to raise funds for famine hit areas in Africa.
23/05/86	The EP Environment Committee decided to draw up a Report on bloodsports and appointed Mr Gerhard Schmid (S-D) Rapporteur.
13/01/87	Doc. 86/10/014 published by the Commission's Directorate General for Research on bullfighting in Spain and the Community's competence on this question (German language only).

10/04/87   Motion for a Resolution 254/87 by Mrs Castle, Mr Martin, Mr Morris, Mr Newens, Mrs Crawley, Ms Tongue and Mr Griffiths, on the cruelty to animals in Spain.

10/07/87   Motion for a Resolution B2-637/87 by Mr Cottrell on French Channel 4 coverage of bullfights.

              Motion for a Resolution B2-918/87 by Mr Cottrell on the blood spectacles involving animals in Spain.

27/10/87   Petition 309/87 by Llewellyn Smith on behalf of his constituents of South East Wales on a ban on bullfighting and ritual killing.

13/01/89   Report A2-356/88 drawn up on behalf of the Environment Committee on possible legal action against events involving cruelty to animals (based on Motions for Resolution B2-1674/85, 2-1060/84, B2-531/85, B2-254/87, B2-437/87, B2-918/87, B2-995/87 and Petition 309/87). Rapporteur: Gerhard Schmid (S-D).

              Mr Schmid's Report was scheduled for debate by the full Parliament in February 1989, but was referred back to the Committee on the Environment where it was re-adopted without change. The Committee on Agriculture then requested an opportunity to give an opinion.

              Following the European Parliament elections in June 1989 this report was consigned to the archives.

07/92   Motion for a Resolution B3-1758/91 on residual ancestral customs throughout Europe which involve cruelty to animals. Referred to Environment Committee which decided not to draw up report.

3/93   Motion for a Resolution [B3-0111/93] on surviving traditional customs in the Community which involve acts of cruelty to animals, has been referred to the Environment Committee.

3/93   Motion for a resolution on the spread of bullfighting tabled.

18/7/94   Economic and Social Committee publish opinion on proposal for a Council Directive amending Council Directive 90/428/EEC on trade in equidae intended for competitions and laying down the conditions for participation therein. (OJ No. C195, 18.7.94, p. 40)

14/2/96   COM (96) 44 final Commission's proposal for 27 Council Regulations on the price for agricultural products and related measures (1996/1997 Price Package). It proposes to delete the second premium for bulls and to increase the first premium to be given when the bull is 10 months of age. (OJ C.125 27/4/96 p. 29)

30/10/96   The Agriculture Council adopted the Commission's proposals on the beef and veal sector. The Commission proposal in relation to the single premium for bulls is accepted.

ANIMALS IN EXHIBITION SITUATIONS

Existing Legislation

Council Directive 79/409/EEC of 2 April 1979 on the conservation of wild birds restricts the trade in certain wild birds (Article 9).

Council Regulation (EEC) 3626/82 of 3 December 1982 implementing the Convention on International Trade in Endangered Species of Wild Fauna and Flora only permits the import of certain animals for commercial display under specific conditions (Articles 6 and 10.I.b).

Work in Progress

17/3/95   Motion for a Resolution B4-0383/95 by Ken Collins on minimum standards for the keeping of animals in zoos was discussed and adopted. The resolution calls on the Commission to maintain the proposal for a Directive on a European policy on zoos and not to replace it with a Council Recommendation. The Council is asked to adopt forthwith a Common Position on minimum standards for the protection of animals in zoos in accordance with Parliament's aforementioned opinion of 25 June 1993.

12/12/95   COM (95) 619 final Communication from the Commission to the Council and Proposal for a Council Recommendation relating to the keeping of wild animals in zoos.
           Consists of guidelines for the accommodation and care of animals in zoos.
           This proposal will be presented to Parliament for an opinion. The Parliament's Environment Committee has appointed Ian White (PSE-UK) as rapporteur.

24/4/96   Opinion of the Economic and Social Committee on the Proposal for a Council Recommendation relating to the keeping of wild animals in zoos. The Committee argues in favour of a Directive on zoos rather than a Recommendation because of the weakness of the Recommendation as a regulatory instrument, and rejects the principle of subsidiarity with regard to legislation on the keeping of animals in zoos. (OJ C.204 15/7/96 p. 63)

Background

Council of Europe

07/05/87   At the final meeting of CAHPA, the World Society for the Protection of Animals and Eurogroup for Animal Welfare submitted their suggestions for a draft Convention on the protection of animals in exhibition purposes. In view of the five Conventions already covering animal protection, the Committee decided not to elaborate a Convention on animals kept for exhibition purposes.

18/01/88   Motion for a Recommendation by Mr Hardy and others on the situation of zoos in Europe (Doc.5844).

European Community

03/88   Motion for a Resolution B2-75/88 by Sir Jack Stewart-Clark, Mr Collins, Mrs Ewing, Mr Fitzgerald, Mr Lalr, Mrs Lemass, Mrs Llorca Vilaplana, Mr Maher, Mr Roelants du Vivier, Mr Seligman and Mrs Squarcialupi on minimum standards for zoological establishments. Environment Committee decided not to draw up report.

1989   The Commission included the preparation of proposals for legislation laying down minimum standards for zoos in its programme for 1989.

10/07/91   COM(91)177 proposal for a directive laying down minimum standards for the keeping of animals in zoos. Referred to the Environment Committee. Rapporteur: Sir James Scott-Hopkins (ED-UK).

27/11/91   CES 1372/91 ECOSOC opinion on COM(91)177 drafted by Messrs Vidal, Douvis and Masucci.

18/12/91   Initial discussion in the Environment Committee on draft report by Sir James Scott-Hopkins on COM(91)177.

21/1/93   Report by Sir James Scott-Hopkins concerning minimum standards for the keeping of animals in zoos referred back to Environment Committee due to consideration of the subsidiarity principle by the Commission in relation to this issue.

25/6/93	Report [A3-0140/93] by Sir James Scott-Hopkins on COM(91)0177 final for Council Directive on minimum standards for the keeping of animals in zoos adopted with 10 amendments at parliamentary session.
17/3/95	Motion for a Resolution B4-0383/95 by Ken Collins on minimum standards for the keeping of animals in zoos was discussed and adopted. The resolution calls on the Commission to maintain the proposal for a Directive on a European policy on zoos and not to replace it with a Council Recommendation. The Council is asked to adopt forthwith a Common Position on minimum standards for the protection of animals in zoos in accordance with Parliament's aforementioned opinion of 25 June 1993.
4/95	Debate in the Parliament's Environment Committee. MEPs repeated their support for a directive.
10/95	The Commission decided to proceed to a recommendation.
12/12/95	COM (95) 619 final Communication from the Commission to the Council and Proposal for a Council Recommendation relating to the keeping of wild animals in zoos.
	Consists of guidelines for the accommodation and care of animals in zoos.
	This proposal will be presented to Parliament for an opinion. The Parliament's Environment Committee has appointed Ian White (PSE-UK) as rapporteur.
24/4/96	Opinion of the Economic and Social Committee on the Proposal for a Council Recommendation relating to the keeping of wild animals in zoos. The Committee argues in favour of a Directive on zoos rather than a Recommendation because of the weakness of the Recommendation as a regulatory instrument, and rejects the principle of subsidiarity with regard to legislation on the keeping of animals in zoos. (OJ C.204 15/7/96 p. 63)

Appendix I

**CONVENTION ON THE CONSERVATION OF MIGRATORY
SPECIES OF WILD ANIMALS BONN, 23/06/79**

**Convention entered into force 01/11/83
Signatories within the EC and Council of Europe**

	Signed	*Ratified*	*Entered into force*
Albania	–	–	–
Andorra	–	–	–
Austria	–	–	–
Belgium	–	–	–
Bulgaria	–	–	–
Czech Republic	–	–	–
Cyprus	–	–	–
Denmark	23/06/79	05/08/82	01/11/83
Estonia	–	–	–
Finland	(acceded)	03/10/88	01/01/89
France	23/06/79	–	01/07/90
Germany	23/06/79	31/07/84	01/10/84
Greece	23/06/79	–	–
Hungary	(acceded)	12/07/83	01/11/83
Iceland	–	–	–
Ireland	20/06/80	05/08/83	01/11/83
Italy	23/06/79	26/08/83	01/11/83
Latvia	–	–	–
Lichtenstein	–	–	–
Lithuania	–	–	–
Luxembourg	26/03/80	30/11/82	01/11/83
Malta	–	–	–
Moldova	–	–	–
Netherlands	20/06/80	05/06/81	01/11/83
Norway	23/06/79	30/05/85	01/08/85
Poland	–	–	–
Portugal	23/06/79	21/01/81	01/11/83
Romania	–	–	–
Russia	–	–	–
San Marino	–	–	–
Slovakia	–	–	–
Slovenia	–	–	–
Spain	23/06/79	12/02/85	01/05/85
Sweden	23/06/79	09/06/83	01/11/83
Switzerland	–	–	–

Convention entered into force 01/11/83
Signatories within the EC and Council of Europe   (*Continued*)

	Signed	*Ratified*	*Entered into force*
Tfyromacedonia	–	–	–
Turkey	–	–	–
Ukraine	–	–	–
United Kingdom	23/06/79	23/07/85	01/10/85

The EEC RATIFIED the Convention on 01/10/83. The Convention entered into force in the Community on 01/11/83. As at 01/05/92 there are 40 Parties to the Convention and 13 signatories.

CONVENTION ON THE CONSERVATION OF MIGRATORY SPECIES OF WILD ANIMALS BONN, 23/06/79

Convention entered into force on 01/11/83
Other Signatories

	Signed	*Ratified*	*Entered into force*
Argentina	–	–	01/01/92
Australia	–	–	01/01/91
Benin	(acceded)	14/01/86	01/04/86
Burkina Faso	–	–	01/01/80
Cameroon	10/06/80	07/09/81	01/11/83
Central African Republic	23/06/79	–	–
Chile	(acceded)	15/09/81	01/11/83
Egypt	23/06/79	11/02/82	01/11/83
Ghana	(acceded)	19/01/88	01/04/88
India	23/06/79	04/05/82	01/11/83
Israel	(acceded)	17/05/83	01/11/83
Ivory Coast	23/06/79	–	–
Jamaica	20/06/80	–	–
Madagascar	23/06/79	–	–
Mali	(acceded)	28/07/87	01/10/87
Morocco	23/06/79	–	–
Niger	23/06/79	03/07/80	01/11/83
Nigeria	(acceded)	15/10/86	01/11/87
Pakistan	(acceded)	22/09/87	01/12/87
Panama	(acceded)	20/02/89	01/05/89
Paraguay	23/06/79	–	–
Philippines	20/06/80	–	–
Saudi Arabia	–	–	01/03/91
Senegal	(acceded)	18/03/88	01/06/88
Somalia	23/06/79	11/11/85	01/02/86
South Africa	–	–	01/12/91
Sri Lanka	23/06/79	–	–

Convention entered into force on 01/11/83
Other Signatories   (*Continued*)

	Signed	Ratified	Entered into force
Togo	23/06/79	–	–
Tchad	–	–	–
Tunisia	–	–	–
Uganda	–	–	–
Uruguay	–	–	–
Zaire	–	–	–

Appendix II

CONVENTION ON THE CONSERVATION OF EUROPEAN WILDLIFE AND NATURAL HABITATS – ETS 104 BERNE, 19/09/79

Conditions of entry into force: 5 ratifications
Convention entered into force: 01/06/82

Signatories in the EC and Council of Europe

	Signed	*Ratified*	*Entered into force*
Albania	31/10/95	–	–
Andorra	–	–	–
Austria	19/09/79	02/03/83	01/09/83
Belgium	19/09/79	24/08/90	01/12/90
Bulgaria	(acceded)	31/01/91	01/05/91
Czech Republic	–	–	–
Cyprus	21/10/81	16/05/88	01/09/88
Denmark	19/09/79	08/09/82	01/01/83
Estonia	(acceded)	03/08/92	01/12/92
Finland	19/09/79	07/12/85	01/03/86
France	19/09/79	26/04/90	01/08/90
Germany	19/09/79	13/12/84	01/04/85
Greece	19/09/79	14/03/83	01/10/83
Hungary	(acceded)	16/11/89	01/03/90
Iceland	17/06/93	17/06/93	01/10/93
Ireland	19/09/79	23/04/82	01/08/82
Italy	19/09/79	11/02/82	01/06/82
Latvia	–	–	–
Lichtenstein	19/09/79	30/10/80	01/06/82
Luxembourg	19/09/79	23/03/82	01/07/82
Malta	26/11/93	26/11/93	01/03/94
Moldova	(acceded)	24/05/94	01/09/94
Netherlands	19/09/79	28/10/80	01/06/82
Norway	19/09/79	27/05/86	01/09/86
Poland	24/03/95	13/09/95	01/01/96
Portugal	19/09/79	03/02/82	01/06/82
Romania	(acceded)	18/05/93	01/09/93
Russia	–	–	–
San Marino	–	–	–
Slovakia	28/04/94	23/09/96	01/01/97
Slovenia	–	–	–
Spain	19/09/79	27/05/86	01/09/86
Sweden	19/09/79	14/06/83	01/10/83

Conditions of entry into force: 5 ratifications
Convention entered into force: 01/06/82

Signatories in the EC and Council of Europe   (*Continued*)

	Signed	Ratified	Entered into force
Switzerland	19/09/79	12/03/81	01/06/82
Tfyromacedonia	–	–	–
Turkey	19/09/79	02/05/84	01/09/84
Ukraine	–	–	–
United Kingdom	Yes	28/05/82	01/09/82

Finland signed and ratified the Convention prior to becoming a Member of the Council of Europe on 5 May 1989.
The EEC ratified the Convention (Birds element only) on 07/05/82.
Date of entry into force in the EEC : 01/09/82.

CONVENTION ON THE CONSERVATION OF EUROPEAN WILDLIFE AND NATURAL HABITATS – ETS 104 BERNE, 19/09/79

Conditions of entry into force: 5 ratifications
Convention entered into force: 01/06/82
Other signatories

	Signed	Ratified	Entered into force
Belarus	–	–	–
Burkina Faso	(acceded)	14/06/90	01/10/90
Croatia	–	–	–
Monacco	(acceded)	07/02/94	01/06/94
Morocco	–	–	–
Senegal	(acceded)	13/04/87	01/08/87
Tunisia	(acceded)	12/01/96	01/05/96

Appendix III

**CONVENTION ON INTERNATIONAL TRADE IN
ENDANGERED SPECIES OF WILD FAUNA AND FLORA
WASHINGTON, 03/03/73**

**Convention entered into force on: 01/07/75
Signatories within the EC and Council of Europe**

	Signed	*Entered into force*
Albania	–	–
Andorra	–	–
Austria	Yes	27/04/82
Belgium	Yes	01/01/84
Bulgaria	Yes	16/04/91
Czech Republic	–	–
Cyprus	Yes	01/07/75
Denmark	Yes	24/10/77
Estonia	–	–
Finland	Yes	08/08/76
France	Yes	09/08/78
Germany	Yes	20/06/76
Greece	–	–
Hungary	Yes	29/08/85
Iceland	–	–
Ireland	01/11/74	–
Italy	Yes	31/12/79
Estonia	–	–
Lichtenstein	Yes	28/02/80
Lithuania	–	–
Luxembourg	Yes	12/03/84
Malta	Yes	16/07/89
Moldova	–	–
Netherlands	Yes	18/07/84
Norway	Yes	25/10/76
Poland	Yes	12/03/90
Portugal	Yes	11/03/81
Romania	–	–
Russia	–	–
San Marino	–	–
Slovakia	–	–
Slovenia	–	–
Spain	Yes	28/08/86
Sweden	Yes	01/07/75

Convention entered into force on: 01/07/75
Signatories within the EC and Council of Europe   (*Continued*)

	Signed	Entered into force
Switzerland	Yes	01/07/75
Tfyromacedonia*	–	–
Turkey	–	–
Ukraine	–	–
United Kingdom	Yes	31/10/76

In total, 124 countries had become Parties to CITES by 13/08/92.
The EC is not yet a Party to the Convention, which is nonetheless implemented within the Community by Council Regulation 3626/82 (EEC).
* The former Yugoslav Republic of Macedonia.

CONVENTION ON INTERNATIONAL TRADE IN ENDANGERED SPECIES OF WILD FAUNA AND FLORA WASHINGTON, 03/03/73

Convention entered into force on: 01/07/75
Other signatories

	Signed	Entered into force
Afghanistan	Yes	28/01/86
Algeria	Yes	21/02/84
Argentina	Yes	08/04/81
Australia	Yes	27/10/76
Bahamas	Yes	18/09/79
Bangladesh	Yes	18/02/82
Belize	Yes	21/09/81
Benin	Yes	28/05/84
Bolivia	Yes	04/10/79
Botswana	Yes	12/02/78
Brazil	Yes	04/11/75
Brunia Darussalam	Yes	20/08/90
Burkina Faso	Yes	15/01/90
Burundi	Yes	06/11/88
Cameroon	Yes	03/09/81
Canada	Yes	09/07/75
Central African Republic	Yes	25/11/80
Chile	Yes	01/07/75
China	Yes	08/04/81
Colombia	Yes	29/11/81
Congo	Yes	01/05/83
Costa Rica	Yes	28/09/75
Cuba	Yes	19/07/90
Czechoslovakia	Yes	28/05/92

Convention entered into force on: 01/07/75
Other signatories   (*Continued*)

	Signed	*Entered into force*
Djibouti	Yes	07/05/92
Dominican Republic	Yes	17/03/87
Ecuador	Yes	01/07/75
Egypt	Yes	04/04/78
El Salvador	Yes	29/07/87
Equatorial Guinea	Yes	08/06/92
Ethiopia	Yes	04/07/89
Gabon	Yes	15/05/89
Gambia	Yes	24/11/77
Ghana	Yes	12/02/76
Guatemala	Yes	05/02/80
Guinea	Yes	20/12/81
Guinea-Bissau	Yes	14/08/90
Guyana	Yes	25/08/77
Honduras	Yes	13/06/85
India	Yes	18/10/76
Indonesia	Yes	28/03/79
Iran	Yes	01/11/76
Israel	Yes	17/03/80
Japan	Yes	04/11/80
Jordan	Yes	14/03/79
Kampuchea	07/12/73	–
Kenya	Yes	13/03/79
Kuwait	09/04/73	–
Lesotho	17/07/74	
Liberia	Yes	09/06/81
Madagascar	Yes	18/11/75
Malawi	Yes	06/05/82
Malaysia	Yes	18/01/78
Mauritius	Yes	27/07/75
Mexico	Yes	–
Monaco	Yes	18/07/78
Morocco	Yes	14/01/76
Mozambique	Yes	23/06/81
Namibia	Yes	18/03/91
Nepal	Yes	16/09/75
New Zeland	Yes	08/08/89
Nicaragua	Yes	04/11/77
Niger	Yes	07/12/75
Nigeria	Yes	01/07/75
Pakistan	Yes	19/07/76
Panama	Yes	15/11/78
Papua New Guinea	Yes	11/03/76
Paraguay	Yes	13/02/77
Peru	Yes	25/09/75
Philippines	Yes	16/11/81

Convention entered into force on: 01/07/75
Other signatories   (*Continued*)

	Signed	Entered into force
Rwanda	Yes	18/01/81
Saint Lucia	Yes	15/03/83
Saint Vincent and The Grenadines	Yes	28/02/89
Senegal	Yes	03/11/77
Seychelles	Yes	09/05/77
Singapore	Yes	28/02/87
Somalia	Yes	02/03/86
South Africa	Yes	13/10/75
Sri Lanka	Yes	02/08/79
Sudan	Yes	24/01/83
Suriname	Yes	15/02/81
Tanzania	Yes	27/02/80
Tchad	Yes	03/05/89
Thailand	Yes	21/04/83
Togo	Yes	21/01/79
Trinidad and Tobago	Yes	18/04/84
Tunisia	Yes	01/07/75
Uganda	Yes	16/10/91
Union of Soviet Socialist Republics	Yes	08/12/76
United Arab Emirates	Yes	01/07/75
United States of America	Yes	01/07/75
Uruguay	Yes	01/07/75
Vanuatu	Yes	15/10/89
Venezuela	Yes	22/01/78
Vietnam	03/03/73	–
Zaire	Yes	18/10/76
Zambia	Yes	22/02/81
Zimbabwe	Yes	17/08/81

Appendix IV

**EUROPEAN CONVENTION FOR THE PROTECTION OF
ANIMALS DURING INTERNATIONAL TRANSPORT – ETS 065
PARIS, 13/12/68**

**Conditions of entry into force: 4 ratifications
Convention entered into force: 20/02/71**

	Signed	*Ratified*	*Entered into force*
Albania	–	–	–
Andorra	–	–	–
Austria	19/12/69	14/09/73	15/03/74
Belgium	13/12/68	21/11/73	01/07/74
Bulgaria	–	–	–
Croatia	–	–	–
Czech Republic	–	–	–
Cyprus	27/02/76	08/02/77	09/08/77
Denmark	13/12/68	24/06/69	20/02/71
Estonia	–	–	–
Finland	(acceded)	04/02/75	05/08/75
France	13/12/68	09/01/74	01/07/74
Germany	13/12/68	09/01/74	01/07/74
Greece	13/12/68	25/05/78	26/11/78
Hungary	–	–	–
Iceland	13/12/68	01/05/69	20/02/71
Ireland	24/09/69	14/03/75	15/09/75
Italy	25/05/71	03/05/74	04/11/74
Latvia	–	–	–
Lichtenstein	–	–	–
Luxembourg	23/06/71	13/04/72	14/10/72
Malta	–	–	–
Moldova	–	–	–
Netherlands	16/05/75	04/09/80	05/03/81
Norway	13/12/68	25/06/69	20/02/71
Poland	–	–	–
Portugal	16/10/80	01/06/82	02/12/82
Romania	(acceded)	26/04/91	27/10/91
Russia	(acceded)	13/11/90	14/05/91
San Marino	–	–	–
Slovakia	–	–	–
Slovenia	–	–	–
Spain	(acceded)	02/08/74	03/02/75
Sweden	10/09/70	20/10/71	21/04/72

Conditions of entry into force: 4 ratifications
Convention entered into force: 20/02/71   (*Continued*)

	Signed	Ratified	Entered into force
Switzerland	13/12/68	19/08/70	20/02/71
Tfyromacedonia	–	–	–
Turkey	18/04/74	19/12/75	20/06/76
Ukraine	–	–	–
United Kingdom	26/02/69	09/01/74	01/07/74

Finland and Spain both acceded to the Convention prior to becoming Members of the Council of Europe on 5 May 1989 and 23 November 1977 respectively.

Appendix V

ADDITIONAL PROTOCOL TO THE EUROPEAN CONVENTION FOR THE PROTECTION OF ANIMALS DURING INTERNATIONAL TRANSPORT – ETS 103 STRASBOURG, 10/05/79

Conditions of entry into force: Ratification by all Contracting Parties to the Convention Protocol entered into force: 7/11/89

	Signed	*Ratified*
Albania	–	–
Andorra	–	–
Austria	10/05/79	07/11/89
Belgium	10/05/79	11/03/80
Bulgaria	–	–
Croatia	–	–
Czech Republic		
Cyprus	21/10/81	22/07/82
Denmark	20/06/79	20/06/79
Estonia	–	–
Finland	(acceded)	31/01/89
France	10/05/79	10/05/79
Germany	10/05/79	16/01/81
Greece	20/02/81	06/06/84
Hungary	–	–
Iceland	24/04/86	24/04/86
Ireland	06/10/80	06/10/80
Italy	19/02/80	17/12/82
Latvia	–	–
Lichtenstein	–	–
Lithuania	–	–
Luxembourg	10/05/79	11/09/80
Malta	–	–
Moldovia	–	–
Netherlands	04/09/80	03/04/81
Norway	20/09/83	20/09/83
Poland	–	–
Portugal	16/10/80	01/06/82
Romania	(acceded)	26/04/91
Russia	(acceded)	13/11/90
San Marino	–	–
Slovakia	–	–
Slovenia	–	–

Conditions of entry into force: Ratification by all Contracting Parties to the Convention Protocol entered into force: 7/11/89   (*Continued*)

	Signed	*Ratified*
Spain	(acceded)	18/04/83
Sweden	10/05/79	10/05/79
Switzerland	10/05/79	10/05/79
Tfyromacedonia	–	–
Turkey	19/06/85	19/05/89
Ukraine	–	–
United Kingdom	22/07/80	22/07/80

Finland acceded to the Additional Protocal prior to becoming a Member of the Council of Europe on 5 May 1989.

Appendix VI

**EUROPEAN CONVENTION FOR THE PROTECTION OF
ANIMALS KEPT FOR FARMING PURPOSES – ETS 87
STRASBOURG, 10/03/76**

**Conditions of entry into force : 4 ratifications
Convention entered into force: 10/09/78**

	Signed	*Ratified*	*Entered into force*
Albania	–	–	–
Andorra	–	–	–
Austria	23/01/92	22/12/92	–
Belgium	30/04/76	13/09/79	14/03/80
Bulgaria	–	–	–
Croatia	–	–	–
Czech Republic	–	–	–
Cyprus	08/11/76	15/04/77	10/09/78
Denmark	10/03/76	28/01/80	29/07/80
Estonia	–	–	–
Finland	02/12/91	02/12/91	03/06/92
France	03/07/76	10/01/78	10/09/78
Germany	23/07/76	09/03/78	10/09/78
Greece	30/04/76	12/11/84	13/05/85
Hungary	–	–	–
Iceland	27/01/77	19/09/89	20/03/90
Ireland	28/06/78	07/04/86	08/10/86
Italy	23/04/80	07/02/86	08/10/86
Latvia	–	–	–
Lichtenstein	–	–	–
Lithuania	–	–	–
Luxembourg	08/04/76	19/01/79	20/07/79
Malta	29/08/88	26/03/91	27/09/91
Moldova	–	–	–
Netherlands	04/09/80	21/04/81	22/10/81
Norway	28/01/80	25/02/80	26/08/80
Poland	–	–	–
Portugal	20/11/79	20/04/82	21/10/82
Romania	–	–	–
Russia	–	–	–
San Marino	–	–	–
Slovakia	–	–	–
Slovenia	(acceded)	20/12/92	21/04/93
Spain	08/11/85	05/05/88	06/11/88

Conditions of entry into force : 4 ratifications
Convention entered into force: 10/09/78   (*Continued*)

	Signed	*Ratified*	*Entered into force*
Sweden	08/06/76	07/12/77	10/09/78
Switzerland	07/07/76	24/09/80	25/03/81
Tfyromacedonia	(acceded)	30/03/94	01/10/94
Turkey	–	–	–
Ukraine	–	–	–
United Kingdom	10/03/76	08/01/79	09/07/79

The EC ratified the Convention le 18/10/88.
Date of entry into force: 19/04/89.
Accession by: Slovenia (Yugoslavia) on 20/10/92; Bosnia Herzegova on 29/12/94; Croatia on 14/09/94; Former Yugoslav Rep. of Macedonia on 30/03/94.

Appendix VII

ADDITIONAL PROTOCOL TO THE EUROPEAN CONVENTION
FOR THE PROTECTION OF ANIMALS KEPT FOR FARMING
PURPOSES – ETS 145 STRASBOURG, 06/02/92

**Conditions of entry into force: all Parties to the Convention
must become Parties to the Protocol**

	Signed	Ratified	Entered into force
Albania	–	–	–
Andorra	–	–	–
Austria	30/04/96	–	–
Belgium	06/02/92	–	–
Bulgaria	–	–	–
Croatia	–	–	–
Czech Republic	–	–	–
Cyprus	19/10/92	02/06/93	–
Denmark	06/02/92	20/01/93	–
Estonia	–	–	–
Finland	05/06/92	05/06/92	–
France	25/02/92	–	–
Germany	10/06/92	15/11/94	–
Greece	29/04/92	–	–
Hungary	–	–	–
Iceland	–	–	–
Ireland	–	–	–
Italy	–	–	–
Latvia	–	–	–
Lichtenstein	–	–	–
Lithuania	–	–	–
Luxembourg	06/02/92	–	–
Malta	–	–	–
Moldova	–	–	–
Netherlands	–	–	–
Norway	06/08/92	06/08/92	–
Poland	–	–	–
Portugal	04/02/92	08/03/93	–
Romania	–	–	–
Russia	–	–	–
San Marino	–	–	–
Slovakia	–	–	–
Slovenia	–	–	–

**Conditions of entry into force: all Parties to the Convention
must become Parties to the Protocol** (*Continued*)

	Signed	Ratified	Entered into force
Spain	–	–	–
Sweden	06/02/92	06/03/92	–
Switzerland	–	21/12/94	–
Tfyromacedonia	–	–	–
Turkey	–	–	–
Ukraine	–	–	–
United Kingdom	–	–	–

The Additional Protocol is open to signature and ratification by the EC.

Appendix VIII

**EUROPEAN CONVENTION FOR THE PROTECTION OF
ANIMALS FOR SLAUGHTER – ETS 102 STRASBOURG, 10/05/79**

**Conditions of entry into force: 4 ratifications
Convention entered into force: 11/06/82
Signatories in the EC and Council of Europe**

	Signed	*Ratified*	*Entered into force*
Albania	–	–	–
Andorra	–	–	–
Austria	–	–	–
Belgium	10/05/79	–	–
Bulgaria	–	–	–
Czech Republic	–	–	–
Cyprus	25/07/86	–	–
Denmark	20/06/79	23/02/81	11/06/82
Estonia	–	–	–
Finland	02/12/91	02/12/91	03/06/92
France	10/05/79	–	–
Germany	10/05/79	24/02/84	10/09/87
Greece	12/11/84	12/11/84	13/05/85
Hungary	–	–	–
Iceland	–	–	–
Ireland	06/10/80	10/12/81	11/06/82
Italy	19/02/80	07/02/86	08/08/86
Latvia	–	–	–
Lichtenstein	–	–	–
Lithuania	–	–	–
Luxembourg	10/05/79	24/07/80	11/06/82
Malta	–	–	–
Moldova	–	–	–
Netherlands	25/02/81	27/06/86	28/12/86
Norway	06/04/82	12/05/82	13/11/82
Poland	–	–	–
Portugal	18/12/79	03/11/81	11/06/82
Romania	–	–	–
Russia	–	–	–
San Marino	–	–	–
Slovakia	–	–	–
Slovenia	(acceded)	20/10/92	21/04/93

Conditions of entry into force: 4 ratifications
Convention entered into force: 11/06/82
Signatories in the EC and Council of Europe   (*Continued*)

	Signed	*Ratified*	*Entered into force*
Spain	–	–	–
Sweden	28/11/79	26/02/82	27/08/82
Switzerland	10/05/79	13/11/93	04/05/94
Tfyromacedonia	(acceded)	30/03/94	01/10/94
Turkey	–	–	–
Ukraine	–	–	–
United Kingdom	10/05/79	–	–

EUROPEAN CONVENTION FOR THE PROTECTION
OF ANIMALS FOR SLAUGHTER – ETS 102
STRASBOURG, 10/05/79

Conditions of entry into force: 4 ratifications
Convention entered into force: 11/06/82
Other signatories

	Signed	*Ratified*	*Entered into force*
Bosnia Herzegova	(acceded)	29/12/94	30/06/95
Croatia	(acceded)	14/09/94	15/03/95
Former Yugoslav Rep. of Macedonia	–	30/03/94	–

Appendix IX

EUROPEAN CONVENTION FOR THE PROTECTION OF VERTEBRATE ANIMALS USED FOR EXPERIMENTAL PURPOSES AND OTHER SCIENTIFIC PURPOSES – ETS 123 STRASBOURG, 18/03/86

Conditions of entry into force: 4 ratifications
Convention entered into force: 01/01/91

	Signed	Ratified	Entered into force
Albania	–	–	–
Andorra	–	–	–
Austria	–	–	–
Belgium	18/03/86	20/12/91	01/07/92
Bulgaria	–	–	–
Croatia	–	–	–
Czech Republic	–	–	–
Cyprus	09/12/93	09/12/93	–
Denmark	18/03/86	–	–
Estonia	–	–	–
Finland	14/06/90	14/06/90	01/01/91
France	02/09/87	–	–
Germany	21/06/88	19/04/91	01/11/91
Greece	18/03/86	27/05/92	01/12/92
Hungary	–	–	–
Iceland	–	–	–
Ireland	06/12/90	–	–
Italy	–	–	–
Latvia	–	–	–
Lichtenstein	–	–	–
Lithuania	–	–	–
Luxembourg	–	–	–
Malta	–	–	–
Moldova	–	–	–
Netherlands	04/08/86	–	–
Norway	18/03/86	09/07/86	01/01/91
Poland	–	–	–
Portugal	–	–	–
Romania	–	–	–
Russia	–	–	–
San Marino	–	–	–
Slovakia	–	–	–
Slovenia	–	–	–

Conditions of entry into force: 4 ratifications
Convention entered into force: 01/01/91   *(Continued)*

	Signed	*Ratified*	*Entered into force*
Spain	11/08/88	12/09/89	01/01/91
Sweden	18/03/86	15/09/88	01/01/91
Switzerland	29/05/89	03/11/93	01/06/94
Tfyromacedonia	–	–	–
Turkey	05/09/86	–	–
Ukraine	–	–	–
United Kingdom	18/03/86	–	–

The EC signed the Convention on 10/02/87.

Appendix X

EUROPEAN CONVENTION FOR THE PROTECTION OF PET ANIMALS – ETS 125 STRASBOURG, 13/11/87

Conditions of entry into force: 4 ratifications
Convention entered into force: 1/5/92

	Signed	*Ratified*	*Entered into force*
Albania	–	–	–
Andorra	–	–	–
Austria	–	–	–
Belgium	13/11/87	20/12/91	01/07/92
Bulgaria	–	–	–
Croatia	–	–	–
Czech Republic	–	–	–
Cyprus	09/12/93	09/12/93	01/07/94
Denmark	13/11/87	20/10/92	01/05/93
Estonia	–	–	–
Finland	02/12/91	02/12/91	01/07/92
France	16/12/96	–	–
Germany	21/06/88	27/05/91	01/05/92
Greece	13/11/87	29/04/92	01/11/92
Hungary	–	–	–
Iceland	–	–	–
Ireland	–	–	–
Italy	13/11/87	–	–
Latvia	–	–	–
Lichtenstein	–	–	–
Lithuania	–	–	–
Luxembourg	13/11/87	25/10/91	01/05/92
Malta	–	–	–
Moldova	–	–	–
Netherlands	13/11/87	–	–
Norway	13/11/87	03/02/88	01/05/92
Poland	–	–	–
Romania	–	–	–
Russia	–	–	–
Portugal	13/11/87	28/06/93	01/01/94
San Marino	–	–	–
Slovakia	–	–	–
Slovenia	–	–	–
Spain	–	–	–
Sweden	14/03/89	14/03/89	01/05/92

Conditions of entry into force: 4 ratifications
Convention entered into force: 1/5/92   (*Continued*)

	Signed	*Ratified*	*Entered into force*
Switzerland	03/11/93	03/11/93	–
Tfyromacedonia	–	–	–
Turkey	–	–	–
Ukraine	–	–	–
United Kingdom	–	–	–

Belgium: Confirms reservation made at time of signature on Article 10.1.a.
Finland and Germany: Reservation on Article 6 and Article 10.1.a.
Luxembourg: Withdrew reservation on Article 10.1 made at time of signature.

Appendix XI

Articles within the Treaty of Rome used for Community legislation on issues related to animal welfare are as follows:

Article 36

The provisions of Articles 30 to 34 shall not preclude prohibitions or restrictions on imports, exports or goods in transit justified on grounds of public morality, public policy or public security; the protection of health and life of humans, animals or plants; the protection of national treasures possessing artistic, historic or archaeological value; or the protection of industrial and commercial property. Such prohibitions or restrictions shall not, however, constitute a means of arbitrary discrimination or a disguised restriction on trade between Member States.

Article 38

1. The common market shall extend to agriculture and trade in agricultural products. 'Agricultural products' means the products of the soil, of stockfarming and of fisheries and products of first-stage processing directly related to these products.

2. Save as otherwise provided in Articles 39 to 46, the rules laid down for the establishment of the common market shall apply to agricultural products.

3. The products subject to the provisions of Articles 39 to 46 are listed in Annex II to this Treaty. Within two years of the entry into force of this Treaty, however, the Council shall, acting by a qualified majority on a proposal from the Commission, decide what products are to be added to this list.

4. The operation and development of the common market for agricultural products must be accompanied by the establishment of a common agricultural policy among the Member States.

Article 43

1. In order to evolve the broad lines of a common agricultural policy, the Commission shall, immediately this Treaty enters into force, convene a conference of the Member States with a view to making a comparison of their agricultural policies, in particular by producing a statement of their resources and needs.

2. Having taken into account the work of the conference provided for in paragraph 1, after consulting the Economic and Social Committee and within two years of the entry into force of this Treaty, the Commission shall submit proposals for working out and implementing the common agricultural policy, including the replacement of the national organisations by one of the forms of common organisation provided for in Article 40(2), and for implementing the measures specified in this Title.

These proposals shall take account of the interdependence of the agricultural matters mentioned in this Title.

The Council shall, on a proposal from the Commission and after consulting the Assembly, acting unanimously during the first two stages and by a qualified majority thereafter, make regulations, issue directives, or take decisions, without prejudice to any recommendations it may also make.

3. The Council may, acting by a qualified majority and in accordance with paragraph 2, replace the national market organisations by the common organisation provided for in Article 40(2) if:

   (a) the common organisation offers Member States which are opposed to this measure and which have an organisation of their own for the production in question equivalent safeguards for the employment and standard of living of the producers concerned, account being taken of the adjustments that will be possible and the specialisation that will be needed with the passage of time;

   (b) such an organisation ensures conditions for trade within the Community similar to those existing in a national market.

4. If a common organisation for certain raw materials is established before a common organisation exists for the corresponding processed products, such raw materials as are used for processed products intended for export to third countries may be imported from outside the Community.

Article 100A

1. By way of derogation from Article 100 and save where otherwise provided in this Treaty, the following provisions shall apply for the achievement of the objectives set out in Article 8A. The Council shall, acting by a qualified majority on a proposal from the Commission in cooperation with the European Parliament and after consulting the Economic and Social Committee, adopt the measures for the approximation of the provisions laid down by law, regulation or administrative action in Member States which have as their object the establishment and functioning of the internal market.

2. Paragraph 1 shall not apply to fiscal provisions, to those relating to the free movement of persons nor to those relating to the rights and interests of employed persons.

3. The Commission, in its proposals envisaged in paragraph 1 concerning health, safety, environmental protection and consumer protection, will take as a base a high level of protection.

4. If, after the adoption of a harmonisation measure by the Council acting by a qualified majority, a Member State deems it necessary to apply national provisions on grounds of major needs referred to in Article 36, or relating to protection of the environment or the working environment, it shall notify the Commission of these provisions.

   The Commission shall confirm the provisions involved after having verified that they are not a means of arbitrary discrimination or a disguised restriction on trade between Member States.

   By way of derogation from the procedure laid down in Articles 169 and 170, the Commission or any Member State may bring the matter directly before the Court of Justice if it considers that another Member State is making improper use of the powers provided for in this Article.

5. The harmonisation measures referred to above shall, in appropriate cases, include a safeguard clause authorising the Member States to take, for one or more of the non-economic

reasons referred to in Article 36, provisional measures subject to a Community control procedure.

Article 235

If action by the Community should prove necessary to attain, in the course of the operation of the common market, one of the objectives of the Community and this Treaty has not provided the necessary powers, the Council shall, acting unanimously on a proposal from the Commission and after consulting the Assembly, take the appropriate measures.

Declaration on the Protection of Animals

In December 1991 the European Council meeting in Maastricht adopted a Declaration on the Protection of Animals calling upon the European Parliament, the Council and the Commission, as well as Member States, 'when drafting and implementing legislation on the common agricultural policy, transport, the internal market and research, to pay full regard to the welfare requirements of animals'.

The Declaration is appended to the Final Act of the Treaty on European Union agreed in December 1991 and signed at Maastricht by all EC Heads of State on 7 February 1992. (OJ C.191 29/7/92, p. 103)

Index